Pamela Kalloway

HISTORY alive

STANDARD 9

General Editor Peter Kallaway

Contributors James Campbell
Justin Hall
Sue Krige
Cynthia Kros
Hugh Lester
Robert Morrell
Rosemary Mulholland
Bruce Murray

Shuter & Shooter PIETERMARITZBURG

Shuter & Shooter (Pty) Ltd
Gray's Inn, 230 Church Street
Pietermaritzburg, South Africa 3201

Copyright © Shuter & Shooter (Pty) Ltd 1986

All rights reserved. No part of this publication may be
reproduced or transmitted, in any form or by any means,
without permission of the publishers

First edition 1986 (ISBN 0 86985 907 2)
Second edition 1989

ISBN 0 7960 0158 8

Set in 10 on 12 pt Century Roman
Printed by The Natal Witness
Printing and Publishing Company (Pty) Ltd,
Pietermaritzburg
8171L

Please refer to your syllabus for the choices in this book.

The material is arranged to allow an overview or a more detailed treatment of a particular theme. The material which is bordered is usually enrichment material and may be omitted if the theme is being studied in outline only.

Bold type indicates questions or activities for the pupils.

Acknowledgements

The publishers and authors wish to acknowledge the use of material from the sources listed below. The publishers have made every effort to contact the relevant copyright holders in each instance, and regret that in some cases this has proved impossible.

The Road to the North by H.A.I. Agar-Hamilton, published by Longman Group Limited. *Industrialization and Social Change in South Africa* by S. Marks and R. Rathbone, quoting T Matsetela, published by Longman Group Ltd. *Japan: The Years of Triumph* by L. Allen, published by BPC Print House. *Kings, Commoners and Concessionaires* by P.L. Bonner; and *The Destruction of the Zulu Kingdom* by J. Guy; both published by Ravan Press. *The Industrial Revolution* by D. Knox; and *Bismarck* by M. Booth; both part of the Harrap World History Series; permission kindly granted by Thomas Nelson and Sons Ltd. *Documents and Descriptions in European History 1815–1939* by R.W. Breach, published by Oxford University Press. *The Rise and Fall of the South African Peasantry* by C. Bundy, published by Heinemann Educational Books, 1979—adapted quotation. *A History of Germany* by W. Carr, published by Edward Arnold (Publishers) Ltd. 'Lobengula, Jameson and the Occupation of Mashonaland 1890' by J.R.D. Cobbing, published in *Rhodesian History* No. 4; and 'Volunteers and the Profit Motive in the Anglo-Ndebele War, 1893' by P. Stigger, published in *Rhodesian History* No. 2; both magazines published by the Historical Association of Zimbabwe. *Germany 1866–1945* by G. Craig, published by Oxford University Press. *Select Documents* by G.A. Cranfield, B.J. Dalton and F.G. Stanbrook, published by McGraw-Hill Book Company Australia Pty Ltd—quoting from *Dokumente der Deutschen Politik und Geschichte*, edited by J. and K. Hohlfeld. *An Ambassador of Peace* Vol. II by Viscount d'Abernon, published by Hodder & Stoughton Ltd—permission kindly granted by the Executors of the Estate of the Right Honourable the Viscount d'Abernon. *The Right to the Land* by T.R.H. Davenport and K.S. Hunt (eds), published by David Philip Publisher (Pty) Ltd. *Senior History* by C. de Fowler and G.J.J. Smit; and *History for Standard 9* by G.J.J. Smit; both published by Maskew Miller Longman (Pty) Ltd. *South Africa. A History of South Africa* by C.W. de Kiewiet; and *The Oxford History of South Africa*, Vol. II, edited by M. Wilson and L. Thompson (adapted quotation); both published by Oxford University Press. *Southern Africa since 1800* by D. Denoon, published by Longman Group Ltd. *Russia in Revolution* by E.M. Halliday, published by Cassell Ltd, 1967 — cartoon on page 199. *History of the 20th Century* Numbers 45 and 48, published by Macdonald & Co (Publishers) Ltd. *Russia in Revolution 1890–1918* by L. Kochan, published by The New American Library, Inc. *Bismarck and the Two Germanies 1866–1870* by H. Kurtz, printed in *History Today* Vol. 20, No. 7, published by History Today Ltd. *A History of Russia and the Soviet Union*, revised edition, by D. Mackenzie and M.W. Curran, published by The Dorsey Press, Illinois. *Africa Undermined* by G. Lanning and M. Mueller (Pelican Books, 1979) p. 19, copyright © Greg Lanning and Marti Mueller, 1979—Reproduced by permission of Penguin Books Ltd. Cartoon by Sir David Low, printed in *The London Evening Standard*, 3 July 1934, reprinted by permission of The London Standard—p. 117. *The German Delegation at the Paris Peace Conference* by A. Luckau, published by Columbia University Press. *The Fall of Kruger's Republic* by J.S. Marais, published by Oxford University Press, 1961. *Men and Their Times: Bismarck and Modern Germany* by W.N. Medlicott, published by Hodder & Stoughton Educational. *Bismarck and the Development of Germany* by I.R. Mitchell, published by Homes McDougall Ltd, 1980. *The Man Without Qualities*, Vol. I, by Robert Musil, published by Picador. *Pan Books Ltd. The South African Economy* by J. Nattrass, published by Oxford University Press Southern Africa. *Japan's Modernization* by E. O'Connor, Harrap World History Programme, published by Harrap Ltd — permission kindly granted by Thomas Nelson and Sons Ltd. *A New History of Southern Africa* by N. Parsons, published by Macmillan, London and Basingstoke. *The Unification of Germany 1848–1871*, edited by O. Planze, published by R.E. Krieger Publishing Company Incorporated — cartoon on p. 18. *Peacemaking 1919* by Harold Nicholson, published by Constable & Co Ltd. *The Causes of the Anglo-Boer War* by D. Robinson. *Travel and Adventure in South East Africa* by F.C. Selous (Rhodesiana Reprint), published by Books of Zimbabwe Publishing Co (Pvt) Ltd. *A Source book for Modern History*, by N. Sheffe and W.E. Fisher, published by McGraw-Hill Ryerson Ltd — permission kindly granted by Norman Sheffe. *The Rise and Fall of the Third Reich* by W.L. Shirer, published by Martin Secker and Warburg Ltd. *The Rise and Fall of Adolf Hitler*, by Judith Steeh, published by Bison Books. 'The Sanitation Syndrome: Bubonic Plague and Urban Native Policy in the Cape Colony' by M. Swanson, printed in the *Journal of African History*, No. 3, published by Cambridge University Press. *Japan in the Twentieth Century* by R. Tames, published by B.T. Batsford Ltd. *The Unification of South Africa* by L.M. Thompson, published by Oxford University Press, 1960. 'An Eye-Witness Account of the Occupation of Essen'; 'The Situation in the Ruhr, March, 1932'; and 'The Situation in Western Germany, May, 1932'; all printed in *The Times*, published by Times Newspapers Limited. 'States and Colonies in South Africa, 1854–1902' by M.C. van Zyl, in *Five Hundred Years: A History of South Africa*, edited by C.F.J. Muller, published by Academica Publishers. 'South Africa in a comparative study of industrialization', printed in *Journal of Development Studies*, III, April 1971. *A Peoples History of the United States* by Howard Zinn, published by Longman. *Black Culture and Black Consciousness* by Lawrence Levine, published by Oxford University Press, New York. *Hitler and the Rise of the Nazis*, by D.M. Phillips, Archive Series, Hill and Fell, published by Edward Arnold Ltd, London. Quotation from *Der Führer* by Konrad Heiden. Copyright 1944 by Konrad Heiden. Copyright renewed 1971 by Bernhard E. Bartels, Executor of the Estate. Reprinted by permission of Houghton Mifflin Company, Boston.

We are indebted to the following sources for the use of illustrations: the Johannesburg Africana Museum; the Killie Campbell Africana Library; the Don Africana Library; the Cape Archives; the Ullstein Bilderdienst, Berlin; the Institute of Contemporary Art and Wiener Library; and the BBC Hulton Picture Library.

Contents

General Introduction

GENERAL HISTORY SECTION

Introduction to contemporary world history (or general history) 1860–1930s

1. The emergence of the nation state in central Europe: The unification of Germany 1
   by Sue Krige

2. The First World War 36
   by Jim Campbell

3. Some consequences of the First World War 79
   by Bruce Murray, Hugh Lester and Justin Hall

4. The United States of America, 1783–1900 121
   by Bruce Murray

5. The emergence of the modern nation state: Japan in the Nineteenth and Twentieth Centuries 159
   by Cynthia Kros

6. The emergence of the modern nation state: Russia in the Nineteenth Century 194
   by Rosemary Mulholland

Composite chronology of general history 221

SOUTH AFRICAN HISTORY SECTION

Introduction 227

7. The economic and social effects of the discovery and mining of diamonds and gold: 1870–1910 229
   by Peter Kallaway

8. Imperialism, Republicanism, and the incorporation of the African Kingdoms 269
   by Robert Morrell

9. Reconstruction to Union 314
   by Robert Morrell

Chronology of Southern African history: 1870–1910 339

General Introduction

HISTORY AS EXPLANATION

History is not the same thing as *the past*. An account of 'the past', if it could be known to human beings, would amount to an account of *everything* that had ever happened. History is our reconstruction and interpretation of the events of the past. It is based on the sources of evidence available from the period we wish to study: often on the writings of the people who lived at the time, and on the research of historians since then. These historians have each attempted to reconstruct that history in their own way—each influenced by his/her own attitudes, beliefs and understanding, and by the circumstances and environment in which they lived.

In a sense, therefore, *the past* is unchanging and unchangeable—and a lot of what happened is unknowable because we have no record of the events that occurred. *History* is by definition what we know about the past, but what we know is itself selected from a vast amount of evidence potentially available to us. As we select we make decisions about what is important and what is to be left out of consideration. In the process of writing history we therefore leave out much more than we include. In that process of selection, the historian consciously or unconsciously *interprets* the evidence and gives his/her own version of what happened and why it happened. The ongoing process of interpreting the evidence is affected by the system of ideas and beliefs (or ideology) of the historian.

There is therefore no such thing as absolutely *objective* history, or history without bias of some kind. All history, because it is written by human beings, individually or collectively, bears the stamp of their personalities and their political, cultural or economic assumptions or beliefs.

School textbooks, generally, tend to obscure one of the important issues raised above—namely that interpretations of history are continually debated, contested and revised by historians. There is very little consensus among 'the experts' regarding the interpretation of the past!

The difficulty of writing an historical summary or survey for a textbook is that any attempt to condense historical debates tends to remove the sense of conflict between historians over the material at hand. In attempting to summarize and condense the writings of historians so as to make them conform to a syllabus and be accessible to students, there is a danger that interesting debates and important points of disagreement will be glossed over, or lost, to the readers. There is a fundamental conflict for the writer of a textbook between, on the one hand, the need to dramatically condense and simplify the writings of historians, and on the other hand, the need to keep alive and impart some of the flavour of the craft of the historian.

In this text we will try to show history as a *process of explanation* rather than a body of received information. Without being able to enter into lengthy explanations at every turn our intention will be to highlight various interpretations of history.

We have attempted to write history by asking questions about past events and attempting to answer those questions—*history is presented as an interrogative process or a dialogue*. In the text we will stop periodically to frame the questions to the best of our ability, drawing on a variety of written sources which will be indicated at the end of chapter. Other questions might strike

This history series, which spans the century between 1870–1970, attempts to move away from a purely chronological (so-called 'factual') approach to textbook history, and to emphasise lines and themes of interpretation. The focus is avowedly explanatory. Rather than drown students in hundreds of pages of information, it is our endeavour to provide a grid for understanding the structure of the subject. We have also attempted to include a wide variety of source materials in the text (photographs, primary and secondary documents, maps, tables and diagrams), in order to give readers a feeling for the 'raw materials' of the historian's craft.

We undertook to write this book on the assumption that there are many teachers in Southern Africa who teach, or wish to teach, vivid, creative, critical history, and that there are many students who seek a wider vision than that provided by a purely chronological presentation of information. We direct our efforts to aid those who find themselves in such learning contexts, accepting that our own presentations and formulations of history may well be challenged or refuted.

What more could we hope for than that our youth should be willing and able to challenge conventional wisdom about the formulation of the past! In this challenging they should acquire the critical tools of the historian's trade; and in doing so they will come to understand the past more comprehensively and be able to plan for the future.

We cannot understand the present or plan for the future without a keen sense of where we have come from, what forces have acted upon our society, and why we find ourselves in the circumstances we do. The critical study of history helps us to understand our world a little more clearly, to decode the complexities of the past, and to appreciate the motives which lie behind our own actions and the actions of others, whether they be in the past or the present.

To assist you in the process of coming to grips with this rather complex material each chapter or section has appended:

(a) a glossary of unfamiliar terms (note that an asterisk after a word in the text indicates that the word is defined in the glossary; also bear in mind that the terms are defined in the specific *context* in which they are used in the chapter — they are not necessarily universal definitions);

(b) a set of exercises to help you appreciate the nature of historical evidence (documents, pictures, maps etc.), and to test your understanding of key issues;

(c) a chronology of the period and content covered;

(d) a bibliography of recommended reading for those who wish to move beyond the limits of our treatment of the subjects covered.

It is our intention to bring history alive and help you to participate in some of the excitement that comes of knowing about other ages and other circumstances. The process of learning how to think historically is of particular importance to our education when it helps us to understand how the modern world came to be made in the way it was and how the past influences the present.

In addition, against the background of considerable experience with the JMB Matric History examination, we would argue that those candidates who have mastered an explanatory and interpretative approach are also those who will achieve well in the examination room.

you as important, and you should use the reading indicated in the bibliography at the end of each chapter to assist you to find answers to those questions.

PETER KALLAWAY
Education Policy Unit,
University of Cape Town
October 1985

General History

Introduction to contemporary world history

(or GENERAL HISTORY) 1860–1930s

We live today in a world different, in almost all its basic preconditions, from the world in which Bismarck lived and died. How have these changes come about? What are the formative influences and qualitative differences which are the distinguishing marks of the contemporary era?

(Adapted from G. Barraclough, *An Introduction to Contemporary History*)

This section is concerned not merely to recount the course of events between 1860 and the 1930s, or to simply expand history from a European focus to represent events on a world-wide scale. Such an account would, in itself, be unlikely to result in a better understanding of the forces at play in the world during this era *unless* we are aware at the same time of the underlying structural changes that were occurring. What we have attempted to provide, in addition to an account of the key events of this era, is *a framework for understanding world history*.

In addition we have tried in places to indicate how the general history section links up with the section on Southern African history.

It is surely more than sheer coincidence that the emancipation of the serfs in Russia and the emancipation of slaves in the USA took place within the same decade at the beginning of this era. How is this to be explained? What concepts do we need to use to make sense of events that replaced centuries-old traditions and opened the way to 'new' human societies as diverse as the democratic, free enterprise market economy of the USA and the socialist, planned economy of the USSR?

It is undeniable that these events, along with the changes that united Germany, or dramatically transformed feudal Japan, must to a large extent be attributed to the new forces of capitalist industrialization, imperialism and the rise of the modern nation state.

Any attempt at crude simplification of these complex events should be rejected — the historical forces at work in Germany, Japan, Russia and the USA *cannot* all be fitted into any simple model of historical development or progress. Yet to understand the significance of the events that took place we are obliged to *explain* what the links are and thus how we are to understand such an apparent coincidence as the emancipation in the USA and the USSR mentioned above. The formal study of history has often fought shy of that obligation and taken refuge in descriptive accounts of historical events, leaving the student mystified regarding the meaning or significance of events under review.

We are not suggesting that teachers would have easy answers to these complex questions. We are simply suggesting that it is necessary to raise the questions if a satisfactory understanding of the complex nature of history is to be developed, and the tools necessary for such understanding are to be made available to learners.

The section on world history in this book is an approach to the study of the past which places an emphasis upon the thematic treatment of key developments. *Chronologically*, the era under review in this book takes on meaning if we think of it as encompassing the period which began with the reign of Kaiser Wilhelm I of Prussia and ended with the rise of Adolf Hitler and the Third Reich; or alternatively as the period which began in the era of slavery in the USA and serfdom in Russia, and ended with the creation of the world's largest free labour economy in the former, and the great socialist experiment of a planned labour economy in the latter. *Conceptually* understood it was an era of nationalism, imperialism and industrialization — forces which wrought changes of the utmost significance. Technology and science transformed the nature of production, communications and warfare. Urbanization changed age-old social patterns and gave rise to problems of housing, health, schooling, welfare and social control that had hitherto been inconceivable.

The transformation of agricultural and industrial production gave rise to new economic and political processes which had their origins in the earlier industrial revolution and the French Revolution — changes which led to a struggle between three forces: the declining traditional aristocracy; the rising bougeoisie or the middle classes; and the emerging working classes. Tensions arising out of these conflicts gave rise to domestic upheavals in all of the countries studied below.

The emergence of a world economy was a key aspect of the trade agreements, political alliances and rival imperialisms that emerged. War, industrialization, technology, colonialism, the expansion of big business and modern means of communication all helped to make the world a 'smaller' place, but often failed to promote better relationships between people.

For all these dramatic changes, the experience of the First World War was a blow to the self-confidence of modern people, and it gave rise to the understanding that 'progress' did not always take place simply with the passage of time. With World History, or total history, it is no longer sufficient to write only about the famous, the wealthy or the powerful. World History should deal with all segments of society and people in all corners of the World, not simply out of a sense of curiosity, but because we are all in a sense part of history.

Total history is the ideal, and we are only partially successful here — in part due to the constraints of the syllabus; in part due to the limitations on the length of this book. Neglected aspects of our attempt to write a total history include the history of colonialism in Africa, Latin America and Asia, the history of racism, the rise of organised labour, and the struggle for women's rights — to name but a few aspects.

In short, what is mainly reflected in the syllabus, and therefore in our selection of content, is a history which tells about the activities of those who have achieved success in history — the histories of those people, nations and groups who were successful in progress and modernization. Such success must of course in itself be assessed critically — for it was that very success which also provided an important ingredient for the advent of the First World War and the rise of Nazi Germany.

1

The emergence of the nation state in central Europe:
THE UNIFICATION OF GERMANY

Introduction 2
The industrial revolution in western and central Europe 3
The transformation of the German area up to 1862 4
   Prussian dominance in German economic affairs
Consequences of the transformation of Germany 8
   The challenge of the German middle class
   The changing balance in the Bund
   Prussia and reform
   The Iron Chancellor and his historians
The process of political unification, 1862–1866:
The exclusion of Austria 15
   Bismarck and the Prussian liberals
   The failure of the Frankfurt meeting
   Prussia and Austria on a collision course: Schleswig and Holstein
   The Austro-Prussian War
   Results of the war
   Europe's reaction to the changing balance of power in Germany
   The peace with Austria and the formation of the North German Federation
   The defeat and defection of Prussian liberals
The process of political unification, 1866–1871:
The incorporation of the south German states 24
   Relations between the south and north German states after 1866
   The quarrel with France
   The south German states and the war between Prussia and France
   Results of the Franco-Prussian War
   The Peace of Frankfurt
   The German Empire
   The German Empire, Europe and the world
   Revision Questions
   Chronology
   Glossary
   Bibliography

Introduction

The revolutions of 1848 in western and central Europe can be seen as an attempt by leaders of the growing middle class* to challenge the political systems created by the Congress of Vienna in 1815. The arrangements concluded then had left Germany* divided into thirty-nine independent states under the control of the German *Bund**. This 'springtime of the peoples', as many saw it, promised much — the end of absolute monarchy, the removal of political power from conservative aristocracies, and the passing of this power to the middle class. The revolutionaries also wanted to break down the political and economic barriers which divided people who shared the same language, culture and traditions and unite them as different 'nations'.

This challenge was unsuccessful. The revolutionaries were divided among themselves about the details of liberal reform or unification. They were unable to mobilize peasant or worker support for their cause, partly because they feared the masses as much as they feared the armies of the absolute monarchs. In central Europe the armies of the Kings of Prussia, Austria and Russia crushed the revolutionary movements in Berlin, Prague, Vienna and Milan. Those who had looked upon the period as a springtime of the peoples seemed to have been premature in their judgement.

Just over twenty years later, the nation states of Germany and Italy had been created. During the period 1850 to 1871 there were no more attempted revolutions such as had occurred in 1848. Instead this period was notable for a number of short but bloody wars which were waged by the professional armies of France, Britain, Prussia, Austria and Russia. These wars played an important part in the process of national unification. Closer examination of the period reveals that these wars were fought against the background of massive economic and social changes taking place in western and central Europe.

In this chapter we will discuss the creation of the nation state of Germany. To find out how this happened we will try to answer a number of questions. First we will examine what sort of economic and social changes took place in west and central Europe in the first half of the Nineteenth Century. Then we will

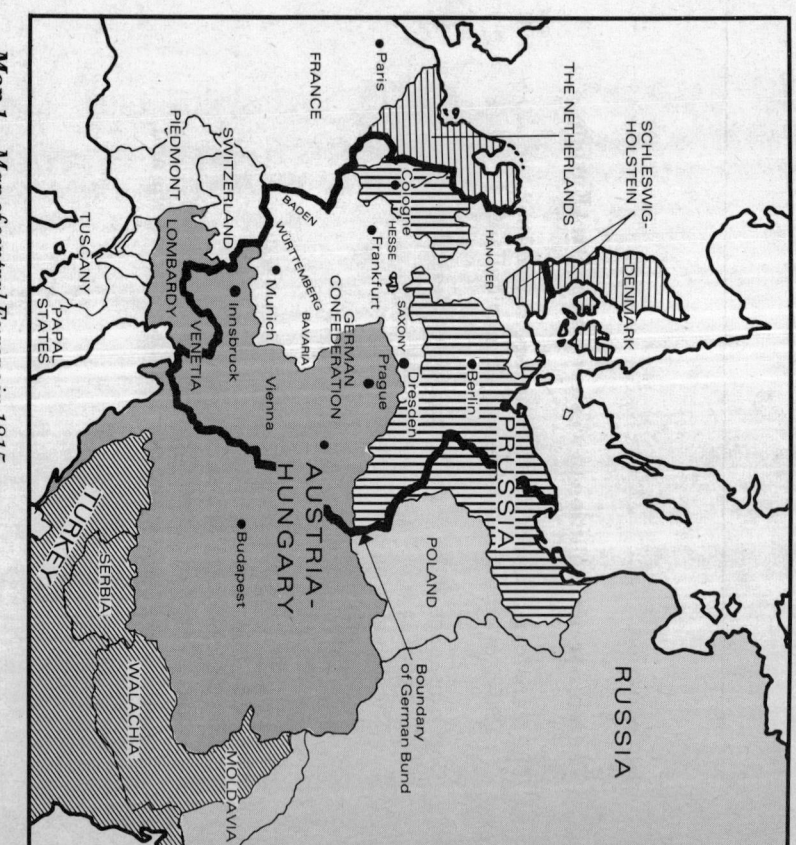

Map 1 — Map of central Europe in 1815.

discuss how these changes affected the German area in particular. Once we have seen how these changes affected Germany, we can examine the process of political unification over the years 1862–1871, under Kaiser Wilhelm I (1861–1888). Finally, we will look at what kind of nation state came into being in 1871, when the German Empire was proclaimed.

The industrial revolution in western and central Europe

One historian has remarked that after 1848, 'political revolution retreated and industrial revolution advanced'. It was this industrial revolution which transformed the economic, social and political structures of the countries of western and central Europe. In Britain the process had begun in the Eighteenth Century, and was based originally on the expansion of the cotton industry. This led to the development of new methods of production for textiles, which in turn stimulated the exploitation of coal and iron resources. These resources were used for providing more efficient ways of transporting goods such as railways and steamships. They were also used to improve machinery used in textile production.

The British produced textiles more cheaply than manufacturers or the continent. British competition began to affect the less advanced textile industries of France and Germany. In response, continental manufacturers began to develop machinery which could also produce goods cheaply and efficiently. Initially they made use of machines and technical experts imported from Britain. From 1802, war between Britain and France forced French and German manufacturers to become more self-reliant, and it stimulated the utilization of natural resources like coal and iron used for the making of machinery. After 1815, France suffered a set-back when it lost valuable coalfields and iron mines located in territories given to Belgium and Prussia. Prussia began exploiting the coalfields and iron ore in earnest.

Perhaps the most spectacular symbol of this exploitation was the railway, which has been called the crowning achievement of the early industrial revolution. Both coal and iron were used in its manufacture, and the expansion of railways made further exploitation of such resources possible. By cheapening transport costs, the railways boosted the production of textiles and other manufactured goods, as well as agricultural goods. Until well into the second half of the Nineteenth Century, railways represented the single most important 'heavy' industry in Europe. The financing of railways required large amounts of capital.

This need led to the growth of an efficient banking system and the formation of powerful national banks, especially in France and Prussia. (It is interesting to compare this process with the 'transport revolution' in South Africa in the late Nineteenth Century. This is discussed in Chapter 7.)

Steamships revolutionized water transport in the same way that railways had revolutionized land transport. Steam engines in factories, mines and forges increased steadily in numbers. Some of the profits made from industrial development were used for research into newer and better methods of production. The mid-Nineteenth Century saw the beginnings of the utilisation of cheap steel through the invention of the Bessemer Converter. Electricity was investigated as a possible alternative power source to coal. Large companies like Siemens in Prussia were directly involved in research into the improvement of steel manufacture and the generation and use of electricity.

The development of railways, and the use of steamships which sailed the huge wide rivers of Europe and the oceans of the world, meant that Europe, and indeed the world, seemed to shrink. New methods of communication such as the telegraph contributed to this. Areas once distant and inaccessible were now easily linked, and everyone felt the impact of this industrial revolution in one way or another.

Before industrialization, the economies of the countries of western and central Europe had been based on wealth created by the sale of agricultural produce. In general this land was owned by aristocrats who also had occupied positions of political power for hundreds of years. Industrialization led to the creation of a class of wealthy people (capitalists) whose money came from their control of the mines, forges, factories, railway companies and banks. These people challenged the fact that political power in most of Europe lay in the hands of absolute monarchs, supported by conservative landowner aristocracies. They began to demand forms of government which were more sensitive to their interests. In general they favoured some form of parliamentary representation which would give them political power. They also saw political unification as the best means of developing their economic interests. Many of the revolutionary leaders of 1848 were drawn from their ranks.

Not all the revolutionaries of 1848 sought to secure purely middle class interests. A minority favoured more radical changes — the extension of the franchise to the ever growing numbers of workers in the cities. Industrialization had led to the creation of a working class in the cities whose interests (such as higher wages and better working conditions) were often at odds with their employers. By the mid-Nineteenth Century socialist ideas had begun to take root among working people. The newly rich middle class faced opposition from both the traditional holders of economic and political power, and from those who had no economic or political power.

It is important to discuss how these changes in the economic, social and political life of Europe affected Germany, for they played an important part in its unification.

The transformation of the German area up to 1862

This section will begin by presenting you with two maps and two passages which deal with German industrialization. Study the material carefully and answer the questions which follow.

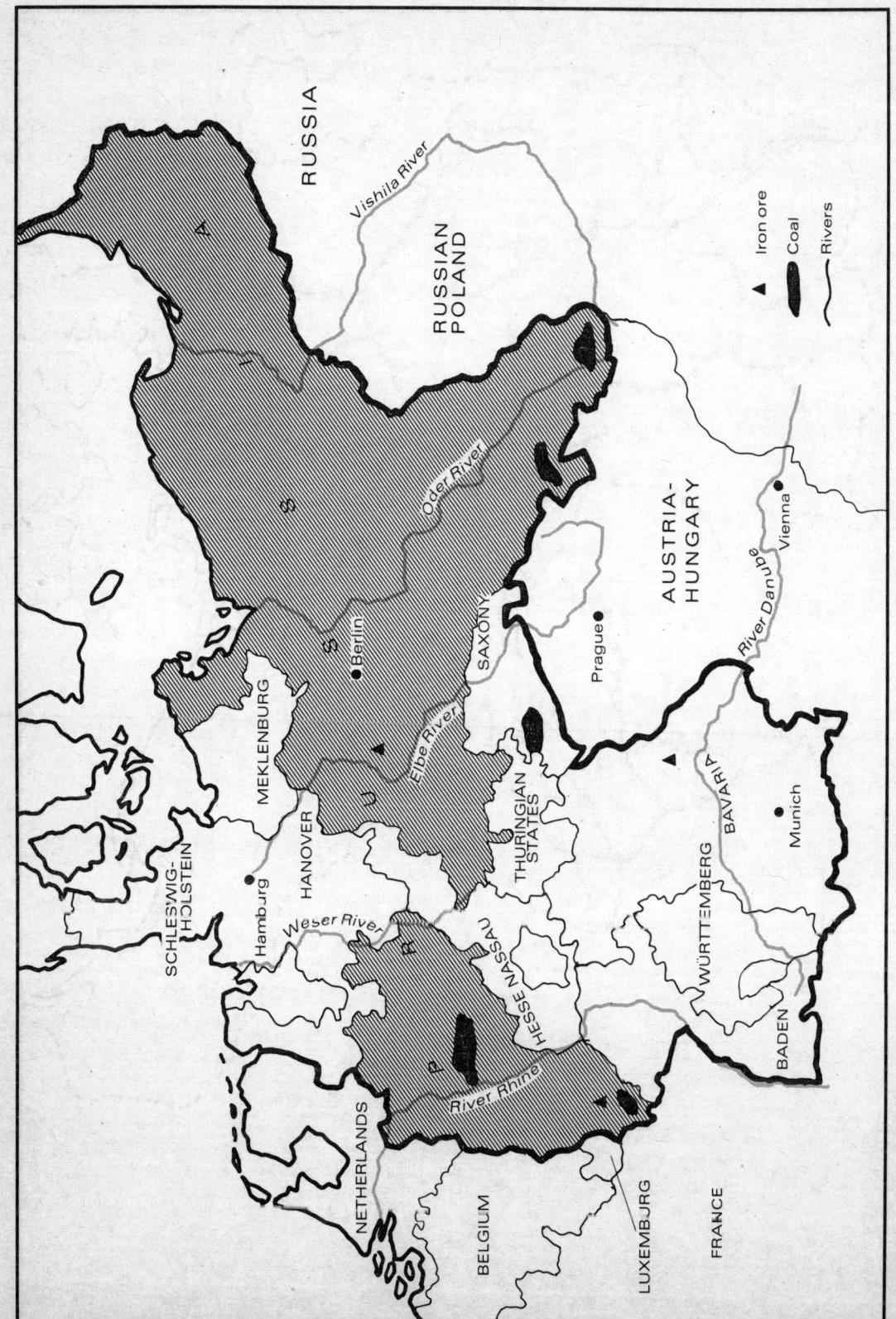

Map 2 — Map of the German area, showing major rivers and coal and iron deposits.

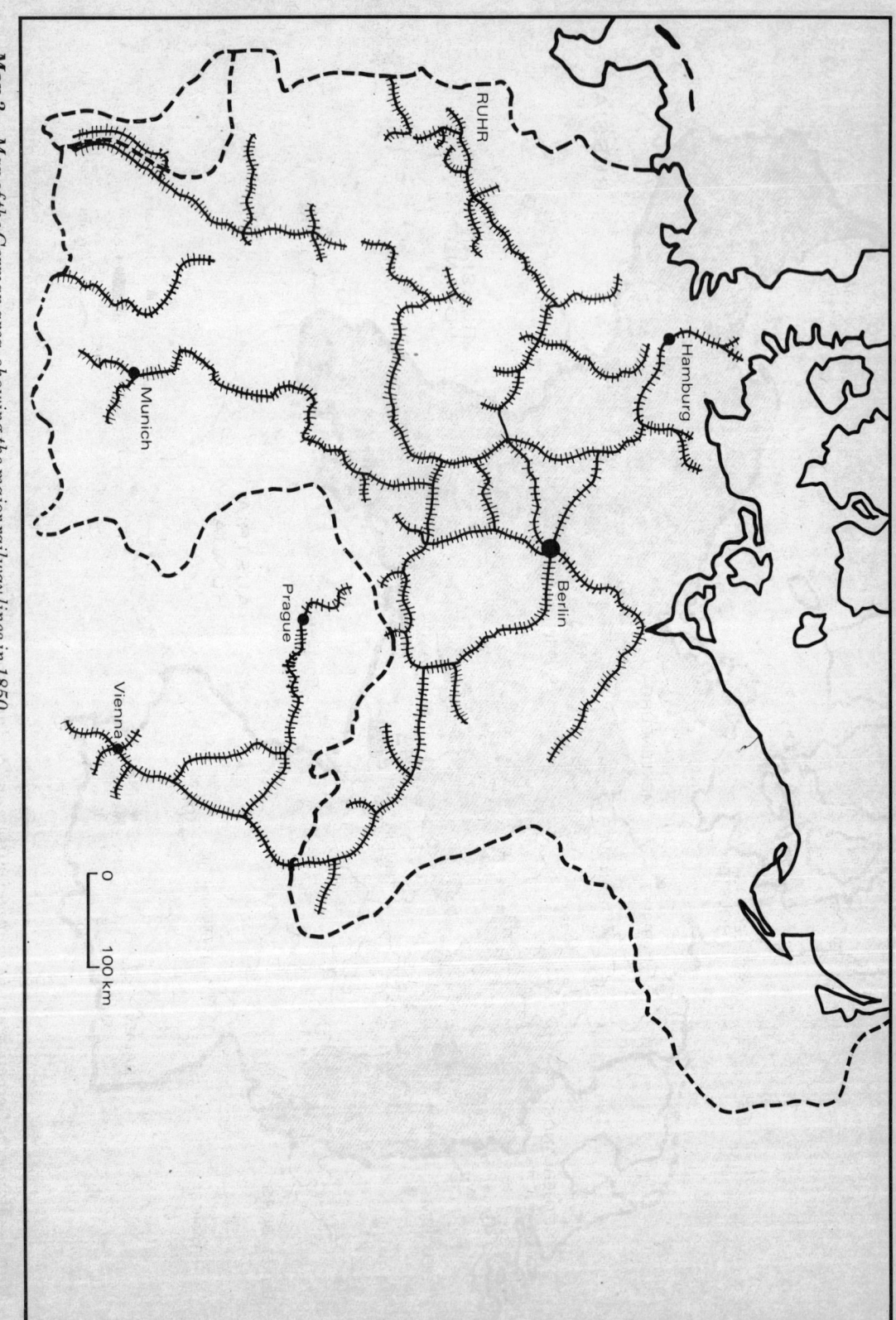

Map 3 — Map of the German area, showing the major railway lines in 1850.

Here is a description of industry in the Rhineland, written in 1846 by an Englishman called Thomas Banfield.

The district of the Ruhr is remarkable for the manufacturing activity which is found there and which promises to increase rapidly and to prove durable ...

A visit to the docks and workshops of Haniel, Huyssen and Jacobi must not be ommitted by any who would inform themselves of the state of machine manufacture in Germany. The greater part of the steam-tugs now plying on the Rhine have been built in this house ... The order, quiet and business-like arrangements were quite English; but it was not very English to hear that every pound of iron used had been raised at their own mines, smelted, rolled and finished at their own works ....

A great variety of experiments have been made by scientific men, and manufacturers, to find a shorter and cheaper mode than the ordinary one for turning the iron of this country into steel. For some uses it is unsurpassed. For instance, the steel foils* of Solingen are sent all over the world as combining toughness with elasticity in the highest degree known.

We have noticed a cast-steel manufactory at Essen, belonging to Mr Krupp, in which the English method of making steel is retained. The steel of this factory is in great demand and is often sold for English. There are few markets susceptible of so much extension as that of steel.

(Quoted in Knox, pp. 23–24)

Below is an extract from a report written in 1854 describing the boom in German industry.

Eighteen new societies and companies for mining and smelting have been already formed; Rhenish coal is already being sent in regular deliveries to Belgium, Rhenish coke to Munich; miners' wages have risen ... labour is in short supply; home and foreign capital is engaged in a mighty onslaught upon the black timber of our mountains; blast furnaces rise one after the other and light up the region when night draws her veil about the mountains ... The 'Phoenix' iron and coal company exceeds all previous enterprises in splendour and size; its fine premises are rapidly approaching completion, two furnaces in Dilldorf and two in Ruhrort are in full blast, and the building of the fifth and sixth furnaces is already far advanced; altogether, it is intended to erect twenty blast furnaces.

(Pollard and Holmes, *Documents of European Economic History*, Vol. 1, quoted in Booth, p. 25)

Questions

1. (a) Both extracts mention one area which was undergoing rapid industrial development. Which was it? RUHR
   (b) To which German state did this area belong? PRUSSIA
   (c) Using the maps and extracts, explain why you think the area was especially noted for its rapid industrialization. RAILWAYS/RIVER

2. (a) The second extract mentions the manufacture of 'steam tugs now plying on the Rhine'. On Map 2 find the Rhine and two other major rivers which flowed through the German area.
   (b) Using the maps, extracts and previous parts of this chapter, discuss the importance of railways and steamships for the development of the German economy.

3. (a) What important new product was being manufactured from iron? STEEL
   (b) Why was it important? SOLD OVERSEAS

4. *Using information provided by the maps and extracts, explain which state in the German area was likely to be the centre of German industrial development.*

As you have seen from your answers to the above questions, parts of the German area were rapidly becoming industrialized. The state of Prussia had developed the most in this direction by the mid-Nineteenth Century. We are going to look more closely at how Prussia came to dominate German political and economic affairs.

PRUSSIA'S DOMINANCE IN GERMAN ECONOMIC AFFAIRS

As was mentioned on page 3, industrialization in Europe was first stimulated by competition from cheap British goods. Prussia's two chief exports were cotton and linen, and both were affected by British competition. Even though Prussian manufacturers began to mechanize their industry by the middle of the Nineteenth Century, they still could not compete with British goods on the open world market. British goods were of higher quality, and were also cheaper.

Prussian businessmen therefore turned to expanding their home market. Internal customs barriers between the Prussian provinces hindered trade by doubling or trebling prices. These barriers were removed. Similar customs barriers existed between all the states of the German Bund (see Map 1). Some smaller German states removed trading restrictions. By 1834 seventeen German states, both large and small, had joined with Prussia to form a customs union or *Zollverein*. This meant that the raw materials of German industry, which were situated at long distances from each other, could be transported quickly and cheaply from one part of Germany to another.

The emphasis in industry moved from textile production to heavy industries such as railway construction, and later engineering and electricity supply. Parallel businesses like banking thrived as industrialists like Krupp and Siemens seemed to need a never ending amount of capital. The formation of the Zollverein, and the consequent growth of heavy industry, gave Prussia the chance to exploit its abundant resources of coal and iron. In doing so it became the most economically powerful state in the German area. Austria, the largest empire in central Europe, was a member of the German Bund, but was excluded from the Zollverein. Austria was short of resources and capital. Therefore its economists favoured protection of its agriculture and newly created industries, rather than the free trade system operating in the Zollverein.

Consequences of the transformation of Germany

THE CHALLENGE OF THE GERMAN MIDDLE CLASS

Prussia's economic dominance of Germany was seen as a positive development by the emerging middle class both in and outside Prussia itself. Why this was so will become clear once we have looked at who the German middle class were and what their particular interests were.

We have noted that industrialization led to the creation of a class of people whose wealth was based on the control of industry in Germany. As in much of Europe, these people challenged the existing political structures which denied them political power. After 1848 industrialists, merchants and professional people formed political pressure groups (such as the *Deutsche National Verein*) or political parties (such as the Progress Party in Prussia). They were committed to three main things: free enterprise, political unification and constitutional reform.

As far as free enterprise was concerned, much progress had been made. The Zollverein met some requirements for free trade. Even the most reactionary governments of the Bund showed that they were capable of promoting free enterprise within their borders. Government controls over mining were removed and bureaucratic restrictions on the formation of companies were eased.

But the German Bund remained a loose federation of thirty-nine states, each with its own laws regarding industrial development and trade. Differences in postal, telegraph and railway systems, in money and coinage, and in weights and measures hindered the more efficient use of resources. Political unification was seen as a way to promote economic growth. The German historian and political philosopher, Engels, commented on the connection between the economic interests of the German middle class and the demand for political reform.

The existence of a mass of petty German states, with their many differing commercial and industrial laws was bound to become an intolerable fetter on this powerfully developing industry and on the growing commerce with which it was linked.

One can see ... that the desire for a united 'fatherland' had a very material foundation. It was the demand arising from the immediate commercial needs of practical businessmen and industrialists for the elimination of all the historically outdated rubbish which obstructed the free development of trade and industry.

(Quoted in Mitchell, p. 51)

These 'practical businessmen and industrialists' believed that a united Germany should be a constitutional monarchy. The German Kaiser and his Ministers should be responsible to a parliament elected by men of property or money. Under such a system the political power of landed aristocrats would gradually become less as the men of new wealth increased in numbers. A restricted franchise would exclude workers and peasants. (See page 13.)

Another important consequence of industrialization was the change in relations between states of the Bund. The consequence of the economic revolution was that it upset the traditional friendly relationship between Austria and Prussia, and this affected the other states.

THE CHANGING BALANCE IN THE BUND

Even though the creation of the German Bund in 1815 reduced the number of German states to thirty-nine, the Bund itself was designed to perpetuate the division of Germany rather than to speed up unification. The *Diet** to which the states sent representatives to discuss matters of common concern, was really nothing more than a debating chamber. It had none of the powers associated with a central government, such as raising an army, imposing taxes or passing laws. Each of the thirty-nine states performed these tasks separately. Indeed, many of the rulers of the German states were autocratic princes who valued their own power and autonomy much more than the idea of unity.

From 1815 Austria's position as the dominant power in the Bund was guaranteed by the constitution which stated that Austria's Prime Minister would be chairman of the Bund. (When this post was occupied by the ruthless Prince Metternich, Austria's dominant position seemed unshakeable.) But the source of Austrian domination went deeper than a clause in a constitution. Many of the German states had strong religious and cultural ties with Austria. The Reformation had left Germany with deep religious differences. Most northern states were Protestant and the southern states were mainly Catholic. Austria was strongly Catholic and so many Catholic German states were drawn to it. The emergence of Prussia in the Nineteenth Century, strongly Protestant and militaristic, reinforced the traditional loyalty of many of the smaller German Catholic states to Austria.

Austria's main rival in the Bund was Prussia — the only state comparable in size, wealth and population. Between 1815 and 1848 Prussia did not really challenge Austria's political domination of the Bund. Prussia's rulers concerned themselves more with economic development. However, it was this economic development and the formation of the Zollverein which effectively increased Prussia's power in the Bund. The smaller German states were now economically dependent on Prussia, even though their traditional loyalties lay with Austria.

This was how Engels summed up Prussia's position in the mid-Nineteenth Century. Read the passage carefully and answer the questions which follow it.

Prussia, in order to put an end to the tariff barriers which divided its two halves [see Map 1], invited the adjoining German states to form a Customs Union [in 1834]. This is how the Zollverein came into existence....

The Zollverein was a great success for Prussia. That it signified a victory over Austrian influence was the least important aspect of it. The most important thing was that it ranged the bourgeoisie* of the small and medium-sized principalities on the side of Prussia.... And the more the Zollverein expanded ... the more the burgeoning* bourgeoisie of these states got used to Prussia as their economic, and potentially their political, leader.

(Quoted in Mitchell, p. 10)

Questions

To answer these questions, use information in the passage and in previous parts of this chapter.

1. *Explain how the Zollverein was formed in the German area.* 1818 in Prussia 1834 17 states

2. *Why was Austria not a member of the Zollverein?*

3. *Engels made two main points about the results of the formation of the Zollverein. Write out these points in your own words.*

① Explain the difference between the K.D. + the G.D solution + which group favoured each

Prussian economic strength was undermining Austria's political dominance of the Bund. The middle class people of the smaller German states began to look to Prussia not only as economic leader of the Bund but as the future leader of political unification. There had been some debate among the middle class about whether or not Austria should be included in a united Germany. There were those who wanted to include Austria, possibly without the non-German parts of its Hapsburg

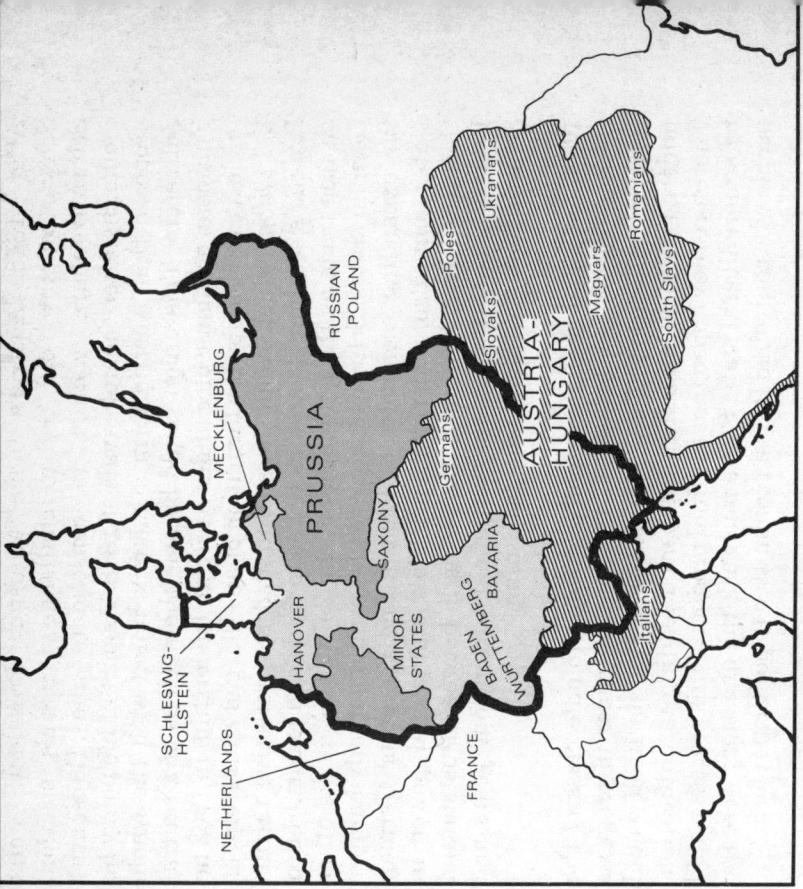

Map 4 — *The Klein Deutsch Solution.*

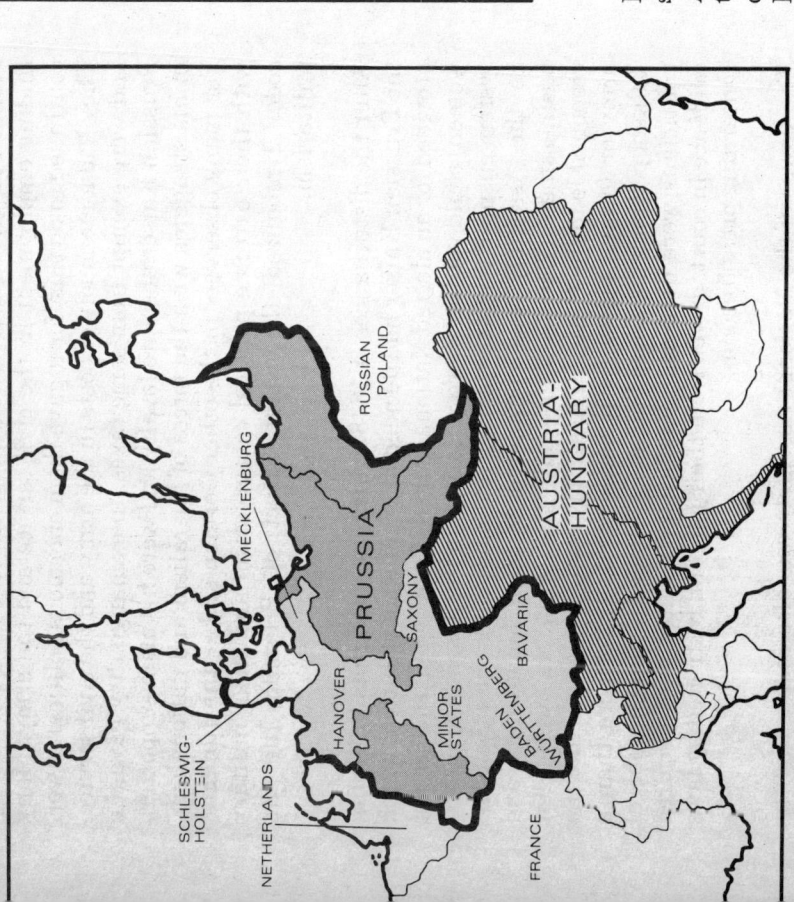

Map 5 — *The Gross Deutsch Solution.*

Empire, which extended into eastern Europe. They favoured the so called *Gross Deutsch* solution. Others wished to exclude Austria altogether. This was the *Klein Deutsch* solution. From the 1850s onwards, more and more members of nationalist organizations supported the Klein Deutsch option, because of Prussia's obvious economic superiority and potential political power. Maps 4 and 5 illustrate these two proposed solutions.

After 1848 Austria's new Minister President, Felix Schwartzenburg, did try to challenge Prussia's position. Schwartzenburg wanted to consolidate the Hapsburg* monarchy after the upheavals of 1848. As part of his policy he proposed that Austria form a customs union with the whole Zollverein. This union would become the nucleus of a central European economic bloc under Austrian leadership. In 1862 he made a proposal for the formation of an enlarged Zollverein, or *Zollunion*, which would be surrounded by protective tariffs. Prussia's economy, geared as it was to trade and export, relied on free trade as the foundation of the Zollverein, as did other German states. Schwartzenburg's plan would not only hamper Prussia's status and power in Germany. As it happened, the struggle between Austria and Prussia was settled on the battlefield within four years and Schwartzenburg's plans came to nothing.

We have noted that the rapidly growing middle class of the German states saw Prussia as the natural leader in progress towards unification. They assumed that Prussia itself would undergo political reform in the period leading to unification. Therefore they hoped that the final product of this process would be a more liberal state. So we must ask the question: were the people who controlled Prussia committed to political reform?

PRUSSIA AND REFORM

One historian has described Prussia as a 'militarized bureaucracy'*. After 1815, Prussian reformers had concentrated on the development of an extremely efficient bureaucracy which could run the state, and on the re-organization of the professional army which protected the state. Both these were staffed by men who came from the conservative, landowning class, the *Junkers*. They were concentrated in Prussian lands east of the Elbe River, where their estates were worked by landless descendants of conquered Slav people.

In general, these estates were not large and had to be carefully worked and managed to provide a profit. The growing needs of industry demanded that these estates be more productive, and many of these Junkers became successful businessmen as a result. For years Junkers had supplemented their incomes by finding employment in the civil service and the army. Many continued to do this, for it gave them enormous political power. They had a monopoly of posts in the army and the civil service, and were exempt from some taxes. In exchange they gave the Prussian Kaiser absolute loyalty and were his main supporters in his struggles with the forces of liberalism and nationalism. For many observers in the other German states, the Junkers, with their extreme political conservatism and strict military code, symbolized the worst aspect of Prussian life, its militarism.

After the disturbances of 1848, which included riots in Berlin, the Prussian Kaiser had decided to grant a constitution, which provided for an elected National Assembly. All men (though not women) could vote for representatives in the Assembly, but the system ensured that the wealthy had more votes than the poor. So the Assembly was dominated by rich landowners and businessmen. The Kaiser and his Ministers were not responsible to the National Assembly regarding issues like the army or foreign policy, so it ended up as little more than a 'talkshop' which discussed budgets. Outside parliament, liberal politicians were harassed by police, persecuted with perjured evidence in court, driven from their jobs and restricted by laws concerning press freedom.

The power of the National Assembly was also reduced by the existence of an Upper House which consisted mainly of landed nobility appointed by the Kaiser. Here is a diagram of the political structure of Prussia.

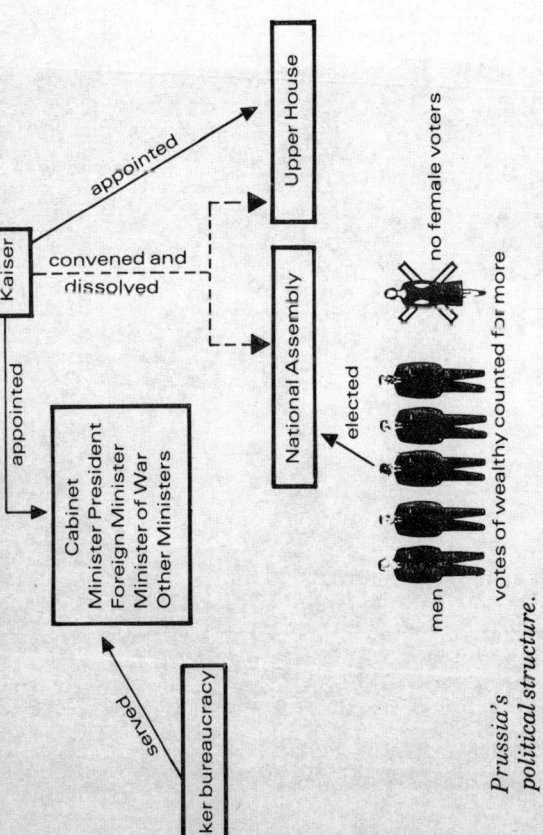

Prussia's political structure.

In spite of the fact that the Kaiser and the Junkers dominated Prussia's political life, Prussian industry developed and boomed. The Prussian state proved that it was quite capable of modernizing without fundamentally changing its political structure. The efficient Junker bureaucracy which administered Prussia had promoted the construction of the infrastructure of roads, railways and waterways, which in turn had led to Prussia's economic development and assured Prussia's domination of the German area. Political and economic liberalism did not necessarily go hand in hand. The historian Hobsbawm remarked that:

> ... the men who officially presided over the affairs of the victorious bourgeois order were deeply reactionary* country noblemen ...
>
> (Hobsbawm, p.3)

As we have seen, the Junkers had a monopoly of posts in the army. Industrialization in Prussia had a profound effect on the military. The construction of efficient railway systems revolutionized the mobilization of troops. Now they could be transported quickly from one place to another and launch surprise attacks on a slower enemy. Large amounts of money which were poured into industrial research resulted in the invention of new weapons and the development of heavy artillery. The needle gun* was far more efficient than the older muzzle-loading rifles. The Krupps arms factory produced cannons which could fire shells over long distances. Speed and advanced technology gave Prussia the basis for a modern army.

Industrial development also made Prussia wealthy enough to wage three wars in the period 1863–1871 without facing financial collapse. State funds were invested in the development of timber and tobacco industries. In addition the state gained revenue from import and export duties, taxing of businesses and royalties from mining rights.

By 1860 Prussia was a rapidly modernizing state, but the people who controlled it in the government, army and civil service remained conservative. The appointment of Otto von Bismarck as Minister President of Prussia in 1862 finally committed Prussia to the path of conservative modernization. If Prussia led the German states to unification, it was likely that this pattern of modernization would be imposed on a united Germany as well.

Before we examine the period 1862 to 1871, it is important to take a look at Otto von Bismarck himself, and at the historical debate that surrounds his role in German unification. Many books written in the last hundred years about German unification focus on the part played by Bismarck in this process.

13

THE 'IRON CHANCELLOR'* AND HIS HISTORIANS

Bismarck was born in 1815 in Prussia, the son of a Junker nobleman. He first came into contact with liberal and nationalist ideas while at university from 1832. He was attracted by nationalist ideas but rejected liberalism. He made this clear after he was appointed as Prussia's representative to the United Diet of 1847. Scornful of the attempts of the liberals of 1848 to unite the Germans, he concentrated on making a career for himself in politics. He became Prussia's representative in the German Diet for a number of years. Here he developed a reputation for being extremely conservative.

He was dedicated to preserving Prussian interests when they came into conflict with those of Austria. He quickly became known as an enemy of Austria in the Diet. He spent time as Prussian ambassador in Austria, Russia and, briefly, in France. He was in Paris when he was called to Berlin to become the Minister President and Foreign Minister of Prussia in 1862, as part of a strategy to strengthen the control of the new, conservative, Kaiser of Prussia, Kaiser Wilhelm I. After the creation of the German Empire, Bismarck became German Chancellor until he resigned in 1890.

During his retirement he wrote his memoirs in which he claimed that his life's work, the unification of Germany, had followed an orderly, long-term plan. This view of unification was accepted uncritically by some early historians of the period, who saw him as a political and diplomatic genius, the architect of German unity. Later historians continued to concentrate on Bismarck's political and diplomatic manoeuvres. However they moved away from the idea that one man was capable of such long-term planning or orderly implementation. Instead they argued that Bismarck had Prussian Junker interests at heart

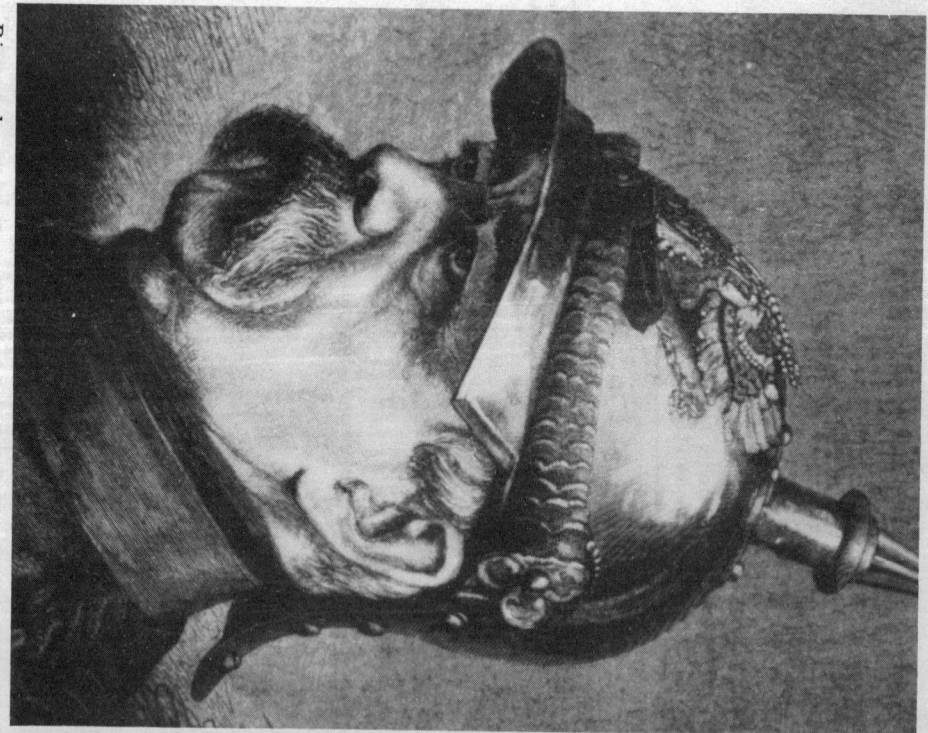

Bismarck

rather than German nationalist interests. Bismarck, they said, was not always master of events in the period 1862–1871, but as a clever opportunist, he often managed to turn them to Prussia's advantage. The German Empire created in 1871 was 'truly an enlarged Prussia'.

While many of the insights discussed above remain useful, in recent years the debate has moved onto a different level. Recent historians have accused their predecessors of ignoring the social and economic history of the time, which is as important as political and diplomatic history. They say that an analysis of German unification must take into account the economic and social transformation of Germany and relate this to political changes. Bismarck, while remaining on stage, is no longer at its centre.

In spite of the shift by many historians away from the study of 'great men', it would be impossible to write about German unification between 1862–1871 without finding that one needs to devote a lot of space to Bismarck.

> *Just as Germany came to dominate Europe during this period, so did Bismarck dominate and tower above his political contemporaries. Even though historians might now argue that this domination was based more on Germany's growing economic and military strength than on Bismarck's personality, his intellectual and diplomatic skills still dwarf those of his contemporaries, and continue to cast a spell. Even the most eminent of his contemporaries, such as Disraeli, fall into shadow beside him. There is not a crisis in Europe during this period into which he and Germany were not drawn: Bismarck was everywhere.*
>
> (Mitchell, p. 2)

We have previously stated that the appointment of Bismarck committed Prussia to the path of 'conservative modernization'. If Prussia managed to dominate the actual process of unification, it would probably impose this pattern on a united Germany. We have already seen how Prussia dominated the economic life of the German area, and that no other state could match its military strength, which was based on massive industrial development. In the next section of this chapter, we are going to see how Prussia did in fact conquer the rest of Germany. The most important figure in this process was Bismarck.

The process of political unification, 1862—1866: The exclusion of Austria

BISMARCK AND THE PRUSSIAN LIBERALS

When the Prussian Minister of War, von Roon, sent for Bismarck in September 1862, he hoped that the conservative Junker would be able to sort out a constitutional crisis in the Prussian National Assembly. Kaiser Wilhelm I was involved in a dispute with the National Assembly about the financing of the army. Behind the question of money lay the question of the army's structure and control. Von Roon wanted to change the structure and size of the army. He wanted it not only to become stronger and better equipped, but also to be rid of liberal elements which had crept in among younger officers of the national guard*. Both von Roon and the Kaiser remembered that it was the army which had restored order during the upheavals of 1848.

The liberals in the Assembly did not oppose the strengthening of the army as such, but they wanted it to be less of a 'personal guard' of the Kaiser and more a national army. More important, they believed that the Kaiser should be answerable to the National Assembly when it came to matters like the army. When von Roon presented his budget for his proposals, the liberals refused to pass it. The Kaiser, who felt that the army was his responsibility alone, decided his authority was being undermined and threatened to abdicate. Von Roon sent for Bismarck.

Bismarck was from the Junker class himself, and his views on the relationship between Kaiser and Parliament partly reflected this background. He believed that the crown should occupy the dominant position in government through control of the army and foreign policy. Therefore the Kaiser should not be answerable to parliament concerning the army budget. But Bismarck was not a typical Junker in his attitude to the liberals and nationalists. He saw the necessity for dealing with them flexibly, because they represented important interests. Whereas the Junkers saw the National Assembly as an affront to the absolute authority of the Kaiser, he saw it as a valuable place for his opponents to let off steam. He realized that the 'process of industrialization reinforced those groups which were seeking to alter the structure of the state' (Hamerow, *Age of Bismarck*, p. 6, quoted in Mitchell, p. 131). But he also believed that unity, with its economic benefits, was more important to them than civic reform and political power.

Engels summed up Bismarck's position in the following way:

> *What Bismarck needed . . . was to make clear to the German bourgeoisie . . . where the real power lay, to get rid of their liberal illusions in the most violent manner, but to carry out those of their national demands which coincided with Prussian aspirations. If he could fulfil the wishes of the bourgeoisie against its will, by making unification a reality, then the [constitutional] conflict would disappear and Bismarck would become the idol of the bourgeoisie.*

(Quoted in Mitchell, p. 19)

It is against this background that we can understand the statement he made to the National Assembly soon after his appointment:

> *Not by means of speeches and majority verdicts will the great decisions of the time be made — that was the great mistake of 1848 and 1849 — but by iron and blood.*

(W. N. Medlicott and D. K. Coveney (eds), *Bismarck and Europe*, quoted in Booth, p. 24)

Bismarck then announced that, because there was a deadlock, the Prussian Government, backed up by the army, would collect taxes to finance army reforms, without the consent of the National Assembly. Bismarck ruled Prussia for the next five years without a fixed budget.

Having dealt with opposition at home (for the time being), Bismarck turned his attentions to Prussia's relations with Austria.

THE FAILURE OF THE FRANKFURT MEETING

The historian, Hobsbawm, commented that 'Bismarck could consider a united Germany only if it was neither democratic nor too large to be dominated by Prussia. This implied the exclusion of Austria . . .' (Hobsbawm, p. 73.) An earlier part of this chapter examined how Austria tried to challenge Prussia's emerging economic and political dominance of the Bund by attempting to create a Zollunion in 1862. In 1863 Schwartzenburg, Austrian Minister President, called for a meeting of the princes of the German states to discuss reform of the Bund. It was to take place in Frankfurt. Bismarck saw this as a direct challenge to Prussia's position. He persuaded the Prussian Kaiser, Wilhelm I, not to attend the meeting. Without Wilhelm the meeting could not take place. From this point on Austria and Prussia were on a collision course, for Bismarck was determined to preserve Prussia's position by excluding Austria from the Bund forever. As we have seen, this Klein Deutsch solution was favoured by most German nationalists as well.

PRUSSIA AND AUSTRIA ON A COLLISION COURSE

In 1864 the future of the strategically important duchies of Schleswig and Holstein became a focus for Austro-Prussian rivalry. The duchies were ruled by the King of Denmark, even though Holstein was a member of the German Confederation. (Find these duchies on Map 1.) When the King of Denmark died in 1863, a number of rivals claimed the right to rule the duchies, but the Duke of Augustenburg's claim received the most support from the German states. Bismarck was alarmed by this, as he believed that a new state formed by these duchies was more likely to support Austria than Prussia in the Confederation. He had decided at this point to annex the duchies to Prussia. This would mean conflict with Austria.

Surprisingly, Austria agreed to join Prussia in direct intervention in the dispute, and to attack Denmark in February 1864. Austria appeared to fear the creation of a new pro-Prussian state as much as Bismarck feared the opposite. The important thing to note about this alliance is that it alienated Austria from many of the smaller German states which looked to Austria rather than Prussia in the Confederation. They saw that the invasion was not the joint effort of German armies liberating German-speaking people from Denmark, but one carried out by two conservative powers, each intent on securing its own 'loot' and its own future.

The Danes surrendered in October 1864. The territories of Schleswig and Holstein had been liberated but Austria and Prussia could not agree on their future. As the historian Golo Mann put it, the war which resulted from their dispute was a war 'to decide who should rule Germany'.

In the same year Austria was finally refused admittance to the Zollverein. This event signalled Austria's final exclusion from German economic life and was important in preparing it for its final political exclusion two years later.

The decision to split the administration of the duchies by the Convention of Gastein in 1865 solved nothing. All it did was to emphasize that the German Confederation was completely excluded from all decisions affecting the duchies. This further alienated the smaller states from Austria.

Possibly in an attempt to win back the support of the smaller German states, Austria allowed supporters of the Duke of Augustenburg to campaign in Holstein. Prussia, alarmed by this, accused Austria of not administering Holstein properly and therefore indirectly of breaking the Convention of Gastein. On 1 June 1866, again seeking the support of the smaller German princes, Austria asked the Federal Diet of the Bund to sort out the future of the duchies. Prussia responded by marching into Holstein. Prussia also put forward plans to the Diet for a united Germany which excluded Austria. On 12 June Austria and Prussia broke off diplomatic relations and war had begun by 16 June.

THE AUSTRO-PRUSSIAN WAR

In the middle of June 1866 Prussia went to war not only against Austria, but also against some German states—Saxony, Hanover, Hesse and Cassel in the north and Bavaria, Württemberg and Baden in the south. Many of the other German states maintained a hostile neutrality to Prussia.

Up to now this chapter has emphasized the economic forces which bound the German states to Prussia. Austria's loss of German support over the Schleswig-Holstein question was also discussed. This last point probably explains why the German states did not form alliances with Austria, even though they fought the same enemy. But the question remains—why did some German states go to war against Prussia?

In spite of economic ties, many German states, especially the south German ones, disliked and feared Prussia's militarism. Also traditional religious divisions between north and south still played an important role in alienating German states from Prussia. In addition, many German states still retained a basic traditional loyalty to Austria, which they saw as their protector against the newly strengthened Prussia. The strength of Catholicism in much of the Austrian Empire also meant that some German states had strong religious bonds with Austrians. So the war, which in the long-term was to be a step towards German unity, was at the time actually a civil war in which German fought German. This was certainly not what German nationalists had striven for.

The war was short, lasting only six weeks. Map 6 shows the main lines of battle. The Austrians suffered a major defeat on the battlefield between the village of Sadowa and the fortress of Königgrätz, north-east of Prague. This result came as a surprise to many, including Napoleon III, the French Emperor, who

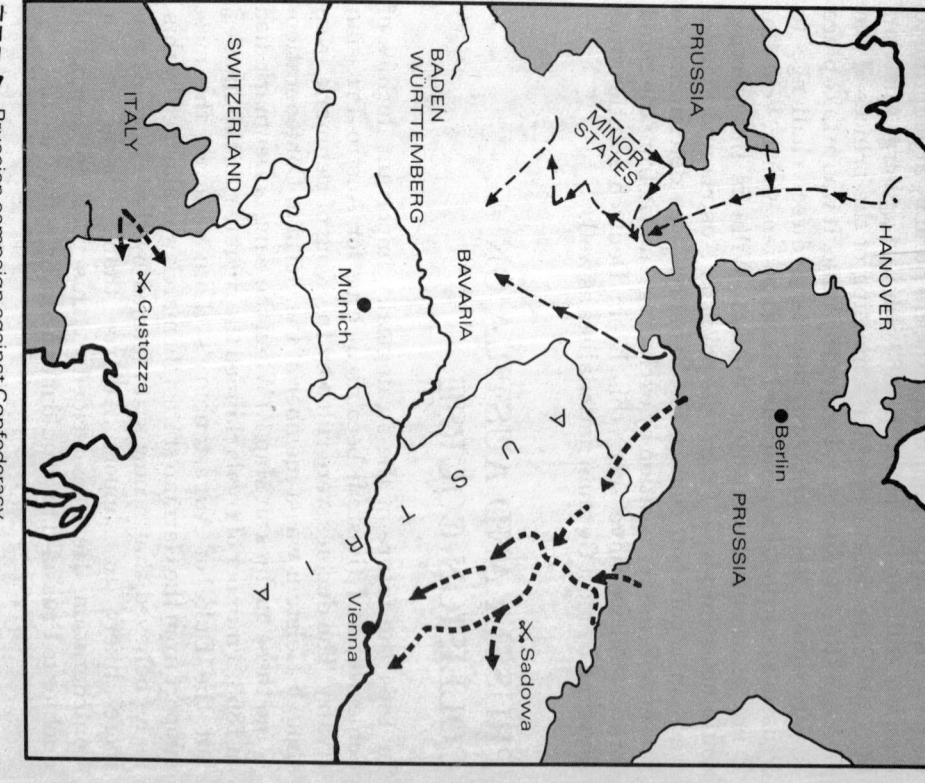

Map 6—The Austro-Prussian War of 1866.

thought that Austria's military might was superior to Prussia's. But certain factors favoured the Prussians. They had a well developed system of railways which meant they could mobilize rapidly. Their use of the newly invented needle gun gave them technical superiority. Perhaps most important was the fact that the campaign was efficiently planned and organized by the Prussian Chief of Staff*, von Moltke, who had been building up the army since he obtained money to do so in 1862.

Another factor was that Austria was forced to fight a war on two fronts, as the Italians attacked from the south. In doing so, they carried out their side of the bargain made earlier with Prussia.

"Watch out that we don't get separated! We're coming to a dangerous point!" Austrian Foreign Minister Rechberg (left) cautions Prussian Foreign Minister Bismarck.

The cartoon opposite appeared in a German magazine in March 1864. Study it carefully and then answer the questions below.

Questions

1. (a) *What do the trains in the cartoon represent?*
   (b) *Why has the cartoonist chosen to show them travelling on two parallel railway lines?*
   (c) *What is the cartoonist's attitude to Bismarck?*
   (d) *What does this tell you about the cartoonist's attitude to the quarrel shown in the cartoon?*

2. *Given the date of the cartoon, explain why Rechberg says, 'We're coming to a dangerous point!'*

3. *How did the 'trains' negotiate this 'dangerous point' in 1864?*

4. *Explain why the 'trains' finally separated two years later.*

RESULTS OF THE WAR

Europe's reaction to the changing balance of power* in Germany

So far this chapter has concentrated on events and relations within the German area. However other states of Europe were also concerned with the outcome of these crises, for changes could directly affect them. The countries most obviously affected by such changes were Italy and France, and, to a lesser degree, Russia.

The main enemy of the Italian nationalists in Italy had been Austria, so any Austrian weakness would be to their advantage. By 1866 the Austrians had been driven out of most of Italy and only held the territory of Venetia in northern Italy. The Italians were easily persuaded to join an alliance with Prussia against Austria, which would give them Venetia, thus completing Italian unification. In the event of a war, the Austrians would have to fight on two fronts.

The Emperor of France, Napoleon III, was well aware that a Prussian victory over Austria could mean the establishment of a large, powerful German state on his doorstep. He was determined to try to control these events as far as possible, so that France could take advantage of them and remain secure. From the time the Schleswig-Holstein question emerged, Napoleon III made it clear that he wanted to be seen as arbiter* of central European affairs. Before the invasion of Denmark and again after the Convention of Gastein, Napoleon indicated that France needed compensation for its non-interference in the crisis. In 1865 Bismarck went to see Napoleon at the French resort of Biarritz, where he made him vague promises of territory along the Rhine in exchange for his neutrality in the event of a war with Austria.

Russia's preoccupation with restoring its position as a power after its defeat in the Crimea in 1856 meant that it was unlikely to become involved in a central European conflict. Bismarck's open support for Russia's crushing of a rebellion in Russian Poland in 1863 ensured that Russia was well disposed towards Prussia. Prussian loans to Russia for the financing of the first stages of industries reinforced this attitude.

The historian Hobsbawm argues that Bismarck's 'technical brilliance' in the area of foreign policy was important in the process leading to unification. But he also argues that Bismarck was given an unusual amount of freedom in his diplomatic manoeuvres by the 'absence of uncontrollable international rivalry'.

The Peace with Austria and the formation of the North German Federation

Kaiser Wilhelm and the military commanders wanted to continue the war with Austria by marching on Vienna, its capital. Bismarck decided to end the struggle with the defeat at Sadowa. The Kaiser was furious, and army commanders felt that Bismarck was interfering in what was still an entirely military question.

Bismarck wrote to his wife explaining his reasons for limiting the war and treating Austria leniently:

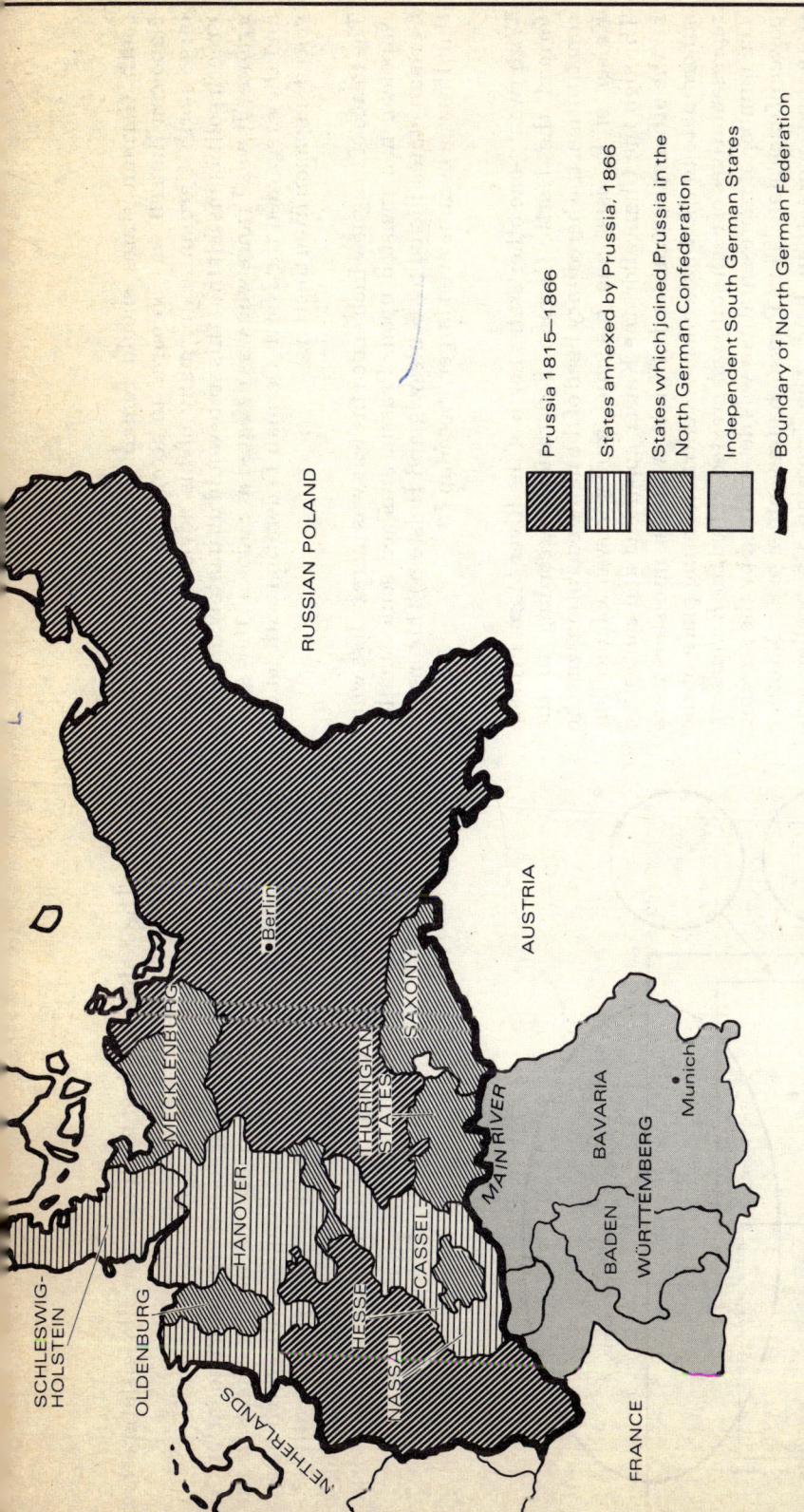

Map 7 — *The North German Federation showing Prussia's increased size in 1867.*

> If we are not excessive in our demands and do not believe that we have conquered the world, we will attain a **peace that is worth our effort**.... I have the thankless task of pouring water into the bubbling wine and making it clear that **we do not live alone in Europe**....
>
> (Adapted from Craig, p. 4) (Our emphasis)

Bismarck was particularly concerned about the attitude of France to the Prussian victory. Napoleon made it clear that he wished to arbitrate and that he wished to limit the outcome of the war. He would accept the exclusion of Austria from Germany, but not a continued war of conquest. He said he would agree to the formation of a North German Federation, but the south German states should remain independent. Though Napoleon himself was prepared to accept the formation of a large north German state, many of his advisors and other French politicians felt that this state would ultimately threaten France. 'It was France who was defeated at Sadowa', they said, and they regarded the North German Federation with loudly voiced suspicion from then on.

The Peace of Prague which ended the war was more or less what Napoleon had insisted upon. Prussia annexed some smaller German states including Schleswig and Holstein. This meant that Prussia became even larger. (See Map 7.)

With twenty-one other states north of the River Main, Prussia formed the North German Federation. According to the constitution, the hereditary head of the new Federation was the Kaiser of Prussia, and his chief minister was Chancellor. Through the Chancellor, the Kaiser appointed and controlled all the other ministries and officials. All these ministers were subordinate to the Chancellor. A central meeting place of the representatives of each state was created, called the *Bundesrat*. The number of representatives was determined by the size and power of each state. Thus Prussia had seventeen seats. No other state had more than four. The Prussian Chancellor was President of the Bundesrat.

The Bundesrat was rather like the upper house of the central parliament of the Federation. The lower house was the *Reichstag*, which was elected by all men over the age of twenty-five. This must have surprised many of the liberals, some of whom did not favour universal male suffrage. However, the practice of not paying Reichstag members meant that only the wealthy could stand for election. More important, the powers of the Reichstag were very limited. It had no control over the army or foreign affairs. These areas were the sole responsibility of the Kaiser. The Kaiser also had to countersign all legislation that emerged from the Reichstag.

The south German states had to remain independent of the north. Austria 'undertook to claim no further share in the organization of Germany' (D. Thomson, p. 313), which meant that it was shut out of German affairs permanently. As Bismarck wished, Austria was not treated harshly by having to pay a huge fine or by losing a lot of territory. Its only territorial loss was Venetia to Italy.

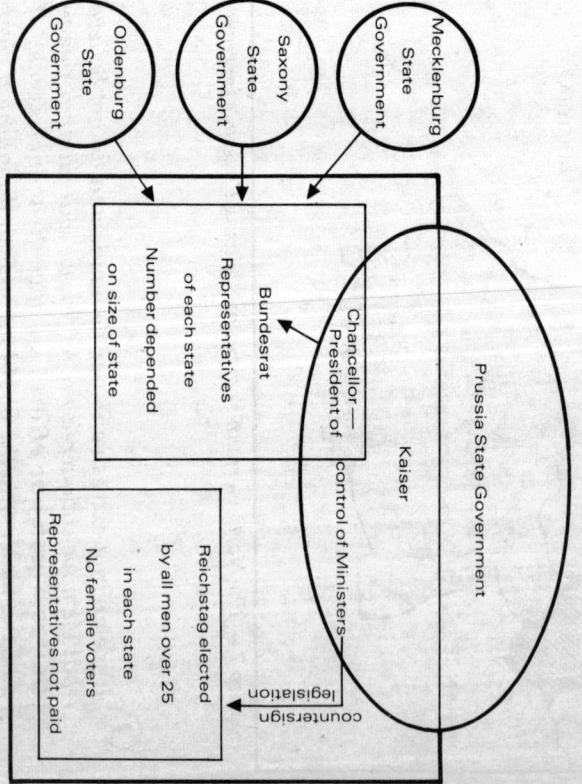

Diagram of the political structure of the North German Federation.

Question

The historian Thomson states that 'as Chancellor of the North German Federation, Bismarck now virtually governed the whole of Germany north of the River Main'. Explain how the constitution of the North German Federation made this possible.

The defeat and defection* of Prussian liberals

In Prussia itself there were indications that the war against Austria was popular with the electorate. On the day of the battle of Sadowa, a new National Assembly had been elected, in which the conservatives, who had supported von Roon's army programme, gained one hundred and forty-two out of three hundred and fifty-four seats, and the liberals only eighty-five. Even these liberals had begun to think that unity was a greater good than parliamentary responsibility and freedom, and they looked forward to the increased economic benefits of unity. When Bismarck came to the National Assembly and admitted that he had been wrong to collect taxes without the members' consent, many liberals as well as conservatives accepted this belated apology. They did so by giving him a retrospective* grant of the funds he had spent since 1862. A large number of liberals split from the Progressive party, which had originally opposed the budget, and formed the National Liberal party, which gave Bismarck backing for his policies from then on. Only a few liberals on the left continued to speak up against the retrospective grant of funds, but their protests were not heard.

The historian Hobsbawm argues that Bismarck was able to dominate Prussian and German politics so completely because of the lack of an effective opposition, and the absence of any serious revolutionary danger. Nationalist movements in general lacked support among the mass of the population. They were confined to the middle classes. The liberals in the Prussian National Assembly certainly ceased providing an effective opposition when they forgave him for ignoring their opposition for four years.

Interestingly, Bismarck's action in approaching the National Assembly also caused a split in the conservatives. The conservative landowners of East Prussia felt that Bismarck had limited royal power by going to the National Assembly and asking for a retrospective grant. But other conservatives, such as soldiers, state officials, some landowners and businessmen, saw the advantages of Bismarck's policy and approved of his attempts to combine authority and a policy of modernization. There emerged something of an alliance between these conservatives and the National Liberal party — a combination of political and economic power.

Conservative Prussia's dominance of the north alienated many liberals in the south German states from the idea of German unification. Even though the south German states were to remain independent according to the Treaty of Prague, there was a large question mark about how long they could remain independent.

The process of political unification 1866–1871: the incorporation of the south German states

RELATIONS BETWEEN THE SOUTH AND NORTH GERMAN STATES AFTER 1866

There were a number of things that indicated that a union of the south with the north could take place soon. Firstly, during the peace negotiations after the war with Austria, Bismarck had persuaded Bavaria, Württemberg and Baden to agree to an offensive-defensive military alliance with Prussia. This meant that in the event of war they would place their armies and railways under Prussian control. There was an element of force in this agreement. Both Bavaria and Württemberg had to pay large fines to Prussia for being Austria's allies in the war, and Bismarck threatened Bavaria with further fines and some loss of territory if it did not agree.

Secondly, the south German states were still linked to the north as members of the Zollverein. In 1867 Bismarck began to reorganize the Zollverein so that it now had a bicameral (two houses) legislature which could decide on tariff legislation, negotiations concerning commerce, navigation of rivers and the regulation of certain taxes and excises*. Each of the states would send representatives elected by universal male suffrage*. He hoped that this *Zollparlement* would mean that political union would be a mere formality, and many manufacturers, merchants and chambers of commerce in the south felt the same way.

However there was a large amount of anti-Prussian feeling in the south German states. Old religious differences still caused antagonism. South German princes watched with alarm as some rulers of north German states were deposed and their territories swallowed up by Prussia in 1866. They clung to their traditional positions of power and autonomy, opposing any steps towards unity.

However, much of the anti-Prussian feeling was centred on a fear of Prussian militarism, which appeared to have become stronger than ever. Prussia seemed to have imposed this on the north successfully; a political commentator in Württemberg remarked that the constitution of the North German Federation had only three articles: '1. Pay up. 2. Be a soldier. 3. Keep your mouth shut.' (Craig, p. 18.) After 1866 Prussia attempted to put the terms of the military treaties into practice, by interfering in southern military organization. This was seen as a Prussian attempt to extend militarism southwards.

Apart from fearing Prussian militarism, southern liberals found the constitution of the North German Federation offensive. It ignored the principle of parliamentary responsibility, and entrenched Prussian power which was basically conservative.

This anti-Prussian feeling became clear in the Zollparlement elections of 1868. In each of the south German states, candidates who opposed the extension of Prussian influence in the south were elected. Bismarck himself wrote in 1869 that any attempt to force the issue of unification with the south German states would be a case of 'shaking down unripe fruit'.

Explain the term

The passage below is part of an address Bismarck made to the North German Reichstag in March 1867. It concerns his ideas about a customs parliament for the Zollverein.

> If the German Customs Union is to preserve its present range and scope, institutions must be set up to enable south Germany to participate in customs legislation . . . It is hard to believe that joint bodies of legislation in the field of customs, once they have been set up, would shirk their duties and not achieve measures applicable to the whole of Germany . . .
>
> (Quoted in Kurtz)

Questions

1. (a) What 'institutions' did Bismarck set up so that the south German states could participate in customs legislation?
   (b) How were representatives to these institutions elected?
   (c) Why do you think Bismarck chose this form of suffrage*?

2. What 'measures' could these institutions pass?

3. (a) What long-term aim did Bismarck achieve when he reorganized the Zollverein in 1867?
   (b) To what extent had he achieved that aim by the beginning of 1870?

If there was so much opposition to unity in 1868, why did the south German states agree to join the north only two years later?

Though Bismarck did not believe in 'shaking down unripe fruit', he would not pass up an opportunity which might speed up the ripening process. And Bismarck knew that a war with France might have just such an effect. This is not to say that he deliberately planned war with France from 1866 onwards. It seems clear that the process of unification had reached a point of stalemate by 1870, and that French actions led Bismarck to believe he could provoke a crisis which might lead to war. The south German states were bound to come into the war on the side of Prussia. Unification was likely to follow.

As we have seen, Napoleon III had set himself up as the arbiter of central European affairs and had made sure that the new German state that came out of the Austro-Prussian conflict was limited to the area north of the River Main. However, there were people in his government and in right wing* political parties who saw the North German Federation as a threat to France. Also, Napoleon's position and popularity as Emperor at home depended on his conducting an aggressive and spectacular foreign policy, and he was encouraged in this by his advisors, right-wingers and the French press.

Egged on by those around him, in 1867 Napoleon decided, rather belatedly, to demand the compensation Bismarck had hinted at when he met the French Emperor at Biarritz. He laid claim to the territory of Luxemburg (see Map 1), which was ruled as a Grand Duchy by the King of Holland and garrisoned by Prussian troops. The North German Federation Reichstag reacted strongly against the possible loss of territory which had been part of the old German Confederation. Bismarck was not prepared to go against these nationalist sentiments, and the

25

sale of Luxemburg fell through. (At the same time Bismarck published the text of the military treaties with the south German states which had been kept secret up to then. He hoped to show the south that it would never be at Napoleon's mercy.) In 1869 Napoleon tried to acquire railway lines in Luxemburg and Belgium, with a possible customs union in mind, but this fell through as well.

Napoleon III's attempts to claim compensation united north and south Germany in anti-French feeling, but this did not last. Anti-Prussian feeling in the south continued to be strong. In 1869 there were rumours that the military alliances of 1866 would not be renewed in 1871.

By 1870 Bismarck had two courses open to him. Either to wait, possibly for years, until southern nationalists gained the upper hand in the south and led the south into union, or to speed things up by engineering a crisis with France which would bring the south in on Prussia's side in a war. Bismarck was not unaware that it took very little to enrage French public opinion, the press and the government, which all demanded a more vigorous foreign policy from Napoleon.

When he decided to support the Hohenzollern* candidate for the Spanish throne, Bismarck was aware that it could provoke a crisis with France. And he was sure Prussia could handle the military challenge, for the Prussian army under von Roon had been preparing for such a possibility since 1866.

THE QUARREL WITH FRANCE

In 1868 a revolution occurred in Spain, and Queen Isabella was driven into exile with her whole Bourbon* family. This left the Spanish throne vacant. The Spanish Minister of War, General Prim, took charge of the attempt to find a new monarch. A possible candidate was Leopold von Hohenzollern-Sigmaringen, a distant relative of Kaiser Wilhelm I of Prussia. Bismarck secretly supported Leopold's candidature, to the extent of sending a bribe to the Spanish parliament to accept Leopold as king. If Leopold took the throne, France would have a German monarch on her southern as well as her western borders. Bismarck was aware what reaction this would cause in France, and hoped to have Leopold installed as monarch before the French even found out that he was a candidate.

Leopold was reluctant to accept the candidacy unless Wilhelm ordered him to do so, and Wilhelm's own hesitancy slowed the process down. News of Leopold's candidature leaked out in early July 1870. A new and rather aggressive French Foreign Minister, the Duc de Gramont, had recently been appointed by Napoleon. As soon as he heard, he made a violent speech about the 'existence of a foreign prince on the throne of Charles V* which would 'place in jeopardy the interest and honour of France'. (Quoted in Kurtz, p. 569.) He demanded that Leopold withdraw. Leopold's father, Prince Karl Anton, withdrew his son's candidature on his behalf.

Bismarck denied that Prussia had had anything to do with a 'purely dynastic' affair', and said that the French attitude was one of impertinent interference. In reality, however, Leopold's withdrawal seemed like a major diplomatic defeat for Bismarck, and a triumph for France.

However, French over-excitement at this victory gave Bismarck a chance to goad Napoleon into action which finally led to war. French patriotic feeling ran high. The French wanted to exploit their victory. Napoleon ordered the French ambassador in Prussia, Benedetti, to see Kaiser Wilhelm. He wanted the Kaiser to give an assurance that Leopold would never renew his bid for the Spanish throne. Benedetti met the Kaiser at Ems health spa on 13 July 1870. The Kaiser refused to give Benedetti any assurances that Leopold would not renew his candidature at a later date. He sent a telegram to Bismarck describing what had happened.

Bismarck, in the company of von Moltke and von Roon, took the telegram and abbreviated it. He made the Kaiser's language seem much ruder than it actually was. As a result the Kaiser appeared to have insulted Benedetti. Bismarck sent it to the French and German press, and it caused an uproar on both sides. The historian, Craig, summed up the situation as follows: 'The publication of the Ems despatch and the resultant elaboration of it in sensational newspapers ... created an atmosphere in which reason and compromise were impossible.' (Craig, p. 27.) For the French to retreat would mean an intolerable loss of honour, and if Napoleon wished to preserve his position as Emperor, he could not afford to appear to waver before Prussia.

Napoleon wrote the following note to the French Foreign Minister, the Duc de Gramont, after Leopold's father had withdrawn Leopold as candidate for the Spanish throne. Read it carefully and answer the questions which follow:

1. *Our concern is with Prussia, not with Spain;*

2. *The dispatch from Prince Karl Anton [father of Leopold] addressed to Prim is, as far as we are concerned, not an official document and no one has been commissioned to communicate it to us;*

3. *It is necessary that Benedetti insists on a categorical reply, for the future, not to permit Prince Leopold to set out one fine day for Spain;*

4. *As long as we do not have an official communication from Ems, we cannot be supposed to have received a reply to our just demands;*

5. *So long as we do not have this reply we will continue our military preparations;*

6. *It is impossible to make a statement in the Chambers [the French parliament] until we are better informed.*

(Quoted in Kurtz, p. 572)

Questions

1. The following people appear in Napoleon's note. Write one sentence on each of them, explaining who they were:
   (a) Prince Karl Anton
   (b) Prim
   (c) Leopold von Hollzollern
   (d) Benedetti.

2. What had Leopold renounced?

3. According to the note, why did Napoleon not accept Prince Karl Anton's dispatch as an end to the problem?

4. (a) Why did Napoleon send Benedetti to Ems?
   (b) Why did Benedetti's visit lead to a crisis between France and Prussia?

27

THE SOUTH GERMAN STATES AND THE WAR BETWEEN PRUSSIA AND FRANCE

Patriotic demonstrations against France took place all over the German area, both north and south of the River Main. The south German states did not hesitate to support what they saw as a nationalist cause. They willingly carried out the terms of the military treaties made with Prussia in 1866, and began to mobilise their armies even before the war was officially declared on 19 July 1870.

Bismarck probably realized that the southerners' concerns for their independence 'had not been drowned, although they had been submerged, in the wave of nationalist enthusiasm'. (Medlicott, p. 85.) So he saw to it that negotiations for the entry of the south German states into a new German federation took place during the war while nationalist feeling still ran high. Baden entered the union without difficulty, but Bavaria had to be bribed with secret heavy payments to the bankrupt King Leopold II. Bismarck also promised that Leopold could keep control of certain aspects of local government, and of the army in peace time. Isolated, Wurtemberg could not afford to stay out of the union; but Bismarck also made Wurtemberg's passage easier by granting similar privileges regarding the army and local affairs. Bismarck's sensitivity to southern concerns angered Kaiser Wilhelm, who wanted to force the southern states to enter a new federation and surrender all their previous autonomy. However, Bismarck's views prevailed and the new German Empire was proclaimed on 18 January 1871.

The war with France lasted from July 1870 to January 1871. It can be divided into two phases. The first phase was the war between the French Empire versus Prussia and its allies. It

Look at the British cartoon below. It appeared at the time the Ems telegram was published. Study it carefully and answer the questions which follow.

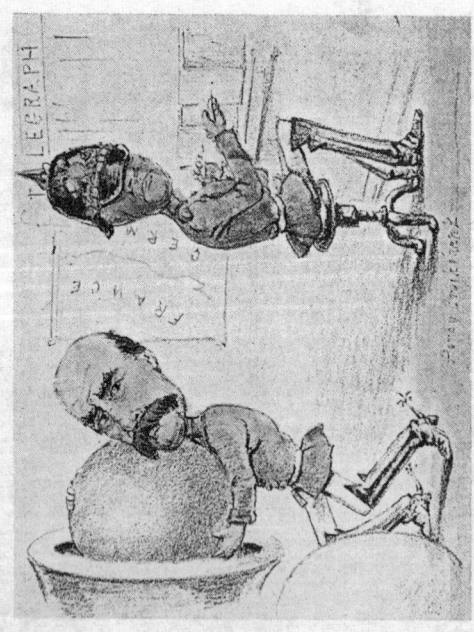

Questions

1. (a) Who was von Moltke?
   (b) Why did the cartoonist show him sitting at a telegraph bench?
   (c) What is the importance of the map behind von Moltke?

2. (a) Why did the cartoonist show Bismarck loading a cannon?
   (b) What is the cartoonist's attitude to Bismarck?

3. Write a paragraph which sums up the cartoonist's view of the events which followed Benedetti's visit to Ems.

ended in September 1870 when Prussia-Germany gained a decisive victory at Sedan, and Napoleon surrendered. From the beginning the Prussians showed their superiority. French mobilisation of troops was partial and chaotic, compared with the almost clockwork precision of the movement of German troops. The first major battle, at Worth, set the pattern for future clashes. French cavalry attacks dissolved in front of Prussian rapid-firing rifles. Prussian heavy artillery destroyed the main French armies. Krupp cannons came into their own during the seige of Metz and the battle of Sedan, where shells caused terrible devastation.

Although Napoleon surrendered, this did not mean the end of the war. A republic was proclaimed in Paris and the new government decided to continue with the war. The German army marched on Paris and laid seige to it. Prussian shells bombarded the city until it surrendered in January 1871. The creation of a radical government in Paris, known as the Paris Commune, delayed peace negotiations for a few months. The Paris Commune demanded far-reaching socialist and republican reforms. It also rejected surrender to the Prussians. It lasted from March to May 1871.

Below are two extracts about aspects of the Franco-Prussian War. Read them carefully and answer the questions which follow. Information for your answers should come both from the extracts and from previous parts of this chapter.

Part of Alfred Krupp's address to his workers at his factory at Essen, 1870.

> Let us prepare the maximum number of shells which can be used by our guns in the event of a battle on the largest conceivable scale. Apart from the 9 inch guns*, we should anticipate the commitment of even the partly finished 11 inch ones ... I expect from the partriotism of all whose services are devoted to cannon, that he will think of nothing except the possible crisis of arms ahead of us, in which our work may be justified and be of incalculable value to the fatherland. I therefore look for the utmost activity.

(Quoted in Booth, p. 25)

A British war correspondent's account of the Seige of Paris.

> The terrible ghastliness of those dead transcended anything I had ever seen, or even dreamt of, in the shuddering nightmare after my first battlefield. Remember how they [the French troops] had been slain. Not with the nimble bullet of the needle gun, that drills a minute hole through a man and leaves him undisfigured ... not with the sharp stab of the bayonet, but slaughtered with missiles of terrible weight, shattered into fragments by explosions of many pounds of powder, mangled and torn by massive fragments of iron.

(Quoted in Booth, p. 27)

Questions

1. Explain carefully what factors made possible the development of Krupp's armaments factory.

2. (a) The second extract refers to the 'nimble bullet of the needle gun'. Explain what the war correspondent was referring to.
   (b) Discuss the importance of this weapon in both the Austro-Prussian and Franco-Prussian wars.

29

the long-term the French developed a strong desire for revenge and for the restoration of Alsace and Lorraine. This humiliation certainly did not make Germany's borders with France secure in the future.

The most important result of the war was the creation of the German Empire. What sort of state came into being in 1871?

The German Empire

The point has been made that the process of political unification between 1862 and 1871 was really the active conquest of Germany by Prussia, under the skilled leadership of Bismarck. By 1862 much of the groundwork had been done. By then, none of the other states in Germany could escape Prussia's economic dominance or match its military strength.

In many of the states wealthy liberals and nationalists supported Prussian-led unification, believing that this would be most beneficial for their interests.

Both Prussia's economic and military strength, and the gradual grudging support Bismarck gained from the representatives of new wealth, gave him a large amount of freedom of movement in embarking on his avowed policy of blood and iron. Also international relations at this time were not nearly as complex as they became twenty years later. Bismarck was able to isolate and conquer his enemies with relative ease.

The Empire that emerged in 1871 was the immediate result of three wars, and so it was based largely on force. After the war of 1866, the north German states had very little option but to join the North German Federation. Some were swallowed up completely by Prussia. Others, which had been allies of Austria,

---

3. In 1870 Krupp's factory was concentrating on the production of different kinds of cannon.
   (a) Describe the role of this kind of heavy artillery in the Franco-Prussian war.
   (b) In the first extract, Krupp's address seems to show that he wanted the workers to regard the production of arms as more than merely doing a job. How did he do this?
   (c) What does this tell you about his attitude to the nationalist cause?

RESULTS OF THE FRANCO-PRUSSIAN WAR

The Peace of Frankfurt

The army and public opinion in Germany demanded that a well dramatized triumph over France was necessary. The German press, supported by Bismarck, launched an aggressive campaign for the annexation of the territories of Alsace and Lorraine, while the war was still in progress. The German historian, Ranke, argues that German-French hostility went back as far as Louis XIV, early in the Eighteenth Century, and that the conditions of peace should be harsh enough to prevent France from ever embarking on a war with Germany again. The Peace of Frankfurt, signed on 10 May 1871, gave Germany the key industrial areas of Alsace and Lorraine. A large fine, or indemnity, was imposed on France, and a German army of occupation was to remain in France until it was paid. This treatment of France might have crushed it temporarily, but in

and therefore defeated by Prussia, were not in a position to reject Prussian plans for unity. The North German Federation was hardly a voluntary association of German states. Many states north of the Main were like vassal states dominated politically and economically by Prussia. The constitution of the North German Federation guaranteed the subordinate position of the German states to Prussia. (See page 22.)

The south German states also joined the north partly as a result of coercion and threats, though there is evidence of genuine nationalist feeling during the Franco-Prussian War. The secret military treaties of 1867 were made on Prussia's terms and caused a good deal of resentment. Bismarck's attempts to extend Prussian influence through the Zollparlement were also resented. The actual incorporation of the south German states was concluded at a psychologically important time, when nationalist feeling ran high. Bribes and threats were nevertheless still necessary to get Bavaria, Wurtemberg and Baden to give up their independence.

The constitution of the German Empire was drawn up mainly by Bismarck. It resembled the constitution of the North German Federation which was also Bismarck's handiwork. (See page 22.) In drawing it up, Bismarck was concerned to create a working relationship between himself (as Chancellor) and the Kaiser, which would allow him almost unrestricted control of German affairs. This would ensure Prussia's political domination of Germany and maintain the pattern of conservative modernization.

According to the constitution, the Prussian Kaiser was always to be Emperor or Kaiser of Germany. The Kaiser had sole charge of foreign affairs and, in war time, of the army. He alone assembled and dismissed the Bundesrat and Reichstag (the upper and lower houses of parliament). Before a law could be effective he had to countersign it, along with the Imperial Chancellor.

The Kaiser's executive really consisted of one person, the Imperial Chancellor, whom he alone appointed. The Chancellor was expected to be the Prime Minister of Prussia. There was no cabinet of ministers. Instead the Chancellor appointed heads of various departments to carry out his orders. In 1871 these were members of the Prussian government.

The structures of the Bundesrat and Reichstag looked much as they had done in the North German Federation. Prussia continued to dominate the Bundesrat in spite of the addition of the south German states. Bavaria had only six representatives compared to Prussia's fourteen. The Imperial Chancellor was also President of the Bundesrat. Even though the Reichstag was elected by universal male suffrage, its powers were extremely limited, as we have seen. Also it represented only the wealthier sections of German society for two reasons: members were not paid, and few new seats had been provided to represent the growing urban proletariat. It was really a sophisticated conservative debating chamber. The Empire was really an enlarged Prussia, with most political power concentrated in the hands of the Chancellor.

To end we will look briefly at the possible effects the creation of the German Empire would have on Europe and the world.

THE GERMAN EMPIRE, EUROPE AND THE WORLD

The statesmen of Europe could not ignore the creation of this huge new Prussianized Empire. Disraeli, the British Prime

31

Minister, remarked that the balance of power in Europe had been entirely destroyed. A great new military power had come into existence which pressed on three international frontiers, west, south and east; frontiers which up to that point had been free from serious military threat. And this power had demonstrated its strength by conducting war in a thoroughly modern and therefore frightening manner. Moreover as the historian Medlicott points out, this did not make the new Germany feel secure:

> *The new state in its turn was threatened from three directions. The Germans, in their earlier disunited position, had always felt insecure; now the mighty Reich gave greater protection, but also a circle of possible enemies, who would soon no doubt copy her military techniques. So with the creation of the Empire, there was created the apprehension that was to haunt it continuously in the future: the fear of encirclement, the nightmare of coalitions**.
>
> (Medlicott, p. 87)

Bismarck himself regarded Germany in 1871 as a 'satiated power'. By this he meant that it had no more territorial claims in Europe or anywhere else.

Bismarck believed that German attempts to obtain colonial territory would upset the situation in Europe. In particular, he did not want to alienate Britain, which could then ally with France. He had little time for the voices which demanded that Germany imitate France and Britain and become a colonial power.

However, these voices belonged to the people who had supported the process of unification and now wished to benefit from the creation of a strong Empire—the capitalists of German industry.

The foundations of German industrial might were laid during the period we have studied. However the process of industrialization in Germany was quite uneven. By 1870 two-thirds of German people still lived off the land. After 1871 German industry took off. Political unification led to full economic unification. The addition of Alsace and Lorraine, with their rich iron ore deposits, and textile and engineering industries, further boosted German economic developments.

As industry became larger in scale, huge amounts of capital were needed to set up manufacturing plants. This meant that the banking system had to be further developed to meet this demand. Business men began to invest their profits in banks, so that the same people often sat on the boards of management of industries and banks.

> *Gradually economic power became concentrated in the hands of the powerful German banking system ... Concentration in banking led to concentration in industry and to the formation of Kartels* [cartels*].
>
> (Mitchell, pp. 55–6)

Cartels were business combinations formed to restrict competition and fix prices. This reduced the risk involved in starting large businesses and ensured a good profit. (It also limited the growth of trade unions.) At the head of these cartels stood wealthy capitalists such as Krupp.

In contrast, after 1871, the economic power of the Junkers was declining. They could not compete with imported foreign grain which was cheaper. They were very short of labour because large numbers of agricultural workers had moved to the towns. Many Junkers went bankrupt. Their days as a political force were numbered. Bismarck 'could not ensure the economic survival of his Junker class — as he had ensured, for a time — their political survival'. (Mitchell, p. 59)

The political influence of the cartels grew after 1871. They backed certain political parties with their money and influence. They also backed specific campaigns which involved their interests. The cartels supported two important campaigns which affected the direction German foreign policy took in the years to come. Firstly they supported the *Flottoverein* which aimed to build Germany into a great naval power. Secondly they backed the *Kolonialverband* which wanted Germany to have an overseas empire. Both these campaigns had important implications for relations between the powers of Europe and the rest of the world, as we shall see.

Revision Questions

1. (a) Explain how Prussia came to be in a position to challenge Austria's domination of the German area by the middle of the Nineteenth Century.
   (b) How was Austria removed from the economic and political affairs of the German area in the period 1860–1866?

2. 'It cannot be said that Bismarck wanted a war in 1870, but thanks to the crisis he encouraged, to Gramont's maladroitness [clumsiness] in handling it, and to the passions it released in French public opinion, that was what he got.' (Craig, p. 27)
   The above passage makes four main points about the causes of the war between France and Prussia in 1870. List these main points in your own words. Then using these points, discuss why the Franco-Prussian War broke out in 1870.

3. 'No responsible politicians in southern Germany believed there was any alternative to fusion with the north ... in the new Europe created by the victory over France. All but the most ardent Prussian haters, knew that the price of independence would be political isolation, economic decline and mounting security costs.' (Adapted from Craig, p. 33)
   (a) Explain why the south German states were reluctant to fuse with the north until 1870.
   (b) Using the ideas contained in the above passage, explain why they were willing to join with the north to form the German Empire in 1871.

4. The economist, J. M. Keynes, argued that 'the German Empire was founded not on blood and iron, but on coal and iron'.
   (a) What did Keynes mean when he altered Bismarck's famous phase?
   (b) Do you agree with him? Give reasons for your answer.

33

Chronology: Germany, 1815–1871

- 1815 Creation of German Confederation of 39 states
- 1819 Carlsbad Decrees
- 1830 Revolts in Brunswick, Hanover, Hesse, Saxony } Expansion and development of the Zollverein
- 1848 Revolts in Austria, Prussia and other German states
  Meeting of Frankfurt Parliament
- 1850 Prussia granted a constitution
- 1862 Constitutional crisis in Prussia. Appointment of Bismarck as Minister President.
- 1863 Schwartzenburg's proposal for a Zollunion
  Austrian attempt to reorganize the German Confederation
  Death of King Frederick of Denmark
- 1864 Invasion of Schleswig/Holstein by Prussia and Austria.
  Final exclusion of Austria from Zollverein
- 1865 Convention of Gastein
  Bismarck's visit to Napoleon III at Biarritz
- 1866 Prussian-Italian Alliance
  Austro-Prussian War; ⚔ Sadowa
  Peace of Prague
- 1867 Creation of the North German Federation
  Napoleon's attempt to claim Luxembourg
  Reorganization of the Zollverein
- 1869 Napoleon's attempt to include Luxembourg and Belgian railway lines in a customs union
- 1870 Crisis over Hohenzollern candidature
  Franco-Prussian War
  Fall of Napoleon III. Control taken by Republican Government
  Paris Commune
  Surrender of France
  Peace of Frankfurt
  Proclamation of the German Empire

Glossary

Arbiter — a neutral third party in a dispute, who attempts to resolve the conflict between the other two.

Balance of power — state of affairs where the military and other powers of different states are roughly the same. The term refers particularly to the preservation of an equilibrium of power among the states of Europe as a security of peace.

Bourbon — the name of the Spanish royal family, which was related to the French royal family that had ruled prior to the French Revolution in 1789.

Bourgeoisie — see middle class.

Bund — the German Bund was a loose federation of thirty-nine states, which was created by the Congress of Vienna in 1815. (See Map 1.)

Bureaucracy — civil servants and officials who administer the laws of a country.

Burgeoning — fast-growing.

Cartel (or Kartel in German) a form of monopoly business enterprise which fixed the prices of goods by controlling the production and distribution of particular articles.

Charles V — the famous Emperor who ruled Spain and the Holy Roman Empire (Austria) from 1519–1555, thereby uniting most of Europe under a single monarch.

Chief of Staff — Head of the army.

Coalitions — alliances.

Defection — to defect means to change sides.

Diet — The Diet (or parliament) of the German Bund was a meeting place for the representatives of the thirty-nine states.

Dynastic — to do with royal families (or dynasties).

Excises — taxes imposed on goods or on licences to carry goods.

Foils — thin, flat pieces of steel.

Germany — when used before 1871, this means the German-speaking part of central Europe.

Hapsburg — 'Hapsburg' was the name of the royal family which had ruled the Austrian Empire for hundreds of years.

Hohenzollern — the Prussian royal family.

9 inch guns — '9 inch' refers to the diameter of the barrel bore.

Iron Chancellor — Bismarck was known by this nickname because of his reference in a famous speech to 'blood and iron' as the key to successful political strategy.

Middle class — a section of society between the aristocracy and the labourers and peasants; a class of people who have made money from trade and industry, rather than from land. Referred to in Marxist terminology as the bourgeoisie.

National Guard — civilian as opposed to professional soldiers.

Needle gun — the first successful breech-loading rifle, adopted by the Prussian army in 1840. ('Needle' refers to the firing mechanism, and not to the size or shape of the bullets.)

Suffrage — the vote.

Reactionary — extremely conservative, in this context favouring absolute monarchy.

Retrospective — a provision made in the present for something which happened in the past.

Right wing — conservative; in this context patriotic supporters of the monarchy.

Bibliography

W. Brown and A. Coysh, *The Map Approach to Modern History* (University Tutorial Press, 1969)

M. Booth, *Bismarck* (Harrap World History Series, 1975)

G. Craig, *Germany, 1866–1945* (Oxford University Press, 1978)

B. Elliot, *Bismarck, the Kaiser and Germany* (Longman, 1972)

E. J. Hobsbawm, *The Age of Capital 1848–1875* (Weidenfeld and Nicolson, 1975)

H. Holborn, *A History of Modern Germany* Vol. 3

D. Knox, *The Industrial Revolution* (Harrap World History Series, 1974)

H. Kurtz, 'Bismarck and the Two Germanies 1866–1870' in *History Today* Vol. 20 No. 7

G. Mann, *The History of Germany since 1789* (Pelican, 1974)

W. N. Medlicott, *Bismarck and Modern Germany* (Hodder and Stoughton, 1976)

I. R. Mitchell, *Bismarck and the Development of Germany* (Holmes McDougall, 1980)

B. Moore, *Social Origins of Dictatorship and Democracy*

O. Pflanze (ed.), *The Unification of Germany 1848–1871* (Robert E. Krieger Publishing Company, 1979)

L. Seaman, *From Vienna to Versailles* (Methuen, 1972)

W. M. Simon, *Germany in the Age of Bismarck* (George Allen Unwin Ltd, 1968)

A. J. P. Taylor, *The Course of German History* (Methuen, 1961)

D. Thomson, *Europe Since Napoleon* (Penguin, 1966)

2 THE FIRST WORLD WAR

Introduction 37

The long-term causes of the First World War 39
  The rise of Germany
  The decline of the old Empires
  The Ottoman Empire
  The Russian Empire
  Austria-Hungary
  Summary: The decline of the old Empires and the Balkan problem
  Colonial rivalry
  The alliance system
  German diplomacy and its consequences
  British fears and the creation of the Triple Entente
  Arms race
  Summary: Long-term origins of the war

The outbreak of the war 53
  Crisis in the Balkans
  The conflict spreads
  War plans

The conduct of the war 59
  The 1914 campaigns
  Trench warfare: 1915–1917
  Technology and tactics
  Total war
  Conscription
  Mobilizing the economy
  Propaganda and the Home Front

Russia leaves the war 68

America enters the war 69

The end of the war 72
  1918 — The failure of the German offensive

Conclusion 73
  Revision Questions
  Chronology
  Glossary
  Bibliography

Introduction

In the Nineteenth Century Western Europe was transformed by industrial and political revolutions. New forms of transportation and communication brought the peoples of Europe closer together than ever before. Industrial production soared, especially in Germany and Great Britain. Commerce, both within and between nations, flourished. For the first time, people began to think in terms of a world economy, with periods of prosperity and depression which affected all countries.

Many Europeans believed that this new economic interdependence made future wars impossible. Socialists spoke of an international working class, where workers of all nations were united by their opposition to capitalism. War was impossible, they argued, because workers in each country would refuse to fight each other. Many capitalists also believed that there would be no more wars in Europe, though for a different reason. War would interrupt trade, and without trade the economies of each of the European powers would grind quickly to a halt. A popular book entitled *The Great Illusion*, written in 1910, argued that this new interdependence meant that there was no longer any advantage to be gained by conquering new territory. War, the author concluded, was therefore obsolete.

Military theorists were less optimistic. In each country they designed elaborate strategies for a war which many expected. Yet the generals also believed that any war would be over quickly. French generals estimated that the next war would take six weeks. By then, they believed, the French army would have thrashed the Germans. In Berlin, German generals predicted victory over the French in the same few weeks. In every country, military leaders clung to a vision of Nineteenth Century war—short, offensive wars, decided by charging infantry and cavalry.

But history has a way of proving our expectations spectacularly wrong. War came, touched off by the assassination of an Austrian Archduke on 28 June 1914. The war was neither brief nor decisive. For over four years the opposing armies slogged through a nightmare of mud and barbed wire. There were no gallant cavalry charges, no glamour of any kind. Instead there was trench warfare, where movement was measured in metres, at a cost of hundreds of thousands of men. The horror soon spread beyond the confines of Europe. Battles raged from Baghdad to South West Africa. Non-European nations, like Japan and the United States, were drawn into the fighting, making the war a truly world conflict.

When the war finally ended on 11 November 1918, twelve million soldiers lay dead. The economies of the countries of Europe were shattered. Europe's three oldest Empires—in Russia, Austria-Hungary and Turkey—were gone. In the years that followed, the survivors, with a mixture of horror and pride, referred to the war of 1914–1918 as 'The Great War'. Only later, following a second great war, did it come to be called by the name we know today: the First World War.

Why did the First World War begin? Even in the first weeks of the war, people argued over that question. Each side accused the other of starting the conflict. Because Germany eventually lost the war, it also lost the argument: At the Versailles Peace Conference in 1919, the defeated Germans were forced to sign a statement accepting blame for starting the war.

This statement, however, has not stopped historians from arguing about the origins of the war. Some historians have argued that 'the Allies'—France, Great Britain and Russia—tried to choke Germany economically, leaving it no choice but to fight. Others have accused Austria-Hungary, Germany's main ally, of acting recklessly, thus dragging all of Europe into a war

37

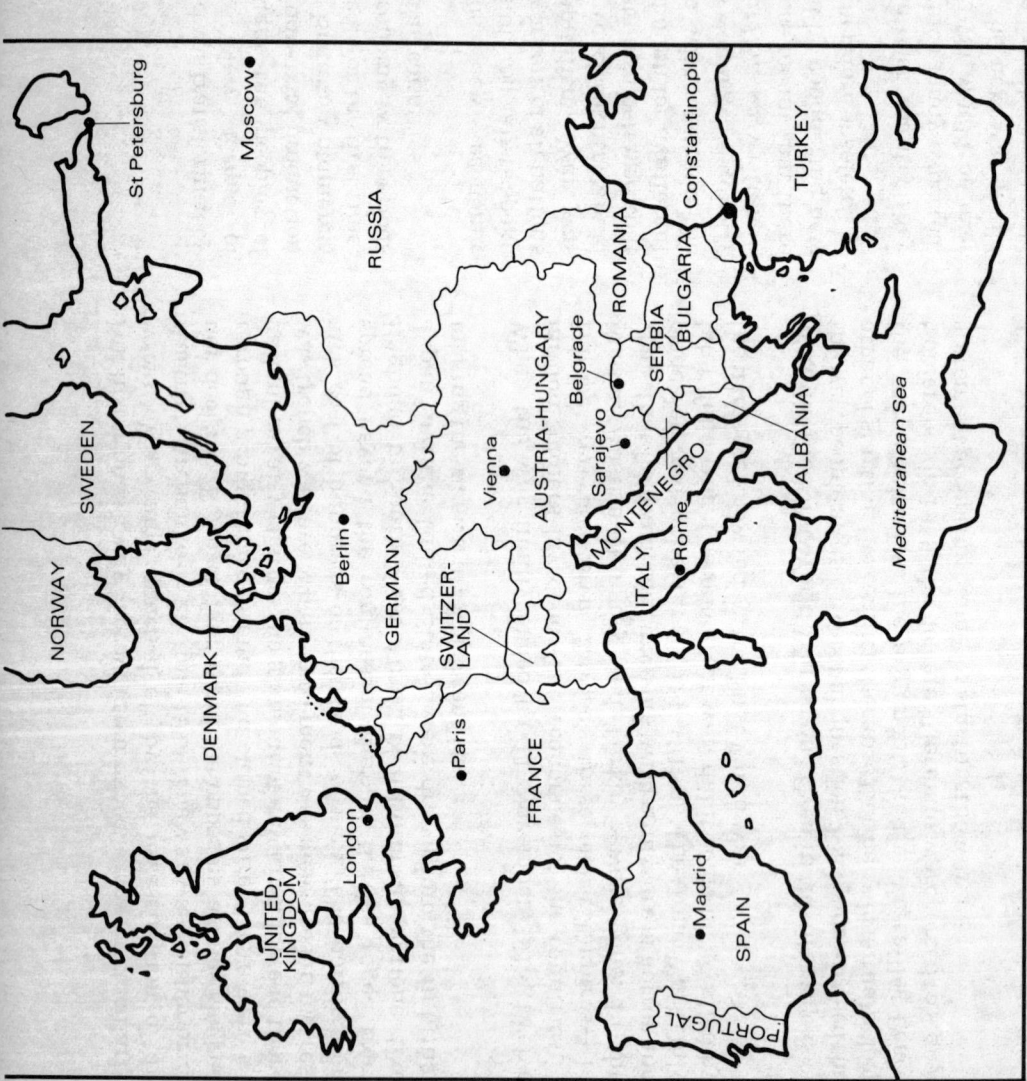

Map 8 — Europe in 1914.

which no one really wanted. A number of historians have laid the blame squarely back on Germany. They argue that Germany in 1914 was 'grasping for world power', and was willing to wage a war to obtain it.

Rather than simply casting blame, we need to focus on the circumstances that led up to the war. In the fifty years preceding the outbreak of war, Europe underwent many profound political and economic changes. These changes improved the standard of

The long-term causes of the First World War

living of many Europeans, but they also made Europe in 1914 a very unstable place—and instability among nations is often a recipe for war. In the first section of this chapter we will discuss four of the long-term sources of instability in Europe. These were:

1. The rise of a powerful, industrial Germany;
2. The slow disintegration of the old Empires of southern and eastern Europe—the Russian Empire, Austria-Hungary and the Ottoman Empire;
3. Competition for the fruits of colonial empire—markets, sources of raw materials and outlets for profitable investment—between the nations of Europe;
4. The ever-tightening network of alliances between European powers—alliances which generated fear, distrust and, eventually, a desperate arms race.

In succeeding sections we will discuss the outbreak of the war; the conduct of the war, both on the battlefield and on the Home Front; and the war's consequences.

THE RISE OF GERMANY

The Congress of Vienna in 1815 created a balance of power in Europe. No single nation could become so powerful that it could endanger all of Europe, as France had done under Napoleon. For fifty years this formula worked fairly well. With a few exceptions, Europe was at peace.

The unification of Germany (described in Chapter 1) destroyed this balance. Under the leadership of Chancellor Otto von Bismarck, thirty-nine German-speaking provinces and principalities were melded into one great nation, with Prussia at its heart. To secure its position, Prussia defeated two of its neighbours, France and Austria, in war.

The new German nation possessed all the ingredients for economic growth. The country had rich natural resources and a large population. Economic power rested securely in the hands of an industrial-capitalist class, which enjoyed the support of a strong central government. Almost immediately, Germany's economy boomed. Germany's steel and chemical industries were soon among the most productive in the world. A network of railroads carried goods throughout the country, and German commerce with other countries expanded rapidly. By 1880, Germany was the dominant economic power on the continent.

The rise of Germany had two important consequences. First it created among the French an undying hatred of Germany. The French neither forgot nor forgave their defeat in the Franco-Prussian War, and they hated Germany for stealing the rich iron and coal fields of Alsace-Lorraine. The French dreamed of avenging their defeat and recapturing their lost provinces. This conflict between France and Germany remained the central division in Europe between 1870 and the beginning of the First World War in 1914.

Germany's fantastic economic growth had a second, less obvious, consequence. Germany's new economic power gave it an unmatched capacity to wage war. Factories producing steel for bridges and trains could just as easily produce guns and

39

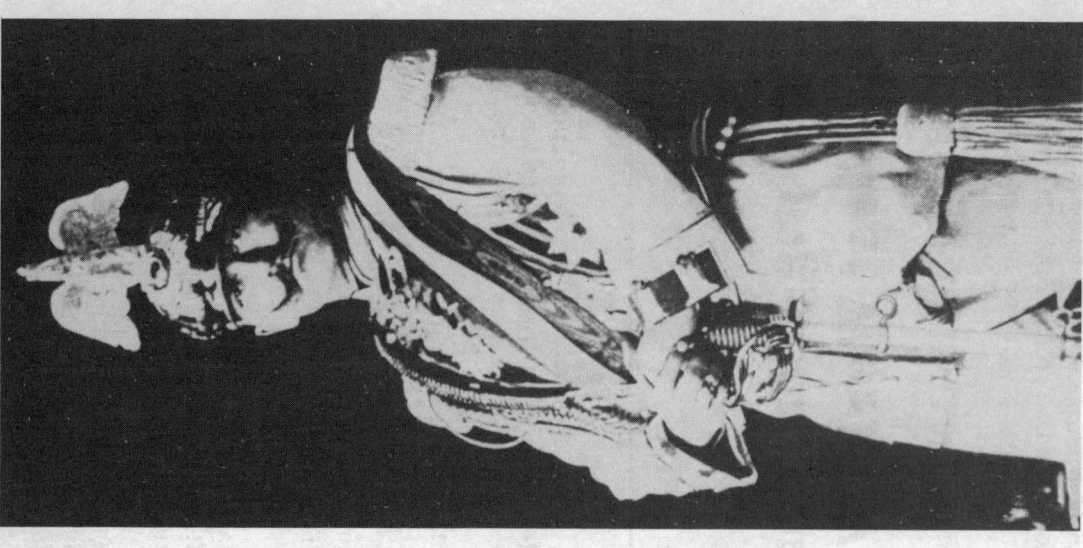

The German Kaiser, Wilhelm II, ruler of the German Empire from 1888 to 1918.

ammunition. The chemical industry had the expertise to produce new high explosives and poison gas. The nation's rail network could quickly shuttle troops and equipment to a battlefront. In sum, the *industrial* power of the new Germany translated directly into *military* power. For the first time since the reign of Napoleon, Europe possessed a single power capable of dominating the continent. The balance of power had been shattered. In the decades that followed, many conflicts would arise over Germany's efforts to assert its newly acquired power.

THE DECLINE OF THE OLD EMPIRES

Germany's rise to power introduced an element of instability to Europe. A second element of instability was added by the continuing decline of the old Empires of southern and eastern Europe. If Germany represented the new order, then the Ottoman (Turkish) Empire, the Russian Empire and the Austro-Hungarian Empire all represented the old. These Empires were autocracies*, ruled by the Turkish Sultan, the Russian Tsar and the Austrian Emperor. The power of these Empires rested not on industry or commerce but on their claims to vast territory. Each was centuries old. The Ottoman Empire stretched back over 600 years; the Austrian Empire had its roots in the Middle Ages; Russia had been ruled by the Tsars for over a thousand years. Yet by the end of the Nineteenth Century, these old Empires were growing weaker. The rulers in each found it increasingly difficult to hold their vast Empires together. The result was a series of conflicts in south-eastern Europe, as each Empire tried to restore its dwindling prestige at the expense of its neighbours.

The Ottoman Empire

At its height, the Ottoman Empire stretched from Algeria to the Persian Gulf. But by the Nineteenth Century, the Empire was the 'sick man of Europe'. The economic and political changes which had made Germany a world power scarcely touched Turkey. Economically, the Empire had little industry or commerce and few railroads. Most wealth was in the hands of a few traditional 'notables'. Politically, power lay with a Sultan, who ruled by decree, more or less according to Muslim traditional law. In the 1870s, the Sultan experimented briefly with a constitution and parliament, but suspended both after one year.

By the end of the Nineteenth Century, the central Government was so weak and inefficient that it was not even able to collect taxes in many parts of the Empire. The army, which had enabled previous sultans to conquer and rule vast areas of Europe and Africa, was in a shambles.

As the Ottoman Empire expired, neighbouring states hovered over the carcass. Generations of Russian Tsars dreamed of 'liberating' Constantinople, the Turkish capital. Constantinople was the holiest city in the Russian Orthodox religion. More important, it controlled the passage from the Black Sea to the Mediterranean. Control of these straits would allow the Tsar to spread Russian commerce and power deep into Europe. (In the Nineteenth Century Russia fought four wars with Turkey, yet it never managed to obtain the straits.) Other European powers were equally interested in the fate of Turkey. Austria-Hungary hoped to spread its own influence into the old Ottoman territories in the Balkans. Even very young nations, such as Italy and Serbia, schemed to expand their influence at the expense of the dying Ottoman Empire.

The Russian Empire

Russia hungrily watched the slow death of Turkey, but in reality it was very ill itself. In 1900, Russia was still by far the largest Empire in the world. It stretched more than eight thousand kilometres west to east and commanded the largest population in Europe. But, in terms of real power, Russia was no match for the more industrialized Germany.

Like the Ottoman Empire, Russia never felt the full effects of the political and industrial revolutions that swept across western Europe. Economically, Russia remained an agricultural nation. Most people lived on the land as peasants, while the nation's wealth was concentrated in the hands of a class of conservative nobles. These conditions prevented any significant industrialization. Put simply, in the late Nineteenth Century Russia had no capitalist class to build factories and no urban working class to work in them.

Different Tsars in the Nineteenth Century had taken a few halting steps towards modernising Russia. Serfdom was abolished in 1861. The State began to build railroads—the greatest project was a trans-Siberian railway linking Russia's western cities with its far eastern frontier. A few industries began to grow in the 1890s — petroleum, textiles, and even a small steel industry to meet the needs of railroad construction. To speed up industrialization, the Tsar passed laws encouraging foreign investors to build factories in Russia. The Tsar even flirted briefly with representative government but, like the Turkish Sultan, he remained suspicious of the experiment.

By the beginning of the Twentieth Century, Russia began to pay the price for its partial modernization. People came to the cities, but often they could not find jobs. They formed a restive and

41

occasionally violent class. Liberal and radical parties appeared, demanding more political rights. In 1905, a revolution broke out in St Petersburg and spread throughout the country. Only with difficulty was the Tsar's army able to restore order.

The Tsar was losing control of his country. But instead of dealing with the country's internal problems, he continued to concern himself with Russia's territorial expansion. Perhaps he hoped that new conquests would quiet the unrest at home. In 1904 Russia's expansion in the east led to a conflict with Japan, another expansionist power. In the Russo-Japanese War of 1904–05, the Japanese inflicted a humiliating defeat on the Tsar's poorly equipped army and navy, which added further fuel to the dissatisfaction at home. Blocked in the east, Russian ambitions turned back to the west, to the decaying Ottoman Empire. Russia watched for an opportunity to extend its power in the Balkans, always with an eye to opening the Black Sea passage. The Russian Empire remained hungry, even as it died of indigestion.

Austria-Hungary

Russia's ambitions in the Balkans brought it into conflict with the Austro-Hungarian Empire. Ruled by the Hapsburg family since the Thirteenth Century, the Austrian Empire had once held territory all over Europe. But in the Nineteenth Century it too was an Empire in decline. In a series of wars it lost territory in Denmark and Italy, and was weakened further by German unification. Even so, the Empire still covered a large, diverse territory in 1900.

Like the other old Empires, Austria-Hungary lacked the strong government needed to manage its Empire. It did have a parliamentary system, with one Parliament for Austria and one for Hungary, but the Austrian Parliament was often suspended. It also possessed a skilled bureaucracy to handle many of the day-to-day affairs of government. Most political power, however, remained in the hands of the Emperor, Franz Joseph. Franz Joseph embodied the old world. By 1914 he had ruled for 66 years, having ascended to the throne as an eighteen-year-old in 1848. Economically too, Austria-Hungary was less than modern. In the late Nineteenth Century the government began taking steps to create a unified, industrial economy. It imposed uniform customs duties throughout the Empire in order to encourage commerce. It began laying railroads. A few industries developed in the Austrian portion of the Empire, although Hungary, with a powerful class of conservative landowners, remained unindustrialized. Given time, Austria-Hungary might have developed a stronger, more modern economy. But time was a resource the Empire did not possess.

Like the Ottoman Empire, the old Austrian Empire included many different peoples. Even after losing Italy and Denmark, it still included ten distinct ethnic groups, speaking nineteen different languages. By the late Nineteenth Century the Empire was being torn apart by the demands of these different blocs. The Austrians solved one of these problems in 1867, by granting limited self-government to the Magyars of Hungary. (Thereafter the Austrian Empire was known as Austria-Hungary.) This arrangement solved the Magyar problem, but soon the Poles and the Czechs in the Empire demanded the same sort of recognition. Without an energetic government or a developed economy there was little to hold these different national groups together.

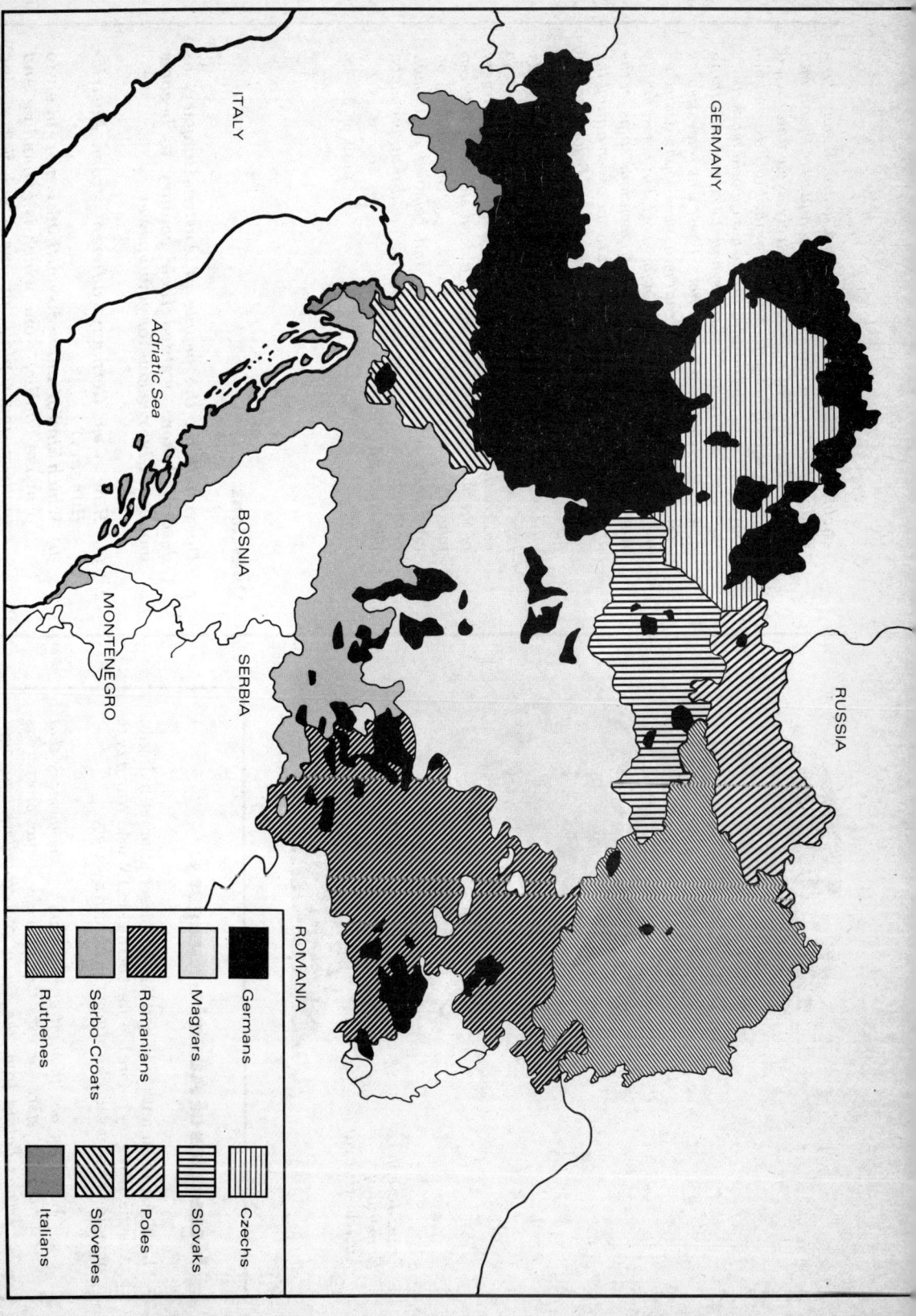

MAP 9—Distribution of ethnic groups in the Austro-Hungarian Empire, 1900.

established order ... Of course cars also drove along those roads — but not too many cars! The conquest of the air had begun here too; but not too intensively. Now and then a ship was sent off to South America or the Far East; but not too often. There was no ambition to have world markets ... the words 'colony' and 'overseas' had the ring of something as yet utterly untried and remote. There was some display of luxury; but it was not, of course, as over-sophisticated as that of the French. One went in for sport; but not in madly Anglo-Saxon fashion. One spent tremendous sums on the army; but only just enough to assure one of remaining the second weakest among the great powers ... Before the law all citizens were equal, but not everyone, of course, was a citizen. There was a Parliament, which ... was usually kept shut ... There were those nationalist struggles ... so violent that they several times a year caused the machinery of the state to jam and come to a dead stop. But between whiles, in the breathing spaces ... everyone got on excellently with everyone else and behaved as though nothing had ever been the matter ... and that, probably, was the ruin of it.

(Musil, pp. 31–35)

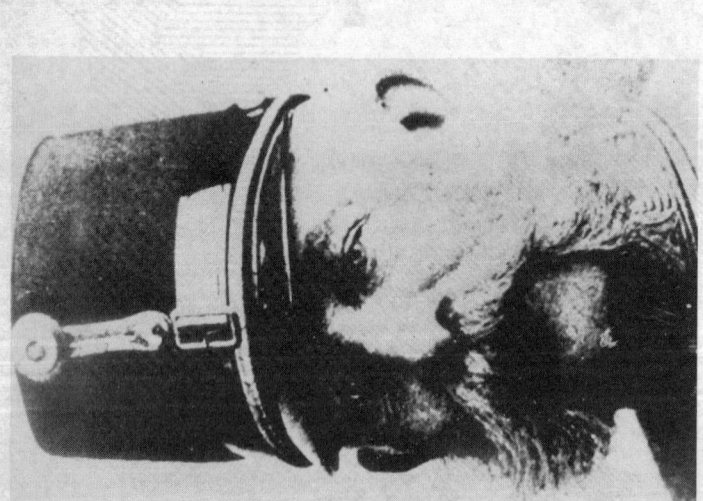

Franz Joseph I, Emperor of Austria-Hungary.

Questions

1. Do you think the people of Austria-Hungary, as described here, wanted their country to become modern? Give reasons for your answer.

2. (a) How was Germany different from Austria-Hungary?
   (b) Which kind of nation do you think is more likely to provoke conflict — one which is expanding and modernising rapidly, or one which is resisting change?

Memories of Austria-Hungary

Read Austrian author Robert Musil's description of living in Austria-Hungary before the start of the First World War. Try to imagine what it was like to grow up in such a society.

Whenever one thought of [Austria] ... the memory that hovered before the eyes was of wide, white, prosperous roads dating from the age of foot-travellers and mail coaches, roads leading in all directions like rivers of

3. (a) What kind of changes—in the form of government or the economy—might have held Austria-Hungary together?
   (b) What sort of structures or ideas are necessary to hold together a nation with many different ethnic groups?

4. The First World War destroyed the Austro-Hungarian Empire. What do you think would have become of the Empire had the war not come? Could it have survived until today?

Summary: The decline of the old Empires and the Balkan problem

At the same time that Germany was growing in power the old Empires continued their slow decline. The three Empires had many similarities. Each covered a large territory with many different peoples, united only by supposed loyalty to Sultan, Tsar or Emperor. All three possessed a class of powerful, conservative landowners who stood in the way of economic development. Industrial and commercial development in each lagged far behind the modern economies of western Europe. Central governments remained weak and inefficient. Put simply, none of these Empires possessed the sinews needed to bind a modern nation state together.

The old Empires shared one other thing in common. By an unfortunate coincidence, each bordered the Balkan region. Once part of the Ottoman Empire, the Balkans now consisted of the nations of Serbia, Romania, Bulgaria and Greece. As Turkish power waned, both Russia and Austria-Hungary hoped to expand their own influence in the region. Meanwhile, the people of the Balkan countries, having just gained independence from the Turks, had little desire to be controlled by yet another Empire. Among many intellectuals in these young nations nationalism* was very strong. In Serbia, for example, many young people dreamed of joining with Serbians living in Austria-Hungary to create a 'Greater Serbia'.

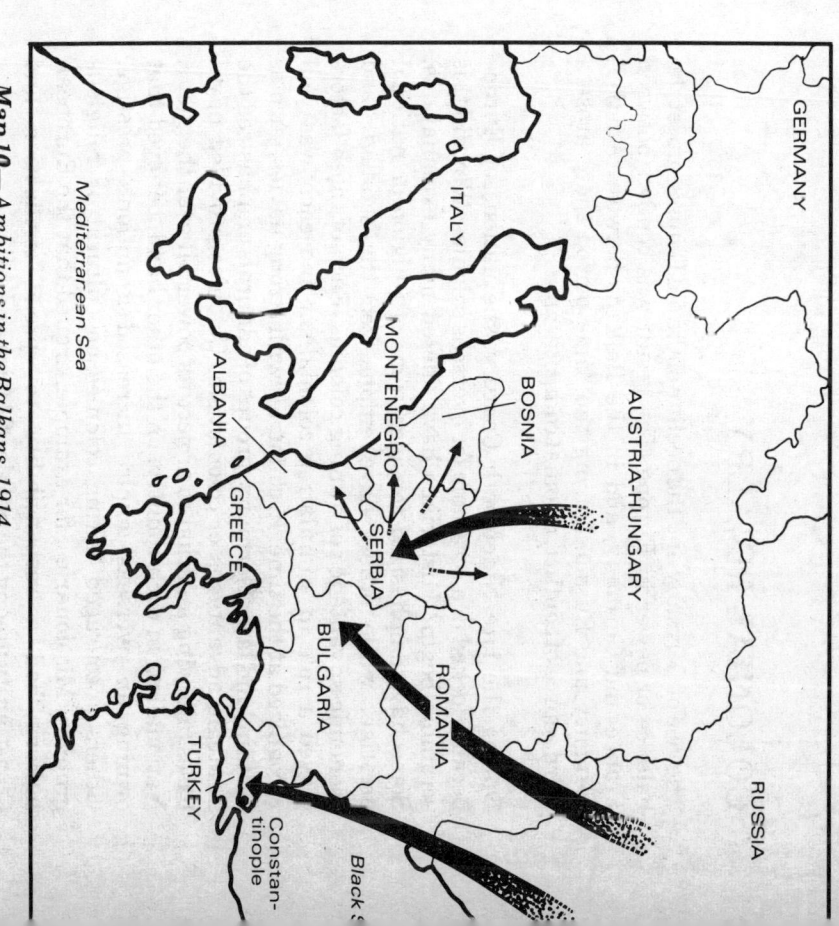

Map 10—Ambitions in the Balkans, 1914.

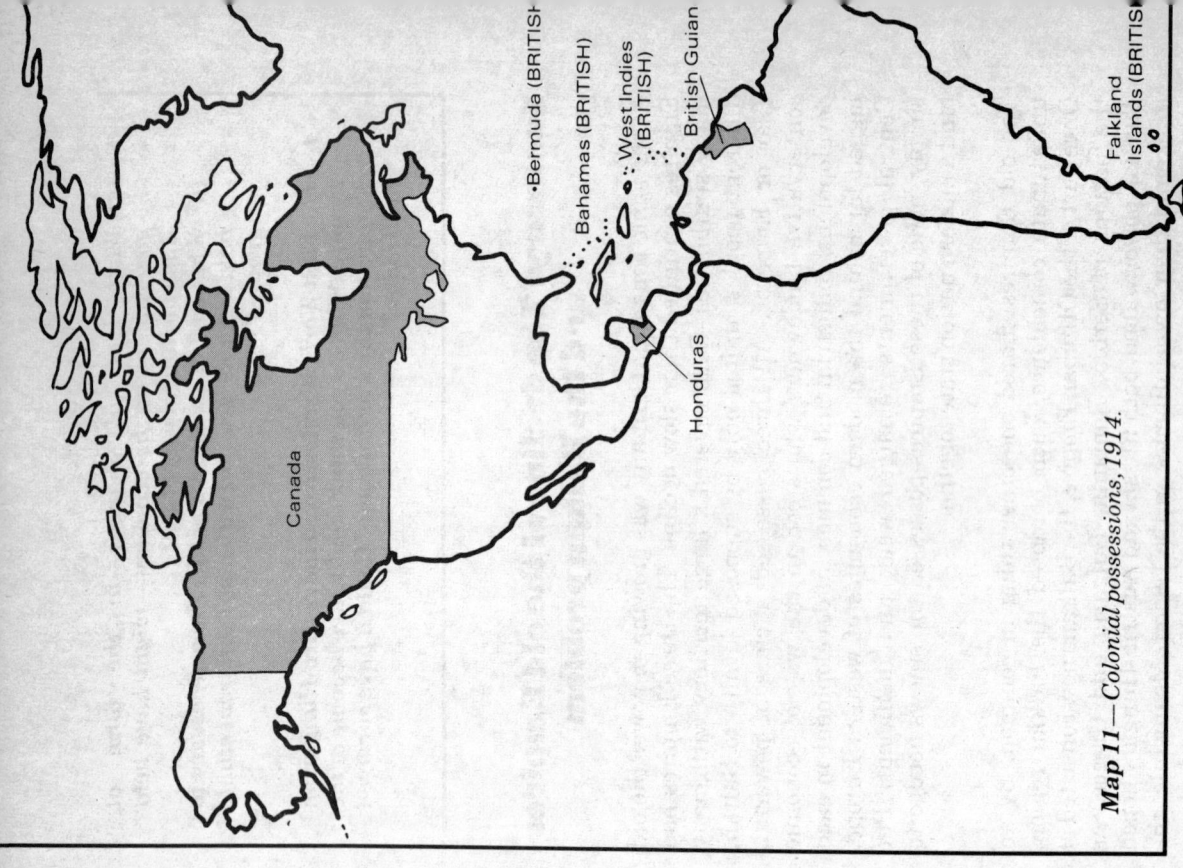

Map 11 — *Colonial possessions, 1914.*

Because of these conflicting ambitions, the Balkans remained an extremely unstable area. By the end of the century, a few leaders began to recognise that instability in the Balkans posed a threat to the peace of Europe. Bismarck, for example, once remarked that war in Europe, should it ever come, would probably be triggered by 'some damned fool thing in the Balkans'. History would prove him correct.

COLONIAL RIVALRY

The rise of Germany and the decline of the old Empires upset the balance of power in Europe. The result was conflict between France and Germany, and in the Balkans between Austria-Hungary and Russia. During the same period there arose a third source of conflict: colonial competition.

During the late Nineteenth Century, the nations of Europe became locked in a scramble for overseas colonies. Why did this scramble begin? Historians have offered many explanations. Some have emphasized considerations of religion or national prestige, while others have emphasized the strategic and economic advantages of owning colonies. Each of these factors played a role in stimulating colonialism and each was well recognized at the time. In countries with strong navies, such as Britain, and later Germany, groups of admirals emphasized the strategic advantages of colonialism. Colonies provided naval bases, allowing a nation to project its power all over the globe. Nationalists in each country, on the other hand, believed that owning an overseas empire increased a nation's prestige. Others encouraged taking colonies on cultural or religious grounds. Missionaries, for example, argued that the European nations had a responsibility to spread civilization and Christianity among the people of Africa and Asia.

46

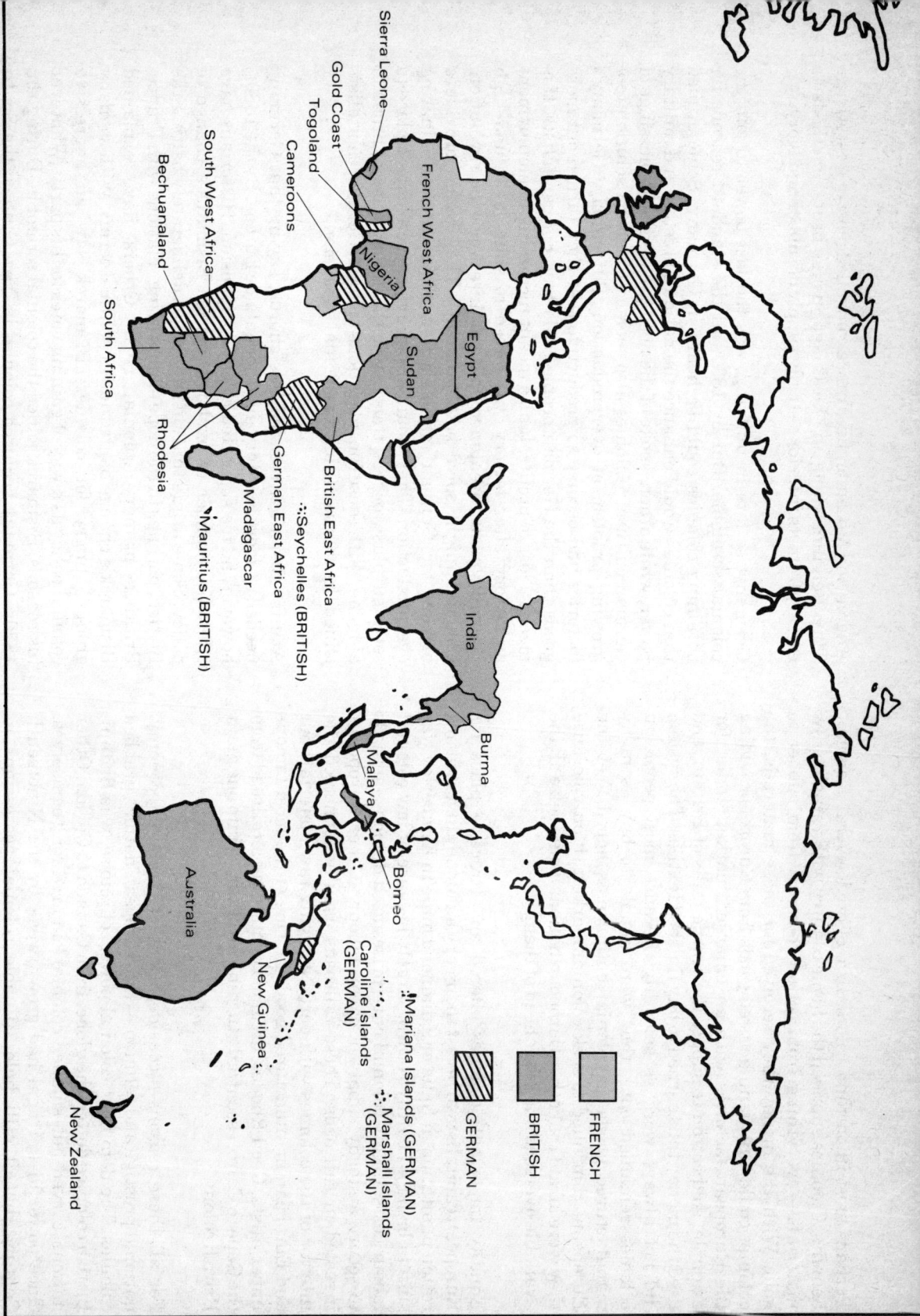

Perhaps most important, colonialism offered several economic benefits. Colonies supplied the home country with valuable raw materials — everything from cotton to cocoa, from rubber to gold. With the money they received for these materials, the colonies could buy manufactured goods from Europe, providing the European factories with an enlarged market. India, for example, sold cotton to supply the textile mills of Britain, and used the money thus earned to buy finished textiles. The system did not always work so smoothly. Because most people in colonies remained poor, they were unable to buy as many manufactured goods as colonial enthusiasts hoped. Yet the Europeans continued to seek colonial markets, if only because they were afraid that other European nations would seize all the available overseas markets ahead of them.

Equally important, colonies offered an attractive place for European capitalists to invest their capital. Money invested in a cotton plantation in India or a diamond mine in Kimberley was sure to bring a healthy return, largely because of low colonial labour costs. (Many colonial enterprises used dubious methods to secure a steady supply of cheap labour.) Other Europeans invested in railroads. These railroads usually connected the interior of the colonies with ports, carrying raw materials out and European manufactured goods in. One of the most famous imperialists, Cecil Rhodes, dreamed of building a railroad from the Cape to Cairo, essentially turning all of Africa into one giant British colony.

For all these reasons — considerations of strategy, economy, national prestige and religion — the European nations grabbed colonies. The dominant colonial power, of course, was Britain. British colonies dotted the globe, from Canada to Ceylon. Other nations carved out smaller colonial empires for themselves. Once powerful Portugal had grown weak by the Nineteenth Century, but it still held valuable colonial possessions in Angola and Moçambique. France controlled most of west Africa. Tiny Belgium clung to the Congo, using brutal methods to extract from its interior a steady supply of rubber and ivory.

Germany, so late in unifying, was the last power to join the colonial scramble. But by 1880, all the standard reasons for obtaining colonies could be heard in Germany. Some argued that colonies would enhance the nation's prestige and military power, while others spoke of the need to extend 'the blessings of German culture'. Colonies also seemed to offer a solution to a growing problem of overproduction. Put simply, Germany's factories had become so productive that they turned out more goods than the German people could buy. For capitalists, this meant a loss of profits. It also meant increasing unemployment as factory after factory was forced to shut down; and high unemployment threatened political unrest or even revolution. Colonies might solve both problems. They would provide a market for German manufactured goods, thus eliminating overproduction. They would also provide a convenient place to settle surplus workers, thus easing the unemployment problem at home. With these considerations in mind, German capitalists joined the chorus calling for colonial expansion.

At first Bismarck resisted this chorus, saying that Germany needed no more territory inside or outside Europe. By the 1880s, however, he too supported colonial expansion. Historians have offered a number of explanations for Bismarck's change of policy. Some argue that Bismarck was deliberately baiting the British, perhaps in the hope of improving relations with France, Britain's primary colonial rival. Others have explained Bismarck's change of attitude in political terms: With so many groups hungry for colonies, Bismarck saw an aggressive colonial policy as a way of gaining votes for his party. Whatever his reasons, Bismarck joined the colonial scramble. During the 1880s, Germany acquired colonies in New Guinea, the South

48

Pacific, Togo, the Cameroons, and east and south-west Africa. The accession of an aggressive young Kaiser, Wilhelm II, in 1888, confirmed this new direction. Germany was bent on obtaining a global empire.

As European colonialism spread across the globe, so too did European conflicts. Colonies inspired jealousy and suspicion between nations. The French wanted Egypt, which had been occupied by Britain since 1880. The British warily eyed Russia, ever fearful that Russia would try to swallow India, its near neighbour to the south. The late-arriving Germans were quick to embroil themselves in colonial conflicts. In 1894, the Germans conspired to deny the British a strip of land in the Congo needed for the Cape to Cairo railroad. A few years later, Britain retaliated in similar vein, scuttling German plans to build a railroad from Berlin to Baghdad.

Colonial competition occasionally almost boiled over into war. A dispute between France and Germany over control of Morocco, for example, almost sparked war in 1905 and 1911. The 1905 crisis was solved by an international conference which gave both France and Germany certain economic rights in Morocco, which remained a French colony. The Kaiser was not satisfied with the agreement, and in 1911 he despatched a German gunboat to the Moroccan port of Agadir. The Kaiser said the gunboat was necessary to protect German economic interests after an indigenous revolt in Morocco, but in reality he hoped to bully the French into surrendering control of much of west and central Africa. France refused, and prepared for war. Only after a warning from Britain did the Kaiser relent. The Germans withdrew the gunboat and in exchange the French ceded over 100 000 square miles of the French Congo to them.

Friction over colonies was so persistent that many historians later concluded that colonial competition was the main cause of the First World War. This view is probably exaggerated. Ultimately most colonial conflicts were settled without shooting. But colonial competition added yet another layer of conflict and instability to an already dangerous situation in Europe. The European nations grew increasingly hostile and suspicious of one another. They used colonial policy to try to enhance their own prestige while humiliating their enemies. Morocco, for example, was in itself hardly worth fighting a war over, but when questions of prestige and national honour intruded both France and Germany were ready to risk war.

Conflict over colonies produced one other important effect. It contributed to the creation and hardening of a network of alliances between the European powers. It is to the alliance system that we must turn next.

THE ALLIANCE SYSTEM

Conflict and instability sent all the European powers scrambling for alliances. Most leaders believed that signing treaties and alliances would make their countries stronger and more secure. In the long run, however, the alliance system had just the opposite effect. It increased suspicion and fear between nations, adding to the general instability plaguing Europe. Worse still, the alliance system forced all the European nations into two increasingly hostile camps. As a result, conflicts between two nations often threatened to spread to all the European powers.

German diplomacy and its consequences

Bismarck once remarked that his sleep was haunted by 'nightmares of coalitions'. France loomed large in his dreams. The French hated the Germans for taking Alsace-Lorraine in

49

1871, and were determined to regain those territories. To check this ambition, Bismarck used diplomacy to keep France isolated and weak. In 1873, he encouraged the rulers of the continent's three major powers—Wilhelm I of Germany, Franz Josef of Austria and Tsar Alexander of Russia—to sign the *Dreikaiserbund* (Three Emperors' League). The league was not a military alliance but it was clearly intended to overawe France. (Much of the three leaders' discussion focused on the 'republican and distinctly socialist nature' of the French government.) Nine years later, in 1882, Bismarck concluded a military alliance between Germany, Austria-Hungary and Italy. This Triple Alliance was again directed against France—the three signatories agreed to fight together if France should attack any of them. Bismarck believed that these treaties, taken together, would keep France too weak to consider attacking Germany. Put simply, there was no power left on the continent for France to ally itself with.

Bismarck had used Russia to keep France isolated, but he still distrusted Russia's expansionist ambitions in the Balkans. Without telling the Russians, he negotiated a secret Dual Alliance in 1879 with Austria-Hungary against Russia. Germany now had one treaty with Russia and one against Russia. As one historian has put it, European diplomacy was a 'tangled web', with Bismarck the spider at the centre. A renewal of the Dreikaiserbund in 1883, followed by a Re-Insurance Treaty with Russia in 1887, further tangled relations. Worse still, each of these treaties was kept secret. Only the Germans knew the exact provisions of each.

Bismarck had exorcized his nightmare of coalitions by signing coalitions of his own—with Germany always at the centre. But political and economic factors soon unravelled Bismarck's system. In 1888, an economic panic caused German investors to withdraw their money from Russia. Up until then, Germany had been the largest lender of money to Russia, allowing the Tsar to begin modernising his industry and army. French investors filled the gap. During 1888–1889, French bankers provided loans worth 2.5 billion francs to help the Tsar build factories and railroads. At the same time, French manufacturers began to sell arms to the Tsar's army. Economic damage to German-Russian relations was doubled by the rise to power of Kaiser Wilhelm II, also in 1888. Many Germans distrusted Russia, but few so fiercely as the young Kaiser. Wilhelm II was determined to make Germany the dominant power on the continent and he saw Russia as his primary obstacle. In March 1890, he forced the resignation of Bismarck, who remained committed to maintaining good relations with Russia. Ten days later the Germans decided not to renew the Re-Insurance Treaty with Russia.

The two continental nations left over, France and Russia, were quick to get together. Fearful that Germany would try to conquer them individually, the two countries signed the Franco-Russian Alliance in 1894. The alliance was defensive in nature—the two nations pledged to fight together should Germany attack either one. France and Russia were an odd pair. To the republican French, the Tsar represented all the evils of the old order, where tyrants enslaved the people. To the Tsar, France represented all the excesses that came of letting the common people try to govern themselves. But diplomacy makes strange bedfellows: The two nations were united by a shared dread of Germany.

There were now two blocs in Europe. The Triple Alliance, centred around Germany, included Italy and Austria-Hungary. Germany's two rivals on the continent, France and Russia, were joined in the opposite camp. For the next few years there was a balance of power on the continent. The balance was short-lived, however, because Britain was at last ready to leave diplomatic isolation.

British fears and the creation of the Triple Entente

While other nations scrambled for alliances, the British concentrated on reaping the profits of their overseas empire. Safe on their island, shielded by the world's most powerful navy, the British saw little reason to join continental alliances. By the 1890s, however, the British began to feel increasingly vulnerable. Russia loomed over India, the 'jewel' in Britain's colonial empire, and threatened other British interests in the Near and Middle East. The French intrigued against the British in Egypt. The Germans, from their newly acquired colony in South West Africa, meddled in South Africa, a region the British considered their own. After the abortive Jameson Raid, for example, the Germans humiliated Britain by sending a message of support to the Transvaal Government. The so-called Kruger Telegram roused a storm in London, where many people saw it as part of a German plot to annex the Transvaal.

Faced with a multitude of threats, the British government began to fear that it was no longer able to defend its empire. Two events in 1898 intensified this feeling of weakness. Germany began building a navy. Urged on by German capitalists, the Kaiser launched an ambitious naval construction programme under the direction of Admiral Alfred von Tirpitz. The naval programme demonstrated Germany's determination to protect its growing overseas interests. It also terrified the British, who depended on naval superiority for their own security, as well as the security of their empire. British feelings of vulnerability were redoubled by the bitter experience of the Anglo-Boer War, which began the same year. If the British army needed three years to quell the outnumbered Boers, how could it hope to withstand the armies of Russia, France or Germany? The condemnation the British received during the war from every European capital only reminded them just how friendless they were.

Driven by fear, Britain cast about for allies. In 1902 the British signed a treaty with Japan. Next they turned to Europe. They first approached the Germans and proposed a settlement of their various colonial disputes. But the Germans played hard to get — they rejected Britain's offer in the hopes of getting a better deal. The Germans were confident that the British had nowhere else to go. They did not believe that Britain would try to negotiate a deal with its traditional enemies, France and Russia.

To the Germans' considerable shock, Britain turned to France. In 1904, the two nations signed the *Entente Cordiale* (Cordial Agreement). France pledged to respect British dominance in Egypt while Britain agreed to allow France a free hand in Morocco. Put simply, the treaty gave the nervous British one less colonial situation to worry about. The entente was not a military alliance but it did demonstrate a new spirit of co-operation between France and Britain. The Entente Cordiale was soon followed by a similar agreement between Britain and Russia. In the Anglo-Russian Entente of 1907, the two nations agreed to split the colony of Persia. The rich northern third of Persia would be a Russian sphere of influence while the middle third was a neutral zone. The southern third, which contained crucial roads to India, was reserved for the British. Once again, one of Britain's major colonial anxieties — about Russian designs on India — was solved by agreement.

The British entered the continental diplomatic game out of a feeling of weakness. They negotiated agreements to colonial disputes because they had begun to doubt their own ability to defend their empire. The move was not aimed specifically at

51

Haunted by fears of encirclement and uncertain of the value of its allies, Germany set out to restore its position. Beginning in 1907, the Germans expanded their naval programme and invested huge sums of money improving their army. This action only served to drive Britain even closer to France and Russia. Britain responded to Germany's new naval schedules with a naval build-up of its own. It entered a new series of military 'conversations' with France, considering ways the two nations' armies and navies could work together in the event of a war. The British also encouraged Russia to accelerate its military build-up. Soon all of Europe was locked into an uncontrolled arms race. Each nation poured money into its military machine in a futile effort to buy security.

The naval race

In the decade leading up to the First World War, the European powers poured massive amounts of money into enlarged and modernized armies and navies. The cost of maintaining these military machines was crippling, especially for Russia, financially the weakest of the Great powers. In 1907, at the suggestion of the Russian Tsar, a disarmament conference was convened at the Hague. Germany, however, facing the combined might of Britain, Russia, and France, refused to consider any reductions in armaments, and the conference ended in failure. Indeed, suspicions about Germany's motivations in refusing gave a further spur to the arms race.

Much of the attention at the time focused on the naval race between Germany and Britain. Germany, by tradition a land power, launched an ambitious naval building programme in 1898 which lifted it from seventh to second among the world's sea powers in scarcely a dozen years. Britain, which maintained only a small standing army and relied on its navy for security,

Germany — indeed, the British approached the Germans first. Nonetheless, many Germans were outraged by the ententes of 1904 and 1907. German nationalists accused the British, French and Russians of conspiring to deny Germany its rightful place in the world. German capitalists complained that they were being encircled by their enemies. The Kaiser spent hours raging about the British betrayal, forgetting that he himself had turned down Britain's initial offer. Newspapers fanned the flames. Although the British had signed no military alliances with either France or Russia, most newspapers soon referred to a Triple Entente, which seemed more than a match for the Triple Alliance of Germany, Austria-Hungary and Italy.

THE TWO ARMED CAMPS 1910	
Triple Alliance	*Triple Entente*
Germany	France
Austria-Hungary	Russia
Italy[1]	Great Britain

[1] Italy declared itself neutral at the outbreak of the war.

Arms race

Now it was Germany's turn to feel threatened. Compared with the combined power of the Triple Entente, the Triple Alliance seemed meagre. Italy was weak and many Germans doubted that it could be counted on in the event of a war. (German suspicions were well founded: when the war began Italy quickly declared itself neutral.) Austria-Hungary was dependable but weak. Its army was large but ill-equipped. In the event of war, Germany might also count on the support of the Ottoman Empire and Bulgaria, but neither offered much comfort.

predictably responded with a naval building programme of its own.

Naval competition centred on dreadnoughts, turbine-powered battleships bristling with big guns. The superior range of the dreadnought's guns enabled it to fire on an enemy fleet without ever coming within range of the opponent's guns. The British launched the first dreadnought in 1906, and the Germans followed suit two years later. With its more developed ship-building capacity, Britain maintained the lead in building dreadnoughts — at the outbreak of the war the Royal Navy boasted twenty-nine dreadnoughts, to only seventeen in the German High Seas Fleet.

The Royal Navy's dreadnoughts enabled the British to maintain control of the seas throughout the First World War. Only once, in 1916, did the German High Seas Fleet venture out into the North Sea to challenge the Royal Navy. After a spectacular but indecisive clash at Jutland, the German navy retired to the safety of its northern ports, where it remained for the duration of the war. Meanwhile the British used their control of the seas to good effect. The Royal Navy convoyed shiploads of American food and supplies to Britain while maintaining a blockade around Germany. Germany's effort to establish a blockade of its own, using submarines to sink Britain-bound merchant ships, never succeeded, though it did claim a devastating toll in men and tonnage. Ultimately Germany's submarine warfare campaign backfired, by drawing the United States into the war on the side of the Allies.

Questions

1. *Why were dreadnoughts important?*
2. *How did Britain's control of the seas contribute to the eventual Allied victory in the war?*

Summary: Long-term origins of the war

The tightening network of alliances and the ensuing arms race were the final ingredients in a recipe for war that was forty years in the making. The alliance system itself was a product of the general instability in Europe — instability rooted in the rise of Germany and the decline of the old Empires. Colonial competition further intensified suspicion and fear between nations, eventually forcing Britain to leave diplomatic isolation. The entry of Britain into the diplomatic equation on the side of France and Russia precipitated a desperate arms race — an arms race which drove frightened allies even closer together. By 1914 Europe was divided into two hostile camps, each armed to the teeth. Conflicts between any two nations could easily spread to all of Europe. As one historian put it, Europe was a "tinderbox" waiting for a spark.

The outbreak of the war

CRISIS IN THE BALKANS

Not surprisingly, the spark came in the Balkans — that region caught between the ambitions of the Austro-Hungarian and Russian Empires. The tiny Balkan nation of Serbia, which had won independence from the Ottoman Empire in the 1830s, had ambitions of its own. In 1912 Serbia led a group of Balkan states to a quick victory in a war against Turkey. Eight months later Serbia crushed neighbouring Bulgaria in a war triggered by conflict over dividing the spoils from the first war. In less than a

53

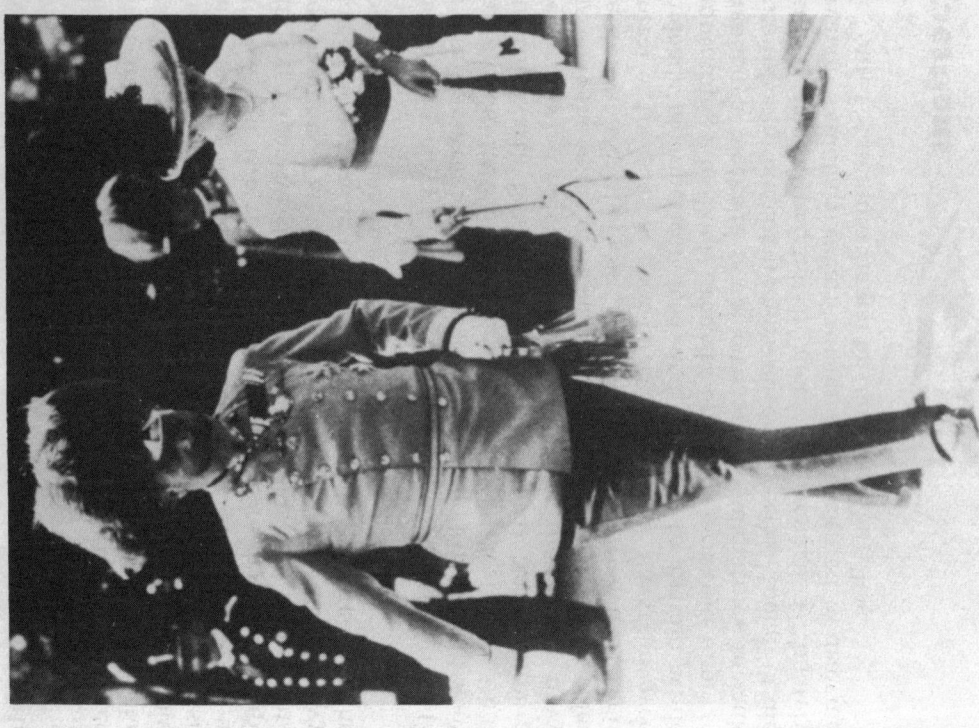

The Archduke and his wife arriving in Sarajevo on the morning of 28 June.

year Serbia doubled its territory and increased its population from three to four-and-a-half million. Serbian nationalists, still dreaming of creating a 'Greater Serbia' which would unite all Serbian people, turned again to Austria-Hungary. They renewed their demands that Austria-Hungary give up the southern portion of its Empire, where almost three million people of Serbian blood still lived. Serbia's ambitions were fed by Russia, which hoped itself to absorb all the Balkan people into its Empire once they had broken clear of Austria-Hungary. Austria-Hungary rejected Serbia's demands.

Then, on 28 June 1914, in a Balkan city named Sarajevo (in what is now Yugoslavia), a Serbian nationalist killed Archduke Ferdinand, heir to the Austrian throne. (See box.) The assassination gave the Austro-Hungarian Government a perfect excuse to do what it had long wanted to do: crush Serbia once and for all. The German Kaiser had been a personal friend of the Archduke and he encouraged his allies in Austria to take their revenge. The Germans understood that any Austrian action against Serbia might start a war with Russia, Serbia's patron, but they were willing to take that risk.

The assassination at Sarajevo

Sarajevo was the capital of Bosnia, a territory once controlled by the Ottoman Empire. Serbian nationalists dreamed of including Bosnia in their 'Greater Serbia', but Austria-Hungary beat them to it: in 1909 the Austrians annexed Bosnia into their Empire. The move infuriated Serbians as well as Russians, who had their own interest in the Balkans. (See Map 10.)

54

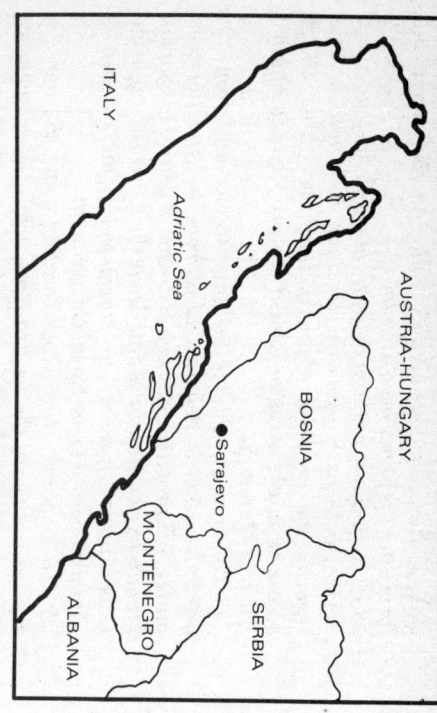

Map 12 — *Bosnia, showing the position of Sarajevo.*

When Archduke Ferdinand, heir to the Austro-Hungarian throne, visited Sarajevo, a group of Serbian nationalists conspired to assassinate him. It was a singularly clumsy killing. In the morning, one of the conspirators threw a bomb at the Archduke's open car. The bomb struck the Archduke's wife, bounced out of the car, and exploded beneath the car behind. The Austrian regents escaped unharmed, except for a bruise on the Archduke's wife's neck.

Later that day, the couple decided to visit a nearby hospital to see a soldier who had been injured in the bomb blast. On the way, their driver became lost. He pulled the car into a sidestreet and stopped. Unfortunately, he stopped right in front of Gavrilo Princip, one of the conspirators. Princip, disappointed after the morning's failure, could hardly believe his good fortune. He drew a revolver and began shooting, killing both the Archduke and his wife.

The killing, more a matter of luck than planning, was the trigger that initiated the world war. Suppose Princip had failed — do you believe that war would have come anyway?

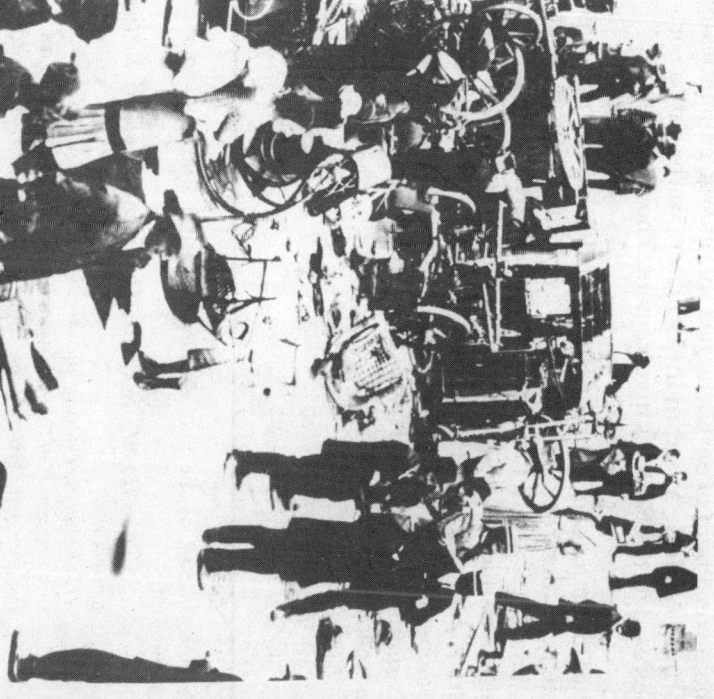

As word of the shooting spread, mobs took to the streets of Sarajevo to punish people suspected of being Serbian sympathizers. Here, a mob's work in a Serbian neighbourhood.

The Austro-Hungarian Government's reaction to the assassination

The Government of Austria-Hungary was convinced that the assassination had been planned by the Serbian Government. The Government of Serbia denied this charge emphatically. At Serbia's request, Austrian investigators were sent to Serbia to seek evidence of Serbia's involvement. They found none.

The Government of Austria-Hungary, determined not to let this chance to destroy Serbia slip away, changed its tack. It now claimed that, even if the Serbian Government had not planned the assassination, it had helped to create a climate of discontent which had led to it. Serbia was thus at least indirectly responsible. On 23 July 1914, Austria-Hungary sent an ultimatum to Serbia. It was deliberately framed so as to be unacceptable.

Here is part of the text of the ultimatum. Judge its tone for yourself.

... The Royal Serbian Government shall further undertake:

1. To suppress any publication which incites to hatred and contempt of the [Austro-Hungarian] Monarchy and in its general bearing is directed against the territorial integrity of that monarchy;

2. To dissolve immediately the society called 'Narodna Odbrana' [a Serbian nationalist group], to confiscate all its means of propaganda, and to proceed in the same manner against the other societies and their branches in Serbia which devote themselves to propaganda against the Austro-Hungarian Monarchy. The Royal Government shall take the necessary measures to prevent the societies from continuing their activity under another name and form after they have been dissolved;

3. To eliminate without delay from public instruction in Serbia, both as regards the teaching body and also as regards the methods of instruction, everything which serves or might serve to foment the propaganda against Austria-Hungary;

4. To remove from the military service and from the administration in general, all officers and functionaries guilty of propaganda against the Austro-Hungarian Monarchy, whose names and deeds the Austro-Hungarian Government reserve to themselves the right of communicating to the Royal Government;

5. To accept the collaboration in Serbia of representatives of the Austro-Hungarian Government for the purpose of suppressing the subversive movement directed against the territorial integrity of the Monarchy;

6. To take judicial proceedings against those of the accessories to the plot of the 28th June who are within Serbian territory;

Delegates of the Imperial and Royal Government will take part in the investigation relating thereto; ...

The Austro-Hungarian Government expect the reply of the Royal Government by 6 p.m. on Saturday the 25th July at latest ...

(Quoted in R. W. Breach *Documents and Descriptions in European History 1815–1939*, pp. 80–82.)

Question

Which of these terms was the greatest threat to Serbia's sovereignty? Give reasons for your answer.

Two days later, the Serbians replied to the ultimatum. Amazingly, they accepted most of its conditions, and sought clarification on others. But Austria-Hungary was determined to punish Serbia regardless. The Austrian ambassador broke off diplomatic relations with Serbia before even reading the reply. On 28 July 1914, Austria-Hungary declared war on Serbia.

THE CONFLICT SPREADS

Faced with the prospect of a general European war, the leaders of Germany, France, Russia and Great Britain briefly drew back. Telegrams flashed from capital to capital with proposals to prevent the conflict from spreading to all the powers. The Germans probed to see if Britain would remain neutral in the event of a war between Germany and Russia. France promised Russia its support but hoped war could be averted. Britain saw little to gain by fighting on the continent and tried to mediate between the powers.

Yet the leaders were unable to stop the spread of war. Why did their last efforts to contain the war fail?

In part, they failed because of the alliance system itself. France, for example, had no real stake in a conflict between Austria-Hungary and Serbia, but it feared the consequences of letting down its Russian ally. The original purpose of joining alliances — increasing security and preventing war — had apparently been forgotten.

Efforts to prevent war were also undercut by the nature of the armies that the countries had assembled during the preceding arms race. The armies in each country were huge, and getting them ready to fight was no easy task. To mobilize* an army of a million men took weeks. To delay mobilization, even for a day, increased the chances that the enemy would attack before one's own army was ready to fight. To speed up the process of mobilization, each nation had devised detailed plans. German plans, for example, included train schedules that were accurate down to the minute. Each day, the Germans were to ship five hundred trainloads of troops and equipment to the Belgian border, where the main German attack was to begin. The whole plan had one flaw. It assumed that each trainload of soldiers would attack as soon as they reached the border. If they didn't, there would be nowhere for the next trainload of soldiers to go. Trains would soon be backed up all the way to Berlin, leaving Germany's elaborate plans for mobilization in ruins. The same problem existed for other nations. There was simply no way to get such massive armies in a position to fight without pushing the first arrivals forward. In effect, this meant that once the order to begin mobilizing was given, there was no way to stop short of war.

Leaders in each nation thus faced a dilemma. To give the order to mobilize meant war. Yet to delay mobilizing gave the enemy a head start, which could mean defeat.

To avoid war in such a situation required that the leaders of each nation have absolute trust in one another. But little trust remained. For more than twenty years they had constantly deceived and humiliated one another. Out of fear they had formed alliances and built enormous armies — armies which were now pushing them forward to war. The leaders of Europe had prepared always for war, giving little thought to the requirements of peace. And now, facing the prospect of war, they did not know how to avoid it.

Russia, with the largest territory, was the first nation to mobilize. The Tsar, nervous to the last, asked his generals if it was possible to mobilize only against Austria without

WAR PLANS

In all the major wars of the Nineteenth Century the side which had maintained the offensive had emerged victorious. World War I generals had been schooled to believe in the importance of attacking at all times. The war plans that each nation developed before the war reflected this thinking. Austria-Hungary's plan called for a massive assault of nearly a million men northward against the Russian army in Poland. Russia planned a two-prong offensive, sending 800 000 men west into Prussia and an equal number south-west against Austria-Hungary. The French, in the immediate aftermath of the Franco-Prussian War, had preferred a defensive strategy, building a line of impregnable fortresses along the German border, which later came to be called the Maginot Line. But they too were soon convinced of the advantages of attacking and devised a new plan calling for an all-out offensive to liberate Alsace-Lorraine. French generals even managed to convince themselves that the gallant French soldier, with his courage and *esprit*, could fight only while moving forward. The generals would soon learn that esprit was a poor match for a machine-gun, and that attacking was no guarantee of victory.

The Germans, too, devised an offensive war plan but their strategy was more subtle. Unlike the other belligerents, Germany faced enemies on two sides — Russia in the east, and France (and probably Britain) in the west. To overcome this situation, the Germans devised the Schlieffen Plan, named after the general who first designed it in the 1890s. Schlieffen realised that Russia, with its vast territory, inefficient government and inadequate railroads, would be slow in getting its massive army ready to fight. Rather than splitting the army between the two fronts, he proposed leaving only a few divisions facing Russia while concentrating the mass of the German army for one hammer blow against France. He gambled that the well-

threatening Germany. The generals told him it was not, and on 30 July the Tsar gave the order for full mobilization. Germany gave Russia 24 hours to stop mobilizing. When Russia refused, Germany declared war. Over the next week the allies joined in: Germany declared war on France, Britain declared war on Germany, Austria-Hungary declared war on Russia. The First World War had begun.

Mobilization: An enthusiastic crowd in Vienna waves goodbye to a trainload of Austrian soldiers bound for the Front. To move a million soldiers into position to fight required precise, inflexible schedules. Some historians have argued that the existence of such schedules made it impossible for European leaders to hold back the tide of war. What do you think?

equipped German army could crush France in six weeks. This would leave Germany ample time to turn to the east and face the slow-to-organize Russians. Having defeated one enemy, the Germans, along with their Austrian allies, could annihilate the Russians at their leisure.

The whole plan depended on gaining a quick victory over France, and Schlieffen devised an ingenious plan to achieve this. He foresaw that France would attack in Alsace-Lorraine. Rather than confronting the French army there, Schlieffen proposed simply to go around it. In Alsace-Lorraine he stationed only enough soldiers to slow down the main French offensive. Meanwhile the bulk of the German army would sweep down from the north, through neutral Belgium. As one historian has put it, the plan was like a giant 'revolving door'—while the French army pushed in the south, the whole German army would just wheel around behind it. By the time the French realised what was happening, the Germans would have knifed down through France and encircled Paris, the French capital and the hub of the nation's rail network. The French army would have nowhere to retreat and no hope of assembling its reserves since the Germans would have control of the railroads. The Schlieffen Plan was a gamble. But if successful it would virtually guarantee German victory. Would it succeed?

Map 13— *Warplans, 1914.*

The conduct of the war

THE 1914 CAMPAIGNS

The war began and each nation rushed forward to disaster. Russia launched an ill-prepared attack into Germany. The Russian commander, Samsonov, hoped to take advantage of Germany's numerical weakness but he succeeded only in leading his army into a German trap. Finding his army surrounded at Tannenberg, Samsonov retreated to the woods and shot himself. In total, the Russians lost a quarter of a million men, killed or captured, in the first battle of the war. The Russians fared better against the Austrians, more by luck

59

than skill. The Austrian army, led by the dashing General Conrad, attacked to the north, allowing half the Russian army to march in behind it. Poorly trained and equipped with 25-year-old guns, the Austrian army barely escaped being surrounded. Three hundred and fifty thousand Austrian soldiers were killed or captured. French soldiers fared little better. They attacked into Alsace-Lorraine, only to be mown down by German machine-guns.

While the other plans foundered, the Schlieffen Plan worked to perfection. The German army crashed through Belgium and down into France. Too late, the surprised French understood the German strategy. Soon the French were desperately retreating toward Paris. The small British army joined the French, but it too was beaten back. On 5 September, only three weeks after beginning its advance, the German army stood just twenty miles outside Paris. Moltke, the German general in charge of the attack, was so confident of victory that he began peeling troops away from the attack to send to the Russian front. In Paris, the French Government considered abandoning the capital. In Berlin, the German Chancellor, Bethmann-Hollweg, sent a memorandum to the Kaiser describing the way in which Germany would re-shape Europe now that the war was won.

But Bethmann-Hollweg spoke too soon. Inexplicably, the general commanding the German's right wing turned south before reaching Paris. Perhaps he thought he could destroy the battered French and British armies without encircling the city, as the Schlieffen Plan directed. A French general saw the error and immediately launched an attack on the exposed rear of the German army. Every available soldier in Paris was poured into the attack. (Because of a shortage of trains, many were carried to the front in Parisian taxi cabs!) Buoyed by the French counter-attack, the British turned and launched an attack of their own. Germany's soldiers had marched as much as 250

British soldiers prepare to attack. Note the sandbagged shelters in which they slept. Note also that someone has jokingly hung a 'King St' sign along one of the trenchlines.

kilometres in three weeks, often without food, and they were too exhausted to resist this double attack. The German advance was broken at the Marne River and soon it was the Germans who were retreating.

The Battle of the Marne destroyed any hope for an early end to the war. The Schlieffen Plan had failed, due to a general's error and the exhaustion of the German troops. In the weeks that followed, the German army retreated northwards, pursued at a safe distance by the equally exhausted French and British. By late October, the opposing lines stretched all the way north to

TRENCH WARFARE: 1915–1917

Following the campaign of 1914, a stalemate existed on the Western Front. The next three years saw some of history's bloodiest battles, but neither side could break through the enemy's trenchline. Elsewhere, both sides enjoyed some success. The Germans conquered Serbia in 1915 and Romania in 1916. The Allies conquered Palestine and Baghdad, and pushed the outnumbered Germans out of South West Africa and German East Africa. On the Eastern Front, the Germans drove the poorly equipped Russians back, inflicting terrible casualties. But on the crucial Western Front, where the army of Germany faced the combined armies of Britain and France, there was no progress.

For the soldiers caught in the trenches, life became an unending nightmare. By day, they moved about in knee-deep mud. At night they slept in shallow caves dug into the walls of the trenches. They shared the trenches with lice and rats and all manner of disease. They lived with the constant shriek of artillery and clatter of machine-guns. They lived with something else as well: the awareness that they were soon to die. For most soon realised that they had little chance of surviving in the trenches. Some felt bitterness at governments which had sent them to pointless deaths. Some tried to remember the world they had left behind — an ordered world where war had seemed exciting and glorious. All felt afraid. Many wrote about their feelings, leaving behind a remarkable collection of journals and poetry that attested to life in the face of savagery.

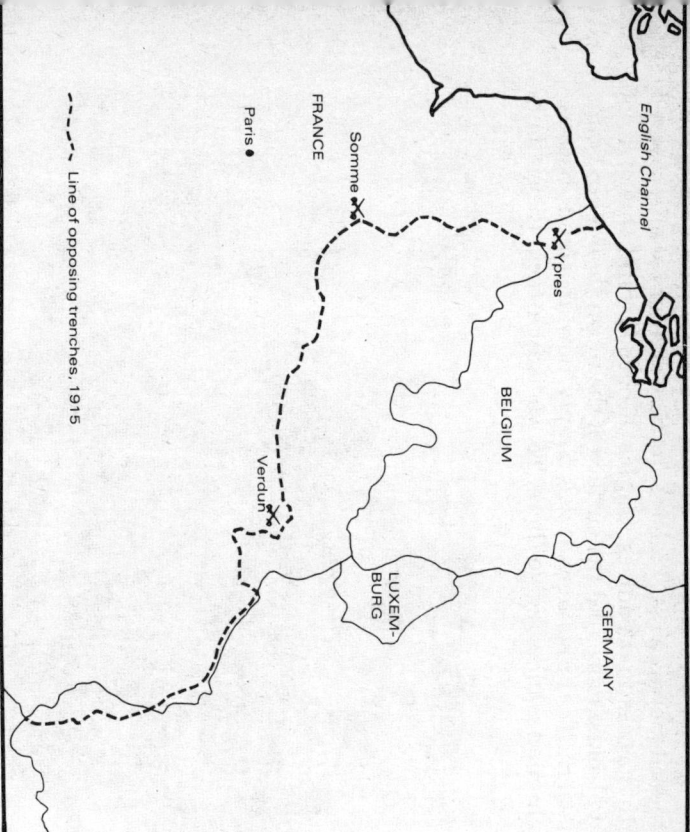

Map 14 — *The Western Front, with major battlefields.*

the English Channel. The Germans made one final, desperate attempt to break through the Allied line at Ypres, a small village in northern Belgium. At Ypres, young German students, recruited *en masse* from their universities, faced the grizzled professionals of the British army. For weeks waves of German soldiers attacked the thin British line, singing old college songs to maintain their courage as they advanced. They made easy targets for the experienced British marksmen, many of whom were veterans of the Anglo-Boer War. Finally the Germans gave up the attack. Both sides dug in, creating two parallel

systems of trenches stretching from the English Channel to the Swiss Alps. For the next three years, that line scarcely moved. The era of trench warfare had begun.

61

TECHNOLOGY AND TACTICS

The soldiers of the First World War were caught between two centuries of warfare. Generals clung to Nineteenth Century tactics which insisted on the importance of attacking the enemy. Yet they fought with Twentieth Century technology, which gave an enormous advantage to the defender. Unfortunately, generals in all countries were slow to recognise the problem. Most continued to believe in attacking at all costs and, as a consequence, millions of soldiers were needlessly slaughtered.

There were two new technological achievements which gave an advantage to the defender. The first was the perfection of the machine-gun. While the machine-gun had already been used with some success, notably by the Japanese in the Russo-Japanese War, its true importance was not understood until the First World War. Operated by two men (one aimed while the other fed in belts of ammunition), the machine-gun made successful attacks almost impossible. One gun could fire hundreds of bullets per minute, laying down an impenetrable steel curtain. Because the gun was stationary, it was of little use for attacking, but for defending it was worth a hundred men. The second new achievement was heavy artillery. First World War cannons were able to shoot high explosives with great accuracy as far as twenty kilometres. Both sides assembled thousands of these guns behind their trenchlines. Whenever one side advanced, the defender could quickly train all his artillery on the spot and shower the attackers with shells. The combination of machine-gun and heavy artillery ensured that even the most determined advances could be stopped.

The difficulty of attacking was increased by the geography of the trench system itself. Both sides carved elaborate networks of trenches, often extending for miles toward the rear. Between the opposing trenchlines lay a narrow strip of land, perhaps two hundred metres wide. Treeless, torn by artillery shells, covered with corpses and endless tangles of barbed wire, this strip of land looked more like the surface of the moon than a landscape on earth. To the soldiers, it was simply 'no man's land', because no human could survive there. To wage an attack, the soldiers

British troops training with a machine-gun. The machine-gun revolutionized defensive warfare. Can you see why it was less useful to attackers?

Generals tried many things to improve the odds for attackers. In 1915 the Germans introduced the use of deadly poison gas. The British and French followed suit and soon both sides launched artillery shells containing chlorine or mustard gas into one another's trenches as a normal prelude to attack. Generals also tried to adapt heavy artillery to offensive uses. They rained explosives down on enemy trenches to 'soften' them for the coming attack. Poison gas and artillery bombardments killed millions of soldiers, but they did not produce a breakthrough on the Western Front.

As generals experimented, casualties mounted. The French experience in the spring and summer of 1915 was a portent. In February and March they launched an offensive against the German line at Champagne. In one month, 50 000 Frenchmen died after pushing the German line back a total of 50 metres. In April they tried another attack at St Mihiel, in which 64 000 French soldiers were killed, gaining nothing. In June, at a place called Loos, over 100 000 French troops died in another futile attack on the German trenches. Other armies insisted on attacking as well, with similar results.

By 1916 many generals had realized that it was impossible to break the enemy's line. So they invented a new tactic: attrition. The idea of attrition warfare was simple: select a spot which the enemy had to defend and then attack it continuously until the enemy ran out of replacements. There was no strategy — the object was simply to kill as many soldiers as possible. The generals realised that they would probably lose an equal number of their own men in the process, but they accepted that fact. This was perhaps the most cruel invention of an extraordinarily cruel war. Both sides would shovel men into a battle until one side ran out. The side with the most soldiers would win.

Digging a field-gun out of the mud at Ypres, 1917.

had to climb ladders out of their own trenches and clamber through the barbed wire of no man's land. All the while they made easy targets for enemy machine-gunners.

Anyone lucky enough to breach the first enemy trench simply faced another trench and then another. By the time a few soldiers had completely broken through the enemy line, the defender had enough time to rush thousands of reserve troops to the spot, often using the rail systems that each side constructed behind its lines. These new arrivals would immediately launch a murderous counter-attack, driving the original attackers back to their own trenches or beyond. Often none of the soldiers in the original attack survived. This pattern was repeated over and over.

The first attrition campaign was launched by the Germans in February 1916 at Verdun. For five months the Germans pounded Verdun in a deliberate effort to bleed France dry. By the end of the battle 350 000 Frenchmen had died, along with 330 000 Germans. Most of the dead were so mutilated by artillery that they were impossible to identify. After the war the bones of all of the soldiers, French and German, were placed in a common mausoleum on the battlefield.

In July the British launched an attrition attack of their own, at the Somme. After a week-long artillery bombardment 60 000 British troops attacked the German line. Most were cut down by German machine-guns after travelling only a few metres. They were followed by wave after wave of attackers through July, August, September and half of October. At the end of the battle,

The Somme, 1916: A soldier killed by artillery.

War poets

The soldiers who experienced life in the trenches left behind a remarkable collection of poetry. Probably the most famous of the war poets was Britain's Rupert Brooke. Brooke, who was killed in 1915, wrote wistfully of a pre-war world of youth and innocence — a world he had left behind for the madness of the trenches. In the following passage, from a poem entitled 'The Dead', he sees this lost world reflected in the faces of soldiers killed in combat:

> *The years had given them kindness. Dawn was theirs,*
> *And sunset, and the colours of the earth.*
> *These had seen movement, and heard music; known*
> *Slumber and waking; loved . . .*
>   *All this is ended.*

Later poets were more bitter, and described the horror of war in terms devoid of nostalgia or romance. Wilfred Owen, in the following excerpt, describes a chlorine gas attack.

> *Gas! Gas! Quick boys . . .*
> *Someone still was yelling out and stumbling*
> *And flound'ring like a man in fire or lime . . .*
> *Dim, through the misty panes and thick green light,*
> *As under a green sea, I saw him drowning.*

> *In all my dreams, before my helpless sight,*
> *He plunges at me, guttering, choking, drowning.*

Many felt bitterness at the governments and societies which had sent them forth to do battle. Siegfried Sassoon, in a poem entitled 'Suicide in the Trenches', railed against the cheering crowds that always gathered to send off the new recruits:

> *You smug-faced crowds with kindling eye*
> *Who cheer when soldier lads march by,*
> *Sneak home and pray you'll never know*
> *The hell where youth and laughter go.*

the German line had been shoved back three miles but was still intact. There were 440 000 German dead, along with 420 000 British and 200 000 French.

By 1917 each side was running too short of men to risk further attrition battles. But casualties remained high. In the summer and autumn, again at Ypres, the British assaulted the German line. The British commander prepared the largest artillery barrage of the war and confidently predicted a breakthrough with few casualties. Over two weeks, 4 500 000 artillery shells fell on the German trenches. Still the British failed to crack the German line. When the assault finally ground to a halt, outside a village called Passchendaele, another quarter million British soldiers had died. As winter set in, the war which everyone had predicted would take six weeks, had dragged on for nearly three-and-a-half years.

TOTAL WAR

In the Nineteenth Century, the effect of war was confined to the battlefield. For non-combatants war remained something far away. That changed in 1914. The First World War was the first total war*. In total war, every resource in the society was devoted to winning the war. Every farm, every factory, produced for the war effort. In a sense, every citizen became a soldier—farmers, workers, capitalists, mothers. And, for the first time, all citizens began to suffer the effects of war at first hand.

Conscription

The major change in the First World War, as compared to previous wars, was in the size of the armies. At the beginning of the Nineteenth Century, all nations had relied on small, professional armies. During the Napoleonic Wars, France revolutionised European warfare by creating a mass army in which all male citizens were required to serve. By the end of the century all the European powers except Britain had followed France's example, imposing some form of mandatory national service. When the First World War began, all the belligerents (again, except Britain) immediately put more than a million men into the field. Yet even these armies proved too small. By 1918, Germany had almost three million men under arms, while France and Britain together fielded nearly four million men. Both sides had already suffered as many casualties in the fighting and each increasingly feared running out of men. Back home, there was simply no one left to call up.

Mobilizing the economy

Once such huge armies were in the field, they had to be fed, clothed and equipped. The entire economy of each nation was turned to the task. Farms supplied food for the men and hay for millions of transport horses. Factories turned out millions of blankets and pairs of boots, as well as an endless stream of guns and ammunition. Germany was quickest in placing its economy on a war footing. By 1915, for example, German factories were producing 250 000 artillery shells per day, while Britain was producing less than a tenth as many. With its industrial base, Britain soon caught up, but neither Russia nor Austria-Hungary had enough factories to meet the demand. By 1915 many Russian soldiers had no ammunition left.

In all the countries, the Governments had to pay for the food and supplies they bought. If they had not done so, workers could not have been paid and the whole economy would have ground to a stop. The war thus placed an enormous financial burden on each Government. Taxes went up, but eventually all Governments had to borrow money from bankers in order to pay the bills.

65

Many banks were ruined and only enormous loans from the United States allowed Great Britain and France to continue fighting the war.

Scientists and engineers were also called to do their part for the war effort. Among their contributions were poison gas and improved aeroplanes. A British engineer invented a mechanical tank, which was essentially a tractor with steel armour. Not until the very end of the war did the British generals realise that here at last was a machine that could break through enemy trenches. This increased role for scientists and engineers set the stage for future wars, in which science and technology would make decisive contributions.

Total war strained every man and woman in the society. Factory workers worked long hours to keep up the flow of goods to the front. In many places, women took industrial jobs to replace the men called to the armies. Farmers watched their crops and horses being taken for the army, never knowing whether they would be paid. Everyone faced shortages—of shoes, blankets and other items needed by the soldiers. High inflation meant that many workers could not buy even those items which were available. Food was rationed in all the countries.

War was no longer just a battle between armies—it became a test of entire societies. The society which could produce more than the other would win the war. Individual governments in each country assumed increasing powers to direct the flow of resources to the war effort. People began to realize that winning the war on the 'Home Front' was the key to winning the war in the field.

Propaganda and the Home Front

To maintain morale on the home front, governments began using propaganda*. Newspapers in every country assured people that their cause was just, that God was on their side. They urged people to continue making sacrifices and promised them that the war would soon be won. People had no way of checking the truth of these claims and usually believed them. Often newspapers contrasted the heroism of their country's soldiers with the cruelty and cowardice of the enemy. British and French newspapers, for example, virtually stopped using the word 'Germans'. Instead they called the Germans 'Huns', equating them with barbarians.

'Tanks', a sketch by Muirhead Bone. The mechanical tank, invented by a British engineer, was able to break through an enemy trenchline. Unfortunately, British generals never fully understood its value until 1918.

A more obvious way to break the people's will was by starving them. As soon as the war began, the British navy blockaded the north German ports. A year later, the British imposed a total blockade, cutting off all shipments of food to Germany. The blockade prevented neutral countries such as the United States from trading with Germany. The blockade, together with a poor harvest in 1915, pushed many Germans to the point of starvation.

The Germans developed their own strategy for breaking the will of the enemy people—strategic bombing*. Beginning in 1915, German Zeppelins began dropping bombs on British cities. The bombing sparked panic in some cities — for the first time, civilians were military targets. The raids did little real damage,

Propaganda: a cartoon from a European newspaper showing the Kaiser devouring the globe. What is the cartoon meant to suggest? Do you think it accurately reflects German ambitions?

Often papers invented stories to warn people about what an enemy victory would mean. A favourite story in Britain and France depicted German soldiers raping nuns and crucifying priests in Belgium. Such fabricated stories made it easier to hate enemies, to forget that they too were human beings.

Propaganda was aimed at keeping up the people's will to fight. It was only natural that each side would resort to tactics designed to break the will of the enemy people. Each country employed people to try to spread rumours and foment revolution among the enemy. Such attempts usually failed.

A German Zeppelin landing after a night bombing mission over Britain. The First World War was the first time that bombing enemy cities was used as a deliberate strategy.

however, and in the long run they probably increased the British people's will to keep fighting. But if strategic bombing had little effect in the First World War, it set an important precedent for the future. In the Second World War, all the belligerents would routinely bomb enemy cities, killing millions. The logical end of this process came in 1945, when America dropped atomic bombs on two Japanese cities.

Atomic bombs were a far cry from Nineteenth Century warfare. The link between the two is found in the years 1914–1918. The First World War was the first total war. It brought mass conscription, mobilization of entire economies, the use of scientists to create terrible new weapons, government propaganda aimed at dehumanising the enemy, and the bombing of civilians. In total war, every member of the society was part of the war effort, whether or not he or she carried a gun. From there, it was only a short step until everyone in the society became a legitimate target.

break Turkey's grip on the Dardanelles, including a disastrous landing at Gallipoli in 1915, failed. The stranglehold on Russia remained.

The shortage of supplies in Russia was compounded by the stupidity of Russia's generals. The campaign of 1914 had begun with a quarter million Russian troops marching into a German trap. (The Germans' task was made easier by the fact that they knew Russia's plans in advance — Russian generals sent all their wireless transmissions uncoded.) 1915 was no better: Russian troops were driven back toward their border, sustaining terrible casualties. In 1916, a million Russian soldiers died in a single campaign! After that, the Russian army was no longer a fighting force. The Germans drove into Russia and the Russian army had neither the men nor the guns to stop them.

Disasters on the battlefield, together with food shortages and inflation on the home front, were too much for the Tsar's Government. In early 1917, a revolution erupted in Russia. By November, control of the revolution had been secured by the Bolshevik party, led by Lenin. The Russian Revolution will be described in a succeeding chapter. In terms of the First World War, the revolution had one enormous consequence: Lenin pulled Russia out of the war. Lenin and his comrades saw little reason to continue fighting in what they believed was a capitalists' war. They called for an immediate end to the war and the return of all conquered territories. The Bolsheviks warned that they would loose the revolutionary power of the working class on any nation which continued fighting. The Germans had already captured huge chunks of Russian territory and saw no reason to give it back. They laughed at Lenin's threats about spreading the revolution to Germany. They continued their march into Russia and the Bolsheviks realized that there would soon be no Russia left for the working

Russia leaves the war

Russia was the first nation to collapse under the weight of total war. To wage total war required industrial might and a strong, efficient central government. Tsarist Russia had neither. Its army entered the field in 1914 poorly equipped, and by 1915 it had run dangerously short of arms and ammunition. Russia's few factories were unable to make up the shortage. Nor were Britain and France able to ship supplies to Russia, because their path was blocked at Constantinople by the Turks, who had entered the war on the side of Germany. All Britain's efforts to

class to rule. Faced with this prospect, they surrendered to Germany. In terms of the Treaty of Brest-Litovsk, signed in March 1918, Russia was forced to give Poland, Finland, the Ukraine and the Caucasus to Germany — virtually doubling the size of the German Empire overnight. In return, Lenin and his party were allowed to continue ruling the now shrunken Russia.

America enters the war

But though Germany had triumphed on the Eastern Front, their situation in the west was extraordinarily bad: in the first week of April, 1917, the United States of America entered the war against Germany. With nearly limitless resources of men, arms and money, America might help the French and British break the deadlock on the Western Front.

Since becoming independent in 1776, the United States had refused to participate in European wars. The country's first President, George Washington, had warned his countrymen against 'entangling alliances' with European nations, and for more than a century Americans had heeded his warning. Most of the American people had fled from Europe to the 'New World' of America and many believed that Europe was sick and corrupt. The outbreak of war confirmed this opinion. As soon as the war began the United States declared itself neutral. The US President, Woodrow Wilson, fearful that the war would cause divisions in American society, especially between German-Americans and Americans of British descent, urged all the people to remain 'neutral in thought as well as in action'.

Neutrality had one great advantage: it left the United States free to trade with everyone. While the other nations battered one another on the battlefield, America could grow rich selling food and equipment. European demand for American wheat and maize drove American farm prices to levels never reached before or since. At the same time, American industrialists grew rich selling manufactured goods not only to Europe but also to Latin America, a region which had been a British market before the war.

Soon, however, America was drawn to the side of Britain and France. In part, this movement reflected the fact that Britain and America were bound by a common language and culture. American sympathies were also affected by reports of German atrocities. The 'rape' of Belgium, widely reported in American newspapers, convinced many Americans that the Germans were barbarians and that France and Britain were fighting to save civilisation. The most important event in converting Americans to the Allied cause was the sinking of the *Lusitania*. On 7 May 1915, a German submarine torpedoed the British liner, *Lusitania*, en route to England from America. Twelve hundred people were killed, including 128 Americans. The Germans insisted that they had the right to sink the ship, arguing (probably correctly) that it had been carrying ammunition. Nonetheless, the sinking produced a wave of outrage in the United States. Wilson sent a stern note to the Germans, demanding that they refrain from sinking non-military ships. Eventually the Germans agreed for fear of provoking American entry into the conflict.

America was also drawn to the Allied side by commerce. Even before the war, America had traded far more with Britain than with Germany. Once the war began, the United States stopped trading with Germany, due to the British navy's blockade. According to international law, the British had no right to interrupt neutral trade of food and non-military supplies to Germany, but this did not deter Britain. The American Government protested the blockade but took no action. Meanwhile, American food and supplies flooded into Britain and American banks provided loans to the British Government to help finance the war.

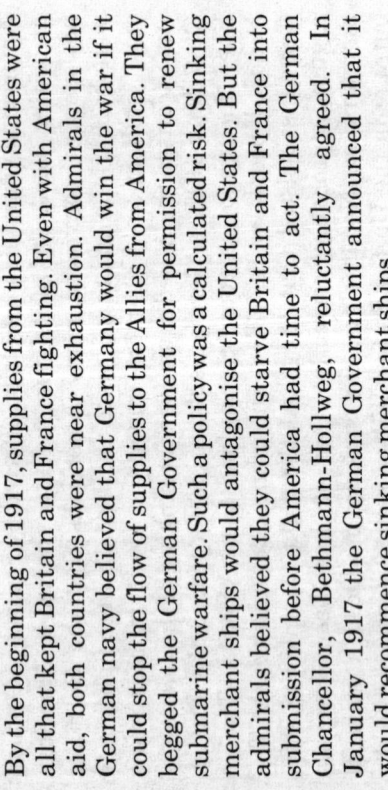

German submarines prowled the Atlantic, preying on ships carrying supplies from America to the Allies. Germany's decision to begin sinking unarmed merchant ships in January 1917 led to American entry into the war three months later.

By the beginning of 1917, supplies from the United States were all that kept Britain and France fighting. Even with American aid, both countries were near exhaustion. Admirals in the German navy believed that Germany would win the war if it could stop the flow of supplies to the Allies from America. They begged the German Government for permission to renew submarine warfare. Such a policy was a calculated risk. Sinking merchant ships would antagonise the United States. But the admirals believed they could starve Britain and France into submission before America had time to act. The German Chancellor, Bethmann-Hollweg, reluctantly agreed. In January 1917 the German Government announced that it would recommence sinking merchant ships.

America's President Wilson faced a dilemma. To continue trading with Britain inevitably meant that ships would be sunk and American lives lost. Each sinking would bring America closer to outright war with Germany. If Wilson were to stop all American ships going to Britain, he could end the sinkings and keep America out of the war. But stopping American exports would also end the period of prosperity being enjoyed by American farmers and industrialists. Without trade, America's economy might even fall into a depression. Wilson was unwilling to risk a depression. He decided to continue trading with Britain, gambling that he could persuade the warring nations to end the fighting by negotiation before America was dragged into the war. He begged both sides to lay down their arms and accept 'peace without victory' — that is, a peace treaty with a return to pre-war borders.

In Europe, Wilson's plans for peace fell on deaf ears. In the Atlantic, German submarines recommenced sinking ships, though never in sufficient numbers to starve Britain into surrender. In America, each sinking brought renewed cries for a declaration of war against Germany. Only a few voices held out for the traditional American policy of neutrality in European wars. Finally, on 2 April 1917, President Wilson asked the American Congress for a declaration of war against Germany.

American entry caused rejoicing in London and in Paris. The French and British people, exhausted and hungry, took heart. More important, the American Government immediately

The Zimmerman Telegram

Two weeks before Germany recommenced submarine warfare against merchant ships, the German Foreign Minister, Arthur Zimmerman, sent a cable to Germany's ambassador in Mexico. The Zimmerman Telegram instructed the ambassador to seek an alliance with Mexico in the event that the United States entered the war. Unfortunately for the Germans, the cable was intercepted by British intelligence, who informed America's President Wilson of its contents. The alliance with Mexico envisioned by Zimmerman never came to pass, but when the telegram was made public in the United States it aroused further calls for a declaration of war against Germany. This was the text of the telegram:

'We intend to begin on the 1st of February unrestricted submarine warfare. We shall endeavour in spite of this to keep the United States of America neutral. In the event of this not succeeding, we make Mexico a proposal of alliance on the following basis: make war together, make peace together, generous financial support and an understanding on our part that Mexico is to reconquer the lost territory of Texas, New Mexico, and Arizona. The settlement in detail is left to you. You will inform the President [of Mexico] of the above most secretly as soon as the outbreak of war with the United States is certain... Please call the President's attention to the fact that the ruthless employment of our submarines now offers the prospect of compelling England in a few months to make peace.

Signed,
Zimmerman.'

Questions

1. Did the Germans expect the United States to be drawn into the war by the submarine campaign?

2. If so, why do you think they were willing to risk renewed submarine warfare?

3. What did they think the submarines would accomplish?

4. Why did British intelligence inform the Americans of the cable?

5. Texas, New Mexico, and Arizona were territories conquered by the United States in a war with Mexico in the 1840s. In 1917, all three were American states. What does Germany's plan to return them to Mexico suggest about the Germans' intentions if they won the war? Can people and territory simply be taken from one country and given to another?

6. How do you think Americans responded to news of the Zimmerman Telegram? Do you think American knowledge of the Zimmerman Telegram made war between the United States and Germany more likely? Give reasons for your answer.

extended huge loans to the British Government, saving Britain from bankruptcy. In all, America loaned Britain $7 billion between April 1917 and the end of the war. But, if the total amount was generous, America's terms were not. First, the British Government was required to guarantee repayment of the loans. Secondly, Britain was to spend the money buying

71

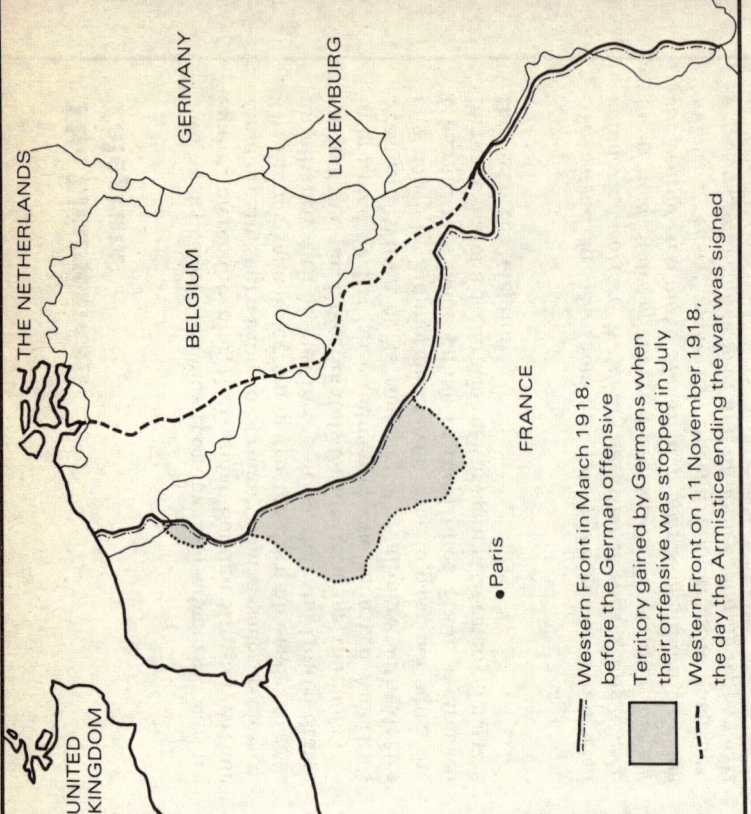

Map 15 — Campaigns of 1918.

- — Western Front in March 1918, before the German offensive
- ▓ Territory gained by Germans when their offensive was stopped in July
- --- Western Front on 11 November 1918, the day the Armistice ending the war was signed

supplies from the United States. In effect, America required that the British repay the loans twice—providing yet another windfall to America's farmers and manufacturers.

The Allies' primary concern, however, was with the arrival of the American army. The United States promised millions of young men to bolster the battered Allied armies. Immediately, the Government began making plans for transporting this massive force to Europe. But such an operation took time, and in that time Germany had one last chance to win the war.

The end of the war

1918: THE FAILURE OF THE GERMAN OFFENSIVE

In the long run, the entry into the war of the United States more than balanced the exit of Russia. But this effect was not immediately felt. American soldiers were three thousand miles from the front. Even after they began arriving in Europe, the American commander, General Pershing, was slow in moving them into the Allied lines. This delay gave Germany a final chance to win the war. With the surrender of Russia, the Germans were at last able to concentrate all their forces on one front. Through early 1918, trainload after trainload of German soldiers arrived on the Western Front from Russia, in preparation for one last, massive assault on the Allied lines. It was a race against time. The Germans needed to attain a quick victory before the arrival of large numbers of American troops swung the balance back against them.

Once again the Germans nearly succeeded. Beginning in March 1918, they launched three huge surprise attacks on the British and French lines. In previous offensives both sides had attacked the enemy's strongest points in order to kill as many soldiers as possible, but in 1918 the Germans decided to strike the enemy at its weakest points. They quickly tore a series of punctures in the Allied line. Soon German soldiers were far behind the front lines and the British and French had to fall back. Germany again seemed on the brink of winning the war.

But Germany no longer had the resources to maintain the offensive. It had no reserve troops left to replace casualties, and the soldiers it did have were hungry and exhausted. The offensive slowly ground to a halt. The French and British rallied, and fresh American troops began entering the fighting at a rate of 300 000 per month. Together they beat the Germans back, using new mechanical tanks to roar through the Germans' hastily built trenches. The German army fought stubbornly, but it no longer had enough men to stop the Allied advance. By September, German generals were urging the Kaiser to seek an armistice* in the desperate hope that Germany would be allowed to keep some of the territory it had already conquered. The Allies insisted on surrender. Soon Germany's last remaining allies, Turkey and Austria-Hungary, admitted defeat. The war was almost over.

The German army might have tried to make one last stand at its border, but it was undercut by revolution on the home front. For four years, the German people had been fed propaganda urging them to make sacrifices, always with the assurance that victory was near. When the truth leaked out, the tired and hungry German people rose up in revolt. An uprising broke out among German sailors in Kiel and spread through the country. On 9 November, the Kaiser was forced to abdicate. With the Government in chaos and the people demanding an end to the war, Germany's army could not hope to keep fighting. On 11 November 1918, Germany admitted defeat. The First World War was over.

The consequences

Twelve million soldiers died in the First World War. This was the war's first and most important consequence. The war claimed almost an entire generation of young men: rich and poor; Christians, Jews, Hindus and Muslims; educated and uneducated. These were men who might have been able to help build a better world, but the world was deprived of their efforts.

The war also changed those who survived. After the war, in each of the countries involved, many books were written by men who had seen the fighting. These books testified to a sense of betrayal, a feeling of rage against the old who had begun a war which the young had to fight. Most of all, these books testified to the gnawing fear felt by all people as they faced a pointless death. Books like Erich Remarque's *All Quiet on the Western Front*, Ernest Hemingway's *A Farewell to Arms*, and Robert Graves' *Goodbye to All That* remain some of the most powerful anti-war novels ever written.

The changes on the map of Europe were equally dramatic. The Ottoman Empire was gone, and Turkey at last became a democracy. The Austro-Hungarian Empire was broken up into separate countries, some with odd, unfamiliar names like Yugoslavia and Czechoslovakia. An old nation, Poland, was restored in territory long contested by Germany and Russia. Even more profound changes, however, occurred inside Russia. The 1 000 year reign of the Tsars was over. Russia began the business of modernisation, but it was directed not by the Tsar but by the Bolsheviks, led by Lenin. Germany, of course, lost the most territory. The territory the Germans had sliced from Russia in the Treaty of Brest-Litovsk was taken away. In the west, Alsace-Lorraine was returned to France. Finally, Germany was stripped of its colonies.

73

Ironically, the war's biggest winner was the United States. America was the only country that emerged stronger in 1918 than it had been in 1914. The Americans had experienced no fighting on their own soil, and they had lost less than 100 000 men, scarcely a fraction of the number lost by other countries. With the boost its economy received from selling food and equipment to the Allies, the United States was now the dominant economic power in the world. A suicidal European war had ushered in what one historian has called "The American Century".

There was one final irony here. The First World War had given civilization a new kind of war: total war. In the process, the war levelled much of Europe. Yet it hadn't solved one of the underlying sources of conflict. Germany was beaten, its dreams of empire shattered. But Germany's factories were far from the fighting and survived the war intact. Potentially, Germany remained the mightiest industrial nation on the continent. And the way the war ended, with a revolution on the home front rather than a final defeat on the battlefield, encouraged some Germans to believe that they had never truly been defeated. As silence settled over the trenches, few foresaw that Germany, scarcely twenty years later, would rise from the ashes and reintroduce the world to total war.

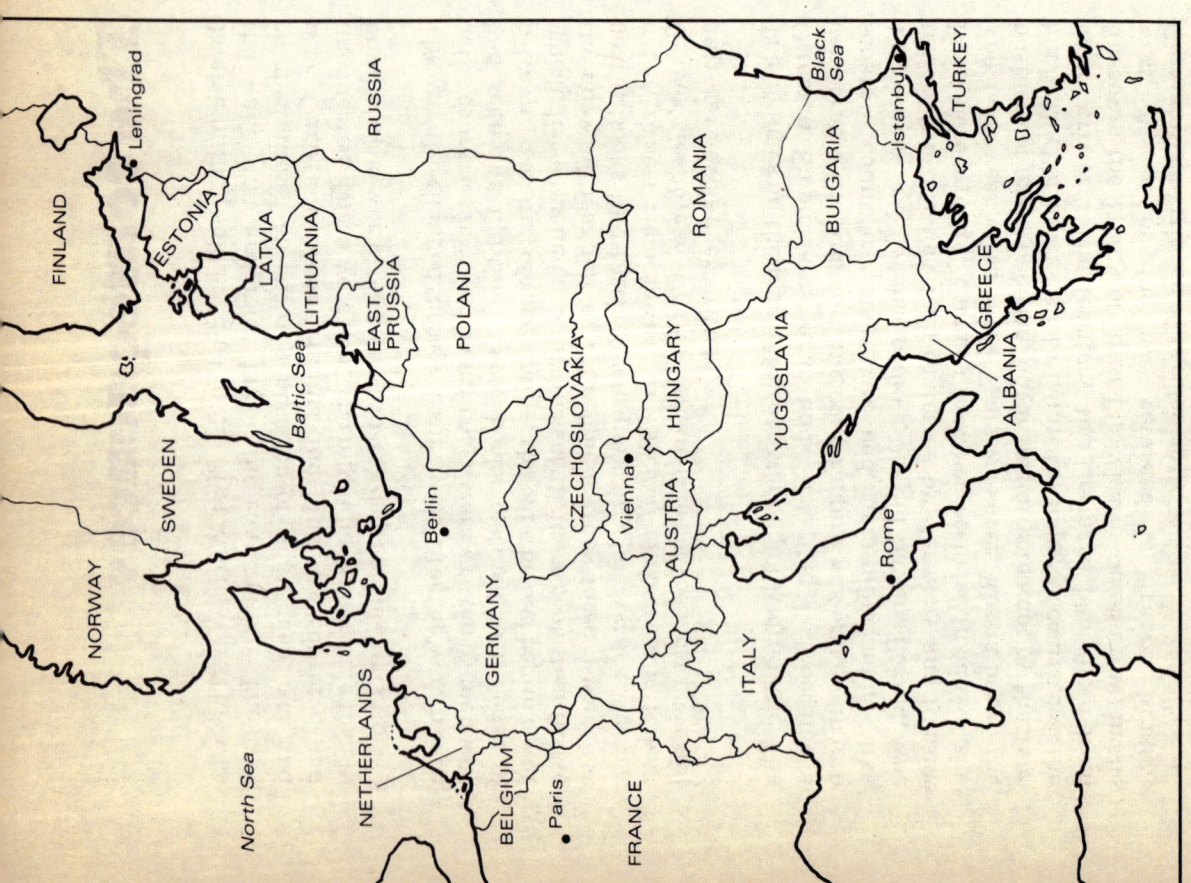

Map 16 — Post-war Europe.

The end of Empires

Germany
The German Empire had only come into existence in 1871, and was rather late in the 'scramble' for colonies, especially in Africa. It had, however, acquired some colonies in Africa: South West Africa and German East Africa; some islands in the Pacific; and spheres of influence in North Africa, China and elsewhere. Days before the end of the war, uprisings in Germany led to the abdication of Wilhelm II — Germany thus lost its overseas empire. In the peace settlement at the end of the war it lost its former colonies became mandated territories under the League of Nations.

Austria-Hungary
Before the end of the war, revolutions brought this Empire to an end, and two separate republics — Austria and Hungary — came into existence. The subject people of the old Empire seized the opportunities presented by military disaster to rise against their former master.

In the post-war settlement both Austria and Hungary lost extensive territory. Austria lost the provinces of Bohemia and Moravia to the newly created state of Czechoslovakia; Hungary also lost over 3 000 000 inhabitants to this new state. The Serbian dream of uniting the southern Slavs was realized and the new state of Yugoslavia came into being. Hungary lost Dalmatia, and Austria lost Bosnia and Herzegovina, to Yugoslavia. Austria lost the Trentino and South Tyrol plus land along the Adriatic coast to Italy, and its Galician provinces went to the newly independent Poland. The total effect of these changes was that the population of Austria was reduced from 22 000 000 to 6 500 000, and that of Hungary from 21 000 000 to 7 500 000.

Russia
The strain of war finally brought down the Russian Empire. In March 1917, revolution forced Tsar Nicholas II to abdicate and Russia became a republic. The Bolsheviks seizure of power in November 1917 led to the outbreak of civil war. Some of the non-Russian people of the old Russian Empire tried to break free from Russia and proclaim their independence. In the case of the Ukraine and Georgia this separate status was short-lived, as the Bolsheviks forced them back into Russia. Poland, however, succeeded in maintaining its independence, as did Finland and the Baltic states of Lithuania, Latvia, and Estonia.

Turkey
Turkey paid the price of backing the losing alliance. It had to cede Adrianople with most of the area around Constantinople to Greece. The only territory left to the Sultan in Europe was the city of Constantinople itself.

In Asia, Turkey lost territory to Greece. Syria became a French mandate and Iraq, Palestine and Transjordan became the responsibility of Britain.

Revision Questions

INTRODUCTION
1. Why did some people in the early Twentieth Century believe that a major European war was impossible?
2. What kind of war did the generals of this time expect?
3. Why was the First World War called a world war?

75

LONG-TERM ORIGINS OF THE WAR

1. What factors enabled Germany to become the most powerful military nation in Europe?
2. What circumstances contributed to the decline of the old Empires of southern and eastern Europe? What changes might have enabled the decaying Empires to restore their power?
3. Why did nations seek colonies? To what extent did the pursuit of colonies contribute to the coming of the war?
4. Why did nations join alliances? Did the system of alliances in Europe before the war make the continent a more stable place? Explain.
5. What is meant by 'balance of power'? Do you think maintaining a balance of power is a way to avoid war? Why or why not?
6. At the Versailles Peace Conference after the war, Germany was forced to sign a 'War Guilt' statement accepting responsibility for starting the war. Do you think that this statement accurately reflects how the war began? Give reasons for your answer.

OUTBREAK OF THE WAR

1. Explain why the Archduke Franz Ferdinand of Austria was assassinated.
2. How did the Government of Austria-Hungary respond to the assassination?
3. Why did the conflict between Austria and Serbia spread to the other European powers?
4. What does mobilization mean? How did the problem of mobilizing armies contribute to the outbreak of the war?
5. Some historians have said that war was inevitable after the Archduke was shot. Do you think this is true? Can you think of anything which some person or nation might have done to stop the spread of the war?

CONDUCT OF THE WAR

1. What did the war plans of all the nations have in common?
2. How did the use of new types of weapons change the nature of warfare? In the First World War, did the attackers or the defenders in a battle have the advantage?
3. What is meant by 'total war'? How was total war different from earlier wars in the Eighteenth and Nineteenth Centuries?
4. What is propaganda? Why did governments use it during the First World War?
5. What contributions did the following groups make to the war effort in each country:

    (a) Bankers; (c) Workers;
    (b) Farmers; (d) Women?

6. What techniques were used to break the enemy people's will to fight? Were these techniques successful?
7. What is meant by attrition war?
8. Why was the First World War important in shaping the history of the United States?

CONSEQUENCES OF THE WAR

1. What were the major consequences of the war for each of the following countries: (a) Turkey; (b) Austria-Hungary; (c) Russia; (d) Germany; (e) the United States?
2. In what countries were most First World War battles fought? Was there any major fighting on German soil? Why do you think this was important for Germany after the war?
3. What effect do you think the war had on those soldiers who saw fighting and survived?

Chronology

1871	German unification
1873	Dreikaiserbund (Three Emperors' League) between Germany, Austria-Hungary, and Russia
1879	Dual Alliance between Germany and Austria-Hungary
1882	Triple Alliance between Germany, Austria-Hungary, and Italy
1887	Re-Insurance Treaty between Germany and Russia
1888	Financial panic; withdrawal of German investments in Russia; beginning of French and Russian *rapprochement*; Kaiser Wilhelm II crowned Emperor of Germany
1890	Bismarck resigns as German Chancellor; Germany refuses to renew Russian Re-Insurance Treaty
1894	Franco-Russian Alliance
1898	German naval-building programme launched; Anglo-Boer War begins
1904	Entente Cordiale between Britain and France
1905	First Moroccan crisis
1907	Anglo-Russian Entente; failure of Hague Disarmament Conference
1911	Second Moroccan crisis
1912	First Balkan War
1913	Second Balkan War
1914	Assassination at Sarajevo; ultimatum to Serbia; mobilization; battles at the Marne, Tannenberg, and Ypres
1915	Stalemate on the Western Front; first use of poison gas; sinking of the Lusitania
1916	Attrition warfare: Verdun and the Somme; Jutland
1917	Stalemate on the Western Front continues; collapse of the Russian army; the Russian Revolution; recommencement of unrestricted submarine warfare by Germany; America enters the war
1918	Treaty of Brest-Litovsk; the German offensive fails; Armistice
1919	Treaty of Versailles

Glossary

Armistice — a treaty ending a war. The treaty signed on 11 November 1918 was virtually equivalent to German surrender.

Autocracy — rule by one person, as opposed to democracy, which is rule by all the people. The old Empires of Europe were autocracies.

Mobilize — the process of getting an army ready to fight. In 1914, assembling all the troops and sending them to the front with all their equipment took each nation at least two weeks.

Nationalism — the belief that people of a common ethnic or national background should be united in their own independent country. Nationalism was strong among some groups in the Balkan region. A Serbian nationalist shot Archduke Ferdinand.

Propaganda — control of information, usually by a Government, to influence the views of the people. Propaganda usually distorts the truth. In the First World War, Governments used propaganda to maintain the people's will to fight.

Strategic bombing — the deliberate bombing of cities in order to break the enemy people's will to fight. Invented in the First World War, strategic bombing killed millions in the Second World War. In both wars it generally failed to break enemy morale.

Total war — war in which every resource of a society is turned to the war effort. The First World War was the first 'total war'.

Bibliography

Fay, Sydney B. *The Origins of the World War; Vol. I: Before Sarajevo; Vol. II: After Sarajevo* (The Macmillan Company, New York, 1930)

Ferro, Marc, *The Great War, 1914–1918* (Routledge & Kegan Paul, London, 1973)

Fischer, Fritz, *Germany's Aims in the First World War* (Chatto & Windus, London, 1967)

Kennedy, David M. *Over Here: The First World War and American Society* (Oxford University Press, New York, 1980)

Kennedy, Paul M. *The Rise of the Anglo-German Antagonism, 1860–1914* (George Allen & Unwin, London, 1980)

Liddell Hart, Basil H. *A History of the World War, 1914–1918* (Faber & Faber, Ltd, London, 1934)

May, Ernest R. *The World War and American Isolation, 1914–1917* (Harvard University Press, Cambridge, 1966)

Mayer, Arno J. *Political Origins of the New Diplomacy, 1917–1918* (Yale University Press, New Haven, 1959)

Musil, Robert. *The Man Without Qualities*, Vol. I. (Picador Pan Books Ltd, London, 1979 — originally published in German in 1930)

Parsons, I.M. (ed.) *Men Who March Away: Poems of the First World War* (Heinemann, London, 1965)

Remarque, Erich M. *All Quiet on the Western Front* (Putnam, London, 1929)

3 SOME CONSEQUENCES OF THE FIRST WORLD WAR

The Paris Peace Conference: A conference of victors, by Bruce Murray and Hugh Lester 80
   The Big Three
   The Treaty of Versailles
   The significance of the Paris Peace Settlement
   The League of Nations
   The Covenant of the League
   Aims and purposes
   The mandates system
   Membership of the League
   The Dawes Plan, Locarno and the admission of Germany
   Disarmament
   The impact of the Great Depression

Germany 1919–1933, by Justin Hall 97
   The weakness of the Weimar Government
   Lack of a democratic tradition
   The Versailles Treaty
   Staggering economic problems
   National apathy
   Some specific problems up to 1923
   Spartacist Revolt, January 1919
   Kapp Putsch, March 1920
   French occupation of the Ruhr
   An improvement in conditions, 1924–29
   The Dawes Plan on reparations, August 1924
   French occupation of the Ruhr ended, November 1924
   The Locarno agreement, 1925
   Germany joins the League of Nations, 1926
   The Young Plan, 1929
   1929 — The beginning of crisis
   The death of Stresemann, 1929
   The Depression
   The rise to power of Adolf Hitler
   Before ...
   ... and after
   Conditions of despair
   Origins of the Nazi party
   The use of violence as a political weapon
   Appeal to the spectacular
   The Munich Braühaus Putsch
   The period 1925 to 1929
   The Great Depression
   The use of propaganda
   Election success
   Consolidation of power
   The Reichstag fire
   The Enabling Act
   The Night of the Long Knives
   The death of von Hindenburg

Revision Questions
Chronology
Glossary
Bibliography

The Paris Peace Conference: A conference of victors

On the afternoon of Saturday, 18 January 1919, two months after the conclusion of the Armistice, the Paris Peace Conference was formally opened. Attending the conference were delegates from 32 states, five of them Great powers: Britain, France, Italy and the two non-European Great powers, the United States and Japan. Apart from delegates from the newly created states of Czechoslovakia and Poland, the conference was confined to the Allied and associated powers who had won the war. It was, in other words, essentially a conference of the victors. Not present were the defeated nations—Germany, Austria, Hungary, Bulgaria and Turkey—and Russia, who had withdrawn from the war following the Russian Revolution. In March 1918, by the Treaty of Brest-Litovsk, Russia had concluded a separate peace with Germany and had thereby lost its status as an Allied power.

When the conference convened it was not the intention of the peacemakers that the defeated Central powers should be permanently excluded from the negotiations. Rather, the original assumption among the victors was that the conference would draw up a preliminary peace treaty which would then be negotiated with enemy delegates at a full congress. But, in the event, this procedure was not followed. What happened instead was that on 7 May 1919, the draft terms of the Treaty of Versailles were presented to the German plenipotentiaries*. They were given three weeks to present written observations on these terms; no oral discussion and negotiation was permitted.

On 16 June the final terms, somewhat revised in the light of the German criticisms, were presented to the Germans and they were given a week to accept the treaty. This they did at the very last minute. On 28 June, in the Hall of Mirrors at Versailles*, the treaty was duly signed without the Germans ever having been permitted to negotiate its terms.

Much the same procedure was adopted for the Treaty of St Germain with Austria (signed on 10 September 1919), the Treaty of Neuilly with Bulgaria (27 November 1919), the Treaty of Trianon with Hungary (4 June 1920) and the Treaty of Sèvres with Turkey (20 August 1920).

A large part of the explanation for the failure of the victors to negotiate with the vanquished was the simple fact that the former did not want to give the Central powers, and the Germans in particular, the opportunity to exploit the differences that had shown themselves on the Allied side during the conference discussions and negotiations. But that was not all. In the spring of 1919 the victors became anxious to secure a rapid settlement with Germany, and it was partly haste that led them to impose the Treaty of Versailles rather than negotiate its final terms with the Germans. This sudden haste was caused by the threat of Bolshevik* revolution in eastern and central Europe.

THE BIG THREE

Up to the conclusion of the Treaty of Versailles with Germany at the end of June 1918, the proceedings of the conference were dominated by the 'Big Three': President Woodrow Wilson of the United States; Georges Clemenceau, the French Prime Minister; and David Lloyd George, the British Prime Minister. Together with Vittorio Emanuele Orlando, the Italian Prime

Minister, they constituted the Council of Four, which served as the inner cabinet of the conference; it provided the overall direction and took the major decisions. As the conference was conducted in English, and Orlando was the only one who did not understand English, his influence proved minimal, and the real direction of the conference was left to the other three.

Questions

1. Explain why there was a 'threat of Bolshevik revolution in eastern and central Europe' in 1919.

2. Is there any other reason (apart from the language problem) why Italy's influence on major decisions at the conference was less than that of the Big Three?

Once the treaty with Germany had been signed, the leading statesmen left Paris, and the function of the Council of Four was taken over by the council of heads of delegations, composed of the Foreign Ministers of the five Great powers. By this stage the major decisions in regard to the European territorial settlement had already been reached; the work of the latter council was essentially in the nature of an epilogue. In short, the substance of the Paris peace settlement was primarily the achievement of the Big Three; it reflected their common desires and interests and also the differences among them that necessitated compromise and concession.

Of the three, President Wilson was by far the most theoretical in approach and outlook. Although a politician of some skill, Wilson was in fact an academic by training and background — prior to entering politics in 1910 he had been a professor of history and President of Princeton University — and he had looked forward to the peace conference as an 'intellectual treat'.

The Big Three: Lloyd George, Clemenceau and Wilson.

Moreover, his whole approach to politics, and even more so to foreign affairs, was conditioned by a strong idealism. 'The force of America,' he asserted on one occasion, 'is the force of moral principle ... there is nothing else for which she will contend.' Quite typically, when in April 1917 he had asked the Congress of the United States to declare war on Germany, he had done so not in the name of American self-interest — although this was being served — but in the cause of making the world 'safe for democracy', and the rights of mankind 'as secure as the faith and freedom of nations can make them'. When Wilson arrived in Paris for the peace conference he believed that the Americans would be 'the only disinterested people' there, and he was determined they should use their power and influence to create a new world order based on justice and peace. 'Tell me what's right,' he urged his advisers, 'and I'll fight for it.'

The programme Wilson brought with him to Paris centred on his Fourteen Points, first announced to the Congress of the United States in January 1918.

Very different in approach and outlook was the French Prime Minister, Clemenceau, known as 'the Tiger'. An old, tired and cynical man, who had been one of the mayors of Paris during the German siege of 1870, he had little patience with Wilsonian idealism. Instead, as a realist who recognised that without the intervention of the United States the Allies could never have defeated Germany, he was determined that the power of Germany should be drastically reduced and that everything should be done to guarantee the future security of France. Clemenceau, the British economist John Maynard Keynes later wrote, had 'one illusion — France; and one disillusion — mankind, including Frenchmen and his colleagues not the least'. Certainly he had little regard for Wilson. 'I do not think he is a bad man,' Clemenceau said of Wilson at the end of the conference, 'but I have not yet made up my mind as to how much of him is good.'

for his consistency of principle and purpose. Before arriving in Paris he had won a general election in Britain by promising to bring the Kaiser to trial and to search German pockets to the 'uttermost farthing' to pay for the war; yet at the conference itself he sometimes appeared as the great champion of a peace of moderation and conciliation. In the main, once basic British demands and interests had been secured, and when he felt it was politically safe for him to do so, Lloyd George did attempt to exercise a moderating influence on the conference.

As it proved, the terms of the peace treaty were severe rather than conciliatory towards Germany; certainly to the Germans it did not appear as the peace based upon justice they believed Wilson had promised in his Fourteen Points. Some historians, mainly American, have argued that what in fact happened at the conference was that the idealistic Wilson was consistently frustrated and hoodwinked by the cynical and ruthless politicians of the Old World, Clemenceau and Lloyd George, with the result that Wilson's projected peace of justice was transformed into a peace of revenge. But this argument is not altogether convincing. What it ignores is that Wilson's concept of justice was a stern one, that he believed Germany had to be punished for her sins. It also ignores the fact that Wilson was totally committed to advancing the cause of the Slavic peoples of Europe and, particularly in the case of the Poles, this could only be done at the territorial expense of the Germans. Gustav Stresemann, a future Chancellor and Foreign Minister of Germany, was one German who had recognized these aspects of Wilson when he wrote just prior to the Armistice: 'As far as I can see, Wilson's Fourteen Points already present the possibility of the loss of Alsace-Lorraine, Upper Silesia, Posen and parts of West Prussia, and in addition an undefined sum for damages, which could very easily be transformed into a war indemnity, however otherwise it may be disguised'.

Question

What did (a) the USA and (b) France have to fear from a revival of German military power? Which country had the most to fear? Explain your answer.

If Wilson could be identified with a set of principles, and Clemenceau with the cause of France, it was not always clear precisely where Lloyd George stood. Known behind his back as 'the Goat', Lloyd George was more highly regarded by contemporaries for his political adroitness and dexterity than

In the final analysis it is difficult to see how, given the objectives of the 'Big Three' and the circumstances of the time, the treaty presented to Germany could have been substantially different. Any treaty would have had to satisfy French demands for security against the possibility of a resurgent Germany, and the demands of the British public for the chastisement of Germany; and any treaty would have had to fulfil Wilson's commitment to an independent Poland with access to the sea, and such access could only have been obtained through German territory.

THE TREATY OF VERSAILLES

In all, the Treaty of Versailles comprised 440 articles, which included the Covenant of the League of Nations (Articles 1–26). For Germany the most important articles related to frontiers, colonies, military forces, reparations* and war guilt.

The purpose of the treaty's readjustment of Germany's frontiers was essentially twofold: to reduce Germany's might and to promote national self-determination for the non-German peoples of the former German Empire. In regard to the first, the treaty was very much milder than Clemenceau had wanted. What he had proposed was that the Rhineland be permanently detached from Germany so as to serve as a buffer state between France and Germany, but Wilson and Lloyd George refused to grant his demand on the grounds that it violated the very principle of national self-determination that the victors were seeking to advance. Instead of creating a Rhenish buffer state, the treaty provided for the demilitarization of the Rhineland for a distance of 50 kilometres from the east bank of the Rhine River, and for an Allied military occupation of the west bank for 15 years. Further, to quieten French fears about a resurgent Germany, the United States and Britain undertook to come to the aid of France in the event of unprovoked German aggression; but as this agreement was never ratified by the United States Senate, it never took effect.

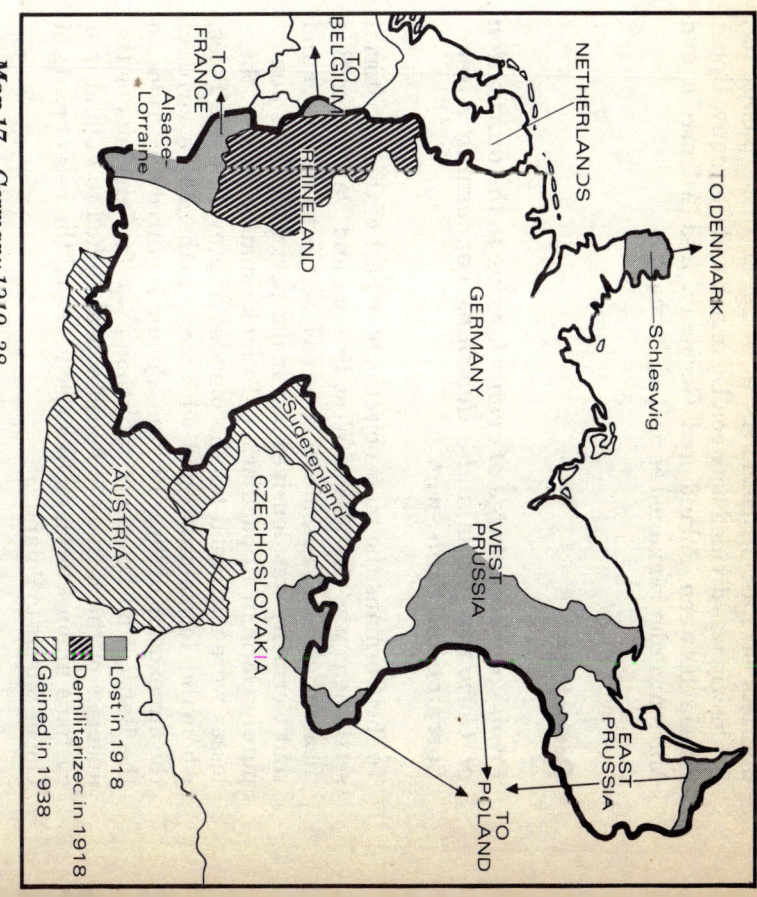

Map 17—Germany 1919–38.

In terms of the treaty Germany was required in the west to return Alsace-Lorraine to France and cede Eupen-Malmedy to Belgium; and in the east to relinquish Posen and West Prussia to Poland, and the cities of Danzig and Memel to the Allied powers. Furthermore, the Saar Basin, which the French had wished to annex to Alsace-Lorraine, was placed under the administration of the League of Nations for 15 years, after which a plebiscite* would be held to decide its future. Immediate plebiscites were to determine the future of Schleswig, Upper Silesia and the Allenstein and Marienwerder

force was prohibited. The stock and manufacture of armaments in Germany was to be regulated by the Allied powers.

Perhaps the most controversial clauses of the Treaty of Versailles related to the reparations Germany was to pay for all damage done to the civilian population of the Allied and associated powers and to their property' during the war. No total was set by the treaty — the actual assessment was referred to a Reparation Commission — but it was clear from the terms of the treaty that the sum would be very large, and this it proved to be. When the Reparation Commission reported in April 1921, it fixed Germany's total liability at 132 000 million gold marks (R13 200 million); an impossible sum, especially in view of the fact that Germany had already been deprived of much of its productive and earning capacity by the treaty. In addition to the cession of valuable territory, Germany was required by the treaty to transfer control of the Saar coalmines to France for 15 years, to surrender almost its entire merchant fleet and to give up all property owned by German citizens abroad.

Question

From the point of view of France, Germany's reparations payments served two major purposes: one was financial restitution for damage done during the war; the other reason, bearing in mind France's security needs, was perhaps even more important. What was this other reason? Give details.

Apart from the losses involved, what infuriated Germans about reparations was that they were based on an enforced German acceptance of responsibility for having caused the war. The reparations provisions of the treaty were prefaced and justified by Article 231, the so-called 'war guilt' clause, which stated:

districts of East Prussia. As a result of these plebiscites, Schleswig was divided between Denmark and Germany, Upper Silesia between Poland and Germany, and Allenstein and Marienwerder remained as part of Germany.

Question

From your knowledge of events leading to the unification of Germany, explain the decisions concerning Alsace-Lorraine and Schleswig.

To the Germans the most objectionable part of this territorial settlement was the loss of West Prussia and Danzig, for this meant that East Prussia was severed from Germany proper and that Germany was deprived of a major port which was almost purely German in population. To make matters worse, these losses were sustained for the purpose of providing the Poles, whom the Germans detested, with access to the sea. By virtue of the annexation of West Prussia, Poland acquired a 'corridor' to the Baltic, and Danzig, established as a 'free city' under the auspices of the League of Nations, was linked to Poland in a customs union. Germans likewise resented the loss of parts of Upper Silesia to Poland.

Altogether, as a consequence of the Treaty of Versailles, Germany lost 13,4 per cent of its former territory, about 14 per cent of its economic productivity, and a little over 10 per cent of its population, some seven million people. Germany was also deprived of all its colonies.

The military clauses of the Treaty of Versailles were designed to help make impossible a German war of revenge. Germany was, in effect, disarmed: the army was limited to 100 000 men, the navy to six battleships and assorted lighter vessels, and an air

THE SIGNIFICANCE OF THE PARIS PEACE SETTLEMENT

The Paris Peace Settlement has been the cause of endless controversy among historians. Its critics have argued that the Treaty of Versailles was a Carthaginian peace — that it was designed to reduce Germany to servitude — and also that the peacemakers committed a fundamental mistake by providing for the balkanization* of central and eastern Europe in accordance with the principle of self-determination. According to the critics, the disruption of the old Empires and the creation of a series of weak successor states, was fatal to the long-term peace of Europe; it created a power vacuum that was bound to attract aggression from Germany and Russia once those powers had regained their strength.

The Allied and associated governments affirm and Germany accepts the responsibility of Germany and her allies for causing all the loss and damage to which the Allied and associated governments and their nationals have been subjected as a consequence of the war imposed upon them by the aggression of Germany and her allies.

To Germans this requirement that Germany avow its guilt was a vindictive falsification and a slur on its honour. The requirement was bitterly resented as such.

Equally humiliating, in the eyes of many Germans, was Article 227 which provided for the trial by special tribunal of Kaiser Wilhelm II 'for a supreme offence against international morality and the sanctity of treaties'. In the event, Wilhelm was never brought to trial; the Netherlands, to which he had fled in November 1918, refused to surrender him for such purposes. He died in Doorn, Holland, on 4 June 1941, aged 82.

Against such criticisms the apologists of the peace settlement have argued that the Treaty of Versailles conformed in its essentials to the Fourteen Points, which the Germans themselves had accepted as the basis for peace, and that the treaty was never as harsh as the Germans maintained it to be, or for that matter, as harsh as the Treaty of Brest-Litovsk which the Germans had imposed on Russia in 1917. Again, the apologists have argued that the territorial settlement of central and eastern Europe promoted more just conditions in the area, certainly in so far as the number of persons under foreign rule was reduced from over 60 million to under 30 million; and they have pointed out that, in the main, the boundaries drawn up in 1919 have stood the test of time.

Consider the above defence in the light of Wilson's Fourteen Points, which follow:

1. *Open convenants of peace, openly arrived at, after which there shall be no private international understanding of any kind but diplomacy shall proceed always frankly and in the public view.*

2. *Absolute freedom of navigation upon the seas, outside territorial waters, alike in peace and in war, except as the seas may be closed in whole or in part by international action for the enforcement of international covenants.*

3. *The removal, so far as possible, of all economic barriers and the establishment of an equality of trade conditions among all the nations consenting to the peace and associating themselves for its maintenance.*

4. *Adequate guarantees given and taken that national armaments will be reduced to the lowest point consistent with domestic safety.*

5. *A free, open-minded, and absolutely impartial adjustment of all colonial claims, based upon a strict*

observance of the principle that in determining all such questions of sovereignty the interests of the populations concerned must have equal weight with the equitable claims of the government whose title is to be determined.

6. The evacuation of all Russian territory and such a settlement of all questions affecting Russia as will secure the best and freest coöperation of the other nations of the world in obtaining for her an unhampered and unembarrassed opportunity for the independent determination of her own political development and national policy and assure her of a sincere welcome into the society of free nations under institutions of her own choosing; and, more than a welcome, assistance also of every kind that she may need and may herself desire. The treatment accorded Russia by her sister nations in the months to come will be the acid test of their good will, of their comprehension of her needs as distinguished from their own interests, and of their intelligent and unselfish sympathy.

7. Belgium, the whole world will agree, must be evacuated and restored, without any attempt to limit the sovereignty which she enjoys in common with all other free nations: No other single act will serve as this will serve to restore confidence among the nations in the laws which they have themselves set and determined for the government of their relations with one another. Without this healing act the whole structure and validity of international law is forever impaired.

8. All French territory should be freed and the invaded portions restored, and the wrong done to France by Prussia in 1871 in the matter of Alsace-Lorraine, which has unsettled the peace of the world for nearly fifty years, should be righted, in order that peace may once more be made secure in the interest of all.

9. A readjustment of the frontiers of Italy should be effected along clearly recognizable lines of nationality.

10. The people of Austria-Hungary, whose place among the nations we wish to see safeguarded and assured, should be accorded the freest opportunity of autonomous development.

11. Romania, Serbia, and Montenegro should be evacuated; occupied territories restored; Serbia accorded free and secure access to the sea; and the relations of the several Balkan states to one another determined by friendly counsel along historically established lines of allegiance and nationality; and international guarantees of the political and economic independence and territorial integrity of the several Balkan states should be entered into.

12. The Turkish portions of the present Ottoman Empire should be assured a secure sovereignty, but the other nationalities which are now under Turkish rule should be assured an undoubted security of life and an absolutely unmolested opportunity of autonomous development, and the Dardanelles should be permanently opened as a free passage to the ships and commerce of all nations under international guarantees.

13. An independent Polish state should be erected which should include the territories inhabited by indisputably Polish populations, which should be assured a free and secure access to the sea, and whose political and economic independence and territorial integrity should be guaranteed by international covenant.

14. A general association of nations must be formed under specific covenants for the purpose of affording mutual guarantees of political independence and territorial integrity to great and small states alike.

(*Congressional Record*, Vol. LVI, pp. 680–81, 1918. Quoted in Sheffe and Fisher, pp. 124–5.)

What is clear is that the Treaty of Versailles was not a success. It was intended to ensure that Germany would not again menace the peace of Europe and in this it failed; twenty years after the treaty, Britain and France were again at war with Germany. Perhaps the fundamental fault of the treaty was that it was sufficiently severe to infuriate the Germans, but not sufficiently severe to ensure that Germany could never seek to overthrow it. In the words of one of its most perceptive critics, the Frenchman Jacques Bainville, the Treaty of Versailles was 'too mild for its severity'. The fact is that despite its undoubted harshness, the treaty left Germany as potentially the greatest power in Europe. Germany was not dismembered by the treaty, and retained the population and economic resources necessary to reassert its Great power status. As General Smuts warned in 1919: 'The fact is, the Germans are, have been, and will continue to be the dominant factor on the continent of Europe and no permanent peace is possible which is not based on that fact.' His warning was not sufficiently heeded.

Where criticism of the peacemakers is distinctly unfair is in holding them responsible for the balkanization of central and eastern Europe: at the Paris conference they had little option but to recognize the new states which had emerged. A more substantial criticism is that, in defining boundaries, the peacemakers gave a dangerously one-sided interpretation to the principle of self-determination. It was consistently applied to the disadvantage and never to the advantage of the defeated Central powers, with the result that millions of Germans and Magyars found themselves living in foreign states, whereas Germany, Austria and Hungary were left with few minority peoples. The danger for the future lay with the new states which contained significant German minorities; the day would come when a revived Germany would actively seek to reclaim these minorities. As Lloyd George forewarned in his Fontainebleau memorandum prepared at the peace conference: 'I cannot conceive any greater cause of future war than that the German people, who have certainly proved themselves one of the most vigorous and powerful races in the world, should be surrounded by a number of small states, many of them consisting of people who have never previously set up a stable government for themselves, but each of them containing large masses of Germans clamouring for reunion with their native land.' It was not a simple matter of Germans who had belonged to the German Empire 'clamouring for reunion.' There were also the Germans who had previously belonged to the Habsburg Empire and who, now that the Empire no longer existed, wished for amalgamation with Germany. In the circumstances it would have been extremely difficult for the peacemakers to grant Germany additional territories on the basis of self-determination. Nevertheless, the Germans were left with a sense of injustice and they were later able to exploit the one-sidedness of the Paris settlement. Eventually Hitler used the fact that Germans were living in Czechoslovakia as a pretext to stir up the Munich Crisis, which was later followed by the outbreak of the Second World War.

In the final analysis, the maintenance of a lasting world peace after the Paris peace conference depended on the existence of an effective international machinery that would provide either for the peaceful and orderly revision of the Paris settlement, or for

Questions

1. **To what extent did the Treaty of Versailles abide by the Fourteen Points? How did it differ from Wilson's plan?**

2. **Refer to Stresemann's comments on the Fourteen Points given on page 82. In the light of the Versailles Treaty, were his comments justified?**

the firm enforcement and defence of that settlement. The League of Nations established by the peace conference was intended to meet this need, but in the event the League failed to serve as an effective instrument for either revising or guaranteeing the international order established at Paris. By the end of 1936 the failure of the League was evident to all, and the post-war international order was in the process of being forcibly overturned.

Here is a description of the atmosphere at the signing of the Treaty of Versailles:

> Suddenly from outside comes the crash of guns thundering a salute. It announces to Paris that the ... Treaty of Versailles has been signed by Dr. Müller and Dr. Bell. Through the few open windows comes the sound of distant crowds cheering hoarsely. And still the signature goes on. We had been warned it might last three hours ...
>
> We kept our seats while the Germans were conducted like prisoners from the dock, their eyes still fixed upon some distant point of the horizon. We still kept our seats to allow the Big Five to pass down the aisle. Wilson, Lloyd George, the Dominions, others. Finally, Clemenceau, with his rolling satirical gait. Painlevé, who was sitting one off from me, rose to greet him ... congratulated him. 'Yes,' says Clemenceau, 'It's a good day's work.' There were tears in his bleary eyes.

(Harold Nicolson, *Peacemaking 1919*.)

Two days after the signing of the peace treaty *The Times* special correspondent in Germany sounded this warning:

> If there is one country that the Germans are determined to get even with it is France.
>
> The Germans will try by every means to foster differences between the Allies. To isolate France, to render the pledges of Great Britain and the United States null and void is the dominating idea of the individual German serving no impulse but his own; and one hears talk about a next war, first with Poland, later with France, when financial stability is restored and the treaty provisions are forgotten ... Never was it more necessary for the Allies to watch Germany closely.

The German press reacted as follows to the signing of the treaty:

Deutsche Zeitung, 28 June 1919.

> Vengeance! German nation! Today in the Hall of Mirrors of Versailles the disgraceful treaty is being signed. Do not forget it! In the place where, in the glorious year of 1871, the German empire in all its glory had its origin, German honour is being carried into its grave. Do not forget it! The German people will with unceasing labour, press forward to reconquer the place among the nations to which it is entitled. Then will come vengeance for the shame of 1919.

Vorwärts, 28 June 1919 (afternoon issue).

> We do not dream of a bloody Revanche like the Pan-German fools, who are now experiencing their 'justice' on their own bodies, but we hope and trust confidently in the victory of right ... Before us lies a struggle for the victory of right, not a battle with bloody weapons, but a battle of the spirit ... On the day of triumph for wrong, we greet the coming peace of right, for which we are going to struggle

Question

Explain why there were tears in Clemenceau's 'bleary eyes'.

Kölnische Zeitung, 29 June 1919.

What shall we Germans do on this black day of our history? To complain and to continue to complain, as is no doubt human in such an hour? To make accusations, as unfortunately it seems natural to many in our fatherland now, and to search for those guilty in the collapse of the Reich? Or in hard recognition of the facts, irrespective of how they came about, to meet the new times with the most tenacious will to life, for us, for Germany? To us it seems that the latter is the only possible and worthy path.

The German Government issued a public statement to explain their signing of the treaty, even though it was horrific to them and to the public:

The Government of the Reich, with the consent of the National Assembly, has decided to sign the treaty of peace. We do so with heavy hearts, under the pressure of the most unrelenting power, and with only one thought: to save our defenceless people from having to make further sacrifices and endure added pains of hunger. Peace has been concluded. Now guard and preserve it.

24 June 1919

Question

Analyse the tone of each of these three German press reports. In each case, explain what the writer proposed as the correct response to the treaty.

---

shoulder to shoulder with our working-class brothers on the other side of the frontiers.

The first demand is that you fulfil the conditions of the treaty. You must bend every effort to fulfil it. It must be carried out, so far as it can be carried out. We shall never forget those who are to be severed from us. They are flesh of our flesh. Wherever it can be done we shall take their part as if it were our own. They will be torn from the Reich, but they will not be torn from our hearts.

The second demand is work. We shall be able to carry the burdens of this war only if no hand is idle. To every unfulfilled obligation our opponents can respond with invasion, occupation and blockade. He who works defends his native soil.

The third demand is faithfulness to the calls of duty. Even as we have remained at our posts, at whatever cost to our self-respect, each and every one of us should do the same. The soldier, whether he be officer or private, the public servant, everyone, must be steadfast in his duty for the sake of the general good, even in this worst day of all. We are compelled to hand over our fellow Germans to foreign tribunals. This is something which we opposed to the last. We know full well how bitter a thing this is for our brave soldiers. But if officers and men alike do not give their full support to the present government, not merely hundreds, but millions of our compatriots will be delivered over to terror, to armed occupation, to annexation. Germany must retain the power to live. If we have no order within, we shall have no work. Without work we cannot meet the conditions of the treaty. If we fail in that, there will be no peace, but a renewal of the war.

If we do not all help, our having signed the treaty will be worthless. We shall then have no ameliorations, no revisions, and no final removal of the gigantic burden. What we leave undone today may cost our children years of servitude. Both government and people must set to work forthwith. There must be no delay and no one must stand

89

aside. There is only one way out of the darkness of this treaty: the preservation of Reich and people through unity and work.

Help us, men and women, to attain that.

(Quoted in Luckau, pp. 496–497)

Question

Briefly sum up the reasons given by the German Government for their decision to sign the treaty, harsh though it was.

THE LEAGUE OF NATIONS

The First World War had both destroyed the European balance of power and greatly assisted the rise of the two Great powers outside Europe — the United States and Japan. It had also made possible the emergence of the first socialist state in the world, Russia. These were developments which called for the creation of a new system of international relations, and the League of Nations represented an attempt on the part of the Paris peacemakers to provide that system. The League was designed by them to replace the old balance of power with a new system of collective security*, and it was intended to provide a framework for the conduct of international relations on a global rather than a purely European-centred basis.

The Covenant of the League

In terms of the Covenant of the League of Nations (which constituted Part 1 of each of the peace treaties), the League officially began its existence on 10 January 1920, when the Treaty of Versailles came into force. Twenty-six years later, on 18 April 1946, the League would be dissolved, having been effectively replaced by the new international organization, the United Nations.

During its existence, the League of Nations offered a permanent machinery for peacefully settling disputes among nations, and for making possible united action by member states. What the League was not, and was never intended to be, was a federation of states or a form of world government. It was rather an association of sovereign, independent states, with each state retaining its essential freedom of action. The League could recommend certain courses of action to member states, but it could not dictate to them.

Aims and Purposes

In terms of Article 2 of the Covenant, action of the League was to be effected through an assembly and a council, assisted by a permanent secretariat. The Assembly, which met annually until the outbreak of the Second World War, consisted of representatives from all member states, each state possessing a single vote. The Council consisted of the major European powers as permanent members and of several lesser powers (the number was progressively raised from four to eleven) as non-permanent members chosen from time to time by the Assembly. Each state on the Council possessed one vote. Except for procedural matters, which could be determined by a simple majority vote, all decisions of both the Assembly and the Council were governed by the rule of unanimity. This meant

Initially it was anticipated that the Council would prove the dominant body in the League, but in the event the lead was taken by the Assembly, and the Council became essentially an executive committee of the Assembly. The chief administrative organ of the League was the Secretariat established in Geneva, the seat of the League, and headed by the Secretary-General appointed by the Council with the approval of the majority of the Assembly. The judicial functions of the League were entrusted to a permanent Court of International Justice, constituted in 1921 and seated at The Hague.

As stated in the preamble to the Covenant, the purpose of the League was 'to promote international co-operation and to achieve international peace and security'. In Articles 8 to 19 of the Covenant, the ways in which the League was to perform its basic task of achieving international peace and security were set forward.

The first of these was by promoting disarmament. Article 8 declared that 'the maintenance of peace requires the reduction of national armaments to the lowest point consistent with national safety and the enforcement by common action of international obligations', and it charged the Council to formulate plans for such reduction. A permanent commission, established under Article 9, was to advise the Council on general military, naval and air questions.

A second way in which the League was to help achieve peace and security was through a system of collective security. In terms of Article 10, members of the League undertook to respect the territorial integrity and political independence of all fellow-members, and to join in protecting them against external aggression. The operative idea behind this undertaking was that of deterring potential aggressors by threatening them with collective action, though Article 10 did not in fact commit members to any specific forms of action against aggressors. What the Article provided was that the Council would 'advise upon the means' by which members should fulfil their obligation in the event of an attack on any of their fellow-members.

Thirdly, under Article 11, the League was given a broad mandate to attempt to salvage world peace should any war break out or threaten to break out. 'Any war or threat of war' was declared to be 'a matter of concern to the whole League', and in this event the League was authorised to 'take any action that may be deemed wise and effectual to safeguard the peace of nations'. Any member of the League had the right to insist on an emergency meeting of the Council in the case of war or threat of war.

Fourthly, Articles 12 to 17 established principles and machinery for the peaceful settlement of disputes and provided for action against members of the League which resorted to war, in violation of the Covenant. Members undertook to submit 'any dispute likely to lead to a rupture' to one of three procedures for peaceful settlement: arbitration, judicial settlement by the permanent Court of International Justice, or inquiry by the Council or Assembly. War was permissible only in certain defined circumstances, as when the Council found that a dispute arose out of a matter 'solely within the domestic jurisdiction' of one of the parties. Any member which resorted to war in disregard of its obligations under the Covenant was to be immediately subjected to economic sanctions and the Council was to recommend to governments what military action should be taken against the 'covenant-breaking state' (Article 16).

that, apart from the actual parties to a dispute, decisions of the Assembly and Council required the agreement of all members present.

91

Finally, the League was encouraged to facilitate peaceful change by Article 19, which empowered the Assembly to 'advise the reconsideration ... of treaties which have become inapplicable and the consideration of international conditions whose continuance might endanger the peace of the world'. It was President Wilson's hope that this Article would be taken advantage of to rectify any injustice in the Treaty of Versailles.

Question

The League of Nations was an attempt to regulate world affairs and to prevent war by joint action. Roughly a century before, after the Napoleonic Wars, an attempt had been made to regulate European affairs and to prevent war by joint action through the 'Congress System'. The statesmen who drew up the Charter of the League of Nations were conscious of the reasons for the failure of the 'Congress System'. What were the differences between the League and the 'Congress' with regard to:
1. Membership;
2. The decision-making process?

The mandates system

Most of the remaining Articles of the Covenant concerned the secondary services of the League, including the supervision of the mandates system established for those colonies and territories taken from the defeated Central powers which were, in the words of the victors, 'inhabited by people not yet able to stand by themselves under the strenuous conditions of the modern world'. These colonies and territories were 'entrusted to advanced nations' for administration as mandated territories under the supervision of the League. Class A mandates,

administered by Britain and France, were established for the Arab territories formerly belonging to the Turkish Empire and which were expected eventually to become independent. Class B mandates were established for the former German colonies of central and eastern Africa and were administrated by European countries as separate territories from themselves. Class C mandates were established for South West Africa and the former German islands in the Pacific and were to be 'administered under the laws of the mandatory as integral portions of its territory'. South Africa was appointed as mandatory for South West Africa, Australia for New Guinea, New Zealand for Western Samoa and Japan for the Micronesian Islands (Caroline, Mariana and Marshall Islands). Each mandatory was to report annually to the permanent Mandates Commission created to 'advise the Council on all matters relating to the observance of mandates'.

Question

Does the Republic of South Africa still have authority over and responsibility for the territory of South West Africa/Namibia? What is the present status of this mandate?

Membership of the League

One of the fundamental weaknesses of the League was that never, at any stage, did it include among its members all the major powers of the world. The United States never joined and at any given time at least one other major power did not belong. To begin with, both Germany and Russia were excluded from membership; Germany was not admitted until 1926, and the Soviet Union not until 1934. By the time the Soviet Union was

92

United States had emerged from the war as the greatest power in the world, and without this power the League was simply not the organization its founders had envisaged. The irony was that the most dedicated and strenuous champion of the League at the Paris peace conference had been President Wilson of the United States; yet it was in his own country that the League idea was first formally rejected. The United States Constitution required that all treaties entered into by the United States receive the approval of a two-thirds majority in the Senate, and in the votes of November 1919 and March 1920 the Senate failed to achieve such a majority for the Treaty of Versailles and the Covenant of the League of Nations. The Senate, retreating from the commitments in Europe undertaken by the Wilson administration, and seeking to preserve a completely free hand for America in international affairs, refused to sanction US acceptance of the obligations of League membership as set out in the Covenant. Following the defeat of Wilson's Democratic party in the elections of November 1920, the question of US membership of the League was never again raised.

The Dawes Plan, Locarno and the admission of Germany

If the failure of the United States to join the League came as a calamitous development to the Covenant's authors, the initial exclusion of Germany and Russia was a deliberate decision on their part. Both were treated as 'outlaw' nations that would have to reform themselves and prove their willingness to abide by the status quo before being admitted to membership of the League. To many in Germany and Russia the League appeared as nothing more than an armed coalition of the victors of the First World War, aimed at preserving the status quo. In fact, that was exactly how the French looked upon the League; they saw it as one among several means for enforcing the Treaty of

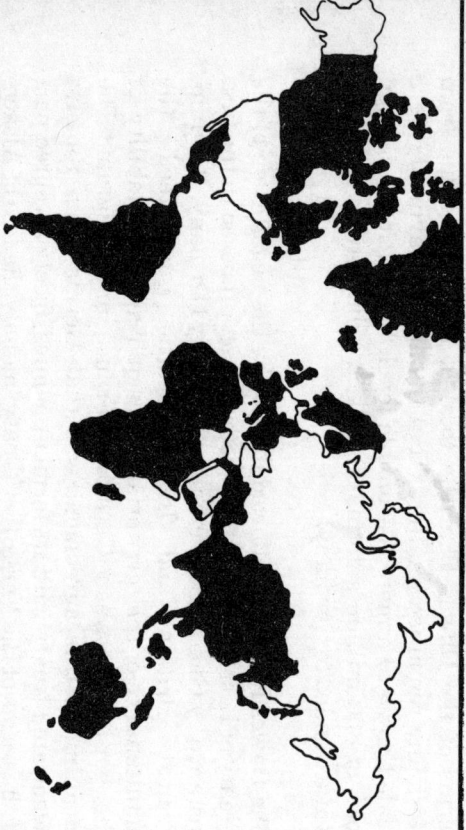

Map 18 — Map of the world showing extent of membership of the League of Nations. (Note that colonies are included.)

At the League's inception the right of membership belonged to the 32 states comprising the Paris Peace Conference and the 13 neutral states invited in the peace treaties to 'accede without reservation' to the Covenant. Thereafter new members required the approval of two-thirds of the Assembly. In 1934 membership of the League reached its peak of 58 states.

From the standpoint of membership, the biggest blow sustained by the League was when the United States refused to join. The

accepted into the League, Japan and Germany had already withdrawn — they both departed in 1933 — and in 1937 Italy also left the League. In 1939 the Soviet Union was expelled for its attack on Finland. In other words, among the major powers only Britain and France were members of the League throughout its career; the League consequently was never truly a world organization.

93

Versailles and keeping Germany down. In Russia, the Allies initially backed the 'White Army'—thus revealing their hostility to the new Bolshevik Government.

In the years 1924–25, a fundamental change was effected in relations between the Allied powers and Germany, a change that resulted in German admission to the League in 1926. This change was made possible by an almost simultaneous reversal of policies on the part of both France and Germany.

In 1924 France, under the direction of Edouard Herriot as Prime Minister and Aristide Briand as Foreign Minister, adopted a more conciliatory approach to Germany. This followed the failure of the uncompromising policy pursued by the government of Raymond Poincaré, culminating in the invasion and occupation of the Ruhr by France and Belgium in January 1923 in response to Germany's default on its reparations payments. The occupation had simply served to underline the futility and dangers of Poincaré's policy. So far from securing German payments, the Franco-Belgian action had prompted a campaign of passive resistance on the part of the Germans and had helped to shake the financial stability of France. After the May 1924 elections, Poincaré's Government gave way to that of Herriot and French policy towards Germany was reversed; France now substituted conciliation for force in its dealings with Germany and the way was thereby opened for the return of Germany to the international community.

On the German side, the statesman who negotiated Germany's re-entry into the international community was Gustav Stresemann, Chancellor in the autumn of 1923 and thereafter Foreign Minister until his death in 1929. In September 1923 Stresemann terminated the policy of passive resistance to France in the Ruhr and thereby initiated the shift in German policy from resistance to what was known as 'fulfilment': the policy whereby Germany would attempt to fulfil the terms of Versailles, hoping to demonstrate to the Allies the impossible nature of their demands and in so doing oblige them to revise the treaty.

The first fruit of the new willingness on the part of France and Germany to negotiate was the adoption in August 1924 of the Dawes Plan for a modified scheme of reparations payments. In terms of the Dawes Plan the total of reparations due from Germany remained unaltered, but the annual payments were scaled down to a more reasonable level. In addition, a foreign loan of 800 million gold marks, raised primarily in America, was extended to Germany.

The Dawes Plan was followed in 1925 by the negotiation of the Treaty of Locarno, a Western security pact proposed in the first instance by Gustav Stresemann. Signed by Germany, Belgium, France, Britain and Italy, Locarno guaranteed 'the maintenance of the territorial status quo' and 'inviolability' of the borders between Germany, France and Belgium. The meaning of this agreement was that Germany, in its first negotiated treaty with its former enemies, freely accepted part of the terms of the Versailles Treaty, namely the loss of Alsace-Lorraine to France; in return, Germany's western frontier was secured, thereby making impossible a repetition of the Ruhr invasion. Germany also signed arbitration treaties with Poland and Czechoslovakia, but in the east there was no general guarantee of frontiers corresponding to that reached in regard to the west. As Stresemann saw it, he had succeeded in gaining security for Germany in the west and at the same time, Germany 'maintained its freedom of action with regard to the eastern frontier'.

The Locarno pacts were by no means entirely reassuring, and in their way they weakened rather than strengthened the

Versailles settlement and the League of Nations. This was because of the marked difference in the nature of the eastern and western settlements. As Britain and Italy undertook in the Locarno pacts to guarantee the frontiers with Germany in the west but not in the east, this implied that the eastern frontiers lacked the same validity and served to undermine the general obligation of all members of the League under Article 10 of the Covenant. Nevertheless, the Locarno pacts did give rise to a new optimism in Europe — the so-called 'spirit of Locarno' was widely hailed — and in accordance with the agreement reached at Locarno, Germany became a member of the League, with a permanent seat on the Council, on 8 September 1926.

With the admission of Germany, the League entered its most promising phase of development. All the major European powers, with the exception of the Soviet Union, were now members, and the League became the focal point for their diplomacy. In accordance with the lead taken by Austen Chamberlain, the British Foreign Secretary, most of the European Foreign Ministers, including Briand and Stresemann, regularly attended the meetings of the League and generally sought to put the League to constructive use.

Disarmament

Germany's admission to the League brought to the fore the whole question of disarmament. As Germany had already been disarmed under the terms of the Treaty of Versailles, and as the disarmament of Germany had been justified as a necessary first step towards a general reduction of armaments, the League was now morally obliged to take action on the disarmament issue. Accordingly, the Council revived earlier plans for a world disarmament conference and set up a preparatory commission to clear the ground for it. The commission soon experienced difficulties, and the world conference was not to meet until 1932. The fundamental problem in any scheme for disarmament was to reconcile disarmament with the need for security: governments could not be expected to reduce their armaments unless the safety of their country was firmly guaranteed; and as yet such guarantees did not exist, even within the League. In the Geneva protocol, presented to the Assembly in 1924, an attempt had been made to provide these guarantees: it called for joint military action by members of the League against any aggressor, and defined an aggressor as a power that chose to make war rather than submit its case to arbitration, or rather than abide by an arbitrator's decision. The disarmament conference had provided for armament reduction. But the protocol was never adopted: in 1925 its fate was sealed when it was rejected by the British Government of Stanley Baldwin.

Thereafter Anglo-French differences proved a major obstacle to progress on disarmament. On the preparatory commission, which first met in May 1926, the French made it clear that they required new and firmer guarantees of their security before they would agree to a reduction in their armaments, while the British were as clearly reluctant to provide any further guarantees for the security of League members. For a short time in 1929, following the negotiation and initial ratification by 15 countries of the pact of Paris (or Kellogg-Briand pact) for the renunciation of war as an instrument of national policy, it seemed that there might be a breakthrough on the disarmament issue, especially when the British supported a plan for extending the sanctions of Article 16 of the Covenant to all wars prohibited by the pact. But the plan was opposed by Japan and the Scandinavian countries and had to be abandoned.

When the preparatory commission finally produced a draft statement of principles in 1930, nothing substantial had been done to satisfy French demands for firmer guarantees of security as a precondition for a major reduction of armaments. The result was that the commission's draft was a disappointment to all advocates of disarmament: it contained no figures for the limitation of armed forces and often did no more than present the opposing points of view on the issues in dispute.

Following the completion of the commission's work, the world conference on disarmament was summoned for 1932. By the time the conference met, the overall world situation had deteriorated to such an extent as to render disarmament a virtual impossibility.

The impact of the Great Depression

What did much to transform the whole international situation at the beginning of the decade of the thirties was the onset of a great world economic depression. It served to usher in a new era of uncertainty and aggression.

The Depression had its immediate origins in the crash on the New York stock exchange at the end of 1929. From Wall Street the crisis spread to the rest of the American economy, and from the United States it spread to the rest of the world. As a consequence of the collapse in the United States, Americans ceased to invest capital abroad, called in their short-term loans and stopped purchasing foreign goods, with the result that a world-wide economic slump ensued. European prosperity, it now became evident, had been heavily dependent on American credit. Then in 1931 the Depression was deepened by the 'crisis within the crisis': the European monetary crisis which followed upon the failure of Austria's largest bank, the *Kreditanstalt*, and which led to Britain's abandonment of the international gold standard in September 1931. In all, by the end of 1932 some 32 currencies had been depreciated in relation to gold since 1929.

In 1932, the worst year of the Depression, the Western world, according to statistics, had at least 30 million unemployed. In the United States alone, 15 million were out of work; in Germany, the hardest hit of the European countries, the figure was 6 million, or some 43 per cent of the labour force. Industrial production in the United States and Germany had been cut in half since 1929.

The impact of the Depression on international structures and relations was enormous. With the adoption of new and higher tariffs, the widespread abandonment of the international gold standard, and the failure of the World Economic Conference of 1933, the old international economy gave way to new systems of economic nationalism and isolationism. The world's international trade fell to one-third of what it had been in 1929. Furthermore, inter-governmental payments, notably reparations and inter-Allied war debts, ceased to be made. In 1932, at the Lausanne Conference, the European powers agreed to cancel reparations payments on condition that the United States also agreed to cancel the Allied war debts owing to it. This the United States refused to do, but the European countries simply ceased paying.

More disturbing, in the long run, than the disruption of the international economy, was the strident nationalism and the militancy that the Depression encouraged in certain countries. In Germany the Depression was an indispensable factor in making possible the rise to power of Hitler and the Nazis. Similarly in Japan, the Depression played a major role in discrediting the liberal groups which had controlled the Government in the 1920s, and in making possible the dominance of the military — developments which resulted in the adoption and execution of an aggressive policy towards China. In September 1931, Japanese troops began the occupation of the Chinese province of Manchuria, and in March of the next year Japan proclaimed it an independent state with the name of Manchukuo; the new state was in fact governed by Japanese 'advisers'. (See Chapter 5.)

In many other countries, including the leading democratic countries, the Depression encouraged a retreat from international involvements and a concentration on domestic economic and social problems. These countries wished to avoid embroilment in foreign adventures, and they certainly had no desire to channel valuable resources into the armaments that such embroilment might require. Indeed, in 1934 the British Treasury questioned the very capacity of Britain's economy to sustain a substantial arms programme.

The Depression, in short, not only helped turn some countries into the paths of aggression, but it also helped to discourage others from resisting forms of aggression that posed no immediate threat to themselves. No effective international action was to be taken against Japan in response to its invasion and occupation of Manchuria.

Question

How did the absence of major powers from the League of Nations, for either all or part of its life, greatly weaken the world body?

Germany 1919–1933

We will look first of all at developments in Germany during this period, and then see how Hitler took advantage of conditions in the country to rise to power.

THE WEAKNESS OF THE WEIMAR GOVERNMENT

Towards the end of the war there was a revolution in Germany. A few days before the Armistice was signed the Kaiser abdicated. Thus the new republican Government had to sign the Armistice. In 1919 the so-called Weimar* Constitution was adopted, and Germany became known as the Weimar Republic. The Weimar Government was beset by so many problems and adverse circumstances that it stood very little chance of survival. Democracy could not have been launched in Germany under more adverse circumstances. The chief weaknesses and problems of the Weimar Government will be considered under the following headings: lack of a democratic tradition; the consequences of the Versailles Treaty; staggering economic problems; and national apathy.

Question

Give possible reasons for Germany's change of name to the 'Weimar Republic', and the transfer of the capital from Berlin to Weimar.

Lack of a democratic tradition

Up until 1919 the German Government had been an autocratic system, with an ineffectual elected Parliament. Thus the Weimar leaders were inexperienced in the workings of a true

97

democracy. From 1919 onwards the republic suffered from a multiplicity of political parties. At no time up to 1933 was any one political party able to dominate the Reichstag — there were always coalition governments, with the Social Democrats being the biggest party.

The other main parties were the right-wing German Nationalist People's party, representing big business, and the Catholic Centre party, both of which formed part of most coalitions. The number of political parties tended to increase, an indication of growing dissent among the people, until by July 1932 there were twenty-four parties.

One of the factors leading to the emergence of so many political parties was the system of proportional representation adopted by the Weimar Republic. By this system, a party gaining, say, 7 per cent of the votes in an election, was entitled to 7 per cent of the seats in the Reichstag. The idealistic theory behind this system was that each political group, no matter how small, should have an opportunity to have its voice heard. In practice, however, it made it virtually impossible for one political party to gain a majority in the Reichstag. The only way a government could be formed was by a coalition of parties. A coalition government is almost invariably a weak government. Being made up of people of differing political opinions, it soon breaks up when different parties emphasise different policies. Germany was thus noted, during this period, for political instability and frequent elections. Governments were usually intent primarily on political survival, and there was little long-term planning as a result.

The Versailles Treaty

As we have seen, Germany was not only defeated in war, but also humiliated in peace. The treaty imposed very harsh terms on Germany.

The Weimar Government was not consulted about these harsh conditions. It was forced to sign the treaty under threat of a continuation of the war — it therefore had no alternative but to sign. However, the Government gained an unfortunate stigma from having signed this humiliating treaty and from having signed the Armistice in 1918.

This led to the false, but widely held belief that the Government had 'stabbed the army in the back' — they were looked upon by many as collaborators with Germany's enemies after the war, as they had to squeeze the country in order to pay reparations. They were thus placed in an impossible position right from the start.

Staggering economic problems

A stable and established government would have battled to solve the economic problems that emerged; for the weak and disunited Weimar Government it was impossible. German industry was crippled by the war and by post-war strikes. Trade was crippled by the war and by the punitive peace terms. There was widespread unemployment and discontent. The Government was hardly in a position to even attempt post-war reconstruction until the mid-twenties.

National apathy

There was a national feeling of apathy, bitterness and disillusionment, coupled with tremendous hardship. This was hardly the climate for a new, idealistic form of government to take root and flourish. More than ever before many Germans wanted strong leadership to shape their destiny.

SOME SPECIFIC PROBLEMS UP TO 1923

Spartacist Revolt, January 1919

This was an attempt to stir up Communist revolution by the Spartacists*. In January 1919 they attempted to seize Berlin. The Government called upon the conservative-dominated army to re-establish control. Peace was restored by General von Lüttwitz. Much uncontrolled violence was directed against the Communists. The Communist leaders, Karl Liebknecht and Rosa Luxemburg, were beaten to death by a mob. Thus the Government survived this attempted coup from the left.

Kapp Putsch, March 1920

The *Kapp Putsch** was an attempted right wing coup led by Wolfgang Kapp and von Lüttwitz. They held Berlin for a few days before the attempt fizzled out and an uneasy peace was restored. The weakness and uncertainty of the Government was revealed by the fact that the putsch leaders were not punished, for fear of offending right wing nationalist elements in the country.

French occupation of the Ruhr

As a result of the above circumstances, Germany fell behind in its reparations payments to France. In January 1923 French troops invaded and occupied the Ruhr industrial region — the industrial heart of Germany. The Government was not able to do anything about this further humiliation. If Germany had resisted, the result might have been war once again. Germany was now cut off from four-fifths of its coal and steel production capacity. This strangulation of the economy contributed to the devaluation of the currency.

French soldiers in the Ruhr (1923).

In 1921 four Marks could buy one dollar; later in 1921 the rate of exchange fell to 75 Marks to the dollar; in 1922 to 400 to the dollar. By August 1923 it took one million Marks to buy a dollar. German currency was worthless. Life savings were wiped out, unemployment intensified and discontent increased. The blame for the French occupation and for the economic crisis fell on the Government, which was led by the Social Democrats. The Government fell, and Gustav Stresemann of the German Nationalist People's party became Chancellor. This party represented conservative political policies and the interests of big business.

Here are the texts of some documents relating to the French occupation of the Ruhr:

An eye-witness account of the occupation of Essen

Essen, January 11th [1923], 4.15 p.m.

Essen was occupied this afternoon by two divisions of French troops... At twenty minutes to two, the main body of the French forces came down the hill to the railway station and chief post office. At the head rode a party of cyclists in dark blue uniform and steel helmets closely followed by five parti-coloured armoured cars. From these grim-looking cars, of which the occupants were invisible, stood out the muzzles of the machine guns, a silent threat to the sullen crowd.

Despite the machine guns, the swords, and slung rifles of the horizon blue cavalry, who came cantering down the street behind the armoured cars, there were angry murmurs from the crowd — many took no trouble to hide the hatred in their hearts. No one thought of his neighbour. Everyone's face was set in the effort to preserve his control or had already lost it in some cry of grief or pain....

The French troops behaved with absolute correctness — there was no hectoring and no jesting. As on a ceremonial parade, these men passed silently through the equally silent lanes of human beings ... The silence was remarkable. Only the clattering of horses' hooves over the cobbles broke it ...

(*The Times*, London, 12 January, 1923.)

The British Ambassador's comment

BERLIN, January 21, 1923 — The French, by their invasion of the Ruhr, and by their imprisonment of mine directors, have done more to bring together all parties and all classes in Germany than it was possible to effect by any other means. The mine-owners and mine-directors who have been imprisoned are becoming national heroes. They do not deserve to be, for the policy they have followed has been certainly selfish and probably short-sighted. They have ruined large classes of their countrymen by their inflation policy, and without doing much good to themselves; but they have achieved the object nearest their heart, which was to avoid the payment of reparations to France. For the moment all class hostility of the workmen against the owners has been submerged by the patriotic wave. The whole country appears to be united.

(Reprinted by permission of the Executors of the late Viscount D'Abernon and of the publishers from *An Ambassador of Peace*, by Viscount D'Abernon, Vol. II, Hodder & Stoughton, p. 159.)

Proclamation by the German Government, September 26, 1923.

... The Ruhr territory and the Rhineland have suffered under heavy oppression. Over 180 000 German men and women, old people and children, have been evicted from house and home. Millions of Germans no longer know what personal freedom is. Countless acts of violence have accompanied the occupation, more than 100 compatriots have lost their lives, hundreds are languishing in prison. A spirit of justice and of patriotism rose up against the illegality of the invasion. The population refused to work under foreign bayonets....

The Reich Government undertook to do its utmost for the suffering compatriots. The means at the disposal of the Reich have been enlisted, to an ever increasing extent, for this purpose. During the past week support for the Rhineland and the Ruhr cost 3 500 billion Mark, in the current week it is expected that this sum will be at least doubled. The former production of the Rhineland and the Ruhr has ceased.

Economic life in occupied and unoccupied Germany is disrupted. The continuation of the present procedure entails the terribly serious danger that the establishment of a regulated currency, the maintenance of economic life and therewith the assurance of a bare existence for our people will be made impossible.

In the interest of Germany's future, and equally in the interest of the Rhineland and the Ruhr, this danger must be obviated. In order to safeguard the existence of people and State we are today faced by the bitter necessity of breaking off the struggle....

(Translated from J. & K. Hohlfeld (eds.), *Dokumente der Deutschen Politik und Geschichte*, Vol. 3, p. 131.)

Question

From the evidence given in these documents, was the French occupation of the Ruhr likely to advance France's aim — namely to force Germany to fulfil its reparations obligations to France? Back up your answer with evidence from the extracts.

AN IMPROVEMENT IN CONDITIONS, 1924–29

Stresemann aimed at economic recovery, reconciliation with France and the rest of Europe, a more satisfactory agreement over reparations, and German admission to the League of Nations. (Germany had not been admitted to the League in 1919 and was thus treated as an outcast among the nations.) He met with some success and improved conditions in Germany and also improved Germany's image in the world. His chief measures were as follows: He ended the strikes among the Ruhr workers who were protesting against the French occupation. At the same time he helped to stabilize the economy by raising loans from the USA in September 1923.

The Dawes Plan on reparations, August 1924

Stresemann requested those who had drawn up the Versailles Treaty to reconsider the annual payments of reparations required from Germany, as the amounts were crippling for Germany. An allied committee (under the chairmanship of an American, Dawes) examined the German economy to assess what Germany could reasonably be expected to pay. As a result, the annual payment was fixed at a more reasonable amount.

French occupation of the Ruhr ended, November 1924

As the result of the above agreement on reparations, Stresemann negotiated the removal of French troops from the Ruhr. This helped to increase his prestige in Germany.

The Locarno agreement, 1925

This was an attempt by Germany to reduce European suspicion of Germany's aggressive intentions in Europe. In the west France, Germany and Belgium agreed to respect one another's frontiers. Britain and Italy agreed to guarantee this agreement. In the east Germany agreed, reluctantly, not to alter by force the frontiers of Poland and Czechoslovakia. France, but not Britain, guaranteed these countries against aggression from Germany.

Here are the terms of the Locarno pact:

Article 1. The high contracting parties collectively and severally guarantee, in the manner provided in the following articles, the maintenance of the territorial status

101

quo resulting from the frontiers between Germany and Belgium and between Germany and France and the inviolability of the said frontiers as fixed by or in pursuance of the Treaty of Peace signed at Versailles on the 28th June, 1919, and also the observance of the stipulations of Articles 42 and 43 of the said treaty concerning the demilitarised zone.

Article 2. Germany and Belgium, and also Germany and France, mutually undertake that they will in no case attack or invade each other or resort to war against each other.

This stipulation shall not, however, apply in the case of—
1. The exercise of the right of legitimate defence . . .
2. Action in pursuance of Article 16 of the Covenant of the League of Nations.
3. Action as the result of a decision taken by the Assembly or by the Council of the League of Nations or in pursuance of Article 15, paragraph 7, of the Covenant of the League of Nations, provided that in this last event the action is directed against a State which was the first to attack.

Article 3. In view of the undertakings entered into in Article 2 of the present treaty, Germany and Belgium and Germany and France undertake to settle by peaceful means and in the manner laid down herein all questions of every kind which may arise between them and which it may not be possible to settle by the normal methods of diplomacy:

Any question with regard to which the parties are in conflict as to their respective rights shall be submitted to judicial decision, and the parties undertake to comply with such decision.

All other questions shall be submitted to a conciliation commission. If the proposals of this commission are not accepted by the two parties, the question shall be brought before the Council of the League of Nations, which will deal with it in accordance with Article 15 of the Covenant of the League . . .

Article 10. The present treaty shall be ratified and the ratifications shall be deposited at Geneva in the archives of the League of Nations as soon as possible.

It shall enter into force as soon as all the ratifications have been deposited and Germany has become a member of the League of Nations . . .

Done at Locarno, the 16th October, 1925.
GUSTAV STRESEMANN
EMILE VAN DER VELDE
A. BRIAND
AUSTEN CHAMBERLAIN
BENITO MUSSOLINI

Great Britain, *Parliamentary Papers*, Vol. XXX, Cmd. 2764. 1926
(Quoted in Sheffe and Fisher, pp. 143–4.)

Question

Was the Locarno pact likely to reduce French and Belgian hostility towards Germany? Give reasons for your answer.

Germany joins the League of Nations, 1926

As a result of a reduction of suspicion, Germany was admitted as a member of the League, and was therefore no longer an outcast among the European and world community.

The Young Plan, 1929

Reparations were still too heavy for the German economy. A new committee (once again under the chairmanship of an American, Young) further reduced reparations. Combined with the agreement was a further large loan, from the USA. Arrangements were made at the same time for the final evacuation of the Allied troops of occupation in the Rhineland, who were to be removed by June 1930.

1929 — THE BEGINNING OF CRISIS

The death of Stresemann (1929)

He was the only really able statesman to emerge under the Weimar Republic. His death left a power vacuum in Germany. Brüning (of the Catholic Centre party) replaced him as Chancellor. He had no majority in the Reichstag, and ruled by emergency decrees in the interests of the aristocracy, army leaders and industrialists.

The Depression

As a result of the crash of Wall Street (the American stock exchange) in 1929, loans from the USA to Germany dried up. This led to a desperate economic crisis in Germany. Trade began to sag, factories closed down and unemployment resulted. In May 1931 the *Kreditanstalt*, Austria's largest bank, collapsed. The Mark was worthless, farmers could not sell their produce, and starvation stalked the land. Germany probably suffered more from the Depression than any other Western country.

The following descriptions give some idea of the effects of the Depression in parts of Germany, and the reaction of people to unemployment and poverty:

The situation in the Ruhr, March, 1932

The stillness that broods over the district appears to be most pronounced at Duisberg-Ruhrort, its natural gateway to the west and the largest river harbour in the world... One may look at docks and channels that have become choked with idle tugs and empty coal-barges, or trace another cemetery for laid-up shipping far along the right bank of the river...

In the foreground stand the smokeless chimneystacks of the Meiderich steelyard, a gaunt array of sleeping sentinels; beneath them the cooled-off furnaces, beyond them a silent acreage of desolate workshops and railway-sidings. It is one of the largest establishments in the Ruhr, from which 6,000 men were paid off when the decision was taken to stop work indefinitely...

Such are the more obvious manifestations of a depression without parallel, the tale of which is revealed in steadily decreasing production and sales and steadily increasing dismissals and unemployment. The output of steel ingots has recently been less than a quarter of what it was two or three years ago... In 1929 the average monthly production of coal was 10,300,000 tons; in the midwinter, and therefore normally good, month of January the output was 8,590,000 tons in 1931 and 6,100,000 tons in 1932. The Ruhr coal industry employed 383,000 men in 1929... It now employs 220,000 each of whom lost on the average 4.32 shifts through short-time working this January. Essen, the capital of the Ruhr, has 80,000 unemployed in a population of 629,000, which means that more than 200,000 men,

103

women, and children are living on relief of one form or another. These figures are typical of the industrial area, with its total population of 4,230,000. At exposed places like Duisburg and Dortmund the proportion of unemployed is a little higher....

Yet the unemployed... do not beg; they do not demonstrate; they do not hang about the streets; they are cleanly and decently clothed. The explanation is that relief is still adequate for the maintenance of orderly German habits, and that everything is being done through theatrical performances, concerts and training courses to keep the younger men, especially, off the streets....

Communism, so far as I could judge, is not the dangerous and disciplined force which the votes of the despairing and the disgruntled sometimes make it appear. The Communist attempts to provoke a general strike early in January were a fiasco.... Keen interest is shown in the defence of the Republic, and all that it implies, against the Nazis and their allies of the Harzburg Front, though in the Ruhr itself the Nazis have not made much progress among the workers...

It seems a fair conclusion to say that the situation in the Ruhr can be kept under control as long as unemployment relief is paid regularly and there continues to be some hope of an eventual world recovery.

(Reprinted by permission from *The Times*, London, 21 March, 1932.)

The situation in western Germany, May, 1932

There has been a recrudescence of violence on the part of the unemployed in Düsseldorf, Cologne, Dortmund, Solingen, Aachen and Wiesbaden during the past few days. Although all public demonstrations have been prohibited by the police, groups of several hundred people organized by the Communist Party have been demonstrating simultaneously, singing the International. On attempting to disperse the demonstrators the police were bombarded with stones and bottles, and in some cases fired at from among the crowd. Several police were injured and many demonstrators arrested, including two women at Dortmund.

(Reprinted by permission from *The Times*, London, 28 May, 1932.)

Question

Both these reports come from the same source, The Times of London, yet they differ in the description of the reactions of the workless to their condition. How do the accounts differ? Think of possible reasons for these differences.

THE RISE TO POWER OF ADOLF HITLER

Before....

The first glimpse we have of Adolf Hitler as a young man gives no hint that one day his name was to be either revered or feared throughout Europe. The future master of Germany was an Austrian of humble birth. His school career was unpromising — in fact he left school early and drifted to Vienna. He certainly did not make his mark in that great city. He described his condition in Vienna thus:

104

The following extract gives an idea of the sort of life he lived between 1909 and 1913 in Vienna:

Hunger was then my faithful bodyguard; he never left me for a moment and partook of all I had ... My life was a continual struggle with this pitiless friend.

(Quoted in Shirer, p. 18.)

On one level he lived the life of a tramp ... he lived in a series of furnished rooms, each dingier than the last. Soon Hitler was reduced to sleeping on park benches and in doorways. In October, when the weather turned cold, he moved to bars, coffee houses, or dismal flophouses. Vienna, the City of Dreams, had become a nightmare of misery and filth.

(Steeh, p. 14.)

He spent some time in a charitable institution for the down-and-outs. Here is how he and a companion made a living:

... they would sometimes pick up a little money doing odd jobs — shovelling snow, carrying baggage at the Westbahnhof, or beating carpets. Hitler even tried begging but turned out to have little talent for it.

(Steeh, p. 16.)

...And After

In January 1933 Adolf Hitler became Chancellor of Germany. Between then and August 1934 he took various steps to make himself absolute master of Germany; at the end of February 1933 he used the SA* and the SS* to destroy all his political opponents. Offices of rival parties were smashed, buildings of critical newspapers were burned down. Hundreds of political opponents were shot, thousands more were thrown into concentration camps. In March 1933 he forced the German Parliament to virtually vote itself out of existence and to give him the power to make all laws without its approval. In July 1933 a law was issued making the Nazi party the only party which could legally operate in Germany. In June 1934, during the 'Night of the Long Knives', Hitler eliminated his opponents within the Nazi party. In August 1934 von Hindenburg, the President of Germany, died. Hitler proclaimed himself to be Chancellor and President, or Führer (leader) of the German people.

No German ruler before or since has wielded such absolute power. A considerable achievement for the one-time Austrian

Adolf Hitler

tramp! How was it possible for Hitler to rise from the gutters of Vienna to the dizzy heights he had reached by August 1934?

There are many factors which help to explain this 'rags to riches' story. Some of these were due to the circumstances of the times — others were due to Hitler's unique ability to take advantage of conditions and events.

We will look at some of the major stepping-stones in Hitler's rise to power.

Conditions of despair

The post-war period was one of disillusionment for most Germans. This feeling plus economic hardship presented an opportunity to politicians who had extreme solutions to the country's problems.

Then, in 1923, the French occupation of the Ruhr turned economic hardship into economic disaster. This extract brings out the effects on ordinary people of rampant inflation.

They all stood outside the pay windows, staring impatiently at the clock, slowly advancing until at last they reached the window and received a bag full of paper notes. According to the figures inscribed on them, the paper notes amounted to 7000,000 or 500 million or 380 billion or 18 trillion marks — the figures rose from month to month, then week to week, finally from day to day. With their bags, the people moved quickly forwards to the doors, all in haste, the younger ones running. They dashed to the nearest food store, where a queue has already formed. Again they move slowly, oh how slowly, forward. When you reached the store,

a pound of sugar might have been obtainable for two millions; but by the time you got there, all you could get for two millions was half a pound ... With the billions you bought sardines, sausages, sugar, perhaps a little butter ... always things that would keep for a week, until the next pay-day, until the next stage in the fall of the mark.

(Conrad Heiden, *Der Führer*)

	Marks to the dollar
July 1914	4
Jan. 1919	9
Jan. 1922	192
July 1922	493
Jan. 1923	17 972
July 1923	353 412
Sept. 1923	4 620 455
Oct. 1923	25 260 000 000
Nov. 1923	4 200 000 000 000

Questions

(a) Study the extract. In the latter part of 1923 in Germany food prices rose daily as the value of money became less. What happened to people if wages did not rise as rapidly as food prices?

(b) If a German had 900 000 Marks saved in January 1919 (worth 10000 US dollars) he would have expected to have financial security for the rest of his life. By November 1923 what were these savings worth? What had happened to his security? Would he have faith in a Government which allowed this to happen? Explain your answer.

Origins of the Nazi party

Against this background of economic failure and national apathy, it is not surprising that many Germans were very discontented with things as they were and had little faith in a Government which seemed incapable of improving conditions. A number of political movements sprang up, each promising solutions to the problems of the day. The Nazi party was one of these.

The Nazi party came into existence in 1919 in the city of Munich, which is in the south German state of Bavaria. Hitler became the seventh member of this tiny party, and very soon he had risen to be its leader. The full name of the party was the 'National Socialist German Workers' party'.

In February 1920 Hitler announced a 25-point programme for the party. This contained the political aims of the party. Some of the more important points were:

1. To unite all German-speakers in Europe into a Greater Germany (there were about eleven million German-speakers at the time in Europe who were not living in Germany);
2. To refuse to accept the harsh terms of the Treaty of Versailles;
3. To deny Jews the right to be citizens of Germany, and to expel all Jews who had come to Germany after 2 August, 1914;
4. To create a strong central Government in Germany.

In the early 1920s there were a number of nationalist and socialist parties competing for the support of the discontented. The Nazis gradually began to make headway against some of these parties in Bavaria (but not elsewhere in Germany at this stage). What accounts for the success of the Nazis? Two important factors were the use of violence and the appeal to the spectacular.

The use of violence as a political weapon

Some of the early political meetings held by the small Nazi party were broken up by thugs from other parties. Hitler came to the conclusion that, if violence was to be used in politics, then the Nazis must use it better than anyone else.

Thus in 1920 the SA came into existence. Many of the recruits to this private army were unemployed ex-soldiers. Their job was to protect party meetings and to forcibly disrupt those of opponents.

These uniformed rowdies, not content to keep order at Nazi meetings, soon took to breaking up those of other parties. Once in 1921 Hitler personally led his storm troopers in an attack on a meeting which was to be addressed by a Bavarian federalist by the name of Ballerstedt, who received a beating.

(Quoted in Shirer, p. 43.)

For this act Hitler spent one month in prison. When he came out of prison Hitler boasted:

We got what we wanted. Ballerstedt did not speak.

(Quoted in Shirer, p. 43.)

Later, Hitler commented on the role of the SA:

Like a swarm of locusts they swooped down on the disturbers of our meetings, without regard for their superior power ... without regard for wounds and bloody victims ...

(Quoted in Bruce, p. 32.)

107

Hitler expressed his scorn for free speech thus:

The National Socialist Movement will in future ruthlessly prevent — if necessary by force — all meetings or lectures that are likely to distract the minds of our fellow countrymen.

(Quoted in Shirer, p. 43.)

Questions

What reasons does Hitler give in the above extracts to justify the use of violence as a political weapon?

Why do you think that Hitler was particularly keen to persuade ex-soldiers to join the SA?

The SA wore a brown uniform and military-style caps. They drilled as soldiers would, and when they marched in party parades through the streets, many onlookers were impressed by their apparent order and discipline.

Appeal to the spectacular

Hitler believed that most of the population were fairly simple-minded people who were easily impressed by the outward trappings. What the party needed was a symbol which was impressive and which could not be confused with anything else. Hitler was the primary influence in the design of the new national flag, which incorporated the swastika, an ancient Germanic rune*.

The flag

The colour red symbolized the social aims of the party, which were to improve conditions for the poor people; the white circle represented the nationalistic aim to make Germany great again; the black hooked cross (swastika) was a symbol representing Hitler's belief in the racial superiority of the German people.

Later large standards, reminiscent of those of ancient Rome, and also incorporating the swastika, were used at Nazi meetings and parades.

This may not have been 'art', but it was propaganda of the highest order. The Nazis now had a symbol which no other party could match. The hooked cross seemed to possess some mystic power of its own, to beckon to action in a new direction the insecure lower middle classes which had been floundering in the uncertainty of the first chronic postwar years. They began to flock under its banner.

(Shirer, p. 44.)

Up to 1923 the Nazis remained a local Bavarian party, little known outside that south German state. How did the Nazi party become known throughout the nation? Strangely enough, this followed a disastrous mistake by Hitler in 1923. Out of this disaster came triumph.

The Munich Brauhaus Putsch

In 1923 Hitler began to realise that the only way to overthrow the Government of Germany was by force. His plan was first of all to seize control of the Government of the state of Bavaria in Munich, and then later to march on Berlin to wrest power from the national Government.

However, Hitler grossly overestimated the support which he would receive, and the *Brauhaus Putsch** in Munich was a dismal failure. Hitler and his leading henchmen were arrested and put on trial for treason. It looked as though Hitler had led his party to disaster and extinction.

However, his trial for treason made his name known throughout Germany. His personality dominated the courtroom and what he said was reported in newspapers throughout the country. He pleaded guilty to trying to overthrow the government, and explained why this was not a crime:

> *I alone bear the responsibility. But I am not a criminal because of that. If today I stand here as a revolutionary, it is as a revolutionary against the revolution. There is no such thing as high treason against the traitors of 1918.*

Hitler believed that, despite the failure of the putsch, it was his destiny to become ruler of Germany.

A Nazi party rally.

(Courtesy of the BBC Hulton Picture Library.)

Question

The Nazis gave an impression of strength and efficiency. Why do you think that many people would be impressed by this in the early 1920s?

109

SA troops in Munich, 1923.
(Courtesy of the Institute of Contemporary History and the Wiener Library, Ltd.)

The man who is born to be a dictator is not compelled. He wills it. He is not driven forward, but drives himself. There is nothing immodest about this. Is it immodest for a worker to drive himself towards heavy labour? It is presumptuous of a man with the high forehead of a thinker to ponder through the nights till he gives the world an invention? The man who feels called upon to govern a people has no right to say, 'If you want me or summon me, I will co-operate.' No! It is his duty to step forward.

He believed, too, that the numbers of his followers would increase to the point where he would be able to resurrect Germany's pride:

The army we have formed is growing from day to day ... I nourish the proud hope that one day the hour will come when these rough companies will grow to battalions, the battalions to regiments, the regiments to divisions, that the old cockade will be taken from the mud, that the old flags will wave again, that there will be a reconciliation at the last great divine judgement which we are prepared to face.

He expressed his contempt for his judges thus:

For it is not you, gentlemen, who pass judgement on us. That judgement is spoken by the eternal court of history. You may pronounce us guilty a thousand times over, but the goddess of the eternal court of history will smile and tear to tatters the brief of the State prosecutor and the sentence of this court. For she acquits us.

(Extracts quoted in Shirer, pp. 75 to 78.)

Hitler dominated the court proceedings to such an extent that it was clear that most of those present, including the judges, were sympathetic to his cause. In the end he received the lightest possible sentence for treason — five years imprisonment. He served only nine months of this sentence before being released.

This trial gave Hitler excellent free publicity. Many Germans who read in newspapers what he had said in court found themselves agreeing with his nationalistic ideas. The Nazis were no longer just a local party, but had become a national party.

While in prison Hitler wrote a book, *Mein Kampf* (*My Struggle*), in which he described his political ideas and his plans for the future of Germany and of Europe.

Question

Read the above extracts. In your own words give the reasons put forward by Hitler for the 1923 putsch.

The period 1925 to 1929

During this period the Nazi party did not gain massive support, despite great efforts to increase membership. The reason for this was that prosperity had returned to Germany. Far fewer people were unemployed and desperate. Under such conditions not many people gave their support to extremist parties such as the Nazis. They preferred more 'respectable' democratic parties.

Hitler did not waste this period. He perfected the party organization and made sure that there were party offices and organizers throughout Germany, even in places where they did not as yet have much support. Hitler was an optimist — he believed that in time economic conditions would get worse!

A measure of the Nazi lack of impact on the public at this time was the Reichstag (Parliament) election of 1928. The Nazis put everything into their campaign to win votes. Meetings and rallies were held throughout Germany and an intensive propaganda campaign was unleashed. When the votes were counted, very little had been achieved. The Nazis only got 810 000 votes out of more than 31 million. This gave them 12 deputies in the Reichstag, which had 491 members. It seemed that the Nazi party was destined to remain a noisy but small party on the lunatic fringe.

The Great Depression

In October 1929 the economy of the USA collapsed. The prosperity of Germany had been largely based on loans from the USA, and very soon the effects of the Wall Street stockmarket crash were felt. Within a short time the country was plunged into despair. Industries ground to a halt, trade virtually ceased, and unemployment figures rose daily.

Unemployment Figures

Year	
1929	1 320 000
1930	3 000 000
1932	5 100 000

Question

Explain why most people are likely to support moderate parties during periods of prosperity, rather than extremists who wish to introduce many changes; and why the opposite often applies in periods of hardship and depression.

Hitler's earlier optimism had been justified. In this sea of human discontent he would certainly catch many fish!

In the ... cut-throat struggle for employment, the inexperienced inevitably lost — and the hatred of the disinherited swelled monstrously — hatred against a social system that had no place for the young. With sixty percent of each new university graduating class out of work, with over half of all Germans between the ages of sixteen and thirty unemployed, young Germany was an easy victim for the patriotic demagogue.

(Edgar Mowrer 'Germany Puts the Clock Back' — quoted in *History of the 20th Century*, No. 45, p.1256.)

The hopeless, workless, restless youths who haunted the streets of Germany turned to this new party [the Nazi party] which offered opportunities for drill and hooliganism, blamed their misery on Jews, Communists, and the Allies, and promised in grandiose speeches glory and prosperity to them as the master race.

(*History of the 20th Century*, No. 48, p.1333.)

111

of the nineteenth-century racialists such as Gobineau and Houston Chamberlain and maintained that history was nothing more than a biological struggle for existence between inferior and superior races. According to them, the one civilising influence throughout world history had been the Aryan race, of which the Germans represented the purest strain; in the present century it was the German racial mission to strengthen the position of the Teutonic people of Europe and to rule over inferior races in the east — a dynamic concept which had radical implications for German foreign policy as will be seen later. Intimately bound up with these racial fantasies was the phenomenon of anti-Semitism. Hitler's hatred of the Jew was pathological*. Jews were not simply members of an inferior race to be despised by pure Aryans; in his eyes they were a 'counter-race' whose aim was the deliberate destruction of the Aryan race by blood-pollution. Jews symbolised all that was evil in Hitler's world; they stabbed Germany in the back in 1918, they were the driving force behind Marxism and monopoly capitalism, they represented a cancerous growth in the racial body which must be destroyed without pity when the time was ripe for a 'final solution' of the Jewish problem. Superb tactician that he was, Hitler must also have realised — even if it was a secondary consideration — that anti-Semitism would be popular in Germany up to a point; middle-class people suffering economic hardship were likely to approve of measures against Jews, who were strongly entrenched in the world of finance and commerce.

Attacks on Jews began as soon as the Nazis were in power, although Hitler moved with some caution at first. Most Jewish officials were soon dismissed, a general boycott of Jewish shops started in April 1933 and in May books by Jewish writers were burnt by members of the NS Studentenbund in Berlin's Opernplatz with the enthusiastic approval of Goebbels. From the early spring of 1933 the Nazi propaganda machine swung into action

The Government of Germany, which since 1919 had been weak at the best of times, found itself incapable of solving the massive problems resulting from the Depression. More and more people became convinced that the existing democratic parties would never be able to restore prosperity. They began to pin their hopes elsewhere.

In Germany, coming on top of the war, defeat and inflation, this last in a seemingly never-ending series of disaster was the last straw. The mood of the German people turned to one of utter discouragement and hopelessness, which was punctuated by periods of wild hope and longing for something completely different.

Hitler was determined that the 'something completely different' which the majority would choose would be Nazism. They would, however, have to be persuaded to do so.

The persecution of the Jews

One of the Five Points of the Nazi programme announced by Hitler in 1920, stated:

> None but members of the nation may be citizens of the State. None but those of German blood may be members of the nation. No Jew, therefore, may be a member of the nation.

Read what the historian W. Carr has to say about Nazi anti-Semitism:

> The xenophobic* nationalism of the Nazi movement was sustained by a fanatical belief in the alleged superiority of the Aryan race. Marx had taught that all history was the history of class struggle; the Nazis revived the arguments

against the Jews, denouncing them openly as 'racial enemies' and flooding the country with the most virulent anti-Semitic propaganda dressed up in pseudo-Scientific language. Persecution of the Jews reached a new stage with the passage of the so-called 'Nuremberg laws' promulgated at the Nazi party congress of 1935; Jews were deprived of full citizenship.

(W. Carr, *A History of Germany 1815–1945*, pp. 180–181.)

Questions

1. How is anti-Semitism in Germany in the period 1920–1934 to be explained? List the long-term and the short-term explanations. Try to place these various explanations in order of priority.

2. How did the Nazis make use of this anti-Semitism to strengthen their own position? What were the consequences of these policies?

The use of propaganda

Hitler became a master of the art of political propaganda. The Great Depression produced millions of bitter people willing to give their support to extremist politicians. It was no accident that so many gave their support to the Nazis between 1930 and 1932. Hitler's great skill as a propagandist had a lot to do with it. As he explained it, the message must be simple and direct:

The receptive power of the masses are very restricted, and their understanding is feeble. On the other hand, they quickly forget. Such being the case, all effective propaganda must be confined to a few bare essentials . . . slogans should be persistently repeated until the very last individual has come to grasp the idea which has been put forward.

(Phillips, p. 28.)

One of Hitler's greatest assets as a politician was his ability as a public speaker and the dramatic effect which he had on an audience, as the following extracts show.

A member of the audience described the emotional atmosphere at a rally attended by 60 000 people:

Every device of music and coloured lights was used to keep the atmosphere tense and the spotlight that played on the giant swastika behind the banners exerted an influence that was almost hypnotic.

The speakers deliberately played on the feelings of the people. At intervals, when something particularly impressive was read out, a curious tremor swept the crowd, and all around me individuals uttered a strange cry, a kind of emotional sigh that invariably changed into a shout of 'Heil Hitler!' It was a definite struggle to remain rational in a horde so surcharged with tense emotionalism.

(Phillips, p. 30.)

Otto Strasser, one of Hitler's followers, commented on Hitler's ability as a speaker:

Adolf Hitler enters a hall. He sniffs the air. For a minute he gropes, feels his way, senses the atmosphere. Suddenly he bursts forth. His words go like an arrow to their target, he touches each private wound on the raw, liberating the mass unconscious, expressing its innermost aspirations, telling it what it most wants to hear.

(Phillips, p. 30.)

113

For the Reichstag elections of 1930 and 1932 the Nazi party used 'saturation' propaganda. Even if he wanted to, the average German could not get away from the Nazi message. As he walked down the street there would be a poster on every lamppost and wall; if he looked upwards to avoid these, he would see a helium balloon with a Nazi catch-phrase stencilled on it; if he closed his eyes, he would hear the Nazi message blaring out from the loudspeaker of a broadcast van. As if this was not enough, he (and every other voter) would receive Nazi propaganda leaflets through the post, as well as a visit from a Nazi propagandist. Every now and then, by day, there would be street parades of marching SA divisions, bearing huge swastika flags and impressive banners, and there were torchlight parades by night. Our average citizen also had the option of attending political meetings or rallies — Nazi leaders addressed hundreds of these throughout Germany in the weeks before an election. After this bombardment, no voter could claim on election day that he did not know who the Nazis were or what solutions they promised to Germany's problems.

The Nazi party became easily the biggest party in July 1932, and, although they subsequently lost some support, they were still the largest party in November 1932.

After the failure of one Chancellor (Prime Minister) after another to form a suitable government, the President of Germany, von Hindenburg, finally asked Hitler to become Chancellor on 30 January 1933.

Question

From the tables on page 111 and on this page, draw graphs of the unemployment figures and the Nazi vote. Comment on the similarities between these two graphs and give as many reasons as you can for these similarities.

CONSOLIDATION OF POWER

Although Hitler was now Chancellor, he was not yet in a position to carry out his Nazi policies because: (a) the Nazi party did not have a majority of the members of the Reichstag; (b) there were opposition groups in the country — especially the large Communist party — which would object to having a dictator; (c) there were some ambitious men in the Nazi party who might threaten Hitler's leadership — especially Ernst Röhm, head of the SA.

Between February 1933 and August 1934 Hitler was to remove these obstacles.

Election success

The effects of the Depression, and the spectacular use the Nazi party made of the desperate conditions of the time, can be clearly seen in the following election figures for the Reichstag:

Election date	Nazi voters	Nazi seats in the Reichstag
1928 (before the Depression)	810 000	12
1930	6 371 000	107
1932 (July)	13 745 000	230
1932 (November)	11 750 000	196

A Nazi propaganda poster. It is titled: 'The Field Marshal and the Lance-Corporal'; and it says: 'Fight with us for peace and equal rights'.

(Courtesy of the Ullstein Bilderdienst.)

The Reichstag fire

Hitler arranged new elections for 5 March 1933. He hoped to stampede voters into supporting him by convincing them that only he could save Germany from a Communist revolution. He waited for the Communist party to make a move which would give him an excuse to crush it. The Communist leaders, realizing this, lay very low. Hitler grew impatient, and thus created an incident. On 27 February 1933, the Reichstag building was burnt down. A simple-minded Dutch Communist, van der Lubbe, was arrested on the spot and accused of the crime. It later became clear that Nazi agents, posing as Communists, had persuaded him to set the building alight in the interests of the Communist party. That night over 4000 people were arrested. These included not only Communists, but leaders of other parties as well. By the morning of 28 February, most organized opposition to Hitler had been smashed. Many Germans were convinced by Hitler that he had indeed saved them from Communist terror.

This is an extract from an official Government statement:

This act of incendiarism* is the most outrageous act yet committed by Bolshevism [Communism] in Germany. The burning of the Reichstag ... was to have been the signal for a bloody uprising and civil war.

The Enabling Act

Despite the fact that only the Nazi party could campaign freely for the elections on 5 March, and the fact that widespread intimidation of voters was used, the Nazis failed to achieve a majority in this election. Hitler now decided to do away with any pretence of democratic procedure. On 15 March 1933, the so-

115

Ernst Röhm

called Enabling Act was passed. What it did, quite simply, was to vote away the power of Parliament for 4 years and to give Hitler the right to make all laws. How was the Reichstag persuaded to virtually vote itself out of existence? Very easily — a two-thirds majority was needed for such an important change — Hitler had enough opposition deputies arrested so that when the vote was taken he had the necessary two-thirds support. He now had the dictatorial power which he wanted.

Question

Give two examples to show that Hitler was quite prepared to act illegally in order to get his own way.

The Night of the Long Knives

By 1934 Hitler had decided to get rid of the SA. This group, which had played such an important role in getting Hitler to power, was becoming an embarrassment. Their 'roughneck' reputation no longer suited the now 'respectable' Government leader, Hitler. There were two other reasons why Hitler decided to get rid of the SA: (1) He suspected that its leader, Ernst Röhm, was too ambitious, and that he was planning to use the SA to overthrow Hitler and take over the Government himself; (2) Hitler wished to build up the army. To do this he needed the support of the army leaders — who despised Röhm and the SA. They hinted that they would not help Hitler with his military plans until the SA had been disbanded. Thus Hitler decided on a blood purge.

The instrument he used was the SS (his by now greatly enlarged personal bodyguard) under Himmler. A carefully prepared secret plan went into operation on 30 June 1934.

SS divisions struck without warning. Ernst Röhm was dragged out of bed and later shot — 150 SA officers were executed by firing squad. Not only SA leaders were killed — others were murdered as 'enemies of the government', or because Hitler or one of his cronies had a grudge against them, or in some cases because they knew too much.

There is uncertainty as to how many died in this purge. In a Reichstag speech, Hitler admitted that sixty-one persons were shot, thirteen more died 'resisting arrest' and three 'committed suicide' — a total of seventy-seven. German refugees in Paris claimed that 401 had been shot. At a Munich trial in 1957, the figure of 'more than a thousand' was given.

Whatever the figure, one thing is certain — Hitler got across very clearly the message that he would tolerate not the slightest opposition, even from among his own supporters.

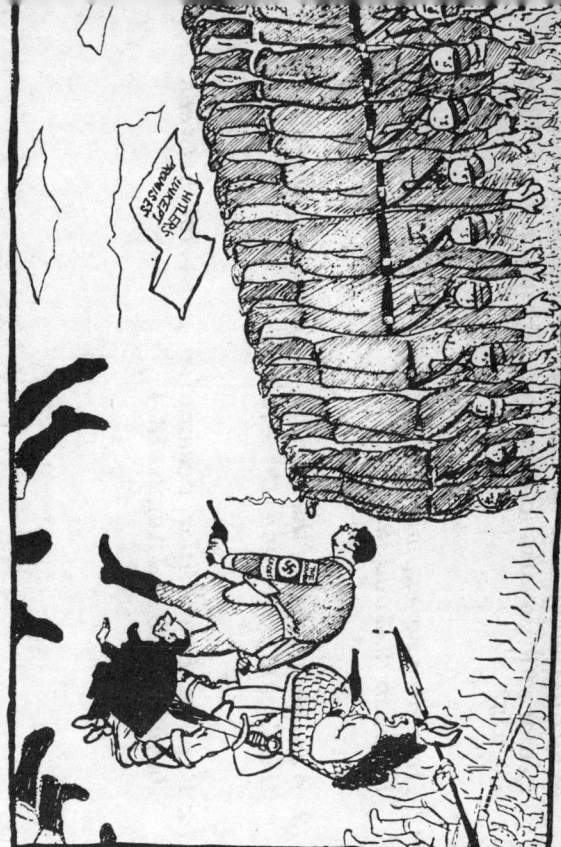

They salute with both hands now.

Hitler demonstrates his triumph over the SA after the Night of the Long Knives, 30 June 1934.

(After a cartoon which appeared in the *London Evening Standard*, 3 July 1934.)

The Death of von Hindenburg

Hitler was by now supreme master of Germany in everything but name. The aged President von Hindenburg was still, in name at least, Head of State. On 2 August 1934, von Hindenburg died. Hitler immediately announced that the offices of Chancellor and President were being combined — he was to be Head of State and President and Commander-in-Chief of the Armed Forces. The last act in the drama was complete. Adolf Hitler had absolute and almost undisputed power in Germany, with the title of Führer.

Revision Questions

1. In what way can the Treaty of Versailles be regarded as a declaration of intent to punish Germany, rather than a document which would prepare the way for future peace and stability?

2. Examine the failures of the League of Nations in the period 1920–1936 and decide to what extent the sovereign independence of the member states contributed to the League's lack of success as a peacekeeping force.

3. Each of the Big Three brought different attitudes to the negotiations at Versailles in 1919.
   (a) Describe the different attitudes expressed by the leaders of the USA, Britain and France.
   (b) Outline how the views of the leaders came to influence the final terms of the Treaty.

4. To what extent did national, strategic and economic interests prevent Wilson's ideals from becoming the guiding principles of the Peace Treaty of Versailles?

5. 'We were journeying to Paris in 1919 to establish a new order in Europe.' (Harold Nicolson) What were the main features of the 'new order' in Europe established by the peace settlements of 1919–1920?

117

6. How far did the League of Nations succeed in its roles of:
   (a) maintaining peace and security through collective action; and
   (b) providing a global system of world government during the period 1920–1933?

7. 'The Treaty of Versailles [1919] had to satisfy the French demand for security against Germany, the British demand for the punishment of Germany, and Wilson's commitment to a new world order.'
   How did the provisions of the Treaty of Versailles attempt to satisfy these demands?

8. 'Historians have emphasized that the League of Nations failed as an instrument of collective security because its members were not prepared to allow it to succeed.'
   Does an analysis of the international crisis which occurred in the period 1920–1933 support the above statement?

9. 'The provisions of the Treaty of Versailles represent a compromise between the victors rather than one between victors and vanquished.' Discuss.

10. Despite his alleged gifts of oratory and leadership, Adolf Hitler would appear to have been an obscure politician with a minority following in 1928. How and why did this circumstance change between 1928 and 1934?

11. Why did the Weimar Republic fail to establish a stable democratic government in Germany in the years 1919 to 1933?

12. How do you explain the growth of the Nazi party between 1923 and 1933?

13. Was the success of the Nazis in 1933 solely the result of the Great Depression (1929–1932)?

14. Explain how Hitler became so powerful between January 1933 and August 1934.

Chronology

1919   Paris Peace Conference
        Treaty of Versailles
        Spartacist Revolt in Germany
1920   Depression in Europe
        League of Nations
        Weimar Constitution in Germany
        Nazi party formed
        Kapp Putsch in Germany
1921   Reparations Commission Reports
1923   French occupation of the Ruhr valley (to 1924)
        The Munich Braühaus Putsch
1924   The Dawes Plan
1925   Treaty of Locarno
1926   Germany admitted to League
1929   Young Plan
        Depression
        Death of Stresemann
        Collapse of Wall Street
1931   Japanese occupy Manchuria
1933   Japan and Germany withdraw from League
        Reichstag fire
        Enabling Act
        Hitler becomes German Chancellor
1934   Russia admitted to League
        Night of the Long Knives in Germany
        Death of von Hindenburg
1937   Italy withdraws from League
1939   Russia expelled from League

Glossary

Balkanization — division of an area into small antagonistic states.

Bolshevik — the name of the Communist party that came to power in Russia in 1917.

Braühaus Putsch — so-called because it started in the *Burgerbraükeller*, a braühaus (beer-hall) in Munich.

Collective security — guarantees of concerted action by all other members; protection against unwarranted aggression towards a member state of an organization.

Incendiarism — the malicious setting on fire of property.

Kapp Putsch — Putsch is a German word meaning an attempt to overthrow a government by force. The Kapp Putsch was an attempt to overthrow the German Government, led by Wolfgang Kapp, one of the leaders of the extreme right wing *Vaterlandspartei* founded in 1917.

Pathological — resembling a disease.

Plebiscite — a general vote by the entire population on a specific, important point.

Plenipotentiary — representative invested with full power of independent action.

Reparations — compensation due under international law to a wronged state from a delinquent state, in this case in the form of cash payments.

Rune — a mystic symbol.

SA — *Sturmabteilung* — a storm division or Storm Troopers.

Spartacists — the name adopted by the German Communists at the end of the First World War. (Spartacus was a Roman gladiator who headed the third revolt of the slaves against Rome in 73–71 BC.)

SS — *Schutzstaffel* — originally similar to the SA, but after 1929, under the command of Heinrich Himmler, it was transformed into an elite force.

Versailles — the great palace of King Louis XIV of France (1643–1715) near Paris.

Weimar — a small town that became the new capital of Germany after the First World War.

Xenophobia — fanatical dislike of foreigners or people who are considered 'alien'.

Zeitung — the German word for newspaper.

Bibliography

Breitenbach, J.J. (ed.) *South Africa in the Modern World (1910–1970)* (Shuter & Shooter)
Bruce, George, *The Nazis* (Hamlyn, 1974)
D'Abernon, Viscount, *An Ambassador of Peace*, Vol. II (Hodder & Stoughton)
Hitler, Adolf, *Mein Kampf* (Hutchinson)
Luckau, A. *The German Delegation at the Paris Peace Conference* (Columbia University Press)
Phillips, D.M. *Hitler and the Rise of the Nazis* (Archive Series, Hill and Fell, Edward Arnold)
Rayner, E. Stapley, R. and Wilson, J. *World Affairs from the Russian Revolution to the Present* (Oxford University Press)
Shirer, W.L. *The Rise and Fall of the Third Reich* (Martin Secker & Warburg)
Speir, Albert, *Memoirs: Inside the Third Reich* (Macmillan)
Steeh, Judith, *The Rise and Fall of Adolf Hitler* (Hamlyn, 1980)
Taylor, A.J.P. *The Origins of the Second World War* (Penguin)

4 THE UNITED STATES OF AMERICA 1783–1900

Introduction 122

From the making of the Constitution to the Civil War 124
The Constitution
The nullification crisis
The South and slavery
Territorial acquisitions
Western settlement and the slavery question
The Compromise of 1850
The coming of the Civil War

Civil War and Reconstruction 135
The war
Slave emancipation
The war and American nationalism
Presidential Reconstruction
Congressional Reconstruction
Redemption
The triumph of Jim Crow

Agriculture and the West 144
Settlement of the Great West
Indian policy
Transportation and mechanization
The farmers' revolt

The rise of industrial and urban America 149
The railways and industrial development
The rise of big business
The emergence of organized labour
Immigration and the cities

Conclusion 156
Revision Questions
Chronology
Glossary
Bibliography

Introduction

In terms of the Treaty of Paris of 1783, which terminated the American War of Independence, Great Britain recognized the independence of her thirteen former colonies as the United States of America. The treaty also awarded to the United States the territory that lay between the former colonies and the Mississippi River. The boundaries of the United States thus extended from the Atlantic Ocean in the east to the Mississippi in the west, and from British Canada in the north to Spanish Florida in the south. Covering approximately one million square miles, the United States was almost equal in area to Western Europe. (See Map 19.)

According to the first United States census, in 1790, the total population of the new country was about four million, including some 700 000 black slaves. The population was overwhelmingly rural in character, with a mere 5,4 per cent being classified as urban. Estimates vary, but at least three-quarters of the population lived directly off the land, whether as plantation owners, commercial or subsistence farmers, farm hands or slaves. Thus in its early years, the United States was basically a farmers' republic. The white population was very largely British in origin, and Protestant in religion.

By the end of the Nineteenth Century the United States had grown enormously, and was being transformed in the process. During the course of that century the United States gained vast new territories, tripling its area. Acquired by a combination of negotiation, purchase, and force, these territories extended the borders of the United States westwards across the entire continent to the Pacific Ocean. A major concern during the Nineteenth Century was the settlement of the West, and its organization into states. By the end of the century all of the

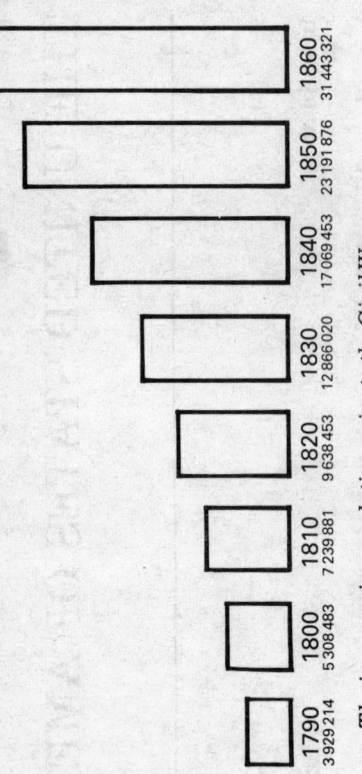

1790	1800	1810	1820	1830	1840	1850	1860
3 929 214	5 308 483	7 239 881	9 638 453	12 866 020	17 069 453	23 191 876	31 443 321

The increase in population prior to the Civil War.

United States had been opened up to organized settlement, and the number of states had grown from the original 13 to 45. Aided by a massive immigration, the population had reached 76 million by 1900, and was becoming increasingly urban. In 1900 some 40 per cent of the American population was classified as urban, and the large city, or metropolis, had already become a major feature of America. New York possessed a population of nearly $3\frac{1}{2}$ million.

Much of the new urban population was recruited from immigrants, and by the close of the century mass immigration had radically altered the overall ethnic and religious composition of the American people. During the course of the century 20 million immigrants poured into the United States. Up to the 1880s this immigration was largely German, Scandinavian, Irish, and British in origin; thereafter it derived chiefly from eastern and southern Europe. As a consequence of this so-called 'new immigration', which was overwhelmingly concentrated in the cities, America became very much more a

Accompanying the main population growth and urbanization in the Nineteenth Century was the process of industrialization. To an extent unparalleled elsewhere, urbanization and industrialization proceeded together in the United States. In Europe, large cities and considerable urbanization had long preceded the Industrial Revolution; in America, the two accompanied and supported one another throughout. Industries, being established in the cities, contributed enormously to urban growth, and the emergence of a mass urban market greatly stimulated industrial development.

Another distinctive feature of American industrial development by the end of the Nineteenth Century was the growing dominance of big business, or the large corporation. The United States pioneered the development of the large corporation. Aided by an upsurge of mergers at the century's end, big business came to overshadow small business in almost all the main industries. The trend was highlighted in 1901 when the banker J. P. Morgan bought out Carnegie Steel to form the giant United States Steel Corporation, the first billion-dollar company. The new corporation consisted of what had once been 138 different companies, and controlled 60 per cent of steel production in the United States.

By the end of the Nineteenth Century the United States had taken its place as the leading industrial and manufacturing nation in the world. In iron and steel production, the basic indicator of industrial strength, the United States had surpassed all rivals in the 1880s; by 1900 America was producing more steel than Britain and Germany combined.

The end of the Nineteenth Century also heralded the arrival of the United States on the world scene as a major political power. The Spanish-American War of 1898, fought ostensibly over Spain's failure to subdue the rebellion against her rule in Cuba,

The early pioneers left the Eastern villages and went to make their homes on the fertile prairie land of the middle West.

'nation of nations', and very much less a Protestant nation. The new immigrants were mainly Catholic, or else Greek Orthodox or Jewish.

Questions

1. What was the increase in the population of the USA between 1790 and 1860?
2. What was the percentage increase of population growth over this period?
3. Account for the rapid increase in population.

From the making of the Constitution to the Civil War

THE CONSTITUTION

The United States is still often regarded as a 'young' country, but it possesses one of the world's oldest constitutions. The present Constitution of the United States was drafted in 1787 by the Philadelphia Convention, and came into operation in 1789, when, in accordance with its provisions, George Washington was elected the first President of the United States.

The Civil War was the central event in Nineteenth Century American history, and much of this chapter will be concerned, in one way or another, with the causes and consequences of the war. It was a struggle over the nature of the Union and the relationship of the states to the federal government; over the place of blacks in American society; over the character of westward expansion; and also in part over the direction of American economic policy and development. To understand the origins of the Civil War, and its significance, we must look first at the Constitution*; then at the South and slavery; and lastly at westward expansion and settlement.

Ever since the War of 1812 with Britain, American security had not been seriously threatened by foreign powers. The United States enjoyed what the historian C. V. Woodward has called 'free security'. Protected from Europe by the Atlantic Ocean and from Asia by the Pacific Ocean, and with relatively weak neighbours on the American continent itself, the United States required neither a large military establishment nor a continuous involvement in international politics in order to safeguard her security. What passed for US foreign policy for most of the Nineteenth Century was the Monroe Doctrine* of 1823, which was itself an affirmation of American isolation from world affairs. It declared that European intervention in the Americas would be treated as an unfriendly act by the United States, and that the United States would not intervene in European affairs. Otherwise, from the perspective of international politics, the wars the US waged with foreign powers, and the negotiations she entered into, were basically isolated incidents, and were chiefly related to the expansionist drive of the US on the American continent itself.

The one major war experienced by the United States in the Nineteenth Century was domestic. The Civil War of 1861–5, waged between the Union forces of the North and the secessionist forces of the South, is often considered the first modern war. It was the first full-scale war of the industrial and democratic age. The victory of the North ensured not merely the preservation of the Union, but turned the United States into a truly national state, in which the sovereignty of the federal or national government was firmly asserted. It also effected a social revolution in the South by destroying slavery.

124

Question

Study the illustration with care. It is a copy of a famous painting which depicts the momentous event of the inauguration of the first President of the USA. Would you say that this was an accurate representation of the event? Could it be used as reliable primary evidence? Explain your answer.

Washington taking the oath as first President of the United States, while the people rejoice.

The Constitution prepared by the Philadelphia Convention replaced the Articles of Confederation, which had served as the first Constitution of the United States. It had come into operation in 1781, in the midst of the War of Independence against Britain, and provided for the permanent confederation of the thirteen states which had declared their independence from Britain. Under the Articles of Confederation the United States was essentially a league of sovereign states. The distinctive feature of the Articles was that sovereignty lay with the individual states rather than with the federal government*. The individual state governments, and not the federal government, possessed the actual powers of government over the peoples of the various states.

The purpose of the Constitution devised by the Philadelphia Convention was to provide for a much stronger central or federal government, giving it real powers of government over people; but at the same time not to reduce the states to mere provinces or administrative units of the central government. The new Constitution was intended to be federal rather than unitary*. Its fundamental achievement was to enable both the central and state governments to act effectively. The central or federal government was given supreme power within its sphere, but that sphere was defined and limited; the remaining powers of government were reserved for the states.

125

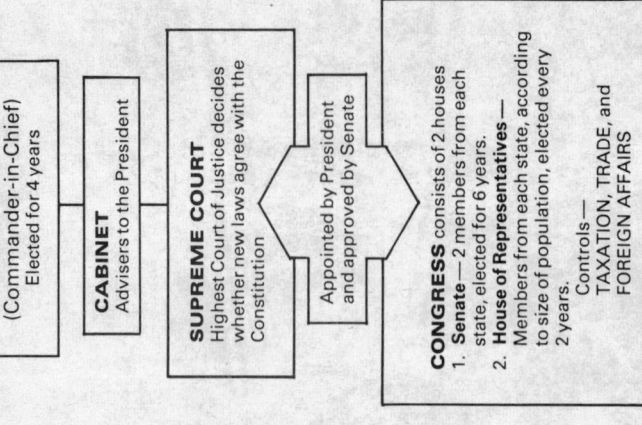

FEDERAL GOVERNMENT

PRESIDENT (Commander-in-Chief) Elected for 4 years

CABINET Advisers to the President

SUPREME COURT Highest Court of Justice decides whether new laws agree with the Constitution

Appointed by President and approved by Senate

CONGRESS consists of 2 houses
1. **Senate** — 2 members from each state, elected for 6 years.
2. **House of Representatives** — Members from each state, according to size of population, elected every 2 years.

Controls — TAXATION, TRADE, and FOREIGN AFFAIRS

STATE GOVERNMENTS

Each state has a GOVERNOR and controls its own Education, Police, Health, etc.

One of the main features of the new Constitution was its attempt to divide power, and in so doing to prevent the possibility of a 'tyrannical' government emerging. The federal system was part of this attempt; so too was the separation of powers, and the system of checks and balances, within the central government itself. The legislative power was vested in Congress, which was checked by its division into two houses — the House of Representatives, which represented the people, and the Senate, which represented the states. Legislation approved by Congress could be vetoed by the President, and his veto could only be over-ridden by a two-thirds majority in both houses. The executive power was vested in the President, who was elected independently of Congress for a term of four years. In the making of treaties and appointments, the President was checked by the Senate; treaties negotiated by him with foreign powers required the approval of a two-thirds majority in the Senate before they could come into force. The judicial power was vested in the Supreme Court and such inferior courts as might be deemed necessary. The judges of the Supreme Court were appointed for life by the President, with the advice and consent of the Senate.

In any system of government, powers can be divided, but ultimate sovereignty cannot be divided, and the new Constitution was ambiguous on the central question of where final political authority or sovereignty lay. In effect, the Constitution declared that sovereignty rested with it. The Constitution itself, and all the laws and treaties made in accordance with it, were declared 'the supreme law of the land'. But the Constitution could be amended. Amendments carried by a two-thirds majority in both houses of Congress, and approved by three-quarters of the states, would become part of the Constitution, and presumably sovereignty lay with those who could amend the Constitution. This was something that later came to trouble the Southern states. Whites there came to fear there might one day be sufficient 'free' states to carry an amendment to the Constitution which would prohibit slavery in the South. There was another problem. If the Constitution, and the laws made under it, were to serve as the supreme law of the land, who was to determine whether a law was indeed in accord with the Constitution? In short, who was to determine what was constitutional and what was unconstitutional?

It seems that many of the Founding Fathers, as the authors of the new Constitution came to be known, assumed that the Supreme Court would exercise the power of judicial review* and pass judgement on whether the acts and laws of Congress and the states were or were not constitutional. However, no direct provision for judicial review was made in the Constitution. In the famous case of *Marbury vs. Madison* in 1803, Chief Justice John Marshall put forward the doctrine of judicial review, and that doctrine has since become entrenched. In his own career, which lasted until 1835, Marshall went far to establish the principle and practice of judicial review, but it was not universally accepted. The notion that the Supreme Court's decisions on constitutional issues were final and binding was challenged in the South. There another doctrine evolved, which held that the states were the sovereign interpreters of the Constitution.

The nullification crisis

In the nullification* crisis of 1832–3, the state of South Carolina declared the United States tariffs of 1828 and 1832 to be unconstitutional and forbade the collection of these duties within the state. Such duties were deemed harmful to the South, which relied on others for its manufactured goods. In declaring the tariffs unconstitutional, South Carolina put into operation the 'nullification doctrine' developed by its leading politician, John C. Calhoun. According to his theory on the nature of the Union, the United States and its Constitution had been established not by the American people, but by the thirteen sovereign states. The Union was the product of a compact among sovereign states; and the federal government was merely the joint agent of those states, which delegated certain powers to the federal government. Should the federal government exceed its powers under the Constitution, should it go beyond its delegated authority, its actions could quite properly be nullified by any or all of the states.

In 1833 the nullification controversy was resolved through compromise: the US tariff was modified in accordance with Southern interests, and South Carolina repealed its nullification ordinance. But the wider constitutional issues raised by the crisis were not resolved, and South Carolina certainly did not abandon its claim to the right to nullify what it deemed unconstitutional legislation.

Although the nullification doctrine was formulated in response to the extremely high tariff duties adopted by Congress in 1828, it was not only the issue of taxation that encouraged Calhoun and South Carolina to advance the doctrine. They feared the prospect of federal government action against slavery in the Southern states, and were consequently anxious to construct constitutional safeguards for the South's 'peculiar institution'. They sensed that a major anti-slavery campaign was getting under way in the North, and they were determined to ward off federal government action against slavery by reserving the right to nullify any such action.

THE SOUTH AND SLAVERY

When the Philadelphia Convention drafted the Constitution in 1787, slavery was already becoming the 'peculiar institution' of the South. Most Northern states had abolished slavery within their borders, and in 1804 New Jersey became the last Northern state to provide for emancipation. Slavery was now confined to the Southern states.

Despite the presence of anti-slavery critics at the Philadelphia Convention, and despite the provision that after 1808 the federal government might prohibit further US participation in the international slave trade, the Constitution positively recognized slavery. It did so in the 'fugitive slave' clause, which required the free states to return runaway slaves when their masters demanded them back.

In anti-slavery circles there was some expectation at the time of the Philadelphia Convention that, regardless of any protection the Constitution might have extended to slavery, it would soon die out even in the South. For one thing, slave-based agriculture was not proving particularly profitable. In addition, it was anticipated that the supply of new slaves would gradually dry up if the US withdrew from the international slave trade. In 1808 Congress did indeed bring US participation in the international slave trade to an end, but thereafter slavery in the South expanded rather than falling into decline. In the first half of the Nineteenth Century the South became the world's most vigorous, expansive, and extensive slave economy.

The vast expansion of slavery in the first half of the Nineteenth Century was based on cotton, which emerged as a highly profitable staple crop, most profitably cultivated on plantations worked by the gang labour of slaves. The South became the world's leading producer of raw cotton, and by mid-century some 60 per cent of its slaves were employed on cotton

(c) *the nature of human relations at the workplace, with specific regard to the nature of relations between master and slave.*

3. *Would you argue that the picture presents an accurate or biased impression of the circumstances of life on a cotton plantation?*

A cotton-gin being worked by Negro slaves.

Questions

1. *The sketch shows Negro slaves working a cotton-gin — a machine for separating cotton from its seeds. What comment can you make with regard to the technology being used here?*

2. *Comment on the artist's perspective of the subject with specific reference to such issues as:*
    (a) *the dress worn by those depicted;*
    (b) *the nature of the work done by slaves on a cotton plantation;*

128

plantations. Four developments made possible this cotton-based expansion of slavery.

The first was the large new demand for raw cotton created by the cotton mills of the Industrial Revolution, particularly in Britain. The second was Eli Whitney's invention in 1793 of the cotton-gin, a machine for cleaning the cotton plant, which made possible the refining of raw cotton on a mass scale. The third was the development of an extensive inter-state slave trade. In the American South, slaves reproduced themselves on a scale unknown in any other slave society; this was a consequence of the near balance of sexes in the slave population, the relative absence of deadly diseases, and, arguably, the milder nature of Southern slavery. The result of this natural increase was that the South was not permanently dependent on Africa for fresh supplies of slaves; in the Nineteenth Century domestic reproduction and the inter-state slave trade maintained an adequate supply of new slaves. In particular, the older states of the upper South developed a major interest in providing slaves for the new areas of slave-based cultivation. By 1860 there were four million slaves in the United States, as against 700 000 in 1790, and all but one per cent had been born in the US. The fourth key development in the first half of the Nineteenth Century was the acquisition of new lands suited to slave-based agriculture, especially cotton.

TERRITORIAL ACQUISITIONS

Between the turn of the century and the outbreak of the Civil War in 1861 the United States made massive territorial acquisitions. These territories were gained by a variety of means. In 1803 President Thomas Jefferson purchased the vast Louisiana Territory, extending from the Mississippi River to the Rocky Mountains, from Napoleon I for 15 million dollars.

The social history of slavery in the South

In recent years historians have begun to reconstruct the social history of Southern slavery — to write the history of everyday life on the plantations. Howard Zinn gives some glimpses of the perspectives that have been explored, which emphasize the strength and vitality of slave culture in the process of resistance.

Also insisting on the strength of blacks even under slavery, Laurence Levine (*Black Culture and Black Consciousness*) gives a picture of a rich culture among slaves, a complex mixture of adaptation and rebellion, through the creativity of stories and songs:

'*We raise de wheat,*
Dey gib us de corn;
We bake de bread,
Dey gib us de crust
We sif de meal,
Dey gib us de huss;

'*We peel de meat,*
Dey gib us de skin;
And dat's de way
Dey take us in;
We skim de pot,
Dey gib us de liquor,
An say dat's good enough for nigger.'

(H. Zinn, *A Peoples' History of the United States*, pp. 174–5.)

129

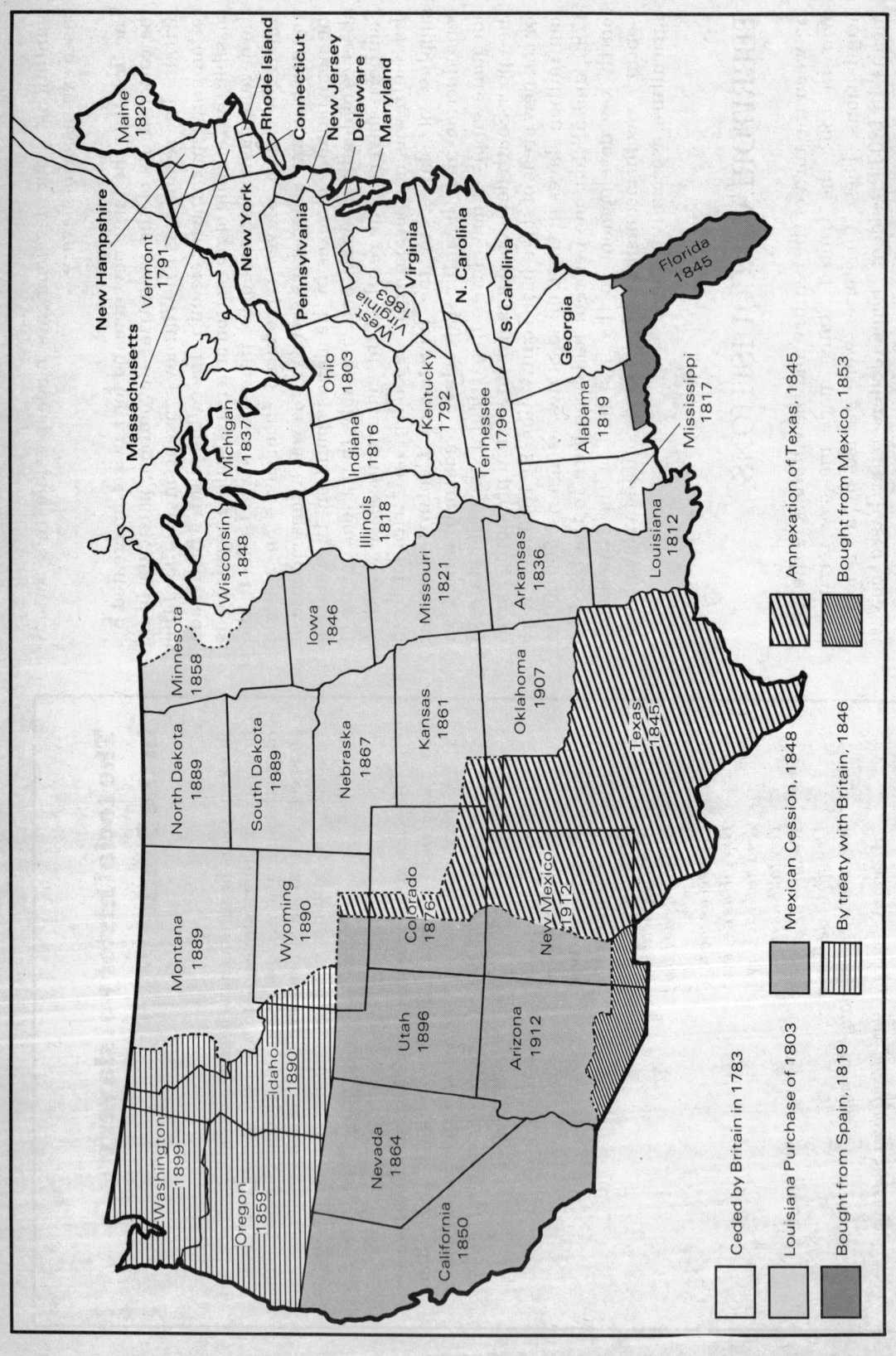

Map 19 — *Territorial growth of the United States. The original 13 states are in bold type. The other states show the date of their admission to the Union.*

Between 1810 and 1819 the US acquired Florida from Spain through war, annexation, and purchase; and in 1845 the US annexed Texas, which had previously declared its independence from Mexico. Following the war between the US and Mexico in 1846–7, the Mexican Government relinquished all claims to Texas north of the Rio Grande, and ceded the Mexican provinces of California and New Mexico to the US. The US had already negotiated the Oregon settlement with Britain in June 1846. With the conclusion of this settlement the US acquired all the land between the Rockies and the Pacific south of the 49th parallel (see Map 19).

The southern reaches of the Louisiana Purchase and Texas were the new areas that proved most suitable for cotton cultivation, and it was here that slave-based agriculture spread most extensively. The great cotton kingdom of the lower South came to extend from the states of South Carolina and Georgia in the east, through Alabama and Mississippi, into southern Arkansas, Louisiana, and Texas to the west of the Mississippi River. In the upper South, where tobacco was the main crop, slavery also spread westwards across the Mississippi, but it was cotton that was the main driving force behind the westward expansion of slave-based agriculture.

WESTERN SETTLEMENT AND THE SLAVERY QUESTION

The first half of the Nineteenth Century produced three major streams of westward migration and settlement in the US. One was a northern stream from New England and the Middle States, which settled in the Great Lakes region; the second was a stream from the upper South that moved north-westwards away from the slave areas; and the third was a southern stream that moved directly westwards carrying slavery with it. This westward expansion of slavery was the central issue which ultimately gave rise to the Civil War.

The Civil War between the North and the slave-owning South arose not out of direct Northern attempts to abolish slavery throughout the United States, but out of Northern attempts to prevent the further extension of slavery. The fundamental policy of the (purely Northern) Republican party, which won the presidential election of 1860, was that slavery must be contained; it was not to be allowed to expand any further.

The question of the further extension of slavery first became a divisive political issue between North and South in the Missouri crisis of 1819–20. Missouri, created out of the Louisiana Purchase, applied for admission to the Union as a slave state, but Northern congressmen insisted that Missouri embark on a programme of gradual emancipation as a condition of entry into the Union. In the end the Missouri Compromise was reached. Missouri was admitted as a slave state, while Maine (created out of the eastern counties of Massachusetts), was admitted as a free state, thereby maintaining the balance between free and slave states in the Union (12 of each). The compromise further provided that in all other parts of the Louisiana Purchase north of parallel 36°30′ (the southern boundary of Missouri) slavery was to be prohibited. Missouri was to the north of any of the existing slave states, and any further northern advance of slavery was to be checked by the terms of the compromise.

In the 1830s, in part as a reaction to the Missouri crisis, a new anti-slavery movement surfaced. This was the abolitionist movement, which was purely Northern, and which demanded the immediate, uncompensated emancipation of the slaves. What the Missouri crisis had served to dramatize was that slavery in the South was not, as anti-slavery groups had anticipated in the late Eighteenth Century, gradually dying out, but rather thriving and expanding. It was a cancer that was

Harriet Beecher Stowe's novel, *Uncle Tom's Cabin*, published in 1852, helped to stir anti-slavery feeling in the North.

spreading, and for the abolitionists the time had now arrived to root it out completely. With Britain's example of abolishing slavery throughout her empire before them, and with the spirit of the religious revivalism of the times to inspire them, the abolitionists embarked on a militant moral crusade to rid America of what they saw as the greatest sin ever perpetrated by man: the sin of slavery.

The Compromise of 1850

The new abolitionism succeeded in giving new prominence to the slavery question, and infused the debate over slavery with a strong moralism, but it never became a major political movement. Politically, the curtailing of the further extension of slavery, rather than its abolition where it already existed, remained the central issue. The whole question once again became urgent following the war with Mexico in 1846–7. Was slavery to be admitted into the territories taken from Mexico? This question served again to divide North from South, both in Congress and throughout the country, and it was again resolved by compromise. In the Compromise of 1850 California was admitted to the Union as a free state, thereby ensuring that slavery was to be excluded from the territory. But when the territories of Utah and New Mexico were established it was with the provision that they might be admitted to the Union as states 'with or without slavery as their constitution may provide at the time of their admission'. It was to be left to the settlers in these territories to decide for themselves whether or not they wanted slavery. This was the principle of popular sovereignty in action.

The Compromise of 1850 applied solely to the territories gained from Mexico. However, in 1854 Stephen A. Douglas, Democratic party Senator for Illinois and chairman of the Senate

Committee on Territories, sought to apply the principles of the Compromise to the remaining 'unorganized' areas of the Louisiana Purchase north of the Missouri Compromise line. In his Kansas-Nebraska Bill for the organization and opening up of the Kansas and Nebraska territories for white settlement, he proposed to repeal the Missouri Compromise prohibition on any further extension of slavery in the Louisiana Purchase north of 36°30', and to extend the principle of popular sovereignty to Kansas and Nebraska. The settlers there were to be free to decide for themselves whether they wanted slavery.

Several Northern Democrats in Congress, reacting against what they saw as Southern control of their party, opposed the bill. The remaining Democrats, supported by the Southerners in the Whig party, secured its passage into law. The result was that the Missouri Compromise was reversed and this made it possible for slavery to enter the Kansas and Nebraska territories.

The repeal of the Missouri Compromise caused a tremendous furore in the North, and led directly to the formation of a new political party there: the Republican party. It was composed of anti-slavery Northern Whigs and Democrats, and other anti-slavery and reform groups, and was committed first and foremost to preventing any further extension of slavery. The repeal of the Missouri Compromise had served to convince many in the North that the South was an aggressive and expansive slave power, prepared even to go back on its previous agreements in its determination to transform slavery from a sectional into a national institution. The purpose of the new Republican party was to thwart the expansionist drive of the South, and block any further extension of slavery.

Northern opposition to the further extension of slavery into the western territories was a compound of a wide variety of influences and attitudes, ranging from moral hostility to the institution of slavery, to outright racial prejudice. Many of those who regarded slavery as a sin, and who wished to see it destroyed throughout the United States, had come to recognize that it was essential first to prevent it from spreading. Containment was the first step along the road towards ultimate abolition. Others had no immediate desire to destroy slavery where it already existed, but were determined to preserve the new areas of settlement for free labour only, holding that slave labour undercut and degraded free labour. Others, again, opposed the further extension of slavery on racial grounds. Slaves were blacks, and they wanted to keep the western territories for whites only.

Kansas was declared open for settlement on 30 May 1854, and what followed there was a minor civil war between pro-slavery and anti-slavery forces. Kansas became the battleground between those who wished to keep the western territories open for slavery, and those who wished to prevent any further extension of slavery. The battle there hardened positions and contributed to the polarization of the nation. The South now began demanding that the federal government extend positive protection to slavery, along with other forms of property, in the western territories, prior to their becoming states. This demand finally split the Democratic party between its Northern and Southern wings, as it was a demand which Douglas and the Northern Democrats would not meet; they continued to insist that the settlers in a territory should be free to exclude slavery if they wished.

As was to become evident in the presidential election of 1860, the issue of the place of slavery in the process of westward expansion and settlement had divided North and South. By 1860–1 the issue was beyond compromise. Instead, it was settled by civil war.

133

THE COMING OF THE CIVIL WAR

The November 1860 presidential election was won by the Republican candidate, Abraham Lincoln of Illinois. Making a purely Northern appeal, directed against the further extension of slavery, he captured every free state except New Jersey, and not a single slave state. As the North commanded a substantial majority of votes in the electoral college, Lincoln gained the presidency. The response of the cotton states of the lower South (South Carolina, Mississippi, Florida, Alabama, Georgia, Louisiana and Texas) to his election was to exercise what they considered their sovereign right of secession: they left the Union. Lincoln and the North recognised no right of secession, and in April 1861 Lincoln sought to assert the rights of the US Government in Charleston harbour, South Carolina. Hostilities resulted, and the four states of the upper South (Virginia, Arkansas, Tenessee and North Carolina) thereupon joined the lower South in seceding from the Union and constituting the Confederate States of America. The Civil War had begun.

Lincoln and his Republican party were not abolitionists in the direct sense that they demanded the abolition of slavery where it already existed. They did not contemplate any action against slavery in the Southern states, and accepted that it was beyond the power of the federal government to abolish slavery there; that was a matter for the individual states themselves. All they called for was the prohibition of any further extension of slavery. At the same time many people, including Lincoln himself, believed that once slavery had been contained, its ultimate doom would be sealed. Containment would, they believed, place slavery on a gradual road to extinction. Lincoln anticipated it might take 'a hundred years at least' for slavery to disappear in the South.

Containment was a threat, albeit long-term, to slavery, which the lower South was not prepared to accept, and they consequently seceded. By the end of 1860 the South generally, and the lower South particularly, was in a very anxious state about slavery and its future. Fears of a slave insurrection had been sparked off in 1859 when the abolitionist John Brown made an unsuccessful attack on the federal arsenal at Harpers Ferry, Virginia, hoping to trigger a slave uprising. White Southerners had become paranoiac about the abolitionists and their influence. The containment of slavery was widely regarded as a death warrant for the institution, and this was seen as a threat to the whole political, social and economic structure of the South. Generally, the lower South took Lincoln's election to mean that slavery would henceforth always be on the defensive within the Union, and rather than tolerate that they preferred to leave the Union. There were already more free states than slave states in the Union (16–15), and with slavery excluded from the western territories, all new states were going to be free states. Thus the South was doomed to a permanent minority position within the Union. The prospect was that the federal government would henceforward be forever dominated by persons and groups hostile to slavery, and consequently the whole system of race relations in the South would come under permanent pressure. Some secessionists predicted that with no new slave states, the day would eventually arrive when there would be sufficient free states to carry an amendment to the Constitution abolishing slavery throughout the United States. The prediction was wide of the mark, but was indicative of the lower South's paranoia. If the fifteen slave states had remained united, they would still today be in a position to block any constitutional amendment, but in 1860–1 the lower South was not in the mood for such rational calculations.

In an effort to rescue the Union in the face of the secession of the lower South, Senator Crittenden of the border slave state,

134

Civil War and Reconstruction

The Civil War began in April 1861 and lasted for exactly four years; on Palm Sunday, 9 April 1865, the war effectively ended when General Lee and the army of northern Virginia surrendered to the Union commander, General Grant, at Appomattox Court House, Virginia. The South had been totally defeated, and the institution of slavery destroyed. There followed a period of military occupation in the South, which ended in 1877 with the withdrawal of the last of the Union troops. This period is known as Reconstruction, because it witnessed both the reconstruction of the Union, with the restoration of the secession states to the Union; and also the attempt on the part of the North to reconstruct or reshape Southern society. This entailed attempts to secure the basic rights of the former slaves or freedmen in that society. The withdrawal of the last of the Union troops in 1877 signified the restoration of full home rule to the South, and the abandoning of the attempt to reshape the South. The freed slaves, left to the mercies of the white South, were thereafter subjected to a process of disfranchisement, discrimination and segregation.

Kentucky, proposed a new compromise in the form of constitutional amendments. On the central issue of the extension of slavery he proposed that in all territories of the United States, 'now held or hereafter acquired', slavery was to be prohibited north of 36°30′, and recognized and protected south of this line. Lincoln and the Republicans would have nothing to do with the proposal. They refused to compromise on their fundamental opposition to the extension of slavery, with the result that there was no compromise settlement in 1860–1 akin to the compromise settlements of 1820 and 1850. As there was no compromise settlement, and as Lincoln and the North were not prepared to allow the lower South to secede, what followed was civil war. The four states of the upper South joined the seven of the lower South in seceding from the Union. The Union managed to hold on to the four border slave states of Missouri, Kentucky, Maryland and Delaware.

THE WAR

The Civil War began as a war to save the Union, or as a war for Southern independence, depending on which side one was fighting; and on both sides it was anticipated that the war would be short. Lincoln began by calling up troops for three months, in the belief it would take no longer to topple the Confederacy. The Southerners, who resorted to a defensive strategy, believed all they had to do was show they were capable of defending themselves and the Northerners would abandon their war effort. In the Southern calculation, the North did not possess the energy and commitment to sustain a prolonged war of conquest, and once the South had succeeded in warding off the initial attacks, the North would soon weary of the war and allow the Confederacy to go its own way. It was a calculation that went horribly wrong. While the Confederacy did mount an effective resistance, the North refused to abandon the effort to restore the Union by force of arms, and the result was to be four long years of war, and a total of over a million military casualties. Military deaths exceeded 600 000, making the Civil War the deadliest war ever for Americans.

135

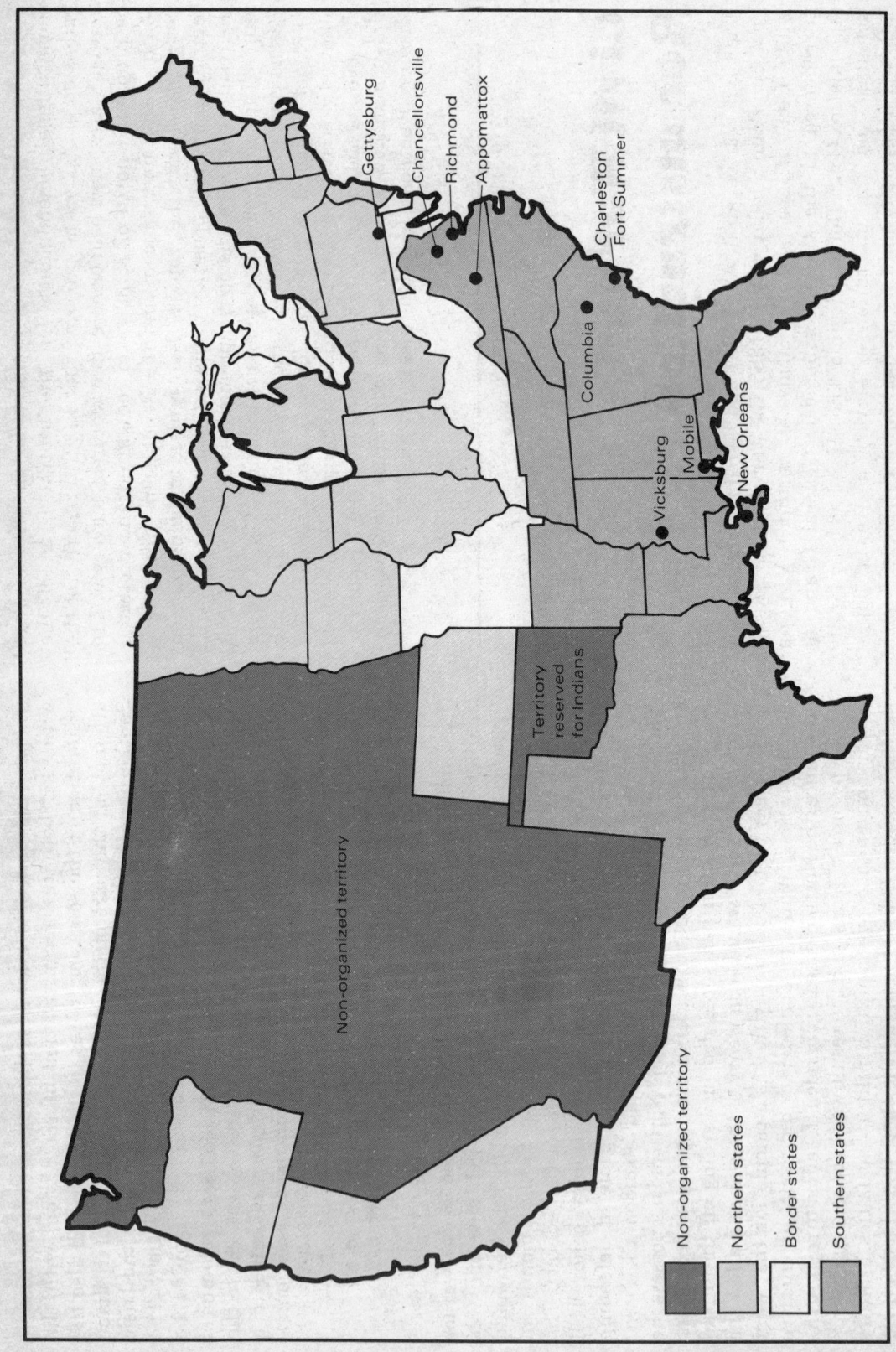

Map 20 — Battle area of the Civil War.

Charleston, South Carolina, 1865, showing the devastation caused by the war.

Before its end, the Civil War had been transformed into a total war, substantially altered in character and purpose. Both North and South began the war with traditional volunteer armies; both ended it with conscript armies, having found themselves obliged to resort to the draft in the effort to mobilize their resources to the full. To the horror of the South, the North even resorted to using black soldiers. In both North and South, the powers of the central government were vastly extended, at the expense of the states as well as the individual. The rights of individual states were severely trimmed by the Confederate government, no less than by the Union government; though it was the policies and actions of the latter that provided the basis for the emergence of a more truly national government in the United States. The demands of the war enabled the federal government to cut through many of the previous barriers to effective national action. The most dramatic example of this was provided by the abolition of slavery, which became one of the Northern goals during the course of the war.

SLAVE EMANCIPATION

Prior to the Civil War it was accepted, even by the abolitionists, that without a constitutional amendment it would be impossible for the federal government to abolish slavery in the Southern states. As the Constitution stood, the preservation or prohibition of slavery was a matter for the states themselves to decide. At the outbreak of hostilities, it was not a declared objective of the North to use the special circumstances of war to force emancipation on the South. The restoration of the Union was the sole official objective of the Northern war effort. By 1863 this had changed, and slave emancipation had become the second major war goal of the North.

It was during the course of 1862 that the Civil War was transformed into a war for the destruction of slavery, with Congress taking the lead. In July 1862 Congress passed a Confiscation Act, which declared free the slaves of all persons in rebellion against the United States. The act, justified as a war measure designed to weaken the enemy, reflected the view of the strongly anti-slavery wing of the Republican party that the war made it both possible and necessary to destroy slavery. The war made it possible in that, under international law, the

137

On 1 January 1863 Lincoln duly issued his Emancipation Proclamation, for which he is remembered as the 'Great Emancipator'. At the time the Emancipation Proclamation did not in fact free a single slave. It *declared* free the slaves in the areas still outside the control of the Union government; however those in the areas under Union control, including the loyal border states, remained in slavery. As Lincoln saw it, the Emancipation Proclamation could constitutionally be justified only as a war measure, directed at weakening the enemy, and hence the areas within the jurisdiction of the United States had to be exempted. He was also concerned not to unduly antagonize the pivotal border states. However, the meaning of the Emancipation Proclamation was clear enough; the emancipation of the slaves in the Confederacy was now a declared Northern war aim, and its realization would almost inevitably lead to an end to slavery throughout the United States. Once slavery had been destroyed in the Confederacy, it would be virtually impossible for it to survive in the border states.

What sealed the fate of slavery was the Thirteenth Amendment to the Constitution, which, with Lincoln's support, was approved by Congress in January 1865. Lincoln and the strongly anti-slavery Republicans had been worried that the courts would not uphold either the Confiscation Act or the Emancipation Proclamation once peace and the Union had been restored, and this ultimately led them to seek a constitutional amendment prohibiting slavery in the United States. Once the Amendment had been approved by Congress, and the South had been defeated, its ratification was imposed on the ex-Confederate states as one of the conditions of their restoration to the Union.

In December 1865 the Thirteenth Amendment was finally ratified. The death of slavery, the very fate the Southern states

federal government was entitled to resort to extraordinary war powers in order to weaken the enemy. Further, the war made it necessary to strike at slavery because the slaves were the greatest single wartime resource of the South; and because slavery was seen as the root cause of the rebellion. In September 1862, President Lincoln followed Congress by issuing his Preliminary Emancipation Proclamation, which declared that on 1 January 1863 all slaves within any state or district then in rebellion against the United States 'shall be then, thenceforward, and forever free'.

Abraham Lincoln

138

THE WAR AND AMERICAN NATIONALISM

In the era of nationalism and the forging of nation states, the Civil War was, in essence, the American equivalent of the Italian and German struggles for national unification. The union of the states, previously insecure, as shown by the Southern secession, was now cemented; and the old dispute as to the nature of the Union had finally been settled, by force of arms, in favour of the sovereignty of the nation against the individual states. The United States emerged from the Civil War more of a nation state, with a central government exercising enlarged and extended powers for the purposes of organizing and developing the United States on a national basis. In conscripting individuals into the army, and in emancipating slaves, the federal government had exercised coercive powers never before envisaged, and the economic policies adopted by the federal government during the war transformed it into a positive instrument for promoting national economic development. With the enactment of the protective tariffs of 1861 and 1864, the vast federal aid given for the construction of a transcontinental railroad, and the creation in 1863 of a national banking system, the old constitutional arguments, mainly Southern-inspired, about the limitations of the powers of the federal government were simply swept aside. The federal government emerged as a distinctly national government, acting directly to promote what it deemed to be the national interest.

The Civil War also greatly stimulated national sentiment in the North. The secession of the South, and the denial of national unity it embodied, provoked in the North a heightened sense of national loyalty and commitment. For the North, the war was above all a war to rescue national unity, to re-forge the nation. The idea of the American nation fragmenting permanently was abhorrent. 'That portion of the earth's surface which is owned and inhabited by the people of the United States,' Lincoln told Congress in 1862, 'is well adapted to be the home of one national family, and is not well adapted for two, or more.'

Regional differences and divisions survived the Civil War, and the bitterness of defeat lingered for a long time in the South; but the victory of the North had ensured that the American future would be determined by those committed to the notion of national unity and the sense of national destiny.

The new assertiveness of the federal government, and the new sense of what was expected of it, were manifested in Reconstruction. It was the federal government which undertook to reshape the South, and this was an enterprise that extended to altering the Constitution itself. Between 1865 and 1870 three amendments were made to the Constitution; they were the first in over sixty years.

had desperately wanted to avoid, had been greatly hastened by secession and war. Not for the last time, the South had proved its own worst enemy, precipitating the disaster it was most anxious to avert. Whereas previously the federal government had not been in the constitutional position to act directly against slavery in the Southern states, the war had created both the opportunity and the excuse for direct federal action to ensure the destruction of slavery.

PRESIDENTIAL RECONSTRUCTION

On Good Friday, 14 April 1865, less than a week after General Lee's surrender, President Lincoln was assassinated while at the theatre by John Wilkes Booth, a demented Virginian. As provided for in the Constitution, Lincoln was succeeded by his Vice President, Andrew Johnson.

The significant feature about Johnson was that he was a Southerner and former Democrat, but never a member of the Republican party. As Democratic Senator for Tennessee he had refused to support secession, remaining with the Union, and for the 1864 presidential elections he had been adopted as Lincoln's vice-presidential candidate in the effort to attract all loyalists to the Lincoln banner.

Although he had never been elected as president, and although he did not belong to the Republican party, which held the majority in both houses of Congress, Johnson took charge of the process of Reconstruction. He considered Reconstruction to be a presidential function, and refused to summon Congress into special session. It was not until December 1865 that Congress met in regular session, and by then Johnson had completed his programme of Reconstruction.

When Congress did finally meet, it refused to accept the results of Presidential Reconstruction as directed by Johnson. The Republican majority in Congress was generally unhappy about its outcome, and about the behaviour of the South. They sensed that the South was unrepentant, that white Southerners had no intention of repudiating their past and mending their ways, and this was intolerable to most Republicans for it suggested that the North had gained little from the sacrifices of four years of war.

The Republicans had two particular objections to the results of Presidential Reconstruction. The first was that it left political control of the South in the hands of its old ex-Confederate leadership. Although Johnson had personally loathed the planter aristocracy that had provided the old South with its leadership, and had refused to associate with them in secession, he proved liberal in granting pardons to ex-Confederate leaders, and allowing them to stand again for public office. In the elections for Congress in the South in 1865, ex-Confederate leaders were returned *en masse*, indicating that the white South had no intention of repudiating the leadership that had taken it into secession and war. Politically, what worried the Republicans was the prospect that this ex-Confederate leadership would soon strike up an alliance with the Democratic party in the North, which would imperil continued Republican dominance in the federal government.

The second objection concerned the white South's treatment of the black population. Under Presidential Reconstruction, the Southern states framed new constitutions that prohibited slavery, but they also enacted 'black codes' that severely restricted the freedom of the former slaves. These codes, usually including vagrancy and apprenticeship laws, were generally designed to ensure that the freed slaves remained on the old plantations either as labourers, tenant farmers, or sharecroppers. In no Southern state were blacks allowed to vote or hold public office. To Republicans in the North, it seemed that Southern blacks had gained little from emancipation, and had been returned to a condition approximating slavery. This was unacceptable to Republicans.

Consequently, when Congress convened in December 1865 the Republican majority refused to allow the Southern representatives to take their seats, and proceeded to develop a programme which would impose more meaningful changes on

CONGRESSIONAL RECONSTRUCTION

A feature of Congressional Reconstruction was that it became increasingly radical in response to the South's unwillingness to compromise. On the central questions of Southern political leadership, and the place of blacks in Southern society, Congress at first required of the South that it repudiate its ex-Confederate leadership, guarantee the civil rights of the former slaves, and extend the franchise to at least some of the blacks. This programme was embodied in the Fourteenth Amendment, adopted by Congress in June 1866. When the Southern states, with the exception of Tennessee, refused voluntarily to ratify the Fourteenth Amendment, Congress resorted to a more radical programme and course of action.

The Fourteenth Amendment disqualified ex-Confederate leaders from holding office, whether state or federal; it prohibited states from passing laws, such as the 'black codes', depriving persons of their due rights as citizens of the United States; and it proposed to reduce the South's representation in the House of Representatives in proportion to the denial of the franchise to blacks. In other words, the South was not forced to enfranchise blacks, but if it failed to do so it would have to accept a reduction in congressional representation. Encouraged by President Johnson, the ten Southern states other than Tennessee refused to ratify the Amendment.

the South. Reconstruction entered its second phase, generally referred to by historians as Congressional Reconstruction, as Congress now began to lay down the terms for the restoration of the Southern states to the Union.

This refusal, together with the resounding Republican victory in the congressional elections at the end of 1866, led Congress to embark on a programme for the fundamental reconstruction of Southern politics and society. The Reconstruction Acts of 1867 embodied the new programme. These acts declared that no legal governments existed in any of the Southern states other than Tennessee, and subjected the South to military government preparatory to the restoration of regular state government and the readmission of the Southern states to the Union. It was in the terms for restoration and readmission that the Reconstruction Acts sought to restructure the South. In each state a constitutional convention, chosen by universal male suffrage, was to set up a state government based on black and white male suffrage. Once the new state legislature had ratified the Fourteenth Amendment, and it had become part of the Constitution, a state would be entitled to take up its seats in Congress. Black suffrage, in short, was now being forced on the South.

By the end of 1868 seven of the Southern states had set up reconstructed governments, and the Fourteenth Amendment had been added to the Constitution. In 1870 the three remaining states, Mississippi, Virginia, and Texas, were reconstructed, and as a condition for their readmission to the Union they were required to ratify yet another amendment, the Fifteenth. Approved by Congress in February 1869, the Fifteenth Amendment sought to provide constitutional underpinning for black suffrage in the South by prohibiting states from depriving any citizen of the vote for reasons of race, colour, or previous condition of servitude. The Amendment became part of the Constitution in 1870.

Congressional Reconstruction represented an initiative aimed at strengthening the power of the federal legislature, at the expense both of the states, which had previously completely

141

controlled suffrage rights, and of the Presidency. Despite President Johnson's attempts to obstruct the policies followed by Congress, including resort to the presidential veto, Congress successfully seized control of Reconstruction from the President. In 1867 Congress even attacked the Presidency directly by having Johnson impeached*. He was saved from conviction in the Senate by a single vote.

In all, Congressional Reconstruction ranks as one of the most dramatic and significant periods in American history. Its enduring significance lies in the enactment of the Fourteenth and Fifteenth Amendments, which might not otherwise have become part of the Constitution. These amendments gave blacks in America a constitutional basis for their struggle for equality. In the short-term, however, these amendments were inadequate to protect the position of blacks in the South. By the mid-1870s it was apparent that Reconstruction had failed to give blacks a viable new place in Southern politics and society.

REDEMPTION

The process by which white conservatives regained control in the South has been remembered among white Southerners as one in which they gained 'redemption' from 'black' Republican government. In no state did blacks ever dominate the government, but the new franchise made possible Republican reconstruction governments throughout the South. Most did not last very long. The development of solid white support for the Democratic party, coupled with intimidation of black voters, ensured that by the end of 1875 only Florida, Louisiana, and South Carolina still possessed Republican governments. The chief agency of intimidation of blacks was the Ku-Klux-Klan, a secret organization founded in 1865 as an instrument for preserving white supremacy in the South. Its tactics included the resort to outright violence and terror. The Force Acts of 1870–1 empowered the new Republican President, General Grant, to suppress these tactics by military force. Some of the violence was checked, but intimidation continued.

The redemption of the remaining three Southern states was finally achieved in the so-called Compromise of 1877. The presidential election of 1876 had ended in dispute, with neither the Republican candidate, Rutherford B. Hayes, nor the Democrat, Samuel Tilden, receiving a clear majority of the electoral vote. The election had to be decided by Congress, and the decision depended on which votes, at the time in dispute, Congress accepted for Florida, Louisiana, and South Carolina, the last states occupied by federal troops. The bargain struck was to allocate their electoral votes to the Republican, Hayes, enabling him to become President; he in turn recalled the remaining federal troops from the South and allowed Democratic party governments to be installed in the contested states.

Reconstruction was over. The South was now solidly Democratic, and the federal government had abandoned its positive attempts to promote and protect the rights of blacks in the South. Blacks were now increasingly left to the mercies of the white South.

That Northern Republicans should ultimately have tired of protecting Southern blacks was perhaps inevitable. The idealism aroused by the Civil War had waned; black voters were clearly not providing the Republican party with an effective base for controlling the South politically; and other questions, notably the economic depression which had begun in 1873, were demanding attention. There was also a general desire in the

North to temper the antagonisms aroused by the Civil War between the North and the white South, and this could only be done by abandoning the cause of the blacks in the South.

The Republican failure in Reconstruction lay not so much in the ultimate abandonment of Southern blacks by the federal government, as in not providing blacks with sufficient means of promoting and protecting their own interests. Crucially, Southern blacks were given no land of their own. Without economic independence, they were at the mercy of the groups which controlled them economically, the landowners and the business groups in the South. All they had was the vote, and that was inadequate when they were easily exposed to intimidation, both economic and physical. Even their right to be registered as voters was not properly safeguarded. The Fifteenth Amendment provided that they could not be disfranchised for reasons of race or colour, but this did not prevent the white South from resorting to other devices, such as literacy and property qualifications, to disfranchise them.

THE TRIUMPH OF JIM CROW

In the American South, segregated facilities and segregation laws were known as 'Jim Crow' facilities and laws. The Jim Crow pattern embodied the white South's own preferred solution to the problem of race relations. The four decades between the Compromise of 1877 and American intervention in the First World War in 1917 witnessed the triumph of Jim Crow practices throughout the South, as blacks were subjected to a continuing process of disfranchisement, discrimination, and segregation.

The process was slow at first, but speeded up once it became evident that the Supreme Court, along with other branches of the federal government, was no longer interested in protecting black rights. From 1883 onwards, when judgement was handed down in the famous Civil Rights Cases, the Supreme Court made a series of rulings that effectively betrayed the principles of equality embodied in the Fourteenth and Fifteenth Amendments. In the Civil Rights Cases the Court refused to enforce the Civil Rights Act of 1875 which had prohibited segregation in public facilities, such as hotels, theatres, and parks. The Court held that the Fourteenth Amendment protected citizens' rights only against infringement by state governments; it did not prohibit discrimination by other agencies and enterprises serving the public. In subsequent cases, the Supreme Court proceeded to rule that state-enforced segregation need not necessarily infringe the Fourteenth Amendment so long as the separate facilities were equal. The Supreme Court upheld the 'separate-but-equal' doctrine in *Plessy vs. Ferguson* in 1896, and in *Cummins vs. County Board of Education* in 1899, when it ruled that separate schools for whites and blacks were constitutionally valid if the facilities were equal. In 1898, in the case of *Williams vs. Mississippi*, the Supreme Court also upheld the validity of the principal methods used by the South to disfranchise blacks. Thereafter, disfranchisement and segregation laws spread rapidly, entrenching white supremacy and reducing blacks in the South to the status of second-class citizens. These were the consequences of leaving the South to settle race issues itself.

It was not until 1954, in the case of *Brown vs. Topeka*, that the Supreme Court was to abandon the doctrine of 'separate-but-equal', and in so doing initiate the contemporary federal challenge to segregation in the South. In 1954 the Supreme Court revised its previous position by ruling that separate facilities were inherently unequal, and that laws requiring segregated schools violated the Fourteenth Amendment.

143

Agriculture and the West

In the thirty years after the Civil War the United States firmly established itself as the world's leading agricultural producer. In these years more land was brought under cultivation than in all the previous history of the nation, and farming itself became a major business, geared to both the domestic and international markets. American agricultural exports, particularly to Europe, rose massively, and as a consequence the United States was able to attain a favourable balance of trade. Between 1873 and 1900 the United States maintained a favourable balance of trade for all but two years, and in this period agricultural products, notably cotton, cereals, meat and tobacco, provided three-quarters of all US exports. Even in South Africa, the production of food cereals was affected by the availability of cheap American grain during this period (see Chapter 9).

An abundance of cheap land, especially in the West, the increasing mechanization of agriculture, crop specialization, and the creation of a modern transport network to convey farm products to urban and overseas markets, all made possible the enormous advance of commercial agriculture in the decades after the Civil War.

SETTLEMENT OF THE GREAT WEST

Between the Civil War and the end of the century, the western half of the United States provided the main focus for internal territorial expansion and settlement. By 1890, with the proclamation of the Oklahoma Territory, the western half of the

Thousands of pioneers travelled westward after the discovery of silver mines in the Rocky Mountains in the 1870s. Here a caravan struggles up a dangerous log road to the mining town of Leadville, Colorado.

country had been opened up in its entirety to organized settlement. As the Superintendent of the Census declared in that year, the US no longer possessed a moving frontier of settlement. 'The unsettled area,' he observed in his annual report, 'has been so broken into isolated bodies of settlement that there can hardly be said to be a frontier line.' Only the Mormon territory of Utah, the desert territories of Arizona and New Mexico, and Oklahoma itself were still in the territorial phase* of development. The remainder of the West had been organized into states, giving a total of 44 states by 1890, as against 33 in 1860.

144

By no means all the western half of the United States was opened up for agriculture. Beyond the Rocky Mountains, reaching westwards to the Sierra Nevada and Cascade mountain system, lay the 'Great American Desert', which was generally too arid for farming. It was developed instead as a mining region. The main new area opened up to agriculture after the Civil War was the Great Plains. This was the vast, dry, treeless, short-grass region extending from western Kansas, where the tall-grass prairies ended, to the Rocky Mountains, and from Texas in the south to the Canadian border in the north. Altogether the Great Plains comprised about one-fifth of the United States. In the generation after the Civil War it was this region that attracted the great rush of white migrants, led by the cattlemen, and followed by the farmers. The previous inhabitants of the Plains, the Indians and the buffalo, were swept aside.

The grasslands of the Plains were ideally suited for grazing cattle, and within a short time after the Civil War virtually the entire area had become a cattle kingdom. From southern Texas, the home of the Texas Longhorn, through to the Canadian border, the land came to be given over to the raising and herding of cattle. The life of the cowboys who watched over the cattle has ever since been romanticized, but as cowboy songs attest, it was often a very lonely and arduous life.

A distinctive feature of the cattle kingdom of the Great Plains at its height was that the range was open. The land was public domain, rather than privately owned, and the cattle were free to roam the Plains with no fences to hamper them. The cowboys rounded them up twice a year, in spring and autumn, for branding or for driving them to the cowtowns, such as Dodge City in Kansas, for shipment to the major meat-packing centres, notably Chicago and Kansas City.

In the mid-1880s the cattle kingdom suddenly collapsed. With the market glutted, prices for beef gave way, and this was followed by a series of natural disasters. Two successive years of summer drought and severe winter decimated the herds. Worse still for the cattlemen was the end to the open range, when sheep-raisers and farmers moved into the Plains as settlers, and enclosed their lands. The enclosure movement, made possible by the introduction of barbed wire fencing, produced bitter feuds between cattlemen and settlers, but its progress marked the death of open-range grazing. Cattlemen were left with the wish that 'the man who invented barbed wire had it all around him in a ball and that the ball rolled into hell.' In the end, the cattlemen were forced to fence in their pastures, and the cowboys were reduced to ranch hands.

Nebraska sod dug-out in 1892.

The Kansas Nebraska Act of 1854 marked the beginning of the process whereby the Great Plains would be opened up for white settlement. In terms of this Act, the policy of maintaining a single large Indian country was abandoned. It was proposed to concentrate the Indians to the north and south of the old Indian country, leaving the centre open for white settlement. Following the Civil War, this policy was further refined, and the Indians were to be herded into smaller tribal reservations, in Dakota territory for the Northern tribes, including the Sioux, and Oklahoma territory for the Southern tribes. The remainder of the Plains would be for whites. Clearing the Plains of Indian settlements and enforcing the reservation policy was achieved in a series of wars, notably against the Sioux, who were finally crushed in 1890.

Together with the reservation policy, the annihilation of the buffalo by white hunters destroyed the traditional life of the plains Indians. The plains Indians were nomads and hunters, rather than farmers, with their livelihood based on hunting the millions of buffalo that roamed the plains. The mass slaughter of the buffalo by white hunters, in search of sport and hides, contributed to forcing the plains Indians to abandon their nomadic ways and reconcile themselves to the reservations.

With the traditional life of the plains Indians undermined, Congress in 1887 passed the Dawes Severalty Act, which determined Indian policy for the next half-century. Indians were now systematically encouraged to become farmers, and to adopt the ways of the white man. The Act provided for the dissolution of the tribes as legal entities, and for distributing the community-owned tribal lands to individual owners. The Act also provided for the extension of US citizenship to those who accepted the allotments. In 1901 the people of the so-called five civilized nations of Oklahoma were all given citizenship.

The advance of the farmers from the prairies into the Great Plains got under way in the early 1870s and progressed rapidly in the next two decades. The population of Nebraska, for example, grew from 123 000 in 1870 to a little over a million by 1890. Many of these farmers were homesteaders, claiming their farms under the terms of the Homestead Act of 1862, which granted free farms of 160 acres to settlers who occupied and improved the land for five years. Given the dry conditions of the Great Plains, 160 acres was generally inadequate for a viable farm, and settlers often simply staked out larger claims for themselves. In the absence of timber, they built their first houses of sod, and burned manure for heat in winter.

Growing cereals in the Plains was made possible by the steel plough, capable of breaking up the tough soil; the windmill, which could pump up water from considerable depths; and the development of dry farming* techniques.

INDIAN POLICY

The opening up of the Great Plains to whites required that they be cleared of Indians, and this led to major changes in US Indian policy. Previously the Great Plains had been reserved as Indian country, and US policy had been to concentrate the Indian tribes in the Plains. In the 1830s several of the eastern tribes had been forcibly removed westwards in what the Cherokee called the 'trail of tears'; one quarter of the Cherokee people died during their removal from Georgia in the winter of 1838–9. Basically, US Indian policy had been one of separate development, supposedly designed to allow the Indians to develop independently of the white man, and escape his corrupting influences, such as drink. The Indian country in the west was duly ringed with a series of forts, to keep the Indians in and white settlers out.

146

TRANSPORTATION AND MECHANIZATION

Also crucial to the opening up of the Great West, and the overall development of commercial agriculture, was the rapid extension of the railway system in the years following the Civil War. The railways spearheaded much of the settlement of the Great Plains by farmers; they railed in the settlers (often recruits from the east of the United States and from Europe), and took their products out.

In 1865 the United States possessed 35 000 miles of railway, almost all of it east of the Mississippi. Within eight years the amount of railway had been doubled, and by the end of the century America's railway network was virtually complete, totalling some 200 000 miles. The network included five transcontinental routes.

The first transcontinental route was completed in 1869, and ran from Sacramento in California to New York, via Chicago. As with the other major American railways, it was built and run by private companies, but they received massive financial aid from government, both federal and state, for construction.

By providing access to markets, the railways gave greater encouragement to regional crop specialization, and specialization together with the advance of mechanization promoted greater agricultural productivity. The Civil War itself had effectively initiated the mechanization of agriculture in the western regions of the North. With many men drawn from farm labour into the army, farmers began resorting to reapers and other new implements in order to maintain productivity, and benefit from the high grain prices. The continued demand and high prices after the war encouraged the further progress of

Expansion of the railways 1830–60

1830	37 kilometres
1840	4 510 kilometres
1850	14 400 kilometres
1860	49 600 kilometres

(Compare these data with those concerning South Africa on p. 248.)

mechanisation, though by the end of the century the mechanisation of American agriculture was still in its early stages. By 1900 the value of farm machines and implements in the US was $750 million. Twenty years later it had jumped to $3 595 million.

THE FARMERS' REVOLT

In the long run the considerable increase in agricultural productivity created a crisis for American farmers. It led ultimately to over-production, and a consequent sharp fall in prices for farm products. The fall began in 1884, and continued

147

The result of the agrarian distress of the late 1880s and early 1890s was the most far-reaching movement of agrarian protest in the history of the United States. This was the Populist* movement, which challenged the existing two-party system with the formation in 1892 of the People's party. The Populist movement succeeded in uniting all the purely rural western and southern states in a campaign for fundamental reforms to assist farmers.

The backbone of support for the Populist movement was provided by farmers who produced for the international market, primarily the wheat farmers of the Great Plains and the cotton farmers of the South. The international market had become highly competitive as a consequence of agricultural advances in other parts of the world, and gluts had a disastrous impact on prices everywhere. Even when American crop yields were relatively low, abundant supplies of crops from elsewhere in the world — wheat from Argentina and Australia, and cotton from India and Egypt — would keep prices down. The problem for American farmers was that their costs remained high. The wheat and cotton farmers were both heavily in debt, at substantial rates of interest, and both faced high transportation costs, being far from their markets.

Currency, credit, and transportation reforms consequently featured prominently in the Populist programme. They demanded an inflationary money policy, so as to increase prices for farm products and enable farmers to pay their debts; a government-funded system for future loans, so as to provide farmers with cheap credit and free them from the grip of eastern banks; and the nationalization of the railways, so as to keep down transportation costs. The complaint of the farmers was that the railway companies charged them extortionate rates.

Farmers adopted steam engines to thresh grain before 1890. Mechanization assisted in developing huge tracts of previously unproductive lands such as the Dakota territory illustrated here.

unchecked until 1896. For farmers in the Great Plains matters were made worse from 1887 onwards by the onset of a prolonged drought. The combination of low prices and drought ruined many western farmers. Between 1887 and 1892 about half the population of western Kansas found themselves obliged to abandon their farms. 'In God we trusted,' they complained, 'in Kansas we busted.'

On the basis of this programme the People's party contested the presidential election of 1892, with its candidate, General Weaver, receiving as much as 8 per cent of the popular vote. For the 1896 presidential election the Populists effectively merged with the Democrats by adopting the Democratic party candidate, William Jennings Bryan. Bryan, 'the great commoner', was the most formidable popular demagogue of his time, and he campaigned vigorously for an inflationary money policy as against the rigid constraints of the gold standard: 'You shall not crucify mankind upon a cross of gold'.

Bryan carried every purely rural state, but he lost virtually every state in which industry was of any significance. He failed to win support among the industrial working classes, who like their employers feared the consequences of an inflationary money policy for its impact on the cost of living and its deterrence to foreign investment in America. The result was that Bryan lost the election to the Republican candidate, William McKinley.

Following Bryan's defeat, and the recovery of agricultural prices after 1897, the Populist movement lost its force. It represented the last attempt by farmers to control the nation politically. The significance of 1896 was that a new America, urban and industrial, was moving into the ascendant.

The rise of industrial and urban America

The dominant trend in the history of the United States in the thirty-five years between the end of the Civil War and the turn of the century was the emergence of a highly industrialized, capitalist, and urban society. By the century's end the United States had developed into the most productive and powerful industrial nation in the world, responsible for some 30 per cent of world manufacturing output. As industries tended to be concentrated in cities, the United States was simultaneously becoming increasingly urban, though it was not until after the First World War that the population became predominantly urban.

Traditionally, the Civil War and its outcome have been regarded as central to the rise and triumph of industrialism in the United States. Historians such as Charles and Mary Beard, in *The Rise of American Civilization*, and Louis Hacker in *The Triumph of American Capitalism*, have presented the Civil War as a period of economic revolution which marked the transition from the agricultural to the industrial era in American history. In the Civil War, Northern industrial capitalism triumphed over Southern agrarianism, and so removed the obstacle of Southern opposition to the adoption by the federal government of policies designed to promote industrialization, such as protective tariffs. Moreover, the war itself acted as a powerful spur to economic growth and industrial development. The massive demand of the military for armaments, transport and clothing, served to revolutionize industrial production in the North, and the profits made by industrialists and bankers from the war resulted in the accumulation of vast sums of capital for investment in further industrial development.

United States was already a major industrial power by 1860, having experienced substantial industrial development in the two decades prior to the Civil War. They argue that the war itself served to disrupt the continuity of industrial progress by diverting resources, notably capital, from industrial development into the war effort. As they see it, American industry would have been in a distinctly stronger position at the end of the decade had there been no Civil War.

Questions

1. What is the main conclusion to be drawn from the three graphs?
2. What political consequences flowed from the changes indicated in the table?

From the statistics it is now evident that, in the short run, the Civil War did retard the process of industrialization in the United States. There was a slower rate of growth in the decade of the 1860s than in the two decades preceding the Civil War and in the two decades following the 1860s. However, the figures for the decade immediately following the Civil War (1865–1875), suggest that the growth rate then was much higher than in the antebellum* era, and that any retarding of industrial development caused by the Civil War was temporary, and soon made up. Short-term considerations aside, there is the question of whether the basic structural changes effected during the war were of significant long-term importance in promoting the process of industrialization. There is no simple answer to this question, but what can be said with certainty is that the Northern victory produced a federal government more responsive to the demands of business and industry, and more

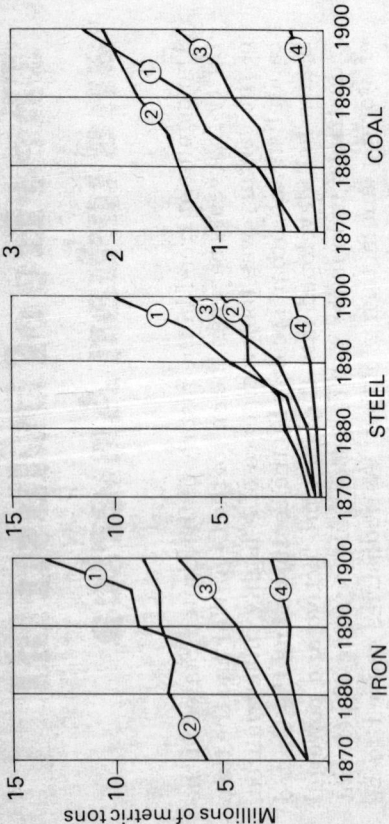

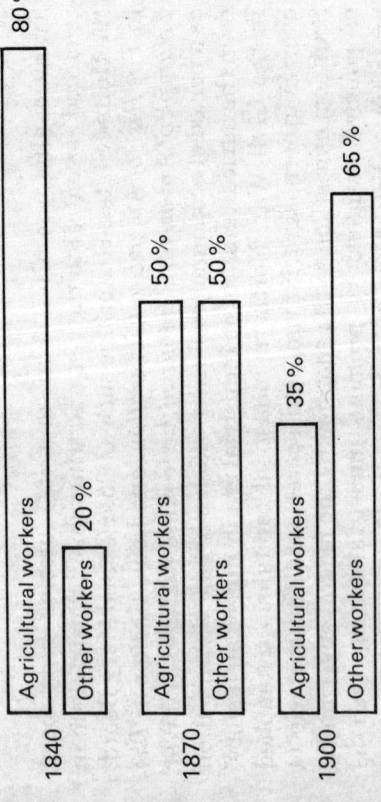

Iron, coal, and steel production, 1870–1900. (1=USA; 2=Britain; 3=Germany; 4=France).

Proportion of agricultural workers to all other workers.

Recent critics of this interpretation, using the extensive statistical evidence provided by the new 'quantitative' economic history, have contended that the Civil War retarded rather than accelerated industrialization. They have demonstrated that the

The notion that the economic growth of the late Nineteenth Century was attained purely by businessmen, without the intervention of government, is a myth. There was a distinct partnership between government and business, and government activity was an important factor in promoting economic growth and industrial development, more particularly during and after the Civil War. It would, however, be a difficult, if not impossible, task to accurately measure government's contribution.

While it is thus evident that the United States had developed into a major industrial power even before the Civil War, there were significant changes in the character and direction of American industrialization thereafter. Prior to the Civil War, American industry had been primarily geared to catering to the needs of an agrarian economy, and it had been mainly regional in nature, dominated by small entrepreneurs. The products of heavy industry, including the locomotives and rails for railway development, had generally been imported, chiefly from Britain. After the Civil War, assisted by protective tariffs, the United States furthered its own heavy industry, based on iron, steel, and coal, and at the same time built up its consumer industries, which catered for a national, and increasingly urban, market. By the end of the century both heavy industry, and the major consumer industries, were beginning to be dominated by big business. Then again, while major inventions, such as the mechanical horse-drawn reaper and the sewing machine, had been made before the Civil War, it was only during and after the war that they were widely applied, leading to the rise of factory-based industries. The acceleration of inventions after the Civil War was to produce some entirely new industries, most notably the electrical industry.

THE RAILWAYS AND INDUSTRIAL DEVELOPMENT

In accounting for American industrial development after the Civil War, a central role has traditionally been given to the construction of the country's railway network. The central role of the railways is now sometimes questioned, but it would be impossible to write a history of the American economy in the late Nineteenth Century without giving substantial attention to the railways.

The railways assisted industrial development and urbanization in a number of ways. First, the building of the railways served as a major catalyst for the growth of heavy industry in the United States through the enormous demand it created for iron, steel, copper, and coal. Second, the construction of a national railway network created a much wider market than before for all goods; it brought into being a truly national market, and further widened that market by substantially reducing transport costs. Third, by expanding the scope of the economy, the railways stimulated urban growth generally, and as a consequence of rate competition fostered the concentration of industries in the larger cities. Industries were encouraged to locate themselves in cities served by several competing railway companies, for at these competitive points railway rates were substantially lower than elsewhere. Fourth, the urban growth promoted by the railways in turn stimulated the development of consumer goods industries. It was chiefly to satisfy the demand

151

prepared to intervene to promote industrial development. High tariffs against certain imported products were used to stimulate certain industries, notably iron and steel, and massive federal aid was made available to the railway companies for the construction of transcontinental routes.

of the growing urban population that the consumer goods industries, such as those involved in food processing, arose.

The railways also had a significant impact on business organization in the United States. As the first truly large-scale enterprise in America, the railways required new methods of business organization, and were pioneers in the development of the large corporation. Not only did the railways take the lead in devising new and larger forms of organization, but by bringing into being a larger national market they made possible the emergence of huge enterprises in other fields.

THE RISE OF BIG BUSINESS

The giant corporate enterprise is a hallmark of modern American capitalism. This has been a development since the Civil War. Prior to the Civil War, American business and industry had been dominated by small firms and partnerships. By the turn of the century the large corporations and combinations were moving into the ascendant. By 1904, aided by a rush of mergers since the late 1890s, there were over three hundred large combinations in existence, with an aggregate capital of nearly $7 billion. Together, they controlled 40 per cent of the capital invested in American manufacturing.

Large companies were sometimes the product of expansion, but more often of mergers* and combinations. These combinations were undertaken for a variety of reasons, but initially the overriding concern was to control and stabilize industries at levels of profit acceptable to the owners. In the case of vertical combinations*, in which a single company came to control the supply of raw materials, the process of manufacturing, and the marketing of the finished product, the object was to ensure supplies as well as stabilize production and control marketing. Horizontal combinations* were combinations of manufacturers in a particular industry, and were usually designed to curb competition, regulate production, and control prices. In all such instances of combination, businessmen also claimed that they promoted greater rationality and efficiency in their industries, thereby reducing waste and costs, and consequently lowering prices. At the end of the Nineteenth Century bankers and financiers, such as J. P. Morgan, came to supersede industrialists in arranging mergers. Very often these financiers were more interested in the profits to be gained by arranging such mergers than in ensuring stability and efficiency in industry.

J.P. Morgan (1837–1913)

The early horizontal combinations were specifically designed to avert ruinous competition in a particular industry. They first took the form of trusts*, a form of business organization pioneered by John D. Rockefeller and Standard Oil. The trust was an unchartered corporation* that held the stock of formerly competing companies in trust, with the board of trustees supervising all the operations of the new combination. In the case of the Standard Oil Trust, formed in 1879 and reorganized in 1882, Rockefeller combined some forty previously competing oil refining companies, with the new organization controlling 90 per cent of the industry. In response to the Sherman Anti-Trust Act of 1890, trusts were reorganized either as huge corporations by means of outright mergers or as holding companies. Essentially, the holding company is another form of trust; it is a corporation empowered to hold the stock of other corporations. It was first given legal form by the state of New Jersey, which passed a series of laws permitting corporations chartered there to own property in other states, as well as stock in other corporations. As a consequence of its liberal incorporation provisions, New Jersey soon gained a reputation as a home for trusts. When Rockefeller reorganized his oil empire in the form of a holding company, it was incorporated as the Standard Oil Company of New Jersey.

By the early Twentieth Century giant combinations existed in communications, the consumer goods industries, and heavy industry. Six major groups controlled much of the country's railway network, Western Union dominated the telegraph business, and the Bell Telephone Company had a virtual monopoly over the new telephone industry. Giant combinations in the consumer goods industries included the American Tobacco Company, United Fruit, the National Biscuit Company, and Swift and Armour, which between them dominated the meat-packing industry. The greatest of all combinations was the United States Steel Corporation, formed in 1901 and including most of the important steel manufacturers.

Public alarm at the growth of giant combinations and monopolistic practices did result in the adoption, before the close of the Nineteenth Century, of the first measures to provide for federal government regulation of business practices. These measures were the Interstate Commerce Act of 1887, which set up a federal commission to regulate railway rates and practices, and the Sherman Anti-Trust Act of 1890, which prohibited trusts and other forms of combination for monopolistic purposes. The federal government, however, rarely invoked the Sherman Act in the 1890s, and it certainly failed to prevent the rush of mergers at the turn of the century.

THE EMERGENCE OF ORGANIZED LABOUR

In comparison with many European countries which were also undergoing industrialization in the Nineteenth Century, the history of the United States has usually been presented as being relatively free of deep class and ideological conflicts. Widescale polarization of its politics along class lines was certainly avoided. In the 1890s the Populists sought to pit the producing against the non-producing classes, but they failed to attract significant support among the industrial working classes.

In a famous essay on the significance of the frontier and of western settlement in American history, written at the end of the Nineteenth Century, Frederick Jackson Turner argued that the existence of the frontier was a major reason why the United States had escaped strident class conflict on the European

153

pattern. The existence of abundant unsettled western land had acted as a 'safety-valve' for social discontent; for the unemployed in industrial regions settlement in the West provided a means of escaping their discontents, instead of channelling them into industrial strife and political agitation. In practice, the frontier rarely served as such a safety-valve. Westward migration tended to swell in good times, and decrease during periods of depression, when the safety-valve was supposed to operate, and few industrial workers ever moved west to become farmers. However, Turner had grasped part of a wider feature of American society. It was an economically abundant and expansive society, in which wages were generally higher than in Europe and the opportunities for mobility much greater. These factors undoubtedly served to temper social conflict in comparison with Europe.

Another major factor that served to retard the development of a powerful working class consciousness, and the emergence of powerful working class movements, was the heterogeneous character of the labour force in America. The great diversity of national and religious groups in the American working class was an obstacle to the formation of a common working class consciousness, and often produced major antagonisms within the working class. As the new immigration from eastern and southern Europe in the late Nineteenth Century was overwhelmingly of unskilled workers, prejudice against them for their national and religious identities served to widen further the gap between skilled and unskilled workers.

Working class political parties consequently failed to develop in Nineteenth Century America, and even the trade union movement progressed comparatively slowly. Employer hostility to unions was part of the explanation for this; powerful employers, as in the steel industry, stubbornly resisted unionization, and they were often assisted by government and the courts. In addition the trade union movement was itself fragile and limited.

The first important formation of trade unions occurred immediately before and during the Civil War, culminating in the foundation in 1866 of the National Labor Union, the first truly nation-wide organization of trade unions in the United States. By 1872 it had a membership of some 300 000, but it then fell apart as a consequence of divisions within the organization, and of the onset of the Depression of 1873. The only major labour organization that survived the Depression of the 1870s was the Knights of Labor. This union attempted to construct a broad-based reform movement incorporating all workers, the unskilled as well as the skilled, women, blacks, and immigrants as well as native-born white males. In the first half of the 1880s membership of the Knights of Labor rose considerably, particularly after the organization of a series of successful railway strikes. By 1886 membership had reached some 700 000, making the Knights by far the largest labour movement of Nineteenth Century America. The failure thereafter of the Knights to mount effective new strikes led to the withdrawal of the more militant unions, and the movement also suffered from the backlash to the Haymarket bomb incident of 3 May 1886. In a confrontation between police and labour groups in Haymarket Square in Chicago a bomb was thrown, killing seven policemen. The incident served to arouse widespread hostility to radical labour organizations, which retreated as a consequence. The Knights were directly affected by this trend, and by the end of the decade membership had fallen to 100 000, and was still declining.

The major labour organization that emerged from the 1880s was the American Federation of Labor, founded in 1886. It differed fundamentally from the Knights of Labor. Whereas the Knights did not confine themselves to labour issues, but aimed at the overall reform of American society, the AFL concentrated solely on labour matters affecting their members, notably wages, working hours, and the protection of jobs. It was a narrowly practical organization, and never contemplated challenging the existing capitalist system. Then again, whereas the Knights recruited their members from all sections of the working class, the AFL largely confined themselves to skilled workers. It was essentially a loose alliance of national craft unions of skilled workers, intent on protecting their skilled positions, and it made no systematic attempt to organize the mass of unskilled workers in the factories. By the end of the century membership of the AFL was about half a million, a small fraction of the overall workforce. By 1914 membership had reached two million, and the AFL was on the way to becoming a more formidable organization.

IMMIGRATION AND THE CITIES

The mass of workers required in the growth industries of the later Nineteenth Century were recruited from two principal sources: the excess rural population, including Southern blacks who began moving into the cities and industries of the North; and immigrants, chiefly from Europe. After the Civil War the pace of immigration speeded up considerably, and the last three decades of the Nineteenth Century saw more immigrants arrive than in the previous seven decades. Almost 12 million immigrants landed in the United States between 1870 and 1900. Increasingly from the 1880s onwards these were 'new' immigrants, deriving not from the traditional sources of western and northern Europe but from southern and eastern Europe; they included Italians, Greeks, Poles, Slovaks, and Russians, and a high proportion of them were either Catholics or Jews. As with the Irish before them, these 'new' immigrants settled overwhelmingly in the cities. In 1900 some two-thirds of the foreign-born population were in towns and cities. They worked in the factories and mines of industrial America, constituting most of the labour force in a number of basic industries, including coal and copper mining, oil refining, iron and steel, textiles, and building.

Significant settlements of recent immigrants were to be found in the great cities, such as Chicago and New York, which came to possess one of the largest Jewish populations in the world. Proportionately, however, they were often much more evident in the newer industrial cities, such as Paterson, New Jersey. American cities came to be distinguished by their immigrant, ethnic, and racial 'ghettos', usually located in the inner city areas, while the middle class, white, native-born Americans moved to the suburbs. It was in the late Nineteenth Century that American cities began to take on their modern social geography.

A feature of American city life in the late Nineteenth Century was the tension that developed between the suburbs and the inner cities. The WASP (white, Anglo-Saxon, Protestant) suburbs believed the inner cities were coming to be dominated by 'alien' groups, and that they were the breeding grounds for all that was undesirable in modern American life. They were regarded as the sources and chief centres for drink, vice, crime, corruption, and violence. The saloon, the gambling den, prostitution and protection rackets, were all located in the inner cities, which were seen as becoming increasingly lawless and violent. The suburbs also resented the inner cities, and their immigrant and ethnic populations, as the base from which the city 'bosses' and their corrupt 'political machines' operated.

The city boss and the political machine, peculiarly American institutions, rose into prominence in the decades after the Civil War, and basically what they did was to turn politics into a business. The boss did not normally hold office, but he and the machine controlled those in civic office, and they used that control to make money by selling franchises* and favours. The basis of their power was control of the immigrant vote. The boss and his henchmen were normally drawn from the immigrant communities; lacking the education and background for careers in business and the professions, they had turned to politics as a means of advancement and profit. Their identification with the immigrant communities, and the services they performed for those communities, in providing houses, parks, and jobs, enabled them to 'deliver' the immigrant vote and determine who would occupy City Hall and control local politics. Control of city offices was used by the boss to distribute jobs to relatives and supporters, and to sell franchises and favours to business, both legal and illegal. Franchises to run public utilities were sold to legitimate businesses, such as tramway companies, and protection from the law was sold to illegal businesses, such as gambling and prostitution operations.

The stranglehold of the bosses on city government, and the corruption of boss government, increasingly outraged the respectable suburbs. At the end of the century a drive to reform city politics, and the inner cities generally, was getting under way. It was to lead to the so-called Progressive movement for municipal reform, and ultimately in the 1920s to immigration restriction and the American experiment in prohibition of the sale of alcohol.

Conclusion

By the end of the Nineteenth Century the United States had acquired the material base to enable her to begin playing a major role in world affairs. Some would argue in fact that material considerations propelled the United States on to the world stage, to secure overseas markets for the goods she was now capable of producing.

America's arrival as a major power in world affairs was signalled in 1898 with the Spanish-American War, purportedly waged by the United States to liberate Cuba from Spanish tyranny. Following the defeat of Spain, the United States acquired Puerto Rico and a protectorate over Cuba in the Caribbean, and Guam and the Philippines in the Pacific, with the latter regarded as a major base for access to the markets of China. Although the hope that American trade would expand rapidly from the Philippines was never fulfilled, the United States had now been established as an influential power in the Far East. In the Twentieth Century the United States was to be drawn, hesitantly, into the affairs of Europe, and her entry into the First World War on the side of Britain and France was to prove decisive in ensuring the defeat of Germany.

Revision Questions

1. *What were the features of settlement, immigration and population in the USA during:*
   (a) *the first half of the Nineteenth Century;*
   (b) *the second half of the Nineteenth Century?*

2. *Explain the fundamental changes in the economy of the USA between 1850 and 1900.*

156

3. Study the diagram on page 126 'The constitution of the USA'. Explain how the arrangements regarding the relationship between the two segments of government—namely federal government and state government—contributed to the causes of the Civil War.

4. How did the colonization of the West affect the history of the USA?

5. To what extent can it be argued that the trends depicted on the graphs and table on page 150 caused the Civil War?

6. What was the role of the USA in international affairs during the Nineteenth Century?

7. (a) To what extent was the Civil War caused by the issue of the emancipation of the slaves?

   (b) How far did the Civil War succeed in gaining civil rights for the black population?

8. How did the various policies followed during the period of Reconstruction reveal the nature of the main forces at work (both political and economic) in US society in the late Nineteenth Century?

Chronology

1823	Monroe Doctrine
1832–33	Nullification Crisis
1846–7	US/Mexican War — annexation of south-western states
1849	California gold rush
1850	Compromise of 1850
1854	Kansas Nebraska Act
1860	Election of President Lincoln
1861	Civil War
1863	Emancipation Proclamation
1865	Lincoln assasinated. Slavery abolished (Thirteenth Amendment)
1865–77	Reconstruction
1869	Transcontinental railway completed
1877	Compromise of 1877
1886	American Federation of Labour organised
1890	Sherman Anti-Trust Act
1890s	Populist Movement
1898	Spanish-American War
1914	Panama Canal opened
1917	US enters First World War
1918	End of First World War

157

Glossary

Antebellum — pre-war.
Constitution — a body of fundamental legal principles, according to which a state is governed.
Dry farming — a farming technique developed in North America, where rainfall is barely sufficient for wheat production. The aim is to accumulate two year's moisture in the soil by allowing the soil to lie fallow in alternate years.
Federal government — where several states form a single nation but retain a considerable degree of independence over internal affairs.
Franchise — a concession to conduct a certain form of business.
Horizontal combinations (or horizontal integration) — the combination of all suppliers in a particular industry; usually designed to curb competition, regulate production and control prices.
Impeachment — accusation and prosecution for treason.
Judicial review — a system whereby laws are subject to review by the courts to ascertain whether or not they are constitutional.
Mergers or combinations — the joining together of firms to form large industrial monopolies.
Monroe Doctrine — first formulated in 1823, during the time of President James Monroe (1816–1824), it signifies the US Government's policy of not agreeing to any European intervention in the political life of the American continent.
Nullification — cancellation.
Populist — in this context, a 'popular' political party which presses for public control of railways, graduated income tax etc. The Populist party was formed in 1892.
Territorial phase of development — prior to becoming a state, an area was organized as a territory under a territorial governor answerable to Congress.
Trust — an organized association of several companies established for the purpose of defeating competition.
Unchartered corporation — a corporation operating without a legal charter defining its rights and liabilities.
Unitary government — where several states form a single nation and pool their identity, with strong power given to a central government.
Vertical combinations (or vertical integration) — where a single company comes to control the supply of raw materials, the process of manufacture, and the marketing of a product.

Bibliography

Billington, R. A. *Westward Expansion*, (Macmillan, 1982)
Brogan, Hugh, *The Longman History of the United States of America*, (Longman, 1985)
Cochran, T. C., and Miller, W. *The Age of Enterprise* (Harper and Row, 1961)
Foner, Eric, *Free Soil, Free Labor, Free Men* (Oxford University Press, 1970)
Genovese, Eugene, *The Political Economy of Slavery* (Vintage)
Higham, John, *Strangers in the Land: Patterns of American Nativism 1860–1925* (Atheneum, 1963)
Jones, M. A. *The Limits of Liberty: American History 1607–1980* (Oxford University Press, 1983)
Oates, D. Stephen B. *With Malice Toward None: The Life of Abraham Lincoln* (Mentor, 1978)
Potter, David, *The Impending Crisis* (Harper and Row, 1976)
Stampp, K. M. *The Era of Reconstruction* (Vintage, 1965)
Vann Woodward, C. *The Strange Career of Jim Crow* (Oxford University Press, 1974)
Wood, Gordon S. *The Creation of the American Republic 1776–1789* (North Carolina University Press, 1969)

5
The emergence of the modern nation state: JAPAN IN THE NINETEENTH AND TWENTIETH CENTURIES

Introduction 160

JAPAN IN THE NINETEENTH CENTURY 162

The beginning of modernization: The breaking of Japan's isolation 162
    Contact with the West
    The Meiji Restoration

The advance of modernization: Domestic policy 164
    Social reforms
    Economic reforms
    Political reforms
    Educational and religious reforms

Modernization and foreign policy: Japan and Asia 172
    The basis of Japanese foreign policy
    Sino-Japanese War (1894–1895)
    Russo-Japanese War (1904–1905)

Conclusion: Japan at the beginning of the Twentieth Century 175
    The effects of the First World War

JAPAN IN THE TWENTIETH CENTURY 177

Liberal government in the 1920s and 1930s 177
    Domestic problems
    Foreign policy as an issue in Japanese domestic politics

Liberal government in crisis: Militarism and expansion 181
    Expansion into Manchuria and China (1931–1939)
    Expansion into south-east Asia and the Pacific (1939–1941)

Conclusion: Japan in the mid-Twentieth Century 189
    Revision Questions
    Chronology
    Glossary
    Bibliography

Introduction

Most of us are familiar with Japanese products. We tend to associate Japan with the mass production of high quality technology. The statistical evidence is impressive. Japan's annual gross national product is currently twice as great as the United Kingdom's, and Japan is the world's largest producer of television sets and motor vehicles.

Japan is one of the most highly industrialized countries in the world and supports a vast population for its size. In 1980 there were 116 million inhabitants. Japan's spectacular success in recent times appears to have been due largely to massive capital investment in new equipment, extensive automation and, currently, to the use of robots in industry. However, within this technologically complex society, there are remnants of an older, pre-industrial Japan.

It is often dangerous to speculate on the 'national character' of a specific people. Such speculations may lead us to stereotype and even to caricature the people we are discussing.

After looking at the extract on the next page, you will see that some scholars believe that it is possible to detect certain forms of 'cultural behaviour' which the Japanese have retained from their past, but which have been modified to meet the needs of the present.

Japanese scholar, Ronald Dore, believes that Japanese society still values courtesy and group harmony more than most westerners do. He tells us that Japanese pupils, for instance, are generally much more deferential to their teachers than pupils are elsewhere. He also describes an incident he observed which demonstrated that children took these values beyond the school. When younger children got off a commuter train at an earlier stop than their seniors, they shouted out in a ritual chorus: 'Excuse us for getting off first.'

People in senior positions are almost equally as polite to their subordinates. Satoshi Kamata, a Japanese journalist who worked in a car factory in the early 1970s, recounts how, even when the conveyer belt was speeded up, sometimes resulting in serious accidents, it was difficult to express antagonism towards the management because his immediate superiors were so helpful and polite. Dore in his introduction to Kamata's account, poses the question: Is it the familial sense of co-operation, actively encouraged by management, which contributes to the high productivity for which Japanese factories are famous?

Japanese levels of productivity have attracted many western businessmen who try to model their factories on Japanese practices. Their imitations are not always very successful because they try to graft Japanese methods on to other societies which do not have the same historical roots. For example, the traditional emphasis on group co-operation expressed in the old Japanese proverb, 'the nail that sticks up gets knocked down,' is at odds with the individualist, 'every man for himself' philosophy of most western countries.

In this chapter we look in more detail at the astounding economic transformation which Japan has undergone since the latter part of the Nineteenth Century. We will try to understand how and why it happened and we will be looking at some of the implications which it had, both for Japanese society and for international relations. Now and then we will pause to consider the ideas which accompanied the various transitions of Japan from one stage to the next. Where did the new ideas come from and what role did they play in the process of change?

> The stress on group harmony [in Japan] is more a matter of positive encouragement than of negative sanctions. People who work together also take their leisure together. Office colleagues regularly go drinking one or two nights a week. Employees of large firms go on holiday to company-owned hotels. At work employees like their boss to take an interest in their personal lives and they will often invite him to family occasions such as weddings and parties. Political factions and university departments often have the same family-like atmosphere, with the leader or professor playing the role of 'parent' to the members of the group, by helping them with promotion or settling their disputes. In return they owe him their loyalty and support.
>
> Many theories have been advanced to explain the Japanese emphasis on the needs of the group. Some scholars have emphasised the historical significance of Japan's 'rice-culture.' For two thousand years the Japanese have had to co-operate in the agricultural tasks of ground-clearing and terracing, planting, irrigating and harvesting rice, and this had led to a wider sense of working together for the good of the community. But if this explanation is right, why is the group emphasis not equally strong throughout the rice lands of East and South-East Asia? And how has it survived in Japan into the age of industrialisation?
>
> Other scholars have pointed out how the Japanese have always been vulnerable to natural disasters such as earthquakes, volcanoes, floods and typhoons. These hazards have forced the Japanese to cultivate a talent for survival and reconstruction, a talent further reinforced by a history which has been marked by periods of anarchy and civil war.

Another school of thought emphasises the closeness of the relationship which has existed for centuries between the rulers and the ruled. In the early seventeenth century William Adams, the first Englishman to live in Japan, remarked that the people were 'very subject to their governors and superiors.' Under the Tokugawa dynasty (1603–1868) public order and stability was the government's main objective and under the Meiji leaders (1868–1912) conscription and mass education were used to make the people into loyal and hard working subjects of the emperor.

Whatever the origins of Japanese 'groupishness,' its importance must never be overlooked. Under a militaristic government the national loyalty of the Japanese was mobilised to serve the needs of war. Since 1945 the Japanese have mobilised themselves for the task of economic reconstruction. At the same time they have managed to combine rapidly rising standards of living, health and education, with a low level of crime and domestic violence. Japan, so often accused of imitation, perhaps deserves to be imitated in return.

(Tames, pp. 8–10)

Questions

1. What does Tames mean by 'groupishness'?
2. Why does Tames think it is important that this 'groupishness' should not be overlooked?
3. Tames gives a number of reasons for the origins of 'groupishness'. Do you find any of them convincing? Support your answer. Look back at this question when you have finished the whole chapter.

Japan in the Nineteenth Century

The beginnings of modernization: The breaking of Japan's isolation

CONTACT WITH THE WEST

The first Europeans to make extensive contact with the Japanese were Portuguese traders and Jesuit missionaries in the mid-Sixteenth Century. Amongst these was Francis Xavier, who lamented the discriminatory nature of the Japanese people's famous politeness. 'They are,' he wrote, 'very polite to each other, but not to foreigners, whom they utterly despise.'

But although the Japanese referred to their visitors as the 'southern barbarians', European commodities, particularly firearms, proved popular, as did Christianity. Weapons were in demand because Japan was embroiled in civil war in this period.

In 1615 peace was restored when the Tokugawa* family managed to unite the warring factions under its rule. In an attempt to rid Japan of divisive influences, the Tokugawa forbade Christianity, and expelled all westerners from the country, except for the Dutch, who were confined to Nagasaki harbour. Travel abroad became a capital offence for the Japanese themselves, and the building of ocean-going ships was banned. For two and a half centuries Japan remained closed to the rest of the world.

During this period of isolation there were many upheavals in Europe, which wrought profound changes in the political and economic structures of certain European countries. Perhaps the most significant of these upheavals was the Industrial Revolution. The Industrial Revolution equipped the countries which experienced it with powerful new technology, which they could use to influence or control other nations. It also impelled them to seek out new sources of raw materials and foreign markets.

For many of the industrializing countries the Far East, with its rich natural resources and large potential market for manufactured goods, was irresistible. Confronted with modern technology the Chinese were forced to submit to western demands and their country was opened up to western exploitation and control.

The United States was able to join in the commercial exploitation of China in the mid-Nineteenth Century, once it had acquired California on the Pacific coast. To the Americans, Japan looked like a useful stop-over point for the refuelling and reprovisioning of their ships on the way to China. But Japan refused initial offers to open trade relations. Therefore, in 1853, the American President sent a squadron of US Navy ships under Commodore Matthew Perry to demand the opening of Japan's ports to American trade.

During the years of isolation, Japan had not kept up with technological advances. The Tokugawa rulers knew they stood little chance of resisting Perry's iron warships. A series of

162

'unequal treaties' followed, first with the US, then with the European countries which came on America's heels. The inequality of the treaties lay in the preferential trading rights* that were granted to these countries, often to Japan's own disadvantage. For example, an important clause in one of the treaties stipulated that the Japanese could only impose very low tariffs on imports from the West.

Most humiliating of all for the Japanese, some historians argue, was a clause which stated that foreigners in Japan, who committed offences, were to be tried in consular courts under their own law. This demonstrated to the Japanese how much contempt the Europeans and Americans felt for their legal system. A British consul at Nagasaki was quite blatant: 'Japan has no known system of law,' he declared.

THE MEIJI RESTORATION

Since the ascendancy of the Tokugawa family, the Emperor of Japan had become a religious figure-head, with no real power. In the period following Perry's arrival many Japanese began to look to the Emperor for relief from an intolerable situation.

The Tokugawa were powerless to keep the foreigners in their place. This increased the resentment that many of the Japanese people, including some members of the ruling class, harboured against the *shogun** and his family.

The shogun, who was a military commander, and his family, who made up the aristocracy, owned huge country estates. The rest of Japan was divided into domains (estates) ruled by *daimyo**. The country was administered by the traditional warrior class, the *samurai**, who besides retaining their military functions, also took on the role of a civilian bureaucracy. The daimyo acted as regional administrators and beneath each of them there was a complex hierarchy of advisers, administrators and military commanders. The peasants and urban dwellers in the areas to be administered (the domains) were divided up into wards under headmen for the purpose of close supervision.

On the whole, the peasants were extremely poor, since between 40 and 60 per cent of their income went in taxes to the daimyo. This, coupled with frequent natural disasters, meant that there was widespread poverty, which often resulted in mass starvation.

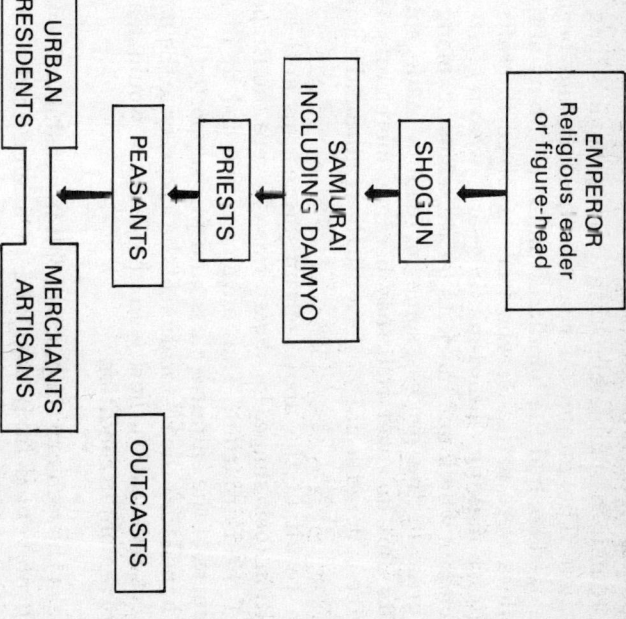

Classification recognized in Tokugawa law and legislation.

163

The advance of modernization: Domestic policy

It would be inaccurate to imagine that the Japanese economy had remained completely static during Japan's long years of isolation. The mining of coal and metals had been slowly developed, as had the handicraft industry. Many of the urban dwellers were artisans, who were involved in crafts such as furniture-making, sword-making, and weaving. It was the merchants who found markets for these goods among the rich samurai. In the process some merchants made substantial profits. But however rich they became, merchants as a class were considered socially inferior to the traditional aristocracy.

As a result of the above circumstances, an anti-Tokugawa coalition took shape. Its slogan was: 'Revere the Emperor and expel the Barbarian.' The movement was led by dissatisfied members of the samurai class, and was supported by peasants who hoped that the restoration of the Emperor to the position of highest political authority in the country would lead to an improvement in conditions.

Some of the rich merchants, who felt increasingly frustrated at being prevented from engaging in foreign trade, as well as socially ostracized within their own country, also joined the coalition. Notable amongst these was the Mitsui family. The Mitsui were so wealthy that they had become money-lenders to samurai who were in debt. The financial backing which they gave to the anti-Tokugawa coalition was valuable.

In 1868 the Tokugawa were overthrown. Although the shogunate was abolished, the Emperor's power was not really increased — he remained a symbolic leader. From now on he was presented as the single most important force for people's loyalty. Since he took the reign name* 'Meiji', the period which followed was called 'The Meiji Restoration'.

Historians often ask of the Meiji Restoration: Was it a revolution?

Some of the men who directed the Meiji Restoration had travelled either to England or to the US. What they observed convinced them that if Japan did not modernize quickly, it would end up as a dependency or colony of one of the great powers, as had already happened to India and China. They believed that it was vital to acquire western knowledge if Japan was to develop into a powerful state. This would in turn help Japan to defend itself against European and US imperialism. But most of the Meiji group did not think that the West was superior. Japan's 'westernization', as you will see, was calculated to 'enrich the country and strengthen the army' (in the words of Foreign Minister Inoue), without reducing Japan to a mere mimic or puppet of the West.

Historian Richard Tames points out that the Meiji were selective borrowers. For example, they based their system of local government on French principles, but relied on the Americans for advice on agriculture and education. The Meiji were, however, wary of becoming too dependent on foreigners. Rather than borrowing huge sums of money from overseas, they raised their own capital through taxes, and they sent foreign advisers back home after Japanese had been trained to fill their places.

If we are to understand the kind of transformation that was initiated by the men who led the Meiji Restoration, we should remember that most of them came from the samurai class. Their

164

education had given them a military outlook. This equipped them to respond to the external dangers confronting Japan. They had also been trained in the Confucian* ideals of loyalty and dedication to society, which was to prove important.

SOCIAL REFORMS

Industrialization in Japan was hampered by rigid class divisions between the traditional aristocracy and other groups, which prevented social mobility. During the Meiji Restoration, the old class structure was broken down. This was part of a deliberate policy to open all occupations to all classes. Under the Tokugawa, peasants, for example, had been excluded from trade or commerce. Now this restriction was abolished. But the disintegration of the old social order also came about as a side-effect of the Meiji leaders' attempts to rationalize and modernize the administration and defence of Japan.

You will recall how complex and lacking in centralization the administrative system was under the Tokugawa. The new government realised the need for a unified and centralized state as the basis for its reforms. The daimyo were persuaded to give up their domains to the Emperor. This patriotic sacrifice was well rewarded by large blocks of shares in government enterprises and the creation of a new peerage*. The domains were reorganized as prefectures, after the French system of local government. Their number was substantially reduced and agents of the central government were sent to the prefectures to issue laws and supervise the carrying out of instructions from the central government.

Despite their important role in the composition of the new government, the samurai lost many of their privileges. For example, they were no longer allowed to kill commoners if they believed they had been insulted. After 1876 they were also prevented from wearing their swords in public. These changes were made possible largely because the samurai's functions had been taken over by the conscript army which had been introduced in 1872. Individuals could buy themselves out of compulsory army service by the payment of 270 yen. This high price meant that the army was comprised largely of peasants because only the rich could afford to buy themselves out of conscription. Compensatory stipends (cash payments) were paid to the samurai, but they were not as easily placated as the daimyo.

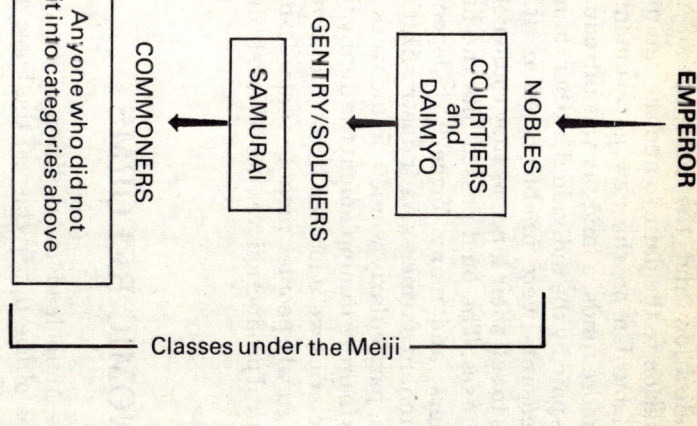

Classes under the Meiji

Industrialization and the payment of millions of yen in compensation to the daimyo and the samurai imposed a heavy financial burden on the new government. In an attempt to provide more funds, a land tax was introduced in 1873. The tax had to be paid by the individual, rather than the landowner, and many peasants were unable to afford it. This forced many peasants to sell their lands as they could not otherwise afford to pay the taxes. The land passed into the hands of the wealthy landowners, and many formerly independent peasants now became tenant farmers. As industrialization proceeded, some peasants, particularly women, found work in nearby mills and factories in order to supplement the family income. The fact that many factories were located in the countryside near the homes of the rural people meant that despite these changes agricultural production was not seriously disturbed.

ECONOMIC REFORMS

With the Meiji leaders' abolition of many of the aristocratic privileges of the upper classes, the basic social conditions for modernization were created. But before economic transformation could take place, financial stability had to be assured. The Meiji government reorganized the national currency on a decimal basis and adopted a central banking system.

The money generated by the new taxes was used to develop steamship lines, railroads, and postal and telegraphic services. In the late Nineteenth Century Japanese children had to learn a song called 'Ten Things to Remember', which enumerated some of the new technological wonders that were being introduced, such as gas lamps, steam boats, newspapers and horse carriages.

The government rewarded enterprising businessmen. This was how the family business, Mitsubishi, expanded into one of the huge commercial empires, known later as *zaibatsu**. The government loaned money to the owners of Mitsubishi, which they used to develop trade with China. With the profits from this trade, Mitsubishi bought the Nagasaki shipyards from the government, and invested in gold and silver mines. Mitsubishi did not forget that it owed its success to the government and continued to be bound to it by strong ties of obligation. Mitsubishi and its fellow zaibatsu, Mitsui, were to play a very important part in the political life of Twentieth Century Japan.

POLITICAL REFORMS

From the account so far, it may seem that the Meiji Restoration was accomplished quite smoothly, and that its achievements were won without the use of force. Yet it is important to note that there was always a degree of resistance, either from the peasants or from members of the old elite. The former saw their freedom being eroded, the latter resented the loss of their privileges. In both cases rebellion was generally crushed by the efficient modern policy or army.

The greatest threat as far as the government was concerned came from the disenchanted samurai. In 1877, a group of traditional samurai, the Satsuma samurai, revolted against their brother samurai in government. But the traditional warriors were no match for the new, conscript army.

In response to the criticisms which were levelled at their government, the Meiji leaders developed new central government machinery, which closely resembled the Prussian model. One of the samurai, Ito Hirobumi, was a great admirer of Bismarck and had consulted closely with him in Germany.

Historians are sharply divided in their opinions as to whether the constitutional government, devised by Ito and his advisers in 1889, was merely meant to appease those who were dissatisfied, without making substantial concessions to them, or whether it represented a genuinely progressive move towards a more democratic system.

The constitution was an ingenious blend of Western, chiefly Prussian, politics and traditional Japanese politics. The Emperor was elevated to the position of sacred monarch, exempt from the laws which governed the lives of his subjects. He could not be touched by criticism or blame.

Ito Hirobumi wrote in 1899:

> Chapter I of the Constitution
> Article III. The Emperor is sacred and inviolable
>
> The Emperor is Heaven-descended, divine and sacred; he is pre-eminent above all his subjects. He must be reverenced and is inviolable. He has indeed to pay respect to the law, but the law has no power to hold him accountable to it.
>
> (Quoted in O'Connor, p. 21)

From the exercise opposite, you will see that the Japanese Parliament consisted of an Upper House of Peers, whose members were chosen by the Emperor, and a lower, elected house (the House of Representatives) which the Emperor could dissolve at will. Their main function was to debate policy decisions on whether or not laws were constitutional when

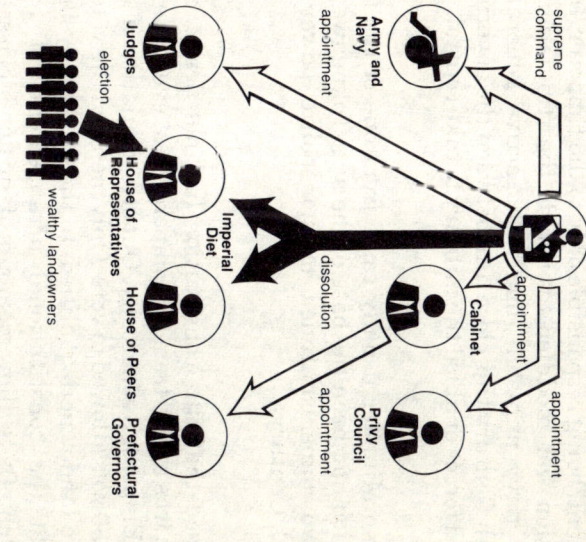

The constitutional structure of Japan (instituted in 1889).

Questions

1. Describe the Emperor's position in the constitutional structure as represented in the diagram.
2. Describe the position of the army and the navy as represented in the diagram.
3. From your study of the diagram, would you say that the new constitutional structure devised for Japan in 1889 provided a basis for democratic government?

made by a separate body called the Privy Council. Ito himself was president of the Privy Council.

The Emperor remained in command of the armed forces. The war and navy ministers could act independently of the civilian government, being responsible only to the Emperor. In 1900 the constitution was modified to include the stipulation that the war and navy ministers had to be active generals. In the Twentieth Century this close link between the government and the armed forces enabled the military to take control.

The Prime Minister usually came from one of the two major clans which had been the base of the anti-Tokugawa coalition. These two clans continued to monopolize power into the Twentieth Century.

Ito stressed that this constitution had not been won by the people. It was a 'gift' from the Emperor. Not everyone benefited from the Emperor's generosity. Out of a population of 40 000 000 only 1 in 80 was allowed to vote. Only men had the vote and only very large landowners qualified. In the final analysis, it would seem that the constitutional arrangements of 1889 were designed chiefly to allow members of the upper classes to 'let off steam', in a manner Bismarck would have approved. (See Chapter 1.)

We can see how the symbolic power of the Emperor was used to sanction much of what happened during the Meiji Restoration. Changes in Japan's economic and social structure were supposedly ratified by him. Yet he was absolved from criticism. Since the Emperor personified the Japanese state, any criticism of the state was seen as criticism of the Emperor. To protest at the changes was to be disloyal to the Emperor.

EDUCATIONAL AND RELIGIOUS REFORMS

The idea of the 'state' was a new one which accompanied the evolution of a strong central government. The Meiji leaders took certain measures to introduce the Japanese people to the concept of loyalty to the state. To make statism* more attractive, they couched it in terms of traditional Japanese beliefs.

Most of the leaders of the Meiji Restoration were determined not to forfeit what they perceived to be the essential Japanese identity. To explain away Japan's apparent deficiencies, they argued that the West's technological superiority was only relatively recent, and they claimed that the bigotry and intolerance which was characteristic of western society did not exist in Japan.

But outside government circles there were many eager converts to western ways. Fashions of the 1870s in clothing, cosmetics and diet show, to some extent, how avidly many of the urban dwellers adopted western ideas. In that period you might have seen Japanese men, dressed in European morning coats, who had hurriedly shaved off their topknots, without worrying about what the rest of their hair looked like. A magazine published in 1875 went so far as to condemn the blackening of women's teeth for beauty as an 'evil' custom, and called for it to be made illegal.

Numerous discussion clubs were formed to debate just how much the Japanese ought to westernize. One of the most influential advocates of thorough-going westernization was Fukuzawa Yukuchi, who maintained that Japan's temporary backwardness was due to the study of Chinese philosophy,

168

which neglected material values. Fukuzawa founded a private school and a newspaper to spread westernization through the elimination of Confucian ideas.

In the 1880s there was, however, a traditionalist reaction. It was probably a fairly widespread revulsion against the extent of western influence. It was certainly exploited by Japan's leaders, who attempted to redirect education to Confucian morals once again. They stressed that, while western material achievements were worthy of study, Japanese ethics ought to be retained.

In the 1880s a series of Education Ordinances were promulgated, which stressed that the supremacy of the state was to be recognised and taught at every level. This had enormous implications since compulsory education had been introduced in 1872. (Mass education was only introduced in England in 1870.) In 1890 the Imperial Rescript on Education was issued and continued to be read on important school days right up to 1945. The Emperor's portrait hung in every school and, if it were lost or damaged, the headmaster might be dismissed.

All textbooks had to be approved by the Ministry of Education, and even the universities were state-orientated. Tokyo Imperial University became the chief training centre for the Japanese bureaucracy. The professors of the University were required to take oaths to the government, in which they pledged to study only those disciplines of most use to the 'practical needs' of the state.

Japan's mass educational system was not designed to produce questioning minds. Its objective was loyalty to the state. (In this Japanese schooling showed marked similarities to the new systems of mass education being evolved in the nation states of Europe and North America.)

An excerpt from the Imperial Rescript on Education, October 1890:

> Ye, our subjects, be filial to your parents, affectionate to your brothers and sisters; as husbands and wives be harmonious, as friends true; bear yourselves in modesty and moderation, extend your benevolence to all; pursue learning and cultivate arts, and thereby develop intellectual faculties and perfect moral powers; furthermore, advance public good and promote common interests; always respect the Constitution and observe the laws; should emergency arise offer yourselves courageously to the State; and thus guard and maintain the prosperity of Our Imperial Throne coeval* with heaven and earth.

(Quoted in O'Connor, p. 24)

Questions

1. After having read the extract from the Imperial Rescript on Education, what evidence do you see of Confucian morals (loyalty, dedication to society)?

2. How is the 'state' presented in the extract?

3. Can you say from your reading of this extract, how the Meiji leaders combined traditional Confucian ideals with statism?

169

Loyalty to the state was further reinforced by the Meiji's declared preference for the Shinto religion. Buddhism, which had coexisted with Shinto under the Tokugawa, was discouraged as an 'obstacle to westernization'. Historian Louis Allen argues that Shinto was made to serve Meiji interests. According to Shintoism, the Emperor could become a *kami* (minor deity) in his lifetime. Shrines were built to his ancestors and to those who had died in the brief civil war which had followed the Restoration.

We have caught glimpses in this section of the Meiji performing a delicate balancing act. They encouraged modernization, which involved extensive adaptation of western techniques. But they could not allow their subjects to follow western examples too closely, especially in the realm which they chose to call 'morals'. The 'Japanese way' was obedience, benevolence and loyalty to the larger community, not criticism or revolution.

Was the Meiji Restoration itself a revolution? There are two major senses of the word 'revolution', namely political and economic. Politically, the Meiji Restoration did involve some reshuffling of the social order. But its impetus came from above, from a section of the ruling class, and as the historian Whitney-Hall, among others, has pointed out, no heads rolled as in the French Revolution. Those who lost their privileges were amply compensated. It is more difficult to assess the economic impact of the Meiji Restoration. Did it amount to a fundamental change in the character of the economy, which would justify the use of the term 'revolution'?

After you have answered the questions in the following exercise, you will be aware of the high proportion of the population which remained involved in the agricultural sector throughout the period of the Meiji Restoration. As you may have observed, cotton and silk continued to be Japan's most important commodities. Both had their roots in the traditional economy. Agriculture persisted as the most important economic sector for many years after the Meiji coup. It provided a solid base for industrialization, by providing raw materials for industry. From this point of view Japan was no different from Britain during its period of Industrial Revolution. In both cases, the rapidity of technological change should not obscure the fact that agricultural activity remained the basis of economic success in the early period of modernization.

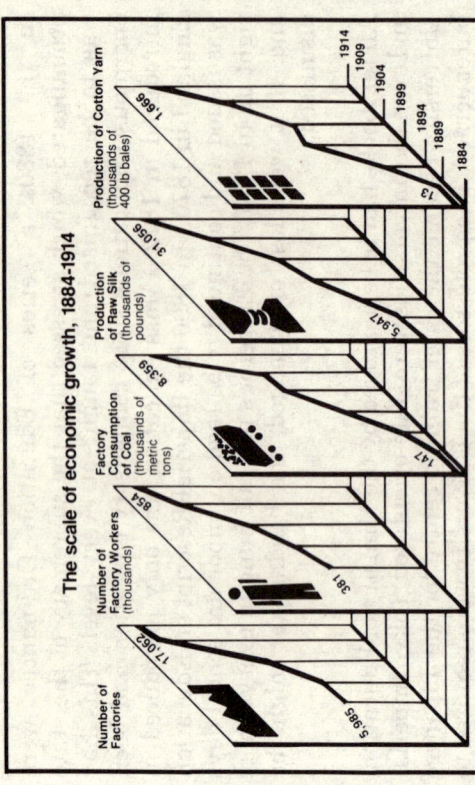

The scale of economic growth, 1884-1914

The development of industry.

CONDITIONS IN THE FACTORIES,
BY W. PETRIE WATSON — From a report written in 1904.
Take the case and the condition of the factory girls of Osaka. Many of them are children of ten, a few of eight, even of six. One account tells us, 'The employees are usually pale and sickly-looking, more especially the younger girls.

'The atmosphere in the mills is oppressive and impregnated with dust and small particles of cotton. There are small pivot windows in the buildings. The manager informed me that these windows are usually opened three or four times per day for a few minutes.'

(Quoted in O'Connor, p. 21)

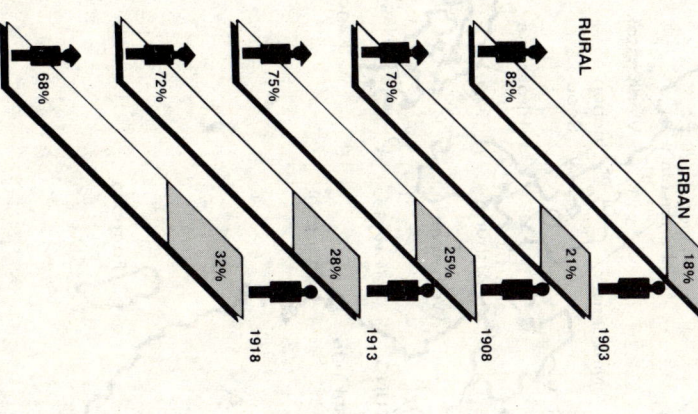

Changes in rural and urban population.

Questions

1. What were Japan's most important commodities, as suggested by the graph which shows the development of industry?

2. What period witnessed the sharpest rise in productivity, according to the graph showing the development of industry?

3. What does the graph depicting changes in rural and urban population show about the changing ratio of urban to rural workers?

4. After considering both graphs, what conclusions can you reach about the nature of Japan's industrialization?

5. After reading the extract, what comparisons can you make with Britain's industrial revolution?

6. Why do you think the labour force in the cotton industry was made up largely of young girls?

171

Map 21 — *Japan in the late Nineteenth Century.*

Modernization and foreign policy: Japan and Asia

THE BASIS OF JAPANESE FOREIGN POLICY

Some historians stress the continuity between Japan's approach to international relations in the Nineteenth and Twentieth Centuries. For these historians, it was Japan's insatiable appetite which led the Japanese to make common cause with Hitler. Other historians point out that Japan did not embark on a course of expansionism for its own sake.

So far, we have seen that the Meiji leaders adopted a programme of modernization in order to protect Japan from exploitation by the great powers. Foreign policy in the late Nineteenth Century was also closely related to Japan's security requirements.

The government's initial efforts in foreign policy were directed at securing respect from the West and the reversal of the 'unequal treaties'. In acknowledgment of Japan's new status Britain was the first country to give up the rights it had acquired under these treaties. An English resident reversed the judgement of Japan's legal system, delivered by his compatriot some forty years before, when he commented:

Japan's laws are excellent and her judiciary is just.

Japan then pursued an imperialist course, not markedly different from that followed by the United States and the powerful European countries. What were Japan's motives for territorial expansion in Asia in the late Nineteenth Century? Begin by looking at Map 21 and the graph above.

Before you study the details of the map, consider the following:

Population growth, 1700–1950
Figures in thousands

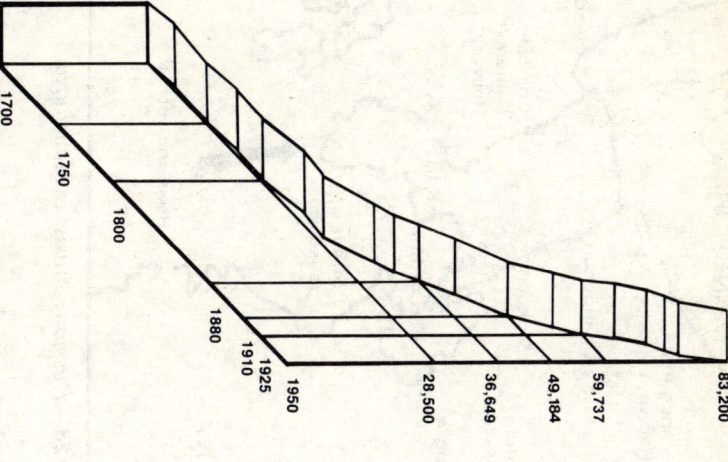

1700
1750
1800
1880
1910
1925
1950

28,500
36,649
49,184
59,737
83,200

The size of Japan;
What the population graph tells you;
What you know about the requirements of a country undergoing an industrial revolution.

What ideas do you have now about the reasons for Japan wanting to extend control over parts of Asia?

SINO-JAPANESE WAR (1894–1895)

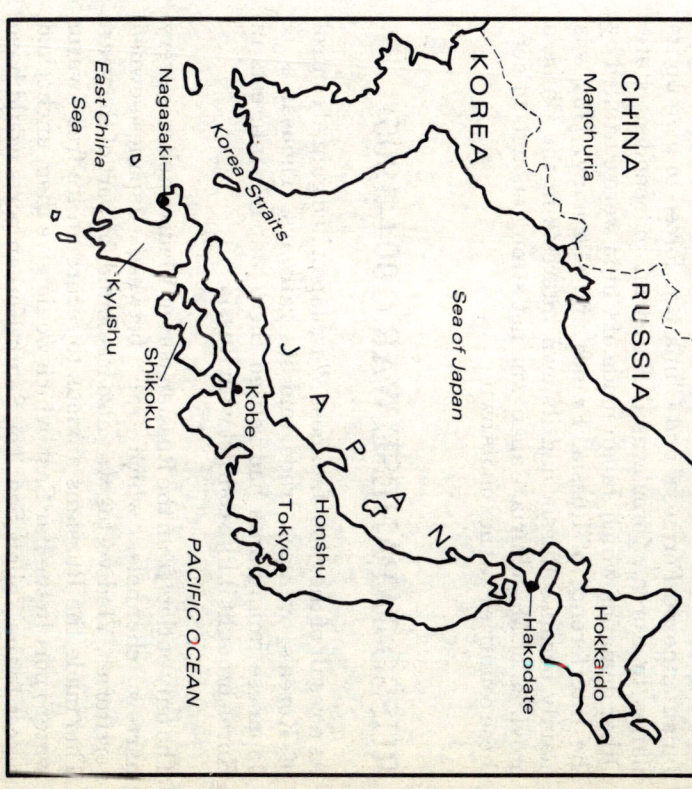

Map 22—*Japan and Korea.*

173

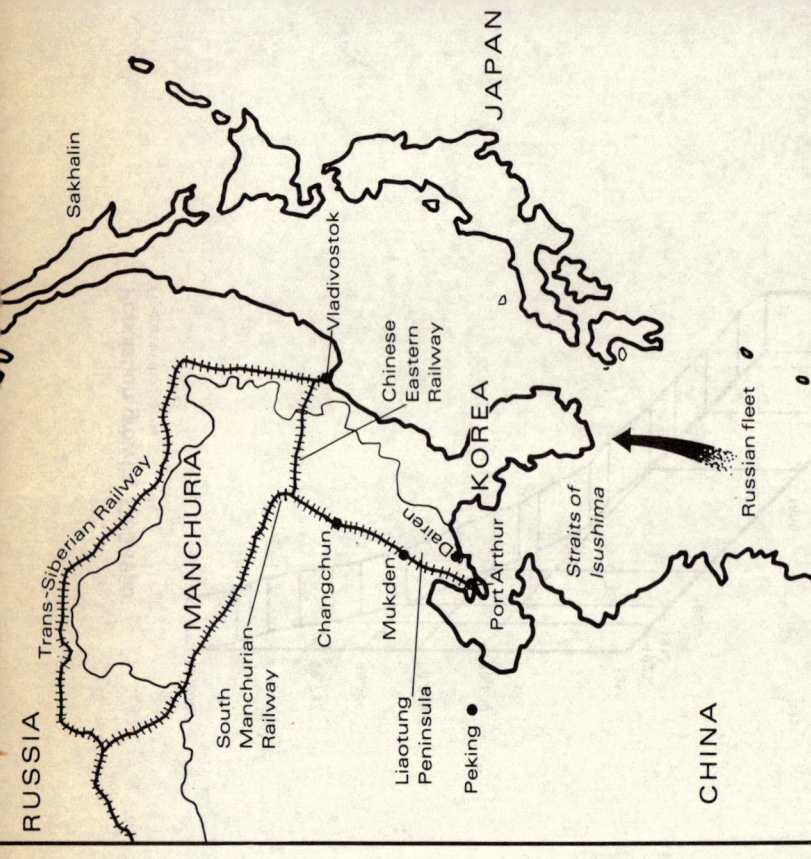

Map 23 — Russian railways in Manchuria.

In 1895 Russia had won a concession from China to build a railway (the Trans-Siberian railway) across Manchuria to Vladivostok (see Map 23). Later the Russians also forced the Chinese to give them a lease on the Liaotung Peninsula and the right to extend their railway to the ports of Dairen and Port Arthur. During the Boxer Rebellion in northern China in 1900, the Russians occupied the whole of Manchuria and subsequently refused to relinquish their position. They were now poised to move into Korea, an intention they took few pains

Both Japan and China had important trading interests in Korea. For centuries China had considered Korea to be its vassal state*. This had security implications for Japan. One of the foreign military advisers said that Korea was 'like a dagger pointing at the heart of Japan'. What do you think he meant by that?

In 1894 the latent tension between Japan and China over Korea came to the surface when both of them intervened in Korea's domestic policies. This led to the Sino-Japanese War, from which Japan emerged as the victor. This victory was due to Japan's increased military strength and her modern army. Japan annexed Formosa, and China was forced to give up its claims to Korea. Korea was declared an independent state. Other demands which Japan made of China were curtailed by the interference of Russia, France and Germany. This was mainly because Russia had its own interests in the Chinese province of Manchuria. Japan was not strong enough to defy these countries' wishes on its own.

RUSSO-JAPANESE WAR (1904–1905)

As a result of the Sino-Japanese War, Japan had gained control of Korea's overseas trade and its railways. Thousands of Japanese immigrants had settled there. Japan's interests in Korea brought it into conflict with Russia.

The only outlets from the Russian port of Vladivostok were very narrow channels, which ran between Japanese-owned territories. Vladivostok was also ice-bound for part of the year. This made the Russians anxious to secure an ice-free ('warm water') port in the Far East, which would give them unchecked access to the Yellow Sea. The South Korean ports would have suited their purposes admirably.

to conceal. With very little subtlety, the Russian envoy to Korea declared that 'Korea must be Russian'.

In 1902 Japan's hand was strengthened, when Japan and Britain made an alliance. This is usually held to be highly significant because it was the first military treaty to have been made between a European and an Asian nation in modern times. But beneath the trappings we must look for the real motives that brought these two countries together. The British were impressed by what they had seen of Japan's action in the Sino-Japanese War and its contribution to the suppression of the Boxer Rebellion. This persuaded them that Japan might be capable of helping to defend Britain's Asian possessions.

The Japanese, for their part, now had an ally, which would enable them to stand up to Russia and its allies. Russia's main ally, France, would be deterred from joining a war between Japan and Russia because of the terms of the Anglo-Japanese Alliance which stated that France would face an attack from Britain if it came to Russia's assistance. (See Chapter 2.) The Anglo-Japanese Alliance also recognized Japan's interests, both commercial and political, in Korea.

In 1904, unresolved tension over Korea and Manchuria led to the Russo-Japanese War. The Russian army was beaten at the battle of Mukden and the Russians' Baltic fleet was totally destroyed by the Japanese navy in the Straits of Tsushima. (See Chapter 6.)

It was an impressive victory for the tiny, newly industrialized country of Japan, but it had imposed a severe strain on the economy. Both Japan and Russia, exhausted by the war, accepted American President Theodore Roosevelt's offer to mediate a peace settlement. In terms of the subsequent Treaty of Portsmouth, New Hampshire, USA:

(a) Japan's paramount interests in Korea were recognized. (This led to the annexation of Korea by Japan in 1910.)
(b) Japan and Russia were to evacuate Manchuria simultaneously.
(c) Japan was to take over Russia's lease of the Liaotung Peninsula from China. Part of the Russian railway, as well as mineral rights, were ceded to Japan.
(d) Japan was granted the southern half of the Russian island of Sakhalin, which had valuable timber and fishing resources.

In the years between the end of the Nineteenth Century and the outbreak of the First World War, Japan was able to consolidate its position as an equal partner of the western great powers. This was best demonstrated when it entered the war as Britain's ally.

Conclusion: Japan at the beginning of the Twentieth Century

THE EFFECTS OF THE FIRST WORLD WAR

By the end of the First World War, Japan was no longer a 'debtor' nation, since it was able to export more than it imported. Obviously the Japanese sustained injuries and material damage in the fighting, but, seen from an overall perspective, the war also brought great economic benefits.

Heavy industry, particularly the mining of coal and the construction of railways and merchant marine ships, was stimulated by the demands of the war. Japan's trading opportunities were also enhanced because European industries were forced to concentrate on war production, thereby neglecting their Asian textile markets. Japan stepped in to fill the gap. Three-quarters of its cotton goods were exported to China. Between 1914 and 1918, Japanese exports of cotton cloth rose by 185 per cent. For the same reason, the Japanese were able to sell two-thirds of their raw silk to the Americans.

The war also enabled Japan to expand its empire. During the war, Japan was determined to concentrate on the Pacific, despite appeals from its allies for troops on the Western Front. In a very short time the Japanese had occupied Germany's Pacific islands—the Marshalls, the Marianas and the Carolines, as well as all the German possessions on the Chinese mainland, including Shantung, which was equipped with a modern port, railways and rich coal mines.

These successes encouraged the Japanese to present the Chinese Government with a series of demands in 1915 which, had they been accepted, would have reduced China to a Japanese colony in all but name. For example, the Japanese demanded the right to control all Chinese towns. After negotiations, the Japanese removed some of the most extreme requests, such as the one just referred to. But they forced the Chinese Government to accept the so-called 21 Demands, which granted Japan important economic privileges, notably an extension on the lease of the South Manchurian railway. Later, an ambiguously worded statement from the US was interpreted by the Japanese as recognition that China was Japan's special sphere of influence*.

Many of Japan's gains were ratified at Versailles (see Chapter 3). There was a growing suspicion on the part of some of the other powers that Japan's ambitions in Asia were reaching alarming proportions. These suspicions appeared to be confirmed when the Japanese sent a huge force into Siberia, as part of the Allied intervention to undermine the Bolshevik Revolution*. The Japanese remained in Siberia until 1922, and in northern Sakhalin until 1925.

So far we have discussed Japan's successes, but there were also hindrances to Japan's progress in the Twentieth Century. We have noted that Japanese intervention in Asia aroused ill-feeling on the part of the other major powers. They found it difficult to accept that Japan could also act as a colonial power. International hostility became an important point of consideration for the government which tried to lead Japan in the 1920s.

The Japanese government of the post-First World War era was also to be beset by domestic problems. The economic benefits of the huge trade boom, which we have described above, were not equally distributed. By 1920, Japan's population had risen to 55 million. Due to industrial expansion, the number of workers in factories had doubled. Trade unions grew as a result of the poor working conditions. Strikes and labour unrest became part of Japanese political life. As the historian Whitney-Hall put it:

> ...Japan was no longer a country which could be dominated by a small handful of politically influential individuals placed in high office.

We now move on to see how the Japanese government of the 1920s attempted to deal both with growing international tension and with the threat of domestic unrest.

176

Japan in the Twentieth Century

Liberal government in the 1920s and 1930s

DOMESTIC PROBLEMS

In the Second World War Japan was to join the Axis powers, so identifying itself with the totalitarian regimes of Hitler and Mussolini. By that time Japan's system of government had many features in common with Fascist Italy and Nazi Germany, such as extreme nationalism and militarism*. (See Chapter 3.)

Historians have been greatly preoccupied with the question of why Japan followed this course, rather than that of liberal democracy. They have posed questions such as whether the ideas of the warrior aristocracy exercised too much power over the minds of the Japanese people. Was the idea of parliamentary democracy too alien to find wide acceptance in Japan? Did Japan resort to totalitarianism* to solve internal problems or to cope with pressures from outside the country?

In an attempt to answer this set of questions, let us now turn to a closer examination of Japan's domestic situation in the 1920s and 1930s.

The Emperor Meiji died in 1912, and by the early 1920s most of the clan-based oligarchy*, which had participated in the Meiji Restoration, had also succumbed to old age or, as in Ito's case, to assassins. Now there was a considerable struggle for the leadership of the country between (a) the military officers and the higher members of the bureaucracy, who considered themselves to be the rightful heirs of the Meiji, and (b) members of the Parliament or *Diet**.

In the broader society there was also intense conflict. The nature of Japan's industrialization had led to the establishment of a few big business combines. They controlled a large portion of Japan's economy, including the many household industries. The powerful position of the combines enabled them to set standardized wage rates and working conditions. Since their main objective was the maximization of profits, hours of work were long and wages were low. Japan's tremendous population growth rate brought with it the continual threat of unemployment. The trade union movement quickly gained momentum in response to these conditions and there were many strikes about wage issues. Lower middle class people also participated in strikes.

Between 1914 and 1918 the price of rice trebled, due, it was widely believed, to poor government planning. In 1918 the fishermen's wives of Toyama Prefecture could endure no more hardship and they rioted. Targets for their anger were rice stores and warehouses. After they had won a ten per cent price cut, other prefectures followed their lead and it took 100000 troops to restore order. The conflict, both within the government itself and outside it, was partially resolved in favour of the new breed of party politicians in the Diet in 1918. Following the rice riots, eleven cabinet ministers resigned and a new government was formed. For the first time the Prime Minister of this government was not chosen by the Emperor's advisers, who had directed Japan from behind the scenes since the Meiji Restoration, but by the Diet. The Prime Minister was a party

177

The Great Depression, which came in the wake of the 1929 US stock market crash, intensified the grievances of a large percentage of the population. The smaller farmers and peasant tenants had already begun to find life difficult in the 1920s, after the relative prosperity generated by wartime demand. The imports of cheaper food-stuffs from Korea and Taiwan undercut their prices. Many of these people supplemented their incomes with silk. The US accounted for a large percentage of Japan's silk exports. After the crash, the Americans cut back drastically on their luxury requirements, including silk. The result was acute poverty for thousands, who drifted into the towns, searching vainly for work.

Farmers' associations, demanding better conditions and more protection for farmers, were formed. These sometimes linked up with workers' groups.

The rural landowners also felt aggrieved since they were still entitled to collect tribute from their tenants, but the fall in the prices of agricultural goods caused by the Depression made it difficult to collect such dues.

Many Japanese workers and intellectuals began to support the small Communist party in this period. But the police tended to apply the provisions of the 1925 Act more strictly to left than to right wing groups. Massive arrests in 1928 and 1932 nearly eliminated the Communist party in Japan. In 1931 and 1932 about 400 Communists were put on trial. Left wing revolution was momentarily checked, but the owners of big businesses knew that they could not exert much more pressure on the workers. Industrial expansion and increased productivity would have to be achieved by other means.

It was the army which provided the answer to these problems and which took Japan towards totalitarianism. The man who owed his position to his support in the Diet. His origins were acknowledged in his nickname, 'Great Commoner'. But it was not as thorough a triumph as it appeared, for the bureaucrats and courtiers still influenced government to a certain extent. As Tames notes, continued in-fighting also often led to hesitant leadership.

Some party politicians argued that the conflict in the broader society could only be eliminated if there was wider representation. In 1925 universal male suffrage was granted and Japan's electorate shot up from 3 million to 14 million.

Western observers interpreted the extension of the suffrage as an indication that Japan was moving towards full parliamentary democracy. But in less than a decade, this proved to be a totally erroneous judgment. What caused democracy to fail in Japan?

The most obvious answer seems to be that democracy in Japan was flawed from the beginning. After 1925 the government no longer represented the interests of the greatly extended electorate.

It was a predominantly conservative government. Both of the major political parties in Japan were closely connected with the zaibatsu, Mitsui and Mitsubishi. These huge commercial empires funded electoral campaigns and sometimes bribed members of the government to take decisions in their interests. Revelations of bribery led to widespread discontent, as other groups in Japan observed the favouritism that was extended to big business. The Peace Preservation Bill, also passed in 1925, gave the police considerable powers to harass groups considered subversive. It was made a crime to belong to a society which advocated the abolition of private property.

178

constitutional position of the army and the navy meant that the armed forces were potentially very powerful (see p. 168). Not only were they themselves independent of civilian control, but each government that came to power had to have a war and a navy minister drawn from the armed forces. The withdrawal of either of these ministers could bring the whole government down.

In the 1930s the army began to exercise its power to an increasing extent. It was not only the constitutional position of the army which allowed the militarists* to eventually take control. As we have pointed out the parliamentary government was fundamentally weak.

The army had close connections with some of the most dissatisfied right wing groups. The vast majority of the soldiers were peasants who belonged to the families which we have mentioned were living on the verge of starvation in the late 1920s and early 1930s. Many of the young officers, on the other hand, came from the class of small and middle landowners, which had suffered as a result of the sharp decline in the price of agricultural goods. There was also a large section of officers of lower middle class origin. All these groups felt they had been deprived of their traditional rights and nursed acute grievances against the party politicians and their big business supporters, whom they blamed for the rapidly deteriorating situation. They were also extremely conservative in their outlook.

At the same time, there was a fundamental tension between the ordinary soldiers with peasant backgrounds and the officers who came from the landowning class, because of their feudal* relationship to each other. This tension could endanger the stability of the army, should it surface. Contemporary observers noted that many of the militarists were actually high-ranking officers, who sought to distract discontented military personnel by appealing for a united effort to overcome Japan's difficulties. Militarist propaganda often exhorted all Japanese, in the name of the imperial past, to work together. Kita Ikki, one of the most famous right wing propagandists, portrayed the army as the defender of Japan's traditions.

By the beginning of the 1930s, the 'Showa Restoration' was being talked of in right-wing circles. 'Showa' was the Emperor Hirohito's reign name. This Restoration would liberate the Emperor from those who had led him astray. The party politicians would be toppled and there would be a purge of western ideas. Proponents of the Showa Restoration talked of 'state socialism' and of placing limits on personal wealth. But, as events were to prove, the militarists were not fundamentally opposed to capitalism.

FOREIGN POLICY AS AN ISSUE IN JAPANESE DOMESTIC POLITICS

One of the most important differences between the party politicians and the militarists was their approach to foreign policy. The militarists saw relief from economic pressure in an expansionist foreign policy. This belief was based on the experience of the benefits that had accrued from involvement in Korea. The civilian government, on the other hand, wanted to curtail Japan's overseas involvements instead of extending them.

During the First World War, Japan had scored a number of resounding victories. Most of its colonial gains were ratified at the Treaty of Versailles in 1919. The Pacific islands, which had belonged to Germany and which Japan had occupied, became Japanese mandates* under the control of the League of Nations.

179

Historians observe that it was chiefly in the matter of prestige that Japan suffered a reversal at Versailles. The Japanese request for a clause promoting racial equality in the Covenant of the League of Nations was rejected, chiefly because the Australian representatives threatened to 'pick up their bags' and leave the conference, if such a motion were accepted. Some years later, Australia and the US added to the insult by passing immigration laws which excluded 'non-whites' from settling in those countries. The racism of the Western powers was a sore point for many of the Japanese militarists who felt that their government ought to do more than protest.

Instead, it seemed that the Japanese Government went out of its way to accommodate the demands of the West. The policy of co-operation that Japan's Government followed in this period was epitomized by the Washington Conference of 1921–2, which gave rise to a number of subsequent international treaties. The most important of these was a treaty which fixed Japan's battleship tonnage at an inferior ratio to that of the US and Britain (5 : 5 : 3), in return for a safety clause in which these two countries, along with France and Italy, agreed not to build any more first-class naval bases within a certain distance of Japan. The Japanese Government followed a policy that was calculated to reduce tension between Japan and the other great powers, especially the alarmingly powerful US.

The old Anglo-Japanese Alliance was dropped in keeping with the League of Nations' prohibition on alliances and Britain, Japan, the US and France made a new treaty of friendship. The historian Tames says of this treaty that, unlike the alliance which it displaced, there was nothing more concrete than goodwill to bind these signatories to their friendship. The new arrangement lacked the security of the old.

Also, under the auspices of the Washington Conference, Japan signed the Nine Power Treaty, in which a number of principal European countries, and the US and China, agreed that 'China's sovereignty, independence and territorial integrity' should be respected.

Despite the use of words such as 'territorial integrity', the Nine Power Treaty did not do very much for China. One of its clauses indicated that the intention of the signatories was to 'uphold the principle of equal opportunity for the commerce and industry of all nations in China', which suggested that the foreign exploitation of China's resources was far from over.

The substance of the Nine Power Treaty was in agreement with the 'Open Door' policy in China, which the US had subscribed to for some years. It meant that China was not to be regarded as the exclusive trading zone of any one nation. This was rather a blow to those Japanese who, in the spirit of the 21 Demands, believed that China was Japan's special sphere of influence. Japan was even pressurized into returning Shantung to China, although the Japanese retained some important economic concessions there.

It was not simply racial slurs and discrimination which led the militarists to react adversely to the conciliatory foreign policy of the politicians. For the militarists, territorial expansion seemed to hold the solution to many of Japan's problems. The acquisition of more territory would create an outlet for the rapidly growing population, which would relieve the tremendous pressure on resources. Territorial expansion would also provide Japan with vital new markets to compensate for the contraction of the old ones. By 1930 Japan had to import all its aluminium, cotton, wool and rubber, and nearly all its lead, steel and oil. These imports had to be paid for by money earned from exports. For the militarist, then, Japan's only route to economic recovery was through an acquisitive foreign policy.

Liberal government in crisis: Militarism and expansion

EXPANSION INTO MANCHURIA AND CHINA (1931–1939)

For many of the militarists, the final humiliation came in 1930 when the Japanese Government signed the London Naval Treaty, which extended the naval agreements made at the Washington Conference. The most famous of the military groups — the Cherry Society — was founded in 1930 by army officers. They wanted to prepare the 'rank and file' of the army to 'wash out the bowels of the corrupt party politicians' who were 'betraying' Japan.

The Japanese army first managed to exercise control in foreign affairs. Its successes in this arena helped it to secure domestic control. How did this happen?

Many of the dissatisfied young army officers, mentioned on page 179, were to be found in the Kwantung army, the garrison that was stationed in the Chinese province of Manchuria. It seemed to them that the 'soft policy' of the Japanese government was endangering their position on the Chinese mainland. China was now ruled by the Nationalists under Chiang Kai-Shek, and committed to ending foreign domination. In the early months of 1931 there was friction between the Japanese and the Chinese authorities in Manchuria. (The Kwantung army also felt menaced by Soviet troops moving along the Amur River.)

Anxiety about the fate of Manchuria was not limited to the more fanatical among the Kwantung soldiers. There were some Japanese who had shares in its railways, mines and agricultural products, and many more who looked to Manchuria as a solution to Japan's economic problems.

To keep Manchuria securely under Japanese control at a time when civilian government appeared so weak, a plot was hatched by officers of the Kwantung army. These probably included a member of the Cherry Society. On 13 September 1931, there was an explosion on the South Manchurian railway, just north of the town of Mukden. The commanders of the Kwantung army accused the Chinese of sabotage, despite the almost certain complicity of their own men. They used the explosion as a pretext to attack the Chinese garrison and later to take over the whole of Manchuria.

In March 1932, Manchuria became the so-called independent state of Manchukuo, with its own Manchu Emperor, Henry Pu Yi. In reality, the state was controlled by the commanders of the Japanese army. The civilian government had lost control over the army's actions overseas. The military take-over of Manchuria was a turning-point in Japan's political and economic development. Its repercussions can be seen in a number of different areas.

What were the consequences? Firstly, Japan's acquisition of Manchuria did help to lift it out of the trough of the economic Depression. But this did not occur immediately.

181

After the seizure of Manchuria the army's continued demand for armaments did stimulate the economy, but it also reorientated production to meeting the needs of a country at war.

The army had managed to sever the 'new state' of Manchukuo from civilian control and was able to try its hand at a 'planned economy', as opposed to the free enterprise system which prevailed at home. Under the army's direction, airports, dams, power plants and thousands of kilometres of railway were constructed. By the beginning of the Second World War, 'Manchukuo' was highly industrialized. Its new capital city had over 300 000 inhabitants. A new port on the coast of Korea linked the 'state' to Japan's industrial heartland. If you look at Map 24 you will see how valuable the addition of Manchuria was from a strategic point of view.

The industrial and military potential of Manchuria was great. The army compelled the zaibatsu to fund its Manchurian projects. As a result, Japan's own economy actually suffered in the process. Nevertheless, the Japanese civilian government used the example of Manchuria as propaganda to exhort the Japanese at home to make a great national effort. In doing so, the civilian government was moving closer to the army. Domestic industry was portrayed as another kind of battlefield in which workers and consumers ought to be prepared to make patriotic sacrifices, just as the soldiers overseas were doing. In the atmosphere of the 'war effort' the government was able to justify taking emergency measures. These contributed to Japan's economic recovery. Japan was the first major country to recover from the Depression — but this recovery entailed a great deal of suffering for the Japanese workers. For instance the government decided to 'eliminate wasteful competition', which resulted in many of the smaller businesses being closed down. The government also decided to abandon the gold standard so as to depreciate the yen. This made Japanese goods attractive on the world market, because of their relative cheapness. Between 1931 and 1936 Japan's exports doubled, but Japanese consumers were at a disadvantage. The general standard of living during this period remained low.

A propaganda poster portraying Manchuria as the land of plenty. (Manchuria had half the population of Japan but three times as much land.)

Questions

1. **What is the message presented in this poster?**
2. **How is the message conveyed?**

The second consequence of the army's take-over in Manchuria was greatly increased support for the military and for a more aggressive foreign policy. The extent of this support was demonstrated in the events of 1932. A director of Mitsui and an ex-finance minister were assassinated by members of an ultra-nationalist association. Later that same year, in an attempted coup, the Prime Minister, Inukai, was murdered by a group of young army and navy officers. All the victims had opposed an aggressive foreign policy. The assassins presented their actions in a patriotic light, as part of the attempt to liberate the Emperor from his evil advisers. The minister of war himself maintained that the murderers had not intended to commit treason. On the contrary, they had believed that they were acting in their country's interests. Widespread sympathy for the assassins led to them being given relatively lenient sentences. From this point on, the army began to exert great influence over the choice of Prime Minister.

For the next 13 years, the army refused to supply a minister of war to a government headed by a party leader. Admiral Saito succeeded Inukai as Prime Minister.

In 1936 there was a more dramatic attempt at a coup, when some members of elite military divisions seized key buildings and murdered a number of men whom they thought were members of the government. Once again they claimed to be acting on behalf of the Emperor, although the Emperor firmly rejected this and denounced them as 'mutineers'. This time the rebels and some of their civilian advisers, including Kita Ikki, were executed.

However, using the incident as evidence of acute dissatisfaction in the ranks, senior officers in the military argued that it was necessary for them to take control of Japan's domestic affairs. Proposals to put liberal ministers in power were vetoed by the army. The Diet lost its short-lived control over the cabinet and reverted to its old form as a glorified debating society. The civilian Prime Minister, Prince Konoye, who was appointed in 1937, commented on the civilian government's relationship to the army: 'We are their puppets.'

A third consequence of the action in Manchuria was the antagonization of the western powers, since it was a violation of the Nine Power Treaty. Britain and the US particularly felt that their own interests in China were being threatened.

The Lytton Commission, set up by the League of Nations in 1932 to investigate the Manchurian affair, was reluctant to find Japan guilty of being the aggressor, but recommended that the state of Manchukuo be refused international recognition. Without any means of coercion at its disposal, the League could do nothing to change the situation, except express moral condemnation of Japan's action. In the end, this only had the effect of angering the Japanese militarists and making them more determined to stake their future on an expansionist policy in Asia.

In 1933 Japan left the League against the Emperor's wishes. Subsequently, the Foreign Office issued the Amau Declaration, which stated that Japan would take responsibility for peace in East Asia and that it would regulate China's relations with the West. This explicit denial of the principles of 'Open Door' set Japan on a dangerous course of head-on collision with the US. At the end of 1934, the navy refused to recognize the Washington Treaty and in 1935 it withdrew from the London Naval Conference.

Having consolidated its position in Manchuria, the Japanese army began to penetrate Northern China, claiming that this was necessary for the purpose of defence. Northern China was an important source of cotton and coal, as well as being a market for Japanese goods.

This extract comes from *The Principles of National Polity* published by the Ministry of Education in 1937. It addresses itself to the concept of *bushido*, that is feudal warrior morality.

The Warrior Code — Bushido

Bushido may be cited as an outstanding characteristic of our national morality. In the world of warriors one can see the spirit of the ancient clans peculiar to our nation. We have followed the teachings of Confucianism and Buddhism, but now we have gone beyond them. That is to say that, though a sense of obligation binds master to servant this has developed into a spirit of self-effacement* and of meeting death with a perfect calmness. It is not that death is made light of. Man prepares himself for death and regards it with esteem.

The warrior's aim should be, in ordinary times, to foster a spirit of reverence for the deities and his own ancestors, in keeping with his family tradition; to train himself to be ready to cope with emergencies at all times; to clothe himself with wisdom, benevolence and valour; to understand the meaning of mercy .... It is this same bushido that shed itself of an outdated feudalism at the time of the Meiji Restoration, increased in splendour, became the Way of loyalty and patriotism, and has evolved before us as the spirit of the Imperial Forces.

(Morris, p. 50.)

Questions

1. What attitude to the nation is expressed in the bushido warrior code?

2. According to the author, how does bushido teach men to regard death?

3. How would this idea have been useful in Japan in the late 1930s?

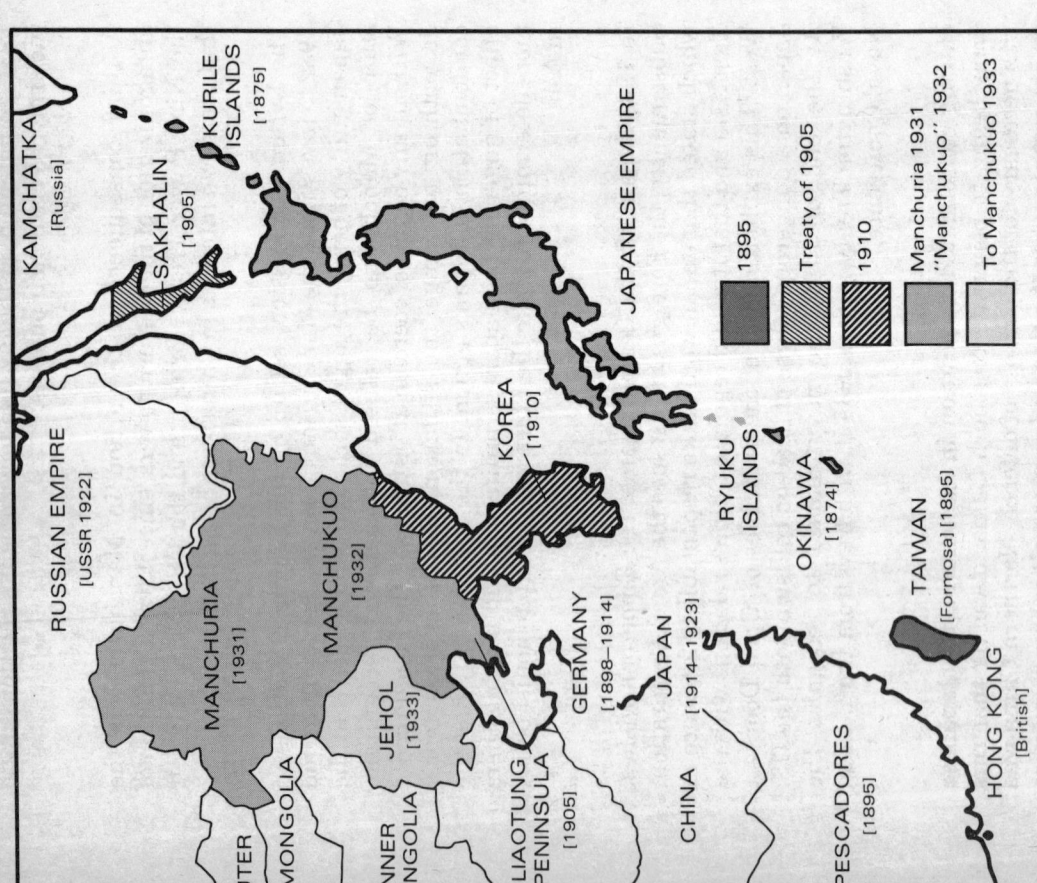

Map 24 — Japan's penetration into northern China up to 1933.

Tension mounted as the Chinese ruler, Chiang Kai-Shek's, determination and ability to resist increased. In 1937 he made an agreement with his opponents, the Chinese Communists, that they would unite to thwart the Japanese. Conflict was sparked off by an incident between a regiment of the Chinese army and a Japanese infantry company on night manoeuvres near Peking at the Marco Polo bridge.

Although Japanese victory seemed likely, the 'Chinese Incident', as it was euphemistically known, was to continue inconclusively until the end of the Second World War. At first Japan moved rapidly, taking Peking, Shanghai and then Nanking, Chiang's capital, where a quarter of a million Chinese civilians were brutally slaughtered. But Chiang was not defeated. He transferred his capital and, when that was seized, moved again. By late 1938 the Japanese controlled China's major cities and railways, but final victory eluded them because of fierce Chinese guerilla warfare that was waged against them in the countryside.

By 1940 the Chinese war was costing the Japanese the equivalent of $4 million a day, but they carried on, believing that this was the only option left to them in an increasingly hostile world. What were the consequences for Japan of the invasion of China?

Japan's involvement in China had a dramatic impact on its own economic and political development. As the war in China became more difficult and more costly, so the Japanese Government was forced to rationalize its resources. Price controls and rationing were introduced. Labour and materials had to be carefully controlled and distributed. In some ways the government approached the 'planned economy' that had been the dream of those who hated the kind of capitalism represented by the zaibatsu. But it was a planned economy which imposed a severe strain on the Japanese. If the national effort was to be maintained, it was essential from the viewpoint of Japan's military leaders that dissidence be stamped out. Shintoism was revived to emphasize, once again, the Emperor's divinity.

In a sense the Showa Restoration, as envisaged by the rebels of 1932 and 1936, had been achieved after all. But Japanese today often refer to the period from the end of the 1930s until 1941 as 'The Dark Valley', meaning that it was a time of repression and extreme conformity.

In 1940 the political parties were persuaded to dissolve and they were replaced by the Imperial Rule Assistance Association (IRAA). Under the IRAA neighbourhood groups were organized for the purpose of monitoring citizens' activities. The IRAA was also responsible for 'spiritual mobilization'.

---

4. In your own words summarize the virtues that the author says are expected of warriors.

5. The author claims that bushido was brought up to date during the Meiji Restoration so as to include elements of loyalty and patriotism. Why do you think that there was no need for a concept such as patriotism under the Tokugawa?

6. Why do you think that the author spells 'Way' with a capital letter?

7. Explain how the extract demonstrates the blending of the old and the new in modern Japan.

8. Write a paragraph to explain how bushido may have been used as propaganda in Japan in the late 1930s.

This was a propaganda campaign to keep morale high and to unite the Japanese in feeling that they were engaged in a special mission to free China from both the Communists and the West. The IRAA promoted a strong anti-westernism. It called for a return to Japan's historical traditions. The historian Whitney-Hall says that anti-westernism even affected the popularity of golf, which the Japanese were encouraged to drop in favour of traditional archery.

It is impossible to make any definite statement about the motives of either the Japanese or the Americans. But it does seem that both interpretations cited above are a little simplistic. The Japanese attack on Pearl Harbor needs to be placed in context.

The full meaning of the attack can only be gauged if it is seen within the context of the deep conflict between Japan and the United States over trade and economic interests in China, south-east Asia and the Pacific.

After 1939, as the Japanese militarists continued their struggle to win the whole of China, so the Americans became progressively more disturbed by what they perceived as a grave threat to their interests in China and, more generally, to American security in the Pacific area as a whole.

Theoretically, the Americans possessed the right kinds of weapons to defeat the Japanese without a military confrontation. Japan's economy was heavily dependent on American supplies of iron and oil. But although the US did attempt to use economic sanctions against the Japanese, they did not prove effective.

Having committed themselves to total victory in China, the Japanese did not find it easy to extricate themselves, in spite of the rising costs of war and antagonism from the United States of America.

The first step which the Americans took to deter Japanese expansionism was the transfer of their Pacific fleet base from San Diego in California to Pearl Harbor on the island of Hawaii in 1940. Lack of agreement on a more aggressive course of action prevented the American Government from taking direct action against the Japanese for some time.

EXPANSION INTO SOUTH-EAST ASIA AND THE PACIFIC (1939–1941)

In September 1939 Hitler's invasion of Poland led to the outbreak of war in Europe. The US remained aloof, committed to its policy of isolationism. But on 7 December 1941 Japan attacked the US naval base at Pearl Harbor in Hawaii. This brought the US into the Second World War and ultimately led to the first atomic holocausts of Hiroshima and Nagasaki.

The attack on Pearl Harbor has provoked extremely contentious historical debate. Some historians have argued that the attack on Pearl Harbor constituted an act of naked aggression on Japan's part. Others have maintained that the American President, Franklin D. Roosevelt, provoked Japan to such an extent that it eventually retaliated with this attack. Some of those historians who argue for the second interpretation believe that Roosevelt was looking for a way into the European war and that he calculated, correctly as it proved, that active Japanese aggression against the US would convince reluctant elements of the American public that participation in the war was necessary.

186

By June 1940, the Japanese were encouraged to be more aggressive as a result of the rapid Nazi victories in the Netherlands and France, which they believed would enable Germany to win the war. The Japanese had signed the Anti-Comintern Pact* with Germany in 1936. Now the Japanese saw the possibility of the immense gains to be achieved by joining Germany in a war against the Allies. The defeat of Russia, the USA, Britain and France, would mean that Asia's rich resources would be free for Japanese exploitation. Under the Greater East Asia Co-Prosperity Sphere Agreement, announced in mid-1940, the Japanese Government visualized Japan as the leader of a union of Asian states, which would provide Japan with tin, rubber, oil and other vital raw materials it lacked. Japan, in turn, would supply these countries with industrial goods. The Japanese cloaked their proposals for the leadership of this Asian union in the rhetoric of anti-colonialism. General Araki, the war minister since 1932, talked of the need to struggle against 'the arbitrariness of white rule' in Asia. From this it was clear just how far the Japanese had gone in their repudiation of their old western partners.

The Americans tried to restrain Japan by withholding exports of aviation petrol. This drew strong protests from the Japanese but it did not deter them from continued expansion in China. It was clear to the Japanese that Chiang would never be defeated unless they could find a way of cutting off the supplies he received from the Allies through neighbouring countries. These supplies came mainly from Indo-China. In July 1940 the Japanese were able to take advantage of the helplessness of France's Vichy* Government to capture French air bases in northern Indo-China. This helped them to intercept Chiang's supplies.

A few months later, the Americans tried to put more pressure on Japan by placing an embargo on scrap iron and steel. They granted the Chinese Nationalists a large loan to further their resistance to the Japanese.

The Japanese signed the Tripartite Pact in September 1940. In terms of this Pact, Japan, Italy and Germany promised each other support if any one of them became the victim of American aggression. Japan's primacy in east Asia was also recognized. This established the so-called Berlin-Rome-Tokyo Axis, and for some time the World War appeared to be progressing in its favour.

In April 1941 the Japanese foreign minister managed to make a neutrality pact with Russia, so blunting the edge of the threat from that quarter. Guaranteed neutrality from Russia freed the Japanese to move south, in the direction of the Asian colonies which belonged to the French, Dutch and English. Their main objectives were British Malaya and the Dutch East Indies. In the next couple of months, the Nazi invasion of Russia put that country firmly in the Allied camp, but the Japanese had no immediate fears while the Soviet troops were so heavily engaged in fighting the Germans. Once again, the Japanese pressurized the Vichy Government to relinquish bases, this time in southern Indo-China.

The American Government now decided to respond more vigorously to Chiang's appeals for support. All Japan's assets in the US were frozen. Japan retaliated by freezing US assets. Trade between the two countries came to a standstill when the Americans imposed a total embargo on exports to Japan in August 1941. Britain and Holland also embargoed exports to Japan. By this stage, Japan's industry was largely directed towards war production, thus the loss of rubber and oil supplies was a serious deprivation. But the repercussions were even wider because Japan's economy was locked into an international trade network.

187

rejected. The Hull Note, which comprised a set of American proposals, was delivered to the Japanese in November 1941. It ordered the Japanese to evacuate these Asian territories and to renounce the Tripartite Pact. The note was written in an aggressive tone which offended the Japanese.

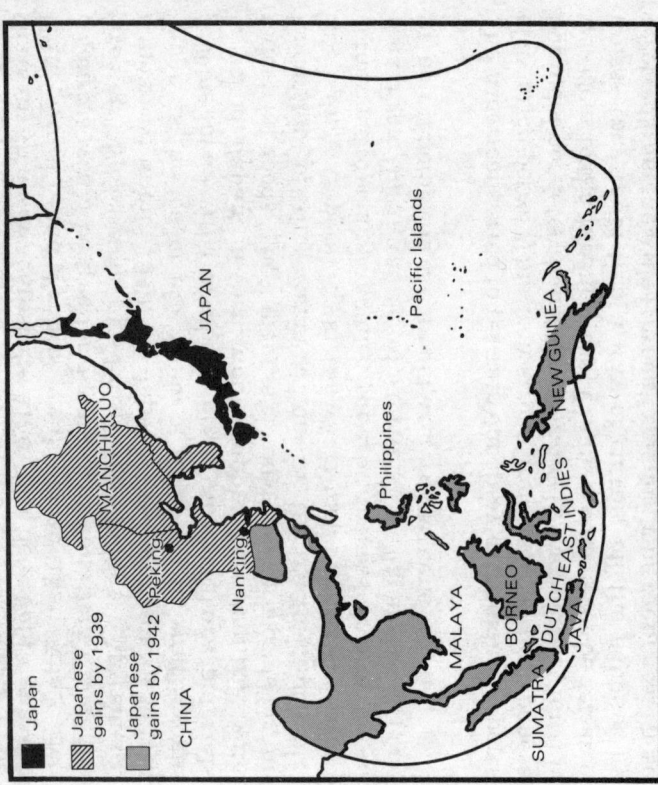

Map 25 — *Japanese conquests up until 1942.*

By November, the Japanese Government had made the decision to attack Pearl Harbor if it did not get its way in China. Tojo and the other leaders were aware of the risks they were taking in defying the US. But for them, their stand on Asia was a matter of survival, especially now that the Americans and the hostile European countries seemed so bent on 'squeezing them

The old currency earning staple, raw silk had fallen to 14% of the total [exports] by 1938 and heavy industry (metals, chemicals, engineering) was assuming a major role. This meant that [Japan] was fully enmeshed in the web of international trade relations and needed overseas supplies as never before in her history: one-fifth of her rice and beans came from overseas, one-third of her fats and oils, four fifths of her iron and steel and all her wool, rubber and raw cotton (she was by now the world's chief exporter of cotton piece goods). One-fifth of her economy, by 1940, was working for war. That economy the USA now deliberately attempted to strangle.

(Allen p. 112)

Japanese military officers calculated that their oil and rubber supplies would only last for another two years. They complained that their enemies were encircling them.

In August 1941, Roosevelt followed up his punitive actions against the Japanese with stern words, advising them that the US would not hesitate to 'take all steps which it may deem necessary toward safeguarding [its] legitimate right and interest'. Negotiations between the Japanese and the Americans which took place during the last troubled months of 1941 foundered because both sides clung stubbornly to their claims to incompatible 'legitimate interests'.

In October 1941, there was an important development in Japan. The Emperor summoned General Tojo, the war minister, to take over the premiership. His instructions were to prepare the army and the navy to act together in the event of war. Although some members of the American Government refused to admit it, Japan had become a fully fledged military dictatorship.

The Americans' offer of favourable trade relations in return for a Japanese withdrawal from China and Indo-China was

188

Kamikaze* pilots about to set off on a suicide mission, 1945.

to death', as they put it. The crisis came to a head on 7 December 1941 when the Japanese launched an air attack on the American base at Pearl Harbor, destroying a large part of the US Pacific fleet and killing over 2000 servicemen.

The attack on Pearl Harbor, and subsequently on the American forces in the Philippines, was conceived of as a temporary strategy to knock the Americans out of the Pacific. This would provide a breathing space in which the Japanese could consolidate their Asian union. With Asia's resources at its disposal, and with a victorious Germany on the European mainland, the Japanese believed that their chances of victory, were good, even if the US did decide to strike back.

Many Japanese did not think this a wise strategy. They realized that large sections of American public opinion were opposed to US involvement in war and saw great danger in making an enemy of a power so great as the USA. We know that there were some misgivings even within the ruling hierarchy. Admiral Yamamoto, chief strategist of the Imperial Navy, confessed: 'I fear we have only awakened a sleeping giant and his reaction will be terrible.'

He was entirely right. Although the attack on Pearl Harbor was militarily impressive, the following day the American Congress voted to go to war against Japan. It was a war which, far from elevating Japan to an even greater imperial stature, devastated it. Once again it was the Americans who were responsible for Japan entering a new phase of its history.

Conclusion: Japan in the mid-Twentieth Century

After a few initial successes during the Second World War, Japan suffered terribly. We know already that Japan was extremely vulnerable once it was cut off from its supplies of raw materials, and its predicament turned out to be insoluble. Scholar Tom Kemp claims that the war also revealed that the process of industrialization in Japan was still incomplete. Half the population was involved in agricultural production and as producers of food they were not available for recruitment into the armed forces.

189

Hiroshima after the atomic bomb.

Finally, there was the physical destruction wreaked on Japan, especially by the two atomic bombs, which led to the Japanese surrender on 2 September 1945. About a million[1] Japanese people lost their lives during the war, including thousands of civilians. Japan's economy was virtually destroyed. Yet forty years later it ranks third among the world's industrial giants. How was this spectacular recovery accomplished?

Tom Kemp describes the war and the subsequent American occupation as clearing the way for a new 'surge' of industrialization. Some of the obstacles to home market expansion were scrapped and industries were reorientated so that their survival no longer depended on the maintenance of overseas territories, as it had done since the days of the Meiji. In the space remaining, it is possible to refer only very briefly to some of the social reforms which allowed for this economic redirection.

Despite the positive assertions made about the role of the US in Japan's economic recovery, Kemp is careful not to attribute too much altruism to American motives. After 1948, Cold War tensions in the Far East worsened and the Americans recognized the value of having Japan as a strong ally. Consequently after 1945 their attention rapidly moved away from the issue of Japan's demobilization to the question of how

---

[1] 3,5 million if the Chinese war is included.

Japan's economic reconstruction could most successfully be accomplished.

Representatives of the Japanese Government arriving on the USS Missouri to sign the instrument of unconditional surrender on 2 September 1945.

The old Japanese leadership was purged and, in tandem with the new leaders, the Americans worked out several measures to help Japan recover its economic stability.

Under the American occupation, substantial land reforms were carried out, which relieved many peasants of their rent obligations. Now they had more money to invest in agricultural machinery, as well as to purchase consumer goods. In this way the conditions for domestic market expansion were created. At the same time, the displacement of large numbers of people because of the war and demobilization meant that there was a large potential labour force.

In the 1950s American economic aid, combined with the conditions described above, allowed Japan to enter a period of sustained economic growth, which has continued up until the present. It was the Japanese state's decision to encourage the new range of consumer industries, responsible for the production of television sets, transistor radios, cameras and later, motor vehicles, for which Japan is best known today.

The Americans, in collaboration with the Japanese Government, tried to abolish the 'morals' courses which pervaded the educational system and the Emperor was required to renounce his divinity over the radio. But some of those influences remain. We are left with the tantalizing question, put by Ronald Dore: Is it social discipline, with its roots in Confucian ideals, or large-scale capital investment in modern equipment, or cheap labour, which accounts most for Japan's success in the latter part of the Twentieth Century?

Revision Questions

1. *The Meiji Restoration has been described as an act of self-defence. Do you think this is accurate? Support your answer.*

2. *Describe and account for the major reforms introduced by the Meiji leaders after 1868.*

3. Account for Japan's shift to totalitarianism in the period 1930 to 1941.

4. How and why did the westernization of Japan influence its foreign policy in the period 1920 to 1941?

5. Explain how and why Japan was able to emerge as a world power by the 1930s.

Chronology

Mid-Sixteenth Century	Portuguese traders made contact with Japanese.
1615	Tokugawa Shogunate established. Westerners expelled. Japan closed.
1853	US squadron under Perry demands opening of Japan's ports to US trade.
1868	Tokugawa overthrown. Meiji Restoration. Emperor Mutsuhito regains power from the Shogun.
1877	Satsuma Samurai revolt occurs and is crushed.
1890	Introduction of constitututional government.
1894–5	Sino-Japanese War.
1902	Anglo-Japanese Alliance.
1904–5	Russo-Japanese War. Treaty of Portsmouth, New Hampshire. Japan's interests in Korea recognized.
1912	Death of the Emperor Meiji.
1914	First World War. Japan joins the Allies.
1915	'21 Demands' presented to China.
1918	Rice Riots — First party Prime Minister.
1919	Treaty of Versailles — material gains mostly ratified, but Japan's prestige was damaged.
1921–22	Washington Conference — several treaties. NB 'Nine Power Treaty' — 'Open Door' Policy in China confirmed. Introduction of liberal government.
1925	Universal male suffrage. 'Peace Preservation' Bill.
1929	Great Depression — severe repercussions on silk industry.
1930	London Naval Treaty — army started to exercise greater control — foundation of Cherry Society. Talk of Showa Restoration. Liberal government crisis: The rise of militarism.
1931	'Mukden Incident' on South Manchurian railway line. Japan occupies Manchuria.
1932	'Independent' State of 'Manchukuo' proclaimed. Domestic 'policy' of assassination. No more party Prime Ministers permitted by army.
1933	Japan withdraws from League of Nations. Issues Amau Declaration.

1934–5   Abrogation of Washington Treaty. Withdrawal from London Naval Conference.
1936   Attempted Coup. Diet loses control over cabinet. Japan signs Anti-Comintern Pact with Germany.
1937   Beginning of Japanese-Chinese War.
1940   Second World War. Rome/Berlin/Tokyo Axis established (Tripartite Pact).
1941   Japan enters war. Pearl Harbour — US enters war.
1945   Hiroshima and Nagasaki — End of war.

Glossary

Anti-Comintern Pact — a pact against Russia.
Bolshevik Revolution — Russian Revolution of 1917 which brought the Bolsheviks under Lenin to power.
Coeval — of the same age.
Confucianism — East Asian philosophy derived from the Chinese sage Confucius (551–479 BC), which tends to view society as a naturally ordained hierarchy.
Daimyo — Lord controlling a territory producing 10 000 koku (approximately 5,2 bushels) or more of rice.
Diet — the two chambers of Parliament.
Feudal — tenant peasants still paid tribute to landlords.
Kamikaze — airmen who flew suicide missions.
Mandate — power given to a state to govern another state.
Militarism — ideology which aspires to military domination of government (and proposes aggressive foreign policy).
Militarist — term used to refer to those people who espoused militarism.
Oligarchy — system in which power is confined to a few persons or families.
Peerage — nobility.
Preferential trading rights — trade agreements which allow the partner special, advantageous rights in competition with other trading nations.
Reign name — name chosen by the Emperor to describe his reign.
Samurai — traditional warrior aristocracy.
Self-effacement — regarding oneself as unimportant.
Shogun — the title of the chief military leader of Japan during the period from the Twelfth until the Nineteenth Century.
Sphere of influence — an area where one power is considered to be most influential.
Statism — ideology in which the state is seen as the most important object of loyalty.
Tokugawa — family name of the shogun.
Totalitarianism — political system or ideology which admits no rival parties or ideas.
Vassal state — a state which owes allegiance to another, more powerful, state (Manchukuo was sometimes also called a 'puppet state').
Vichy Government — a French government which collaborated with the German occupying forces.
Zaibatsu — a big business clique (originally a derogatory term).

Bibliography

Allen, L. *Japan: The years of Triumph* (BPC Unit 75, 1971)
Kemp, T. *Industrialisation in the Non-Western World* (Longman)
Morris, I. *Japan 1931–1945: Militarism, Fascism, Japanism? — Problems in Asian History* (D.C. Heath and Co., 1980)
O'Connor, *Japan's Modernisation* (Harrap World History Programme, Harrap, 1975)
Satoshi, K.; Foreword by Dore, R. *Japan in the Passing Lane* (Unwin Paperbacks, London, 1980)
Storry, R. *A History of Modern Japan* (Penguin, 1975)
Tames, R. *Japan in the Twentieth Century* (Batsford Academic and Educational Ltd, 1981)
Whitney-Hall, J. *Japan: From Pre-history to Modern Times* (Weidenfield and Nicholson, 1970)

6

The emergence of the modern nation state: RUSSIA IN THE NINETEENTH CENTURY

Introduction 195

The Russian Empire: Its territorial growth and foreign policy 200
  Expansion of territory
  Foreign policy
  In Europe
  In Asia

The Russian state: Attempts to consolidate power inside the Empire 207
  Control mechanisms
  Economic change and government response
  The urban working class
  The peasants
  Political opposition and government response
  Bloody Sunday 1905
  Foreign policy prior to the First World War
  Far East
  Europe and the Middle East
  The Balkans

Conclusion 217
  Revision Questions
  Chronology
  Glossary
  Bibliography

Introduction

The more I see of Russia the more I agree with the Emperor when he forbids Russians to travel and makes access to his own country difficult for foreigners. The political system of Russia would not resist 20 years free communication with western Europe.

(Marquis de Custine, *Journey for Our Time*. Quoted in MacKenzie and Curran, p. 293.)

Russia was regarded as the greatest land power of Europe in the early Nineteenth Century. What was it really like? The traveller quoted above suggests the great Russian Empire was isolated, autocratic* and afraid of comparison with the countries of western Europe. A study of its history reveals that there were many weaknesses in the social, political and economic structure.

At that time Russia was industrially backward. Its peasants eked out a living from primitive agriculture on large feudal* estates, and its major towns were essentially cultural and administrative centres that lacked both industry and trade facilities. As a consequence there had been no accumulation of the capital needed for industrial growth, the development of resources or the improvement of communications. The industries which did exist were rudimentary, and economic activity centred around such local raw materials as wool, flax (linen), cotton, leather and sugar-beet. Oil and coal resources were virtually untouched. The foundations for the development of industry were thus lacking. Exports were minimal and by the middle of the century trade stood at only 18 per cent of Britain's total for the same period.

Russia was industrially backward. Its peasants

In the Nineteenth Century rapid social, economic and political change took place in western Europe, but Russia modernized very slowly. The nobles owned the land and exacted payment in taxes or labour from the peasants, who constituted the vast majority of the population. The peasants were serfs, virtual slaves to the landowners. They owned no land, had no rights and could be physically punished by their lord. They were bought and sold with the land, like livestock. Until the 1840s they could be auctioned off, or moved from one estate to the other either with or without their families. There were two classes of serfs, one state-owned and the other privately-owned. Although by the middle of the Nineteenth Century only 51 per cent were still privately-owned, the structure of the society was still essentially feudal, with all rights and privileges reserved for the nobles. The peasantry formed the largest and poorest class and upward social mobility was rare.

The government of such a society was characteristically autocratic. The rulers were dictatorial and there was no constitutional limit* to their power. As late as 1906, Article 1 of the Fundamental Laws of the Empire stated:

> *... The Emperor of all the Russians is an autocratic and unlimited monarch. God himself commands that his supreme power be obeyed, out of conscience as well as fear ...*

The government did little to promote industrial growth during the first half of the Nineteenth Century, when other European powers were rapidly industrializing. The Finance Minister opposed free trade and social change and refused to grant state loans for industry. He preferred, instead, to give loans to the nobles who had become impoverished by lavish spending.

The above quotation shows how out of date the Russian political system was in an era during which most European countries

195

were moving toward forms of constitutional* and democratic government. In Russia the awesome authority of the Tsar was reminiscent of the ancient Mongol Emperors and was combined with a belief in the divine right* of kings. One man conducted the affairs of the nation of over one hundred million people (c. 1900), and determined its laws. The problems of reform and change would confront each Nineteenth Century Tsar in turn. We need to examine their behaviour and determine in what fashion they dealt with the issues of their time.

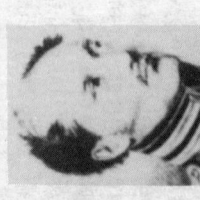

Nicholas I (1825–1855), known as the 'Iron Tsar', used armed force, exile and execution to quell any resistance to his autocracy.

The most serious rebellion against his government was the Decembrist Revolt in 1825. It was the first organized attempt to overthrow Tsarism in the Nineteenth Century. The officer-conspirators had hoped to abolish serfdom and set up a republic governed by a liberal constitution, in keeping with developments in France and elsewhere in Europe in the wake of the French Revolution. The Tsar crushed the rebellion, silenced the rebels and established a new branch of the secret police to assist in the repression of all dissent. His government took control of books and newspapers and enforced strict censorship. Education was carefully supervised, not to ensure quality, but to eliminate all ideas of revolution. A French writer of the time, de Tocqueville, described the Government of Russia as 'the cornerstone of despotism in the world'.

Some historians have argued, on the other hand, that Nicholas I was not so much a reactionary* as a reform conservative*. He seems at times to have recognized the need for change, but his meagre attempts at reform were stifled by a selfish aristocracy, unprepared to give up even a fraction of its privilege. First proclaimed in 1833, the official creed in his reign was 'Autocracy, Orthodoxy* and Nationalism'. The 1848 revolts in Europe frightened him even further away from the idea of reform and increased his conservatism.

But change, however slow, had begun to take place. Towns grew bigger, the urban population slowly increased from 4 per cent in 1795 to 9 per cent in 1858. Factories were built and the peasants began to move off the land. The changing economic structure raised an important question. Could Russia continue to be ruled by the principles and methods appropriate to its old economic and political system? If cultivation of the land took second place to industry as a source of income, could the landowners maintain their political control? These questions arose as a consequence of change. Why was change taking place?

In any historical situation it is difficult to isolate the causes of change. The population of Russia was increasing and the search for new and more efficient means of production became pressing. Western Europe stood as an example of the possibilities of mechanical and scientific progress. Some intellectuals and a few statesmen were conscious of the need for change and encouraged it wherever possible. A major stimulus to change turned out to be military defeat. The Russian army, once regarded as one of the most formidable in Europe, suffered an humiliating defeat in the Crimean War of 1856 at the hands of British and French troops armed with modern weapons. This

The guardians of Orthodoxy: A group of priests of the Russian Orthodox Church in the Nineteenth Century.

workers' leaders. They spoke out against the autocracy, serfdom and the lack of religious freedom, and they complained about the insecurity of person and property in Russian society. Their agitation, reinforced by socialist ideas filtering through from western Europe, resulted in a national mood of discontent and sporadic uprisings. Those who wished for change were able to take advantage of the circumstances and press for reforms. The path of change was a difficult one and the reformers met with much resistance.

Nicholas' successor, Alexander II (1855–1881), understood the need for modernization but failed to find the means to put his plans into action. The mid-century was a period in which reform and conservative interest battled for supremacy. Those who were in favour of modernization were opposed by those who clung to traditional values. Alexander failed to tip the scales in favour of the reformers because he was too dependent upon the conservative aristocracy.

A major issue that emerged at this time, in the context of the need for modernization, was the demand of industrialists for a large labour supply freed from serfdom and willing to work in the new industries for low wages. In order to guarantee such a supply of labour for the factories and to answer the demands for reform, Alexander signed a law for the emancipation of the serfs in 1861.

The poor performance starkly revealed not only the poor quality of the army, but also the country's industrial and technological backwardness. The despotic regime was strongly criticized by the small but growing middle class, and by intellectuals and

land at the time of purchase and pay the balance over fifty years. Emancipated serfs were not permitted to refuse to purchase land, so those who could not afford the full price bought quarter allotments from which they could not hope to produce anything but the most meagre subsistence* crops.

Despite emancipation, the lives of peasants were controlled by their village councils (*mirs*), and if they wished to move from one district to another they had to obtain permits. When working in the towns they were obliged to pay taxes in their home villages. Those who remained in the countryside were given limited, local political rights through the governing bodies of each district — the *zemstvos*. The zemstvos soon became forums for the dissemination and growth of liberal and reform sentiments. The reforms of the 1860s provided the basis for change in the economic and political sphere, but despite the granting of certain limited civil liberties they failed to provide for popular participation in the political process.

Discontent led to the growth of an agrarian socialist movement known as Populism. The leader of the movement, Alexander Herzen, believed that the traditionally communal aspects of Russian agrarian society were a good foundation for a collectivist* socialist* state. He, and others, denounced autocracy, censorship and servitude. Liberalism and capitalism were viewed with distrust. The factory system was denounced as evil and degrading and farming was thought to offer an ideal way of life for all people. The movement's objective was nothing less than the overthrow of the existing political and social order and the redistribution of land to the people.

In Populist thought a naïve faith in the peasantry was contradicted by the belief that the peasants required the leadership of dedicated intellectual revolutionaries. In the 1870s the Populists began to live and work among the peasants,

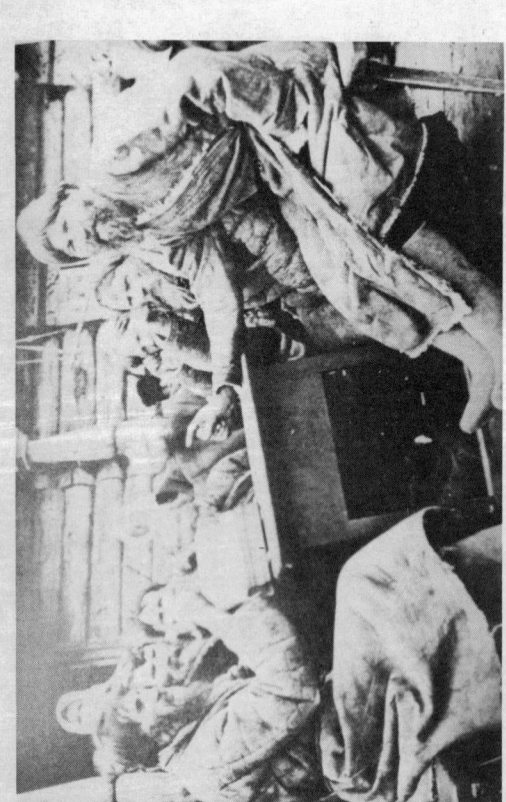

The village council (mir).

Whether Alexander was prompted to make this move by an earnest desire to assist industry in the process of modernization and economic growth, or whether he acted in order to prevent revolution, is a matter of uncertainty. We cannot be sure of his motives. What *is* clear is that the consequences of his actions were extremely important for subsequent Russian history. (Note that the emancipation of the slaves in North America took place at approximately the same time — see Chapter 4.)

Emancipation meant that many peasants were forced to leave the countryside to seek work in the towns. Those who remained in the rural areas were forced to buy inferior land at high prices. It took many years for them to get out of debt — sometimes generations. Where the land was fertile high compensation was demanded by the nobility. In some instances peasants were forced to put down 20 per cent of the inflated selling price of the

preaching and organizing for social revolution. In many areas the peasants viewed them with suspicion and were openly hostile to the idea of revolution against the Tsar, whom they regarded as a potential protector against the rapacious landlords. The radicals turned to terror and sabotage in an attempt to shatter the bureaucratic machinery of the state. They plotted the murder of the Tsar. After seven unsuccessful attempts, the People's Freedom party* assassinated him in 1881, a few hours after he had signed a document promising limited constitutional reform, which would have allowed for elected representation in the government.

Reforms	
Serfs freed	1861
University autonomy granted	1863
Judiciary made independent	1864
Urban communities granted limited constitutional rights	1870

Questions

Study the cartoon.

1. Who are the major figures in the cartoon meant to represent?

2. What is the cartoonist saying about Russian society?

3. From your reading so far, would you agree with this assessment? Give reasons for your answer.

(Halliday p. 29)

The Russian Empire: Its territorial growth and foreign policy

What was the Russian Empire like?

We do not belong to any of the great families of the human race; we are neither of the west nor of the East, and we have not the traditions of either.
(Chaadaev, 1829)

Russia — the word conjures up an image of a vast country, the home of a people who have a common culture, language and religion. Look carefully, however, at the following photographs.

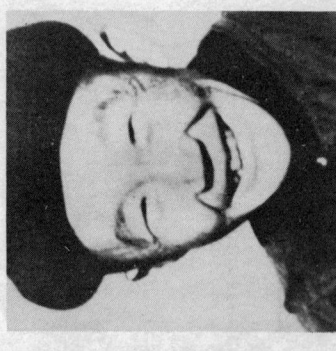

A Yakut tribesman.

A woman from Georgia.

All the people pictured are Nineteenth Century Russians. What do the photographs tell you about the nature of Russian society?

New forces in society began to exert pressure on the old institutions. The country faced a number of problems. The most important of these were:

- How to expand and consolidate territory without provoking a major war. (See 'territorial growth and foreign policy', p. 200.)
- Could the monarchy continue to dominate the political system or would the newly founded radical political parties gain power?
- In a multi-national empire which lacked cohesion or unifying ideology, what was an appropriate political system? (See 'Political opposition and government reform', p. 213.)
- How to accumulate, through taxation, the wealth which was needed for the development of industry, without creating social upheaval. (See 'Economic change and government response', p. 208.)

The above questions highlight some of the tensions in Russian society which were to be resolved in the years 1861–1917.

One of the factors which determine the social and political structures of any country are the needs created by its economy. The economic structure helps determine the ways in which people live and the types of employment they are able to find. These in turn generate relationships between people which determine how power is both used and distributed in a society.

In Russia change created a restive society. Each group — nobles, middle-class, industrial workers and peasants — experienced new life-styles, adopted new ideas and acquired new aspirations. The ensuing attempts at modernization and urbanization would create many new problems. The first to be tackled was the consolidation of territory. Although solving one set of problems, this resulted in a further cultural diversification in the Russian Empire.

A girl from Armenia.

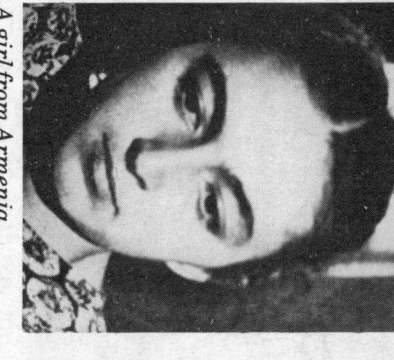

A woman from Turkestan.

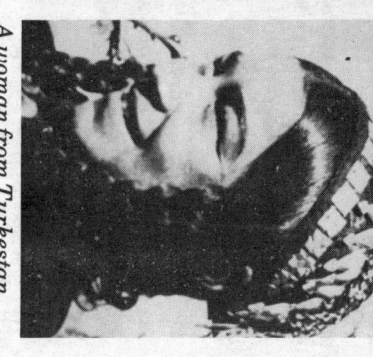

A Kazan mullah.

A Buriat school.

Crimean Tartars learning the Koran.

EXPANSION OF TERRITORY

In the year 1462 the Tsar of Muscovy ruled over a vast area of some 38 000 square kilometres. Over the centuries the kingdom expanded. Major gains were made when the Baltic lands were annexed in the time of Peter the Great (1682–1725). Catherine the Great (1776–1796) annexed territory on the borders of the Turkish Empire. By the year 1914 the Empire had become the home of many different peoples.

There is seldom only one reason why a country attempts to expand its territory. Factors such as the desire for prestige and security, the pressure of population, the acquisition of raw materials and markets, a need for access to rivers or sea-ports, all combine to guide expansionist decisions. Sometimes border territory is acquired by government agents acting without official permission. Thus the motive for each territorial gain must be viewed separately.

Since the Sixteenth Century there have been a desire for more land to secure borders, and a perceived need to create buffer states around the vulnerable heart of the Russian Empire. The country needed raw materials, markets for its goods, railways and access to warm-water* ports. Its rulers realized that territorial expansion would meet some of these needs. The regional army commanders responded to the immediate demands for security in the frontier areas.

The Nineteenth Century was the age of imperialism. It was the time when most European powers maintained overseas empires and a country's stature in world affairs was enhanced by its territorial gains. Russia annexed neighbouring territories for many of the reasons that Britain and France occupied territories in Africa and Asia. The government was conscious of Russia's lack of prestige amongst the established powers of Europe and wished to gain international recognition for its role as a world power.

The pattern of Russian expansion was one of ever-widening circles. Neighbouring territories were annexed over the centuries to create an unwieldy, multi-national empire. Why? One historian suggests that:

> *There was something natural, almost elemental and irresistible, about the long course of Russian colonization and immigration.*
>
> (Rogger, p. 165)

Perhaps this was so: Russian expansionism had greater territorial integrity* and strategic logic* than that of the other European powers. Nevertheless, it is not possible to eliminate commercial self-interest and the geographic imperative* as reasons for expansion. It has already been suggested that Russia was attempting to establish itself as an important imperial power in order to acquire status in its dealings with the other European countries; but this was only one of the reasons. A desire to safeguard its borders from a western European invasion (as had happened in the Napoleonic era) and from raids by border tribes of Asia, also influenced the imperial policy. Once satisfied with its acquisition of buffer states* in the west, Russian policy-makers began to concentrate on gains in the east.

Access to warm-water ports was sought both for strategic reasons and for trade, but the Russians were afraid of committing themselves to any military action, and proceeded with extreme caution. Foreign policy was advanced by negotiation and treaty, and paid respect to the European balance of power* which had been created at the Congress of Vienna.

202

Refer to a map of Russia in an atlas. Knowledge of the geography of the country makes it much easier to understand why Russia considered the annexed territories to be important to its needs.

Consider these facts:

The distance between Vladivostok and Leningrad is 9 329 km. The country covers 11 time zones; to go from the western border to the eastern border the traveller must cross 11 000 km and reset his watch 10 times.

The total area of the country is 22,3 million km². (China = 10 million km²; USA = 7,8 million km².)

Russia has every raw material except rubber.

Most of the soil is poor, the rainfall erratic and Russia has the highest percentage of marshland in the world. This combination makes 88 per cent of the total area unsuitable for cultivation.

Much of the ground is frozen to a great depth. Russia borders on ten seas, most of them frozen for the greater part of each year. This makes the country virtually land-locked.

Russia has borders with thirteen countries — seven Asian and six European.

Questions

Having studied a map and looked at the facts provided, answer the following questions:

1. *What implication does the size of Russia have for communications such as railways?*

2. *If the soil is poor, what will it mean if too many people have to make their living out of farming?*

3. *If minerals are found in frozen ground how does it affect the mining industry?*

4. *What defence and trading problems might result from the fact that the seas are frozen for most of the year?*

5. *If Russia has borders with so many countries, what factors must be anticipated when planning the defence of the country?*

Consideration of these geographical facts should have given you some understanding of why farming in Russia was often not very productive. This had two consequences. It made territorial expansion desirable and, as you will discover later in this chapter, it was to make an accumulation of money (capital*) derived from agriculture difficult. Knowledge of the geographical features of the country also suggests reasons why the rulers thought it safer to incorporate neighbouring countries and gain political control over the people living in those territories. Also, it provides an important explanation for Russia's constant attempts to gain access to warm-water ports. Keeping these factors in mind we will examine the foreign policy of Nineteenth Century Russia.

FOREIGN POLICY

Russian foreign policy was influenced by the country's geographic position. It had borders with western Europe, the Turkish Empire and the lands of the Far East. All were areas of strategic concern, with economic potential, which could also improve Russia's communications with the outside world. But Russian ambition was restrained by a lack of money, industrial capacity, communications and military strength.

Foreign policy decisions were always realistic, and neither nationalism nor religion was used to justify imperialistic actions. Narrow nationalism could not be encouraged in a multi-national empire. Although Russian Orthodoxy was recognized as the official state religion and the Russian Orthodox Church received special consideration, the rulers recognized that many of their subjects were not of the Christian faith.

In Europe

The major aim of Russian foreign policy was to achieve territorial gain without provoking the hostility of the major European powers, with which it had a constantly changing relationship—friendship alternating with suspicion and aggression. After the Congress of Vienna in 1815 Russian influence in European affairs grew steadily and led to the annexation of Poland, Finland and Bessarabia.

One focus of Russian foreign policy between 1860 and 1880 was Prussia. Because Russia needed money for industrial development, the Russians were easily persuaded to remain neutral while the new Germany was created under Prussian leadership. After the unification of Germany, Russia joined Germany and Austria in the *Driekeiserbund* (Three Emperors League) in 1873 and agreed to remain neutral in the event of war. This uneasy alliance was Bismarck's attempt to counterbalance Russian and Austrian ambitions in the Balkans, and to prevent a vengeful France from attacking Germany. Although Russian nationalists disagreed with the policy of friendship with Germany, Foreign Minister Girs continued to pursue it. The alliance was renewed in 1881 and again in 1884.

What handicapped Russian foreign policy most was the Tsar, his inept advisers and the country's military weakness. The country's backwardness was regarded with contempt, and its prestige had sunk so low that in 1885 the weak Austrian Empire was able to seize control of Bulgaria. In 1887 Russia and Germany signed the Reinsurance Treaty, but despite the alliance, Bismarck cut off the flow of German money to Russia and ordered the *Reichsbank* to stop accepting Russian securities. His action led Russia to consider, instead, an alliance with France. In the last decade of the Nineteenth Century these two countries had forged strong economic links, and in 1894, contrary to Bismarck's intention, a Franco-Russian alliance became the main-spring of Russia's foreign policy. It was a treaty that promised mobilization by both parties should either party be attacked.

The Balkan states were another major focus of Russian foreign policy. One of Russia's long-standing ambitions had been to win influence with groups in the Ottoman Empire, and gain control of the Dardenelles and the straits that gave passage from the Black Sea to the Mediterranean. This was the key reason for Russian involvement in Balkan politics and support for local nationalists in their efforts to throw off Turkish rule.

An attempt in the 1850s to expand towards Turkey aroused anger in Britain and France, which were jealous of their own interests in that region and opposed to any Russian attempt to gain influence there.

They united in a war against Russia. The Crimean War of 1856 ended in a shattering defeat for Russia and put a stop to its expansion towards the Dardenelles. It revealed how far that country had fallen behind Britain and France as a military

204

power. The war laid bare Russia's deficiencies as a power and made it difficult to negotiate as an equal among the nations of Europe.

Although the Crimean War had dampened Russia's enthusiasm for Balkan involvement, the massacre in 1875-6 of Bulgarian Christians by Turks and the Panslavic* agitation that followed, encouraged the Tsar to invade Turkey. The protection of Christianity was used as a moral justification for territorial expansion. But Britain sent a fleet to Constantinople (Istanbul) as a reminder of her maritime interests in the area. The Tsar took fright and sought a truce with Turkey. A treaty favourable to Russia was signed at San Stefano in 1878. The interested European powers however forced a review; and a few months later another treaty, much less favourable to Russia, was drawn up in Berlin (1878). Russia had been made to realize that territorial ambitions could, and would, be curtailed by the other European powers.

In Asia

Central Asia

Under Alexander II Russia pacified the Caucasus and acquired secure borders and bases in the south. After 1864 Russian foreign policy turned its attention to the weaker countries of central Asia. The power vacuum in that area was easily filled. The imperial family sanctioned conquests to enhance its prestige, and between the years 1865–1881 annexed Kokand, Bokhara, Khiva, Tashkent and Geok Tepe. Raids by tribesmen anxious to protect their land were used as an excuse, but commercial greed and the need for secure frontiers were the real reasons for conquest. For example, cotton grew well in Turkestan and the area became a major source of raw cotton for the Moscow textile mills.

The territorial gains in central Asia had immediate consequences for foreign policy. By 1877, Europe was again viewing Russia with suspicion. Britain, in particular, was alarmed by the conquests in central Asia which had brought the Russian army to the borders of Afghanistan — beyond which lay India, the 'jewel in the Crown' of Britain's Empire.

East Asia

Some Russian statesmen, such as the finance minister, Sergei Witte (1892–1903), had a sense of mission and espoused the view that Russia could become the power which united West and East. But the reasons for Tsarist expansion into east Asia were, most often, the imperialist drive for glory and economic benefits, both real and potential.

Russia viewed China as a source of raw materials, a place for foreign investment and a route to ice-free ports. China was weak and incapable of resisting the pressure of the European powers on its centuries-old isolation. At first the Tsar's government was divided on the best course of action, but Nicolas II was eventually persuaded to offer the Chinese help in opposing the demands of other foreign nations. China agreed to a Russian occupation of its Amur province, which led to the establishment of the port of Vladivostok. Because Vladivostok suffered from the same drawbacks as other Russian ports, namely that it was ice-bound for a large part of the year, Russia continued its quest for a warm-water port. But before negotiations with the Chinese could be completed, Japan attacked Formosa and annexed Port Arthur on the tip of the Liaotung Peninsula in an attempt to counter the Russian advance. Russia and the western powers threatened Japan and

205

In 1904 Japan launched a surprise attack on the Russian fleet in Port Arthur and involved Russia in a campaign thousands of miles from its heartland. The Russian army was short of all the essentials for modern warfare and its commanders were old men with ideas as old-fashioned as their guns. What equipment it had could only be moved slowly along the single-track trans-Siberian railway. Ill-prepared for its first Twentieth Century test of strength, Russia went recklessly to war.

Russia's humiliating defeat at the battle of Mukden (1905), the annihilation of its Baltic fleet on the other side of the world[1], in the straits of Tshushima, along with the withdrawal of French loans, forced Russia to sign a humiliating peace treaty a few months later. (See Chapter 5.) The ineptitude and corruption of the Tsar's government was revealed for all to see, and it began to come under attack at home. This was the first time since the Crimean War that Russia had blundered into a war created by the perceived need to expand territory. The results within the Empire were profound.

---

[1] The Russian fleet left the port of Liepaja in October 1904. The journey to Japan took 7 months, as the fleet had to travel half-way around the world to get there.

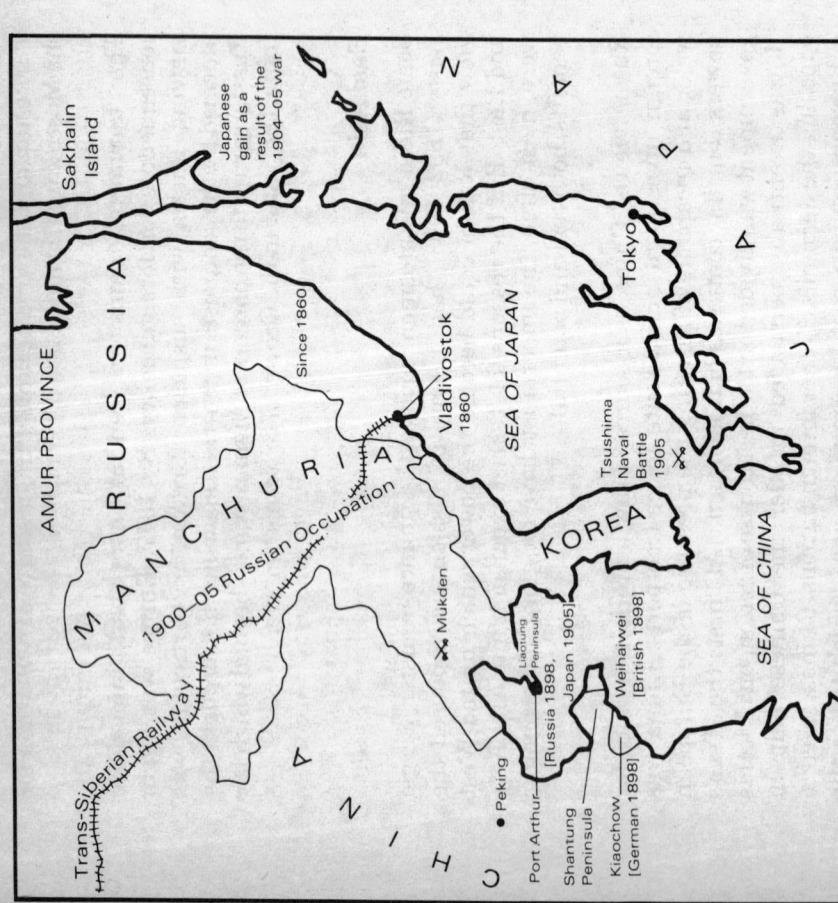

Map 26

Port Arthur was returned to China. The Chinese Emperor gave the Russians the use of the port for twenty-five years and permission to build a trans-Siberian railway through Manchuria. Japan and England formed an alliance because they thought Russia was threatening their imperial interests in China.

The Russian State: Attempts to consolidate power inside the Empire

CONTROL MECHANISMS

Poor foreign policy decisions and the multi-national nature of the Empire had created problems of control within the expanded country. Expansion also helped to maintain the prestige of the Tsarist regime in some quarters and enabled it to resort to ruthless repression. The Nineteenth Century had witnessed the rise of nationalism in many parts of Europe and the diverse peoples of the expanding Russian Empire had also begun to strive for self-determination. They wanted to rule themselves, speak their own languages and follow their own cultural traditions, but whenever they attempted to implement such plans, retribution from the central government was swift and ruthless. An oppressive system of Russification which started in Poland, was repeated in Finland, the Baltic countries (Latvia, Lithuania and Estonia), Transcaucasia and Armenia. The Russian Orthodox Church attempted to impose doctrine on other Christians living in the zones of Russian occupation. School pupils were taught through the medium of Russian, and syllabuses were modified to combat regional nationalism. Local officials were replaced with Russian bureaucrats* whose loyalty to the Tsar was undisputed. Threat and force were freely used whenever persuasion failed, and every effort was made to keep all the divisions of the Empire politically and economically subordinate to the needs of the Tsarist regime.

As often happens in such situations, a vulnerable minority was made an example for all subject peoples who showed any signs of opposition. Of all the non-Christian people in the Empire the Jews were the most vulnerable. They were concentrated in the western and south-western parts of the country. Many were poverty-stricken peasants or factory workers, others were petty traders, tailors, cobblers or cabinet-makers. Centuries of Tsarist persecution had made them politically conscious. Some opposed autocracy and gave support to the idea of representative institutions, while others supported the tenets of socialism. The regime's fear of mass political activity, bolstered by the anti-Semitic preachings of the Orthodox Church, made persecution of the Jews a convenient diversion for the dissatisfied masses.

Jews were confined by edict to an area known as the Pale of Settlement. From the mid-Nineteenth Century onward, pogroms* became commonplace, reaching a peak in 1905 (the year of Russia's humiliating defeat by Japan), when six hundred communities were sacked by mobs under the guidance of Cossack cavalry.

In this period the Jews lost the right to vote and to buy or own land. A strict quota was imposed on the number permitted to enter the professions. In the Pale of Settlement only ten per cent of Jewish children were permitted to attend school or university—outside the Pale the percentage was five, and in Moscow itself, three. The parents of the lucky ones had to pay the school fees for Christian children as well as for their own.

Anti-Semitism became a major ideological* weapon for the state. The Tsars had found a scapegoat for their failures and inadequacies. During the reign of Alexander III the Jews were dismissed from judicial posts, banned from government service and most of the professions, subjected to special taxes and

Jewish people were not the only victims. Stricter control than before was imposed on freedom of speech and organization. Children of the working class were not allowed to attend secondary school and government agents attempted to direct every aspect of life, even in the smallest village. Conversion to the Russian Orthodox Church was vigorously promoted.

These policies stemmed from the very nature of the government. The autocratic individuality which marked the Russian polity* made systems of compromise difficult. It must be remembered, however, that arrests, deportations and executions were relatively sporadic until the advent of the Twentieth Century. The country was too vast for totalitarianism to be uniformly applied.

It is now appropriate to ask which internal political and economic conditions led to the escalation of violence.

ECONOMIC CHANGE AND GOVERNMENT RESPONSE

If the mass of the Russian people had improved their standard of living through industrialization, the effects of government-inspired terror and the harshness of the autocracy may have been partially justified. The government, however, had an ambivalent attitude toward industrial progress. On the one hand it saw it as desirable because it might give Russia parity with other industrial nations. On the other hand, it also recognized that the growth of the industrial, merchant and working classes would challenge the power of the nobility. In the end the government tried to impose a given rate of growth and industrialization and curb any resultant social and political changes which threatened the authority of the autocracy.

Victims of the 1905 pogrom.

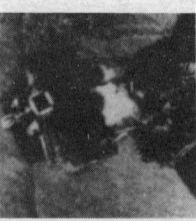

driven into the Pale of Settlement with more vigour than had previously been the case.

The assassination of Alexander II had had the unfortunate, though understandable, effect of making his heir, Alexander III (1881–1894) totally opposed to reform.

The onset of a massive programme of government-inspired industrialization brought with it such tension as left no field of Russian society unaffected.

(Kochan, p. xiii)

At no time in its history was Russia able to produce an agricultural surplus which could be marketed outside the country. Selling crops abroad meant sacrifice at home. The poor quality of the agricultural yield meant that there was little accumulation of capital. Therefore Britain's industrial revolution, which occurred between 1780 and 1850, could not be duplicated in Russia.

Industrialization requires large reserves of money to establish factories and buy machinery. It requires people prepared to risk capital and anticipate a profit from risky ventures. Russia had few such entrepreneurs*. When the government recognized the need to move into the industrial era it found the country tied to a medieval economic structure, based initially on serfdom and later on peasant-type agriculture. Internal demand for manufactured goods was limited as the villagers were too poor to afford them. The peasants were conservative. Change, to them, meant the acquisition of more land, not technological progress. These social and economic barriers to change prevented Russia from reforming her political institutions at the time that other European governments became more and more democratic.

As old-fashioned, conservative policies were pursued, Russia fell further and further behind western Europe, America and Japan in industrial achievement. In 1860 Russia was economically even further behind western Europe than it had been in 1800. Nevertheless, new towns had been built and railway construction was underway. The government intervened periodically and tried to force the pace of industrialization.

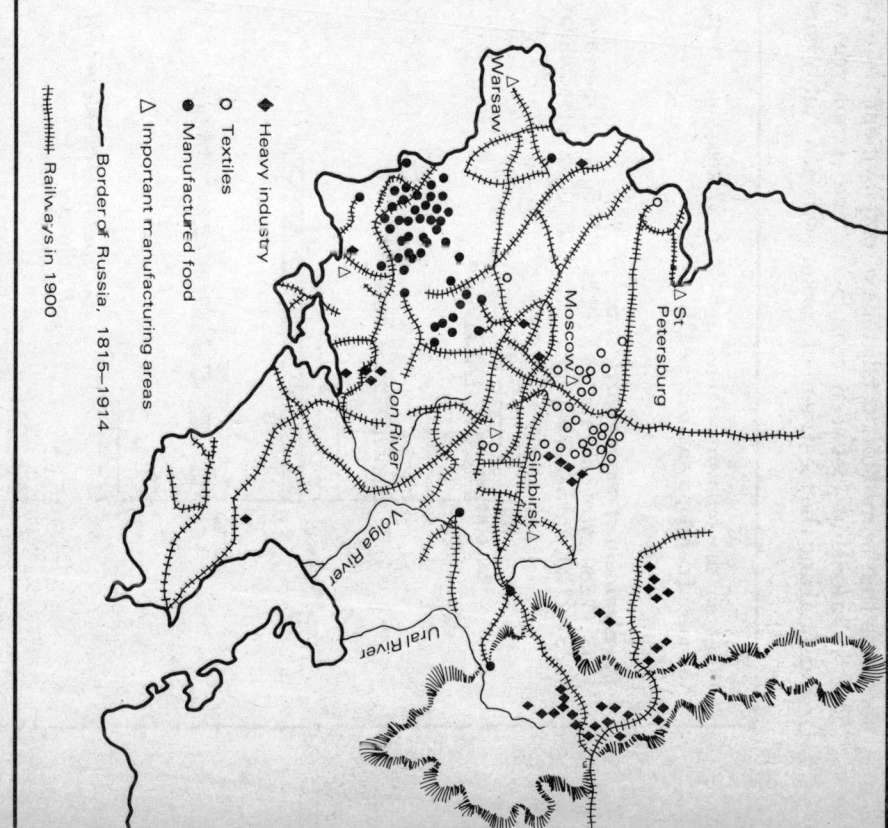

Map 27 — *Industrial development.*

As industries evolved society changed. Peasants became industrial workers with needs and ambitions different from their parents. The government controlled many industrial enterprises, largely financed with foreign capital. In the huge

209

factories that were built conditions of employment were bad. The relationship between employer and employee was impersonal and the treatment of workers was invariably harsh.

What do the following tables and Map 27 tell you about industrial development in Russia?

Development of railways in Russia:
1855 1 360 km of railways 1905 64 000 km of railways
1885 27 200 km of railways 1914 76 800 km of railways

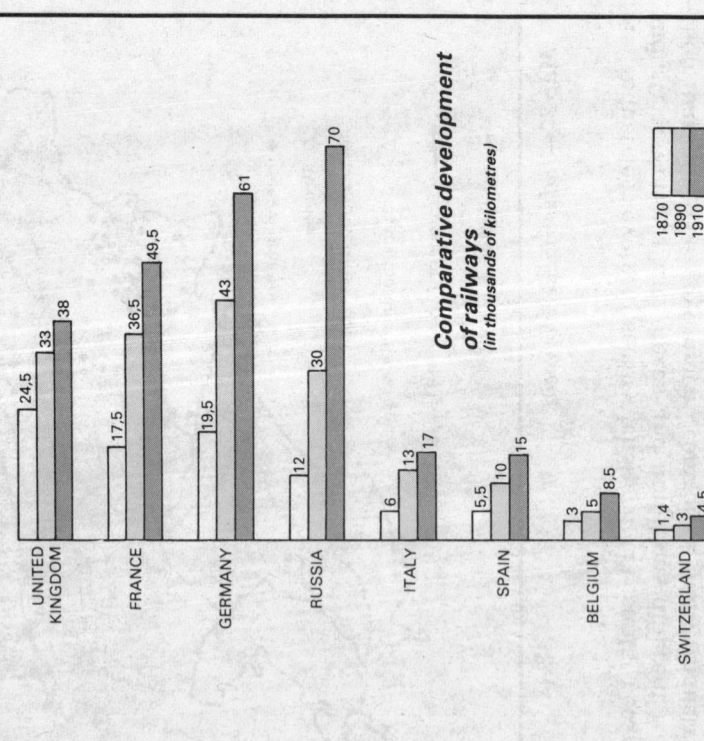

Comparative development of railways
(in thousands of kilometres)

1870 / 1890 / 1910

	1870	1890	1910
UNITED KINGDOM	24.5	33	38
FRANCE	17.5	36.5	49.5
GERMANY	19.5	43	61
RUSSIA	12	30	70
ITALY	6	13	17
SPAIN	5.5	10	15
BELGIUM	3	5	8.5
SWITZERLAND	1.4	3	4.5

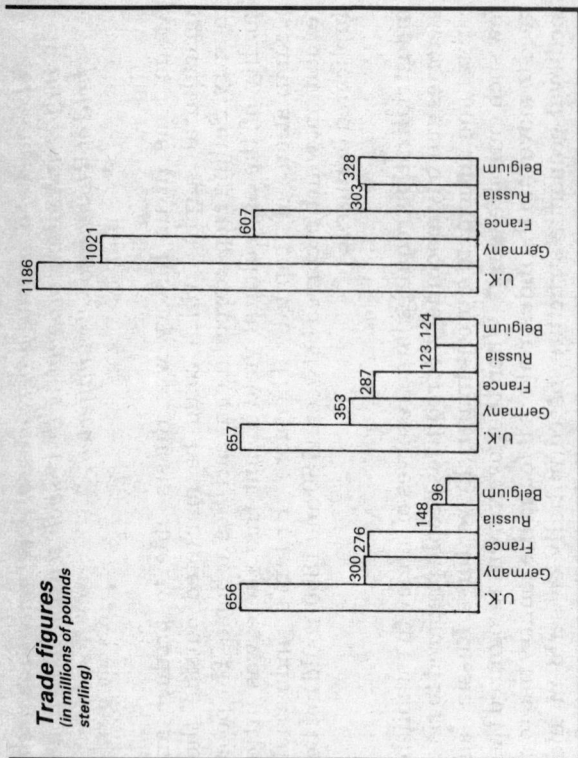

Trade figures
(in millions of pounds sterling)

	U.K.	Germany	France	Russia	Belgium
	656	300	276	148	96
	657	353	287	123	124
	1186	1021	607	303	328

THE URBAN WORKING CLASS

Because of a land shortage in the country areas, young people were forced to seek work in the towns, and with so many of them looking for work, wages remained low. Those who wished to sell their labour in the towns had to obtain the permission of the village council. If permission was granted a pass was issued. The peasant, although allowed to work in town, remained legally tied to the home village and he or his relatives had to pay village taxes. Thus many of the urban workers were migrants living in town without their families. They were housed in unhygienic dormitories, where two or more people shared the same bed — an arrangement made possible by the twelve-hour shifts the factories worked. (These circumstances can in some ways be compared with the evolution of the system of migrant labour in South Africa during the last quarter of the Nineteenth Century. See Chapter 7.) Unhealthy conditions led to outbreaks of cholera and typhus. Trade unions and strikes were forbidden. One of the Tsar's ministers was dismissed for trying to enforce laws that had been designed to protect children in factories from exploitation. Workers were obliged to buy their clothing and food from factory stores which meant that the greater part of their wages went back to their employers. Their discontent led to frequent strikes. Troops were regularly used to smash strikes and disperse workers' meetings.

Strikes	Troops used against workers
1893	19 times
1899	50 times
1901	271 times
1902	522 times

Although the above statistics point to a growing alarm and increased violence on the part of the authorities, it must be remembered that the working class was a small minority. In 1900 there were 3 000 000 industrial workers out of a total population of 133 000 000. The peasants were still potentially the strongest political force in the country.

THE PEASANTS

Far from improving life, the emancipation of the serfs seemed to have worsened conditions for those who remained on the land. Many belonged to communes and were subject to a new set of laws. Their houses were one-roomed log cabins. A single table and a couple of chairs served as furniture. They slept on the floor. Their staple diet was coarse bread and cabbage soup.

What do the following photographs tell you about the Russian peasantry?

Typical peasant hut.

Estonian peasant women.

Family affected by the famines of 1891 and 1899.

Peasant farmers in Oryal.

Peasant family in Siberia.

Farming methods were primitive and good land was scarce. They were heavily taxed and poverty was great. A dramatic rise in population created further difficulties in both industry and agriculture — between 1897 and 1913 the population of Russia doubled. It placed a great strain on the fragile economy; even a more talented and concerned government would have been hard put to supply enough land for the peasants and sufficient jobs in the factories. Although the government had little money for development, the Finance Minister, Witte, saw the need for Russia to advance rapidly. He tried to improve industry and communications and raised large sums of money by levying taxes and exporting food that was needed at home. He gambled on the hope that industrial growth would improve the standard of living of the workers and peasants before they found the tax burden intolerable. Seventy-five per cent of all taxes were collected from the peasants. Items taxed included matches, vodka, tobacco, sugar, tea and kerosene. These items provided 80 per cent of all taxes collected in Russia. A crop failure in 1891 was followed by starvation and disease. The death toll was 400 000. Another famine in 1899 and the world economic recession of 1900–6 led Russia to the brink of disaster.

POLITICAL OPPOSITION AND GOVERNMENT RESPONSE

Moderate reforms had been granted and revoked according to the government's perception of the best way of dealing with immediate problems, and had not formed part of a systematic programme of modernization. The emancipation of the serfs had created unfulfilled expectations of a better life. Industrialization was in its infancy and therefore incapable of significantly improving the economic lot of either the peasants or the workers. Consequent discontent made many sections of society responsive to any political programme which offered the prospect of change. Political unrest grew in an atmosphere of disappointed expectations.

The intelligentsia who often led these movements were described by one historian as 'a thin crust of educated people with a European outlook, intensely self-conscious and profoundly uneasy about the desperate condition of their country in the modern world' (Thomson, p. 335). Amongst the major parties to emerge were the anarchistic Social Revolutionaries (1901), who held that a programme of violence and assassination would gain control of the land for the peasants. The party emerged in the 1890s and helped organize the peasant uprisings in 1902. It won a great deal of support during the dramatic events of 1905. The Social Democrats' (1903) aim was a worker revolution, and the establishment of a Marxist state through the weapon of the industrial strike. The Liberal party (1903) was composed of gentry, middle-class businessmen and professional people who wanted moderate evolutionary reform. Although the parties had few points of agreement all were united in their hatred of the regime.

Nicholas II

The last Tsar of Russia, Nicholas II (1894–1917), continued with his father's repressive policies. He had little knowledge of the realities of Russian society and did not display much interest. He lived in a private world of hunting, yachting and family gatherings, and was oblivious to the heavy responsibility of his position as ruler of one of the largest Empires in the world. He experienced difficulty in making decisions of any kind, but was certain of one thing — the folly of allowing social or political reform in Russia. Weak and insecure, he allowed himself to be influenced by men with selfish interests. Year by year he

Bloody Sunday, 1905. Father Gapon and his followers being cut down by troops.

destroyed the trust and loyalty of his people. The peasants, especially, revered the Tsar. Until 1914 many of them clung to the belief that he was ignorant of the cruelty of his officials. Had he been a politically astute leader he might have turned the very conservatism of the peasants to his own advantage. Their interest was not in revolution, but in securing land. Agrarian reform might have won the peasants to his side and strengthened both the monarchy and the government.

BLOODY SUNDAY 1905

How did the Tsar respond to the pressures which were building up in Russian society after 1904? There had been many disturbances since the turn of the century. Peasant riots and worker strikes had given warning that the people were discontented. Matters came to a head when a general strike was organized in St. Petersburg. On 5 January 1905, 26 000 workers downed tools. Within three days 111 000 were out on strike. On Sunday, 9 January, a priest called Father Gapon led 150 000 people in a march on the Winter Palace. Their intention was to hand a petition to the Tsar explaining their grievances and requesting political reform.

An extract from the petition to the Tsar:

... we working men of St Petersburg, our wives and children, and our parents, helpless and aged men and women, have come to you, our ruler, in quest of justice and protection. We are beggars, we are oppressed and overburdened with work; we are insulted, we are not regarded as human beings but are treated as slaves ... are driven further into the abyss of poverty, injustice and ignorance; we are strangled by despotism and tyranny ... Your Majesty! We are here, many thousands of us; we have the appearance of human beings, but in fact we have no human rights at all ... The workers have no right to organize their own labour unions for the defence of their own interests ...

The Minister of the Interior was given prior notice of the march. The procession was peaceful and the people were unarmed. In bitterly cold weather the workers, singing hymns, made their way past the frozen river Neva and converged on the palace. They were dressed in their best Sunday clothes, and carried religious banners and portraits of the Tsar. At the sight of such a large crowd some of the soldiers lining the route began to panic, someone started shooting and the Cossacks* swung into action. Brandishing huge swords, they bore down on the procession. Hundreds of people died that day and many were wounded.

On the day of the massacre the Tsar was many miles away. His departure made the people think that he had left because he lacked sympathy for the workers' cause, but it is doubtful that he even gave them or their petition much thought.

Strikes and demonstrations erupted. The middle class joined the workers in protest and by the end of January half a million people were on strike. The country was paralysed as railwaymen, factory workers, and university lecturers displayed solidarity with the St. Petersburg workers. All pressed for political reform and the industrialists requested constitutional amendments. Most dangerous to the shaky regime was the formation of the All-Russian Peasants Union in August, 1905. In the countryside peasants despoiled estates and raided store-houses. Anarchy prevailed and no amount of police action seemed able to contain the situation. The urban working class staged a general strike in the autumn, and, as a forewarning of things to come, some of the troops mutinied and joined the strikers. Bad news from the Far Eastern war zone added to the problems of the government. (See pp. 205–6.) The structures of repression were under severe strain.

The Tsar was at last persuaded to issue a political manifesto. It granted fundamental civil rights to all the people and promised

The Tsar's soldiers in 1905.

a representative legislature.* The manifesto caused a split amongst the revolutionaries. Some supported it, many were against it, but amongst the general population opposition to the regime petered out amidst high hopes for a new and just society. The autocracy had proved itself remarkably resilient. It had withstood attack from all sections of society. As soon as he felt secure the Tsar called for pogroms, to divert attention. The Jews in the Pale of Settlement were the first victims, then it was the turn of the socialists and liberals.

By the following year the Tsar's regime was in full control again. Gaol, deportation to Siberia or exile in Europe was the fate of the revolutionary elite who were arrested. Elections were

215

from among the Tsar's favourites. Those ministers who showed themselves willing to solve problems or listen to the people were dismissed.

This disillusion and disappointment was followed by strike after strike. In the year 1912 there were 2 032 strikes throughout the land. Against this background of domestic strife, Russia's rulers attempted to guide foreign policy and maintain some semblance of imperial grandeur.

FOREIGN POLICY PRIOR TO THE FIRST WORLD WAR

Far East

Russia had established a firm foothold in the East when the Trans-Siberian railway was completed in 1903. This gain was off-set by the defeat it suffered in the Russo-Japanese War of 1905. But although its Eastern policy was restricted, Russia had its right to Mongolia recognized, and between 1907 and 1912, Japan and Russia agreed to respect each other's interests in the area.

Europe and the Middle East

Once Bismarck had been removed from office and his policy of friendship with Russia was abandoned by the Kaiser, Russia turned to France for political and financial support. French capital was required for industrial expansion. This was liberally granted and by 1914 French investors held 22 per cent of the stocks in privately-owned Russian banks.

The Kremlin in Moscow — today the seat of power of the USSR Government.

held in April 1906. Despite the limited franchise, of the 497 members elected to the Duma only 44 were conservatives. The composition of the new Duma held promise of liberal change. But the Tsar dissolved the Duma three months later. The second Duma (February–June, 1907) was also dissolved after three months. Next the Tsar changed the electoral system so that only the aristocrats and the wealthy could vote. They chose a conservative Duma which remained in office for five years. Government was exercised by corrupt and foolish men chosen

Britain also had large amounts of capital invested in Russian industry and in 1907 Russia signed a treaty with Britain which was designed to protect their various interests in the Middle East. Russia acknowledged Britain's interest in Afghanistan. It was agreed that Tibet would be left untouched by either power, and Persia was divided into one neutral zone and two spheres of interest—one British and the other Russian.

Russia, Britain and France became partners in the Triple Entente, an alliance poised in dangerous contradiction to the Triple Alliance of Germany, Austria and Italy.

The Balkans

The Balkans was an area where state boundaries were radically redrawn in the late Nineteenth Century. One province after another asserted its claim to national sovereignty and challenged the power of the weak Ottoman Empire. Russia and Austria both stood to gain from the Turkish loss of influence and as a result they were engaged in continuous conflict over the area throughout the latter part of the Nineteenth Century. Russia lent its support to the Balkan League (Serbia, Bulgaria, Greece and Montenegro) when it declared war on the Turks in 1912. Under Russian protection Serbia became a leading state within the region, a state openly hostile to Austria. In such a situation, rife with tension and mutual suspicion, the smallest incident had the potential to trigger off a major conflict. (See Chapter 2 for details.)

Conclusion

In the introduction the question was posed—could Russia expand and industrialize and yet retain the political structures of the Nineteenth Century? We have seen that both expansion and industrialization created tensions in society with which the government was unable to deal. The conservative reforms of the Tsarist government were designed to maintain the autocracy. Consequently, they did not address the problem of political change, and this encouraged many in society to look to revolutionary, rather than evolutionary, solutions to political and social problems.

In the early Twentieth Century alliances were forged that changed the Nineteenth Century European balance of power.

When a Serbian patriot assassinated the heir to the Austro-Hungarian Empire in Sarajevo, imperial Russia, unstable and backward, found itself once again on the slippery road to war. On 1 August Germany declared war on Russia, and Russia's powerful partners in the Triple Entente, France and Britain, became engaged in the war with Germany and Austria. The war, in which 5 million Russians died, would devastate Europe, demolish the imperial autocracy of the Tsars, and install a new political order in Russia.

Revision Questions

1. Do you think the intention of Tzarist reform in the period 1861–1906 was to redistribute political power or to sustain the autocracy? Give reasons for your answer.

217

2. Russia seemed to have both the physical resources and the size of population necessary for rapid modernization in the Nineteenth Century. What were the major factors hampering the rapid industrialization of the country at that time?

3. What social and political problems arose out of the transformation of Russia from an agricultural to an industrial state in the Nineteenth Century?

4. What were the effects of territorial expansion on the foreign and internal policies of the Russian Government in the late Nineteenth and early Twentieth Centuries?

5. 'The Tsarist government's response to tensions in Russian society was inappropriate and ineffectual.' Discuss this statement critically.

Chronology

1825–55	Tsar Nicholas I
1825	Decembrist Revolt
1854–56	Crimean War
1855–81	Tsar Alexander II
1861	Emancipation of the serfs
	Limited reforms
1873	Dreikaiserbund (Germany/Austria/Russia); annexations in central Asia
1877	Russia declares war on Turkey
1878	Balkan Wars
	Treaty of San Stefano
	Congress of Berlin
1881	Alexander II assassinated
1881–94	Tsar Alexander III
1887	Reinsurance Treaty (Russia and Germany)
1892	Finance Minister Witte starts industrial programme
1893	Entente between Russia and France
1894–1917	Tsar Nicholas II
1901	Social Revolutionary party formed
1902	Anglo-Japanese Alliance
1903	Completion of Trans-Siberian railway
	Social Democratic and Liberal parties formed
1904–05	Russo-Japanese War; ⚔ Mukden
1905	Bloody Sunday
1906–07	Dumas
1907	Triple Entente (France, Russia, Britain)
1914–17	First World War
1917	Bolshevik Revolution
1918	Treaty of Brest-Litovsk
	Beginning of civil war

Glossary

Autocracy — absolute, dictatorial government.

Balance of power — the idea that countries could restrain one another from acts of aggression, provided they were of equal strength.

Buffer states — countries which, because of their geographical situation, are used to protect another. Any military attack would have to be made on these states before the controlling state could be attacked.

Bureaucrats — government officials.

Capital — the accumulation of money, which is invariably used to invest in a business venture which will increase the amount of money through profit.

Constitutional government — a means of governing whereby the powers of the rulers are curtailed by those of other members of society.

Constitutional limit — a legal restraint on the actions of rulers.

Collectivism — the ownership of land by all for the benefit of all.

Cossacks — light horsemen of the Russian army.

Divine right — the belief that kings derive their authority from God, and that therefore their authority is independent of the will of the people.

Entrepreneurs — businessmen who supply money and ideas for new ventures.

Feudal system — a social system in which all peasants owed loyalty and tribute to their lord; in return the lord offered protection.

Geographic imperative — when the geographic peculiarities of a country make certain political or military actions seem necessary.

Ideology — a system of ideas which gives a foundation for an economic or political theory or system.

Orthodoxy — meaning, in this instance, loyalty to the Russian Orthodox Church. The Church was of great assistance to the rulers because it instilled the values of obedience, humility and morality into its adherents.

Panslav movement — a movement which aimed at the unification of all Slavs under one government.

People's Freedom party — otherwise known as the People's Will.

Pogroms — organized massacres, especially of Jews in Russia.

Polity — organization of government or state.

Reactionary — ultra-conservative, one who is against any form of liberal change.

Reform conservative — a person who supports only those changes which are designed to maintain the status quo.

Representative legislature — a parliament where the interests of voters are represented.

Socialism — the theory that the community as a whole should own and control the means of production, distribution and exchange, i.e. ownership by all for the good of all.

Strategic logic — when a country finds it necessary to obtain territory, not for the territory's qualities, but in the interest of defence.

Subsistence agriculture — a situation in which sufficient crops are grown, or livestock kept, to meet only the immediate needs of the family. Little, if any, surplus is produced.

Territorial integrity — when a territorial acquisition has a geographic logic, e.g. Russia acquired territory in neighbouring areas — unlike Britain.

Warm-water ports — sea ports which are not iced over for a large part of the year, thus preventing the movement of ships in and out of the port.

Bibliography

Dziewanowski M. K. *A History of the Soviet Union* (Prentice-Hall International, 1979)

Evans, D. *Europe in Modern Times 1900–1975* (Mathew Arnold, 1981)

Falkus, M. E. *The Industrialization of Russia, 1700–1914* (London, 1972)

Fitzlyon, K. and Browning T. *Before the Revolution* (Penguin, 1982)

Halliday, E. M. *Russia in Revolution* (Cassell, 1967)

Hasler, J. *The Making of Modern Russia* (Longman, 1969)

Jackson, N. C. *Russia in the Twentieth Century* (Pergamon Press, 1975)

Kochan L. *Russia in Revolution 1890–1918* (New American Library, 1966)

219

Kochan L. and Abraham R. *The Making of Modern Russia* (Penguin, 1962)
MacKenzie D. and Curran M. W. *A History of Russia and the Soviet Union* (Dorsey Press, 1977)
Rogger H. *Russia in the Age of Modernisation and Revolution 1881–1917* (Longman, 1983)
Thomson, D. *Europe Since Napoleon* (Pelican, 1976)
Troyat H. *Daily Life in Russia under the last Tzar* (Allen & Unwin, 1961)
Weissman, N. B. *Reform in Tsarist Russia: The State, Bureaucracy and Local Government 1900–1914* (New Brunswick, 1981)
Westwood J. N. *Endurance and Endeavour: Russian History* (Oxford University Press, 1973)

Composite chronology of general history

GERMANY	EUROPE	RUSSIA	USA	JAPAN	OTHER	G BRITAIN	SA
1815 Congress of Vienna							
			1823 Monroe Doctrine				
1830 Revolutions		1825–55 Tsar Nicholas	1832–33 Nullification Crisis		1833 Slavery abolished in British Empire	1832 Great Reform Bill	
1834 German Zollverein						1837 Chartist Movement	1835 Great Trek
	1848–49 Revolts in France, Germany and Italy, Hungary		1846–47 US/Mexican War. Annexation of south-western states				
1850 Frankfurt Parliament. Prussian Constitution			1849 Californian Gold Rush				
	1852 Accession of Napoleon III of France		1850 Compromise of 1850				
	1854–56 Crimean War	1854–56 Crimean War 1855–81 Tsar Alexander II	1854 Kansas Nebraska Act	1853–54 Commander Perry forces Japan to open ports to US trade/Treaty of Kanagawa	1857 Indian Mutiny		
	1859–61 Italian War of Unification		1860 Election of Lincoln as President				
1860 Constitutional crisis in Prussia	1861 Unification of Italy	1861 Emancipation of the serfs → Limited reforms	1861 Civil War				
1862 Bismarck becomes Minister President of Prussia			1863 Emancipation Proclamation				
1864 Schleswig/Holstein			1865 Slavery abolished. Lincoln assassinated → Reconstruction				
1865 Convention of Gastein							

221

GERMANY	EUROPE	RUSSIA	USA	JAPAN	OTHER	G BRITAIN	SA
1866 Austro-Prussian War. North German Confederation created. Peace of Prague. Zollverein reorganized. 1868 Spanish succession crisis		← Limited reforms →	← Recon-struction →	1866 Tokugawa Keiki becomes Shogun			1866 Discovery of diamonds
			1869 Trans-continental railway completed	1868 Emperor Mutsuhito regains power from the Shogun	1867 Canada becomes a dominion 1869 Suez Canal opened	1867 Second Great Reform Bill	
1870 FRANCO-PRUSSIAN WAR Unification of Germany under Kaiser Wilhelm	Fall of Napoleon III. Paris Commune Peace of Frankfurt			1872 Compulsory education introduced		1872 Compulsory Education Act	
	1873 Dreikaiserbund (Russia/Germany/Austria) 1878 Congress of Berlin 1879 Dual Alliance 1883 Revival of Dreikaiserbund	1873 Dreikaiserbund (Russia/Germany/Austria) 1878 Treaty of San Stefano. Congress of Berlin 1881–94 Tsar Alexander III	1877 Compromise of 1877 1886 Establishment of American Federation of Labour	1877 Revolt of Satsuma samurai 1887 Reinsurance Treaty	1877 Russo-Turkish War 1884 Berlin Conference on Africa		1879 Destruction of the Zulu Kingdom 1881 First Anglo-Boer War 1886 Gold rush on Witwatersrand
1888 Accession of Kaiser Wilhelm II 1890 Resignation of Bismarck as Chancellor 1898 Beginning of German navy	1893 Franco-Russian Treaty 1902 Anglo-Japanese Alliance 1904 Entente Cordiale (Britain/France)	1894–1917 Tsar Nicholas II 1903 Completion of Trans-Siberian railway 1904–05 Russo-Japanese War≻Mukden	1890 Sherman Anti-Trust Act 1898 Spanish-American War	1894–95 Sino-Japanese War ← Scramble for China → 1904–05 Russo-Japanese War≻Mukden	← Scramble for Africa → 1898 Fashoda	1902 Anglo-Japanese Alliance 1904 Entente Cordiale (Britain/France)	1895 Jameson Raid. Kruger telegram 1899–1902 Anglo-Boer War ← Recon-struction →

GERMANY	EUROPE	RUSSIA	USA	JAPAN	OTHER	G BRITAIN	SA
1905 First Moroccan Crisis		1905 Bloody Sunday / Russian Revolution 1906 Duma			1906 Algeciras Conference in Morocco		
1911 Second Moroccan Crisis 1914 First World War	1907 Anglo-Russian Entente. Triple Entente (France/Britain/Russia) 1912 Balkan Wars 1914 (28 June) Sarajevo — First World War	1914 First World War 1917 Bolshevik Revolution 1918 Treaty of Brest-Litovsk. Russian Civil War	1914 Opening of Panama Canal 1915 Sinking of the Lusitania 1917 US enters First World War 1918 END OF WAR. Wilson's Fourteen Points	1914 Japan joins the Allies in First W.W. 1915 Twenty-one Demands	1911 Chinese Revolution 1917 Balfour Declaration on Palestine		1910 Union 1914 First World War 1918 END OF WAR
1918 END OF WAR 1919 Spartacist Revolt 1920 Weimar Constitution. Kapp Putsch 1921 Reparations Commissions	1918 END OF WAR 1919 Paris Peace Conference/Treaty of Versailles 1921 League of Nations			1919 Treaty of Versailles 1921–2 Washington Conference			
1923 French occupation of Ruhr. Munich Brauhaus Putsch. 1924 Dawes Plan 1925 Treaty of Locarno 1926 Germany admitted to League 1929 Young Plan	DEPRESSION RISE OF FASCISM IN ITALY MUSSOLINI TAKES POWER	1924 Lenin dies 1927 Stalin takes power	1924 Dawes Plan 1929–30 Wall Street crash	1923–29 Introduction of liberal government reforms 1925 Universal male suffrage 1930 Showa Restoration 1931 Japanese occupy Manchuria		1922 Rand Revolt GENERAL STRIKE	1922 Rand Revolt Depression
1933 Reichstag Fire. Enabling Act. Hitler becomes Chancellor	1930 DEPRESSION		1933 'New Deal'	1933 Japan withdraws from League			RISE OF AFRICAN NATIONALISM. RISE OF AFRIKANER NATIONALISM. NEW PHASE OF INDUSTRIALIZATION AND NATIONALIZATION

Reconstruction

GERMANY	EUROPE	RUSSIA	USA	JAPAN	OTHER	G BRITAIN	SA
1934 'Night of the Long Knives'. Death of von Hindenberg		**1934** Russia admitted to League		**1935** Japan withdraws from Washington Naval Conference			
	1937 Italy withdraws from League			**1937** Beginning of Japanese-Chinese War			
1938 Anschluss							
1939 Second World War	**1939** Second World War	**1939** Russia expelled from League		**1940** Tripartite Pact (Germany/Italy/Japan)			**1939** Second World War
				1941 Pearl Harbor. Second World War			

224

South African History

Introduction

When dealing with South African history our intention will be to integrate the interpretations offered by the 'new history' with earlier traditions of Afrikaner nationalist history, and with so-called liberal historical writing.

The Afrikaner nationalist historical tradition tends to emphasise a heroic and patriotic tradition of Boer farmers as victims of British imperialism, locked in a struggle for survival with nature and the indigenous people; their trek to the 'promised land'; their fight for their identity as a people (*volk*); and the flowering of Afrikaner nationalism in the Twentieth Century. As F. A. van Jaarsveld has shown, 'the Afrikaner's interpretation of South African history' arises from a particular set of historical circumstances and was in large part written as an apologia for the political rise of the National Party.[1]

Since the victory of the National Party in the 1948 election, the 'official version' of our history has come to resemble the perspective offered by this Afrikaner tradition and this has had a strong influence on the nature of history taught in schools. School textbooks for all races have come to bear the stamp of the Afrikaner nationalist's version of South African history, in keeping with the doctrine of Christian National Education.

The liberal school of historians, in its turn, focused on the history of the British Empire with special reference to South Africa, and on the economic growth and development of South Africa in a period of modernization. Historians like E. A. Walker, C. W. de Kiewiet, J. S. Marais and W. H. Macmillan had a humane vision for South Africa. Their work showed great sensitivity to the injustices and sufferings of the colonial experience, and their history was infused by an appeal for racial tolerance and humanitarian values.

Where the liberals took note of the major transformations of the post-1870 era and the advent of industrialization and urbanization, they recognized the tensions and conflicts that arose out of those changes. They put much of the blame for them upon the 'irrational political tradition' of Afrikaner nationalism, which they claimed was a brake on true economic and political progress (modernization) for all. Liberals often argued that the 'frontier mentality of the north' (i.e. the Transvaal and the Orange Free State) had come to dominate public life in South Africa after the 1890s, and assumed this 'political factor' to be central to the lack of economic growth or modernization in South Africa up to the 1960s. The liberals assumed that economic growth based on the modern sector (maize, gold and manufacturing) would serve to minimize social and political conflict and create a more equal society in South Africa.

This liberal approach to history put forward the claim that there is a fundamental and historical contradiction between: (i) the politics of racism (usually attributed to Boer and Afrikaner nationalism); and (ii) modern economic growth in a free enterprise society. The assumption that lies behind these claims is that the development of the modern economy necessarily diminishes conservativeness and racism. In other words, the more the economy develops — the more growth — the more, it was assumed, South Africa would be freed from old-fashioned prejudices such as colour-bars, job reservation, miscegenation laws, group areas legislation, petty apartheid, and influx control.

[1] It is important to note at the same time that this is just one possible interpretation for the history of Afrikaners — namely the nationalist version.

On this view the segregationist or apartheid policies of various governments were held to be an out-of-date element in our modern society. Liberal historians and economists called for a return to the idea of a true free market or capitalist economy which, it was assumed, would also accent individual human rights and freedoms, and the distribution of the wealth of society on more equal terms.

Since the early 1970s there have been important developments in the study of South African history. Much of the initial challenge came from South African students studying in Britain, Europe and the USA, but these ideas have now come to have a major influence on historical writing on Southern Africa. Although the 'new history', (sometimes called the revisionist version), has to a large extent grown out of the liberal tradition, it places rather different emphases on the evidence.

Influential in the 'new history' is the Africanist tradition, which stresses the nature and relationships of pre-colonial African societies, the impact of colonialism on Africa, and resistance to imperial powers. This tradition was developed in the universities of Africa in the post-independence era (especially since the 1960s), and provided a scholarly echo to the 'winds of change' which brought the colonial era to an end.

An equally radical departure was reflected in work which focused upon South Africa's role, nationally and internationally, as a colonial, capitalist state, and on the phenomenon of South Africa's industrial revolution in the period from the 1870s. The Afrikaner nationalist tradition largely ignored the massive social and economic transformations affecting South African society in the period from 1860 to 1970, or only noted its effects on 'poor whites'. The liberals saw in this transformation a fundamentally positive development hindered only by the 'political interference' of the state; while the new school saw in this period the development of a systematic and lasting system of control and domination of white over black in the political, economic and social spheres.

The recent emphasis on social and economic history reflects an international trend in historical writing. That emphasis does not in any way imply that political factors are considered to be unimportant or that they can be omitted; on the contrary, the assertion is that political history can only be fully understood if economic and social influences are taken into account and vice versa.

Above all there has been a shift away from the writing of the history of only the rich and the powerful, that is of 'great men history' (e.g. Rhodes vs. Kruger) or the history of specific groups, towards a history which lays its emphasis on the historical experience of the majority of the people — on their daily lives, their work situations and their actions in the political, economic, cultural and social spheres.

The intention of this book is not to focus exclusively on any one of the schools of interpretation mentioned above, but to attempt to introduce the student to the study of South African history as such, in all its richness and diversity. We will draw from each of the perspectives and from the vast areas which lie between these rather rigid classifications. We will attempt to demonstrate points of conflicting interpretation, but it will not be possible to enter into in-depth discussions of all of the issues due to lack of space. We hope that such an approach will give rise to discussion and assist learners and teachers to use the time at their disposal to maximum advantage — above and beyond the necessary requirements of preparation for examinations.

7 THE ECONOMIC AND SOCIAL EFFECTS OF THE DISCOVERY AND MINING OF DIAMONDS AND GOLD: 1870–1910

Introduction 230
The changing nature of the South African economy and society: 1870–1910

Southern Africa before the mineral discoveries 231

The industrial revolution in Southern Africa: 1870–1910 233
The mining revolution
The development of the diamond-fields
The river diggings
The dry diggings
The development of gold mining on the Witwatersrand
The agricultural revolution
The transport and technological revolution
The social revolution: Urbanization and the growth of towns
Why did people leave the countryside and move to the towns?
Why did black South Africans move to the towns?
Why did many Afrikaners move from the countryside to the towns?
The labour revolution: The making of the working class

Conclusion 260
The characteristics of the first phase of modernization or the first industrial revolution
The context of modernization
The price of modernization
The decline of the African economy
The creation of an industrial labour force
Dependency: The limits of industrial development
The unequal distribution of wealth
Revision Questions
Glossary
Bibliography

Introduction

THE CHANGING NATURE OF THE SOUTH AFRICAN ECONOMY AND SOCIETY: 1870–1910

Southern Africa's economic and social development during the period 1870–1910 was marked by a shift from a purely agricultural and trading economy to the first stages of a modern industrial economy. The discovery and mining of diamonds and gold provided the basis for this economic and social transformation. The move from a rural and agricultural economy to a modern industrial economy changed the nature of society.

Economic change was accompanied by major social and political changes. The way people lived, what they believed, and how they earned their livelihood, was radically transformed in a short space of time. As one historian put it:

> ... the mineral revolution which began in the 1860s, and accelerated during the 1870s and 1880s, was the most far-reaching change to have taken place in nineteenth century South Africa — in many ways more revolutionary than the Mfecane and more influential than the Great Trek.   (Denoon, p. 55)

After the mineral discoveries and the industrial revolution that followed, the conditions for the creation of wealth increased dramatically. This was a result both of the expansion of exports and of the increase in size of the local market for agricultural and manufactured goods.

A major feature of that process of change was the emergence of well organized groups of people which controlled the new sources of wealth and power. They were faced by a relatively weak and disorganized, but expanding, labour force. This imbalance in the access to wealth and power enabled the mineowners, in particular, to have a strong influence on political policies and social arrangements out of all proportion to their size as a group.

The industrial transformation of Southern Africa's economy and society took place in two phases, which can for convenience be considered as two phases of the industrial revolution:

Phase 1: *THE FIRST INDUSTRIAL REVOLUTION or the EXTRACTIVE* PHASE OF MODERNIZATION: 1870–1920s*

This phase was dominated by the mining revolution and the extraction of minerals, which focused on the development of gold, diamond and coal mining. This era also saw the beginnings of large-scale modern farming, especially the production of wool, hides, sugar, wine, maize and wheat.

This was the first phase of South Africa's industrial revolution. Major economic developments in South Africa were often closely tied to the needs of the industrial nations of Europe.

Phase 2: *THE SECOND INDUSTRIAL REVOLUTION or the MANUFACTURING* PHASE OF MODERNIZATION: 1930s–1970s*

This phase saw a dramatic increase in the manufacturing industry, in addition to the expansion of mining. During this period South Africa became a fully developed modern industrial state with an economy that included both agricultural and industrial sectors producing for the

Southern Africa before the mineral discoveries

market. Yet South Africa continued to differ from the industrial nations of Europe and North America in important respects. The majority of the black population was still forced to live in the rural reserves*, or in increasingly racially segregated urban townships. They attended segregated schools. They were restricted in the work situation by a range of job reservation* laws which excluded blacks from many jobs.

This chapter will focus primarily on the period prior to 1910, during which South African industry began to modernize. (Stage C (i) in the table opposite.)

What would the key features of Southern African society and economy have been to the eyes of a visitor to the area in the 1860s? This is not a question that can be answered solely by the use of imagination — though this *is* important to historians! The answer is obtainable mainly by the reading of accounts written by contemporary travellers, missionaries, hunters, traders or government officials, who recorded their daily observations of the lives of ordinary people.

In the past people who wrote history tended to concentrate on the deeds of 'great men and women' — politicians, businesspeople, and royalty. Although these historical accounts

The stages of economic development in South Africa

PRE-INDUSTRIAL

Stage A
Pre-capitalist subsistence economy, including agriculture, hunting, stock farming, mining and limited regional trade.

Up to the Nineteenth Century.

Stage B
The early colonial economy or early modern economy/merchant or trade economy — including hunting (especially ivory), agriculture (sugar), pastoral farming (hides, beef, wool) — for profit and export. NB: Linked to the world economy.

Dominant until the 1870s.

INDUSTRIAL

Stage C (i)
The first industrial revolution/(the extractive phase of modernization), dominated by the extraction of raw materials and a mining revolution including diamonds, gold, and coal, and the beginnings of large-scale capitalist* farming.
NB: Wool, maize and sugar.

From the 1870s to the 1920s.

Stage C (ii)
The second industrial revolution (the manufacturing phase of industrialization*); or the phase of manufacturing and the development of secondary industrialization.

From the 1930s to the present.

NOTE: These stages should not be seen as simply following in sequence, one after another. Each stage should be understood to continue into the following stage; e.g. aspects of Stage A were still evident in the mid-Twentieth Century (Stage C (ii)). What is being pointed out is the *main* feature of each stage.

231

wool + Sugar

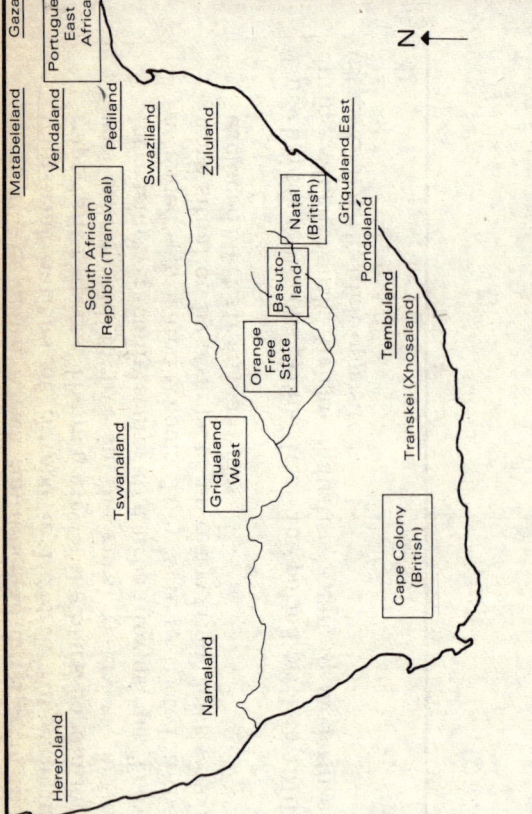

Map 28 — Political map of Southern Africa circa 1876. (Boundary lines are not included because in many cases they were ill-defined and in any case often in dispute.)

In 1876 all the areas underlined were independent — i.e. free from foreign rule. By 1900 all of the region had come under European rule. The names given in the boxes indicate areas of white rule (either British, Boer or Portuguese) in 1876.

The general character of the economy in the 1860s was that of a sparsely populated country largely engaged in pastoral farming and self-subsistence agriculture, too poor to advance rapidly by creating wealth locally and lacking any exploitable resources to attract foreign capital ... The

gave us an important beginning, they only partially helped us to understand our roots. Today we are also keen to discover more about the lives of ordinary people. The histories of church organizations, small rural communities, or peasant groups, for example, have taken on increasing importance as they give us an in-depth understanding of the past.

Politically Southern Africa consisted of a variety of communities or states in 1876. As Map 28 shows, very large areas of land and the majority of the human population still lived beyond the control of the states that were governed by the colonial powers or local white groups. Most 'states'* were in any case groupings of people rather than territorial areas.

The societies of Southern Africa varied greatly in their nature and composition, and it is often difficult or erroneous to generalize about their history or ethnic identity, their social or religious customs, their economic practices or their political institutions or affiliations. Nevertheless, it is probably true, in general, to say that communal social and economic arrangements based on homestead production* for subsistence purposes were still a marked feature of African societies at this time. This was also basically true of Boer societies. Much white farming was still bound to the simple needs of a largely self-sufficient, subsistence economic system — which meant that economic development for the market was very slow. In the Cape and Natal commercial farming was beginning to emerge, but capitalism itself was far from established as the major economic system. The beginnings of a transformation in economic relations also began to change the social life and political practices of the majority of the inhabitants. In the Cape and Natal exports of wool and sugar were beginning to demonstrate what could be achieved. In 1860 wool accounted for over 50 per cent of the Cape's £2 million worth of exports.

232

The industrial revolution in Southern Africa: 1870–1910

Although market-orientated farming, trade, transport, banking and education were gradually being extended to the interior, on the eve of the mineral discoveries things looked far from favourable for growth along the lines of a modern industrial state. South Africa was in the grip of an economic recession and the collapse of the international wool market at the end of the American Civil War was a further blow. A serious drought was also affecting the greater part of the country. This was the state of affairs during the 1860s, when the mineral discoveries on the Vaal River suddenly began to transform the economy and society.

From being a small exporter of wool and sugar (see table p. 235); from providing a very limited market for British exports; and from having been important largely for strategic reasons, because of its location on the sea route between Europe and the East; South Africa became a major supplier of gold, the currency base for the world economy.

economic structure of the region was largely moulded by the fact that the land was no longer abundant, capital and skilled labour were scarce, markets were extremely distant and the means of transport primitive...

(Adapted from *Oxford History of South Africa*, Vol. II, p. 1.)

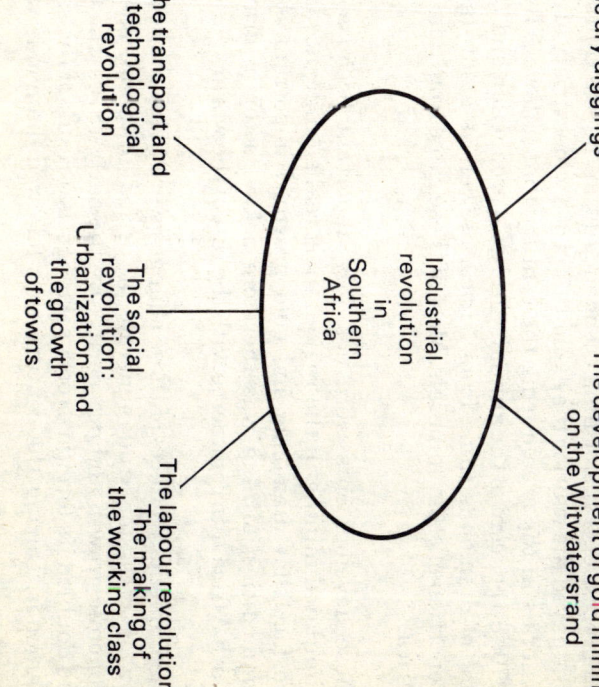

- The mining revolution
- The development of mining on the diamond-fields
 * The river diggings
 * The dry diggings

The development of gold mining on the Witwatersrand

Industrial revolution in Southern Africa

The social revolution: Urbanization and the growth of towns

The labour revolution: The making of the working class

The transport and technological revolution

1865

① land conflicts to urban / industrial conflicts.

⑧ Pre capitalist somewhat agri economy → new political + economic dispensation dominated by white.

233

THE MINING REVOLUTION

For many centuries before the arrival of the Europeans in Africa, minerals were mined by Africans, both for use in African societies, and for export. Although only small amounts of iron and gold were mined in Southern Africa, the level of technology was often quite advanced and the products that resulted were extremely important to the societies that produced them. For example, iron-smelting in the southern Transvaal was vital to the hunting and agricultural economy of the region because it provided efficient weapons and farming implements (such as hoes). The production of such commodities also gave rise to trade with other societies.

The discovery of diamonds near Kimberley in the 1860s and gold on the Witwatersrand in 1886 proved to be major events in the process of transforming economic life on the sub-continent. This paved the way for the exploitation of a wide variety of other minerals in the area during the century that followed. By the 1970s 80 per cent of the annual world gold production and 75 per cent of diamonds came from Africa, as well as a substantial proportion of other minerals. Most of these came from Southern Africa.

These developments were not only important because they stimulated mining in the region; their real significance lay in the fact that diamonds and gold provided important export commodities. Mining was therefore a key factor in drawing South Africa into commerce with the rest of the world.

The immediate effects of these changes were to lift the country out of recession and generate a period of unprecedented economic growth and prosperity. By the early 1870s, the Cape had doubled its foreign export earnings as a result of the sale of diamonds. During the century that followed diamonds worth £700 million were sold, along with some £6–7 000 million worth of gold. These figures, together with those in the table opposite, give a rough idea of the importance of these two minerals to the growth of the economy.

> *The problem for Africa, is whether the activities of the international mining companies are compatible with the continent's economic development, or whether the companies present a major obstacle to development.*
>
> (Lanning and Mueller, p. 19.)

Minerals and mining companies have played an important role in the development and modernization of Southern Africa. From Cecil Rhodes to Harry Oppenheimer, mining magnates have played a dominant role in the development of the politics and economy of the region. There have been at least two important consequences.

1. The industrial revolution brought political upheaval in its wake, but it also changed the nature of political conflict. Prior to the 1890s the main arena of political conflict had centred on the countryside. Now this was slowly overshadowed by urban politics and conflict in the industrial labour market. This conflict took place between owners (the Randlords*) and workers over the distribution of profits; it also took place, especially after 1907, between white and black mineworkers, as they jostled for an advantaged position in the labour market.

2. The restructuring of the economy by the mining companies, the massive exports of minerals and the profits they initiated, largely destroyed the pre-capitalist, subsistence agricultural economies. This transformed existing trade patterns to produce a new economic and political dispensation dominated by whites and, particularly in the period under consideration, by Britain.

Economic consequences of the mineral discoveries in South Africa: 1861–1910

The table depicts the amount of South African produce exported during the period 1861–1910. Three categories of exports are noted: gold, diamonds and all other exports.

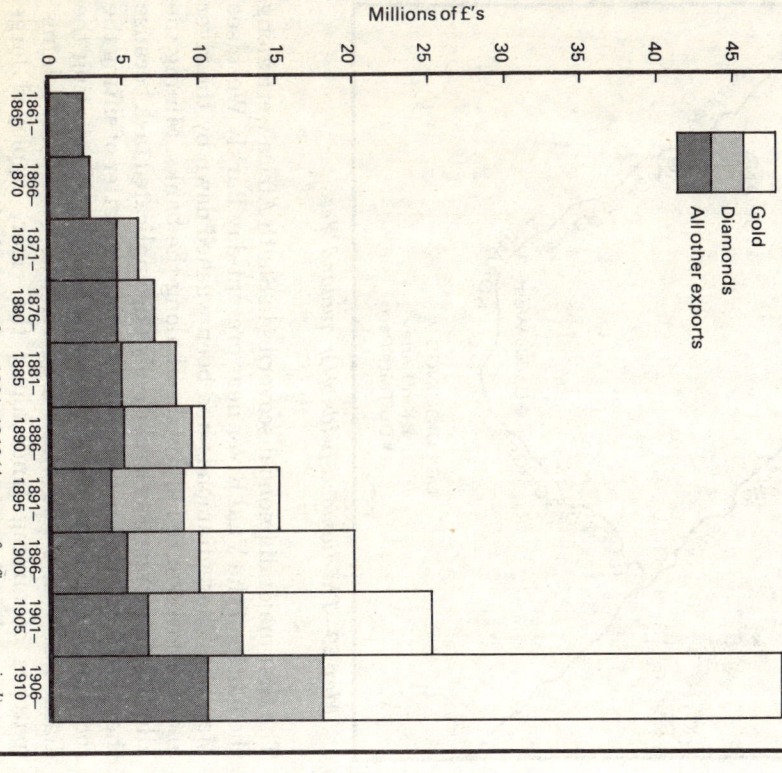

Exports of South African produce 1861–1910 (Average for five-year period).

Questions

1. In the period before 1870 what percentage of South African exports was comprised of minerals?
2. Other commodities exported were wool, hides and skins, sugar, mohair and wine. Give reasons for the overall growth of the agricultural export sector during this period.
3. From the table, what major change in the South African economy occurred in the years between 1870 and 1890?
4. Between 1886 and 1910 the value of diamonds exported remained much the same, why was this so?
5. Comment on the rate of expansion of the gold mining industry during the period 1891–1905. How did this change after 1905?
6. What other economic consequences resulted from the mineral revolution in South Africa?
7. Study the diagram on p. 233 and the table and compile a list of the major consequences of the mineral revolution in Southern Africa.

South Africa's first industrial community was on the diamond fields. There South Africa faced for the first time the modern problems of capital and labour. There South Africa faced a new competition between black and white inhabitants, not for land or capital, but for a place in industry.

(de Kiewiet, p. 89.)

235

THE RIVER DIGGINGS

The consolidation of economic wealth and political power in the hands of whites during the period was sealed in the Union of South Africa in 1910.

> The discovery of diamonds and gold undoubtedly triggered the development of the modern South African economy and society. However, it also laid the foundation for the inequality that is characteristic of present day South Africa.
>
> (Nattrass, p. 135.)

The development of the diamond-fields

In this section, emphasis will be placed upon developments at Kimberley and on the diamond-fields. This is not because they are considered to be more important than those that took place on the Witwatersrand. Clearly the scale of the changes and the effects of events on the Witwatersrand are of far greater general significance to South African history. The reason for our focus is that the nature of the changes is essentially similar, while the smaller scale of events on the diamond-fields makes them easier to understand. In addition, the opening up of the diamond-fields took place first and the documentary evidence for these events in the form of contemporary descriptions is more dramatic and more easily accessible. The effects of the events on the diamond-fields and the trends set in motion there flow into the broader stream of events that add up to the making of an industrial revolution.

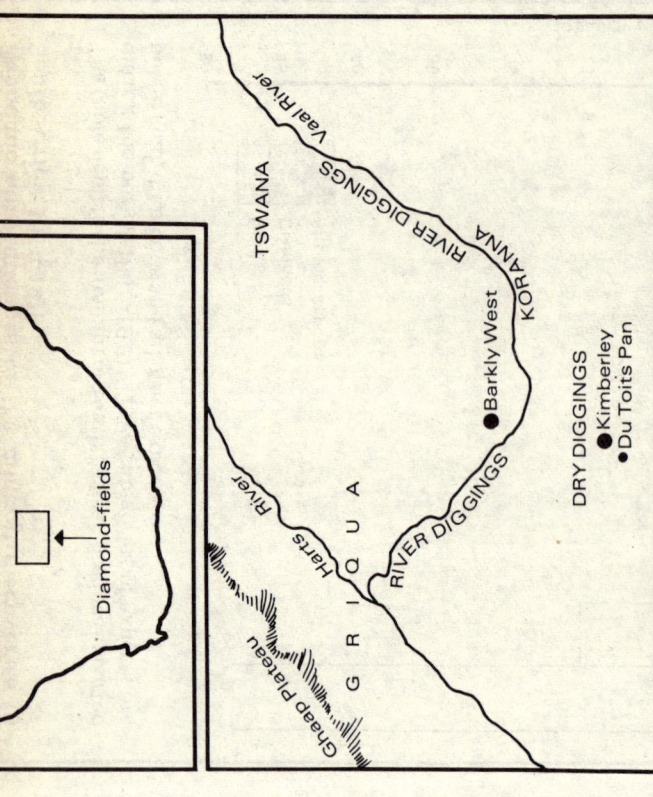

Map 29—*The diamond-fields of Griqualand West.*

The first major diamond discoveries in South Africa were along the banks of the Vaal River near present-day Barkly West (see Map 29). These diamonds had been washed down by the river and deposited in the alluvial soil along the banks. Mining the alluvial diamonds was a relatively uncomplicated task because they were near the surface. It was simply a matter of sifting the rocks and soil along the river bank and then extracting the diamonds. White and black diggers, who owned the 'claims' (patches of mining land) along the river, employed large numbers of black workers to mine and sift the diamond-bearing soil. At first the sifting was done by hand, but machines were soon designed to separate the diamonds from the soil. Only small amounts of capital were necessary to establish such a mine in the early days.

THE DRY DIGGINGS

By the early 1870s diamonds were discovered in much larger quantities away from the Vaal River, at the dry diggings (see Map 29). The first major discovery was at a small hill called Colesberg Kopje. This place later came to be called 'New Rush', or Kimberley, after Earl Kimberley, the British Secretary of State for the Colonies.

Here miners discovered a number of extinct volcanic pipes that had brought the diamonds to the surface from deep in the earth. Colesberg Kopje was itself the top of one of these 'pipes', and the miners soon cut away the kopje and made what was then the biggest man-made hole in the world — the Kimberley 'Big Hole'. If you ever go to Kimberley you can visit this hole at the Kimberley Mine Museum.

Later other 'pipes' or mines were also brought into production at du Toit's Pan, De Beers, Bultfontein and Wesselton, all close to Kimberley.

Surface mining — At first the miners simply dug holes in their claims in order to extract the special soft 'yellow ground' that contained the gems. Later, when they struck the hard 'blue ground', the holes became too deep and too large to work with safety as they kept caving in or getting flooded with water.

Geology and technology combined to defeat the digger who had little capital, while large mining companies were able to take advantage of conditions that developed on the diamond fields from the 1880s.

(Based on Stanley Trapido.)

A new method of mining had to be introduced, namely underground mining.

Underground mining — The diagram on page 244 shows a cross-section of a 'blue ground' volcanic pipe with:
1. the original 'open-cast' mine (which operated from c. 1871 to the 1880s);
2. the development of an underground mining system (which was developed from the early 1880s).

These changes resulted in the framing of new laws relating to claim holding. At first the rule had been one-owner-one-claim. In 1874 one owner was allowed to own up to ten claims. By the end of the 1870s many of these small-scale mineowners were in turn forced to sell out to large mining companies. These companies had the capital to buy out and consolidate claims, and invest in the expensive mining equipment and diamond recovery plants that became necessary under the new conditions. In the early 1870s there were 1 600 claims at the Kimberley Big Hole. By 1880 this number was reduced to just under 400.

First the small-scale individual miners gave way to larger companies. Finally, by the late 1880s, the De Beers Mining Company, under the control of Cecil Rhodes, gained a monopoly of the entire industry. Through the London Diamond Syndicate, de Beers eventually established a world monopoly of diamond sales.

As underground mining developed, skilled European, Australian and American miners were brought in by the big companies. New mining methods were developed and technology improved. As a result, the number of unskilled black labourers declined dramatically, from between 20 and 30 000 at

237

any given time in the period 1871–1875 to under 10 000 in 1888. (For details relating to the issue of labour on the diamond-fields see pp. 254–260.) While the number of people employed on the diamond mines decreased over time, the output of the industry, and the wealth created, have increased dramatically during this century due to improved mining techniques and the greater use of sophisticated mining technology.

The dry diggings circa 1872.
(Illustration courtesy of the Cape Archives.)

A splendid view of the deepening Kimberley mine and the hoisting system which took the place of the earlier roadways running across to the floor of the mine.

(Illustration courtesy of the Cape Archives.)

they seem standing erect as walls, sometimes they descend in steps; here they seem to range themselves in terraces, and there they gape asunder as pits; altogether they combine to form a picture of such wild confusion, that at dusk, or in the pale glimmer of moonshine, it would require no great stretch of imagination to believe them the ruins of some city of the past, that after the lapse of centuries was being brought afresh to light.

But any illusion of this sort is all dispelled, as one watches the restless activity of the throngs that people the bottom of the deep dim hollow. The vision of the city of the dead dissolves into the scene of a teeming ant-hill; all is life and eagerness and bustle. The very eye grows confused at the labyrinth of wires stretching out like a giant cobweb over the space below, while the movements of the countless buckets making their transit backwards and forwards only add to the bewilderment. Meanwhile to the ear the windlasses; there is the hoarse creaking of everything is equally trying; there is the perpetual hum of the wires; there is the constant thud of the falling masses of earth; there is the unceasing splash of water from the pumps; and these, combined with the shouts and singing of the labourers, so affect the nerves of the spectator, that, deafened and giddy, he is glad to retire from the strange and striking scene.

(E. Holub, *Seven Years in South Africa*, Vol. I, pp. 71–2.)

Questions

From the information in the extract, diagrams and pictures, construct a model of a 'diamond quarry' (you can use a small waste-paper bin and waste paper), and use this to identify the various aspects of the mining operation referred to.

Make sure that you can explain in some detail:

1. the nature of the mining operation;

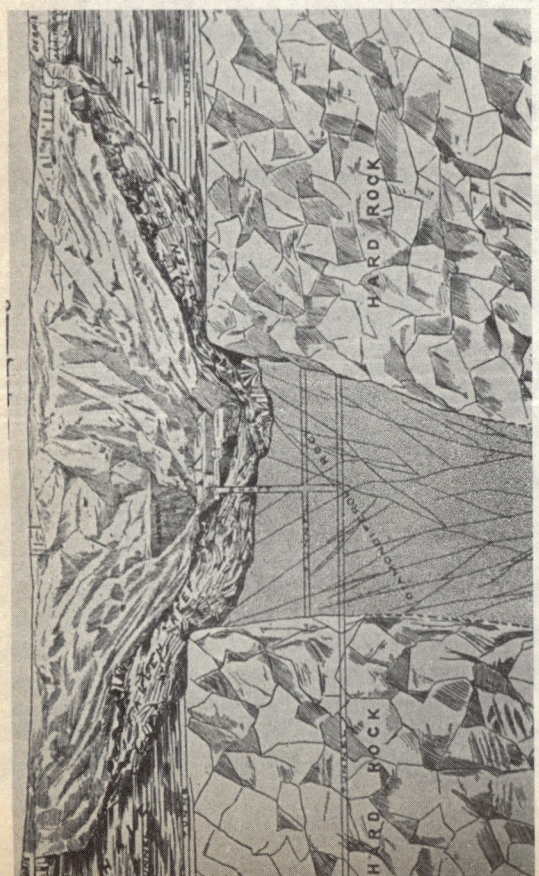

Transverse section of the Kimberley Mine in 1885.

A description of a diamond mine in Kimberley in 1872

Emil Holub, a Czechoslovakian traveller, visited the diamond-fields in 1872, and left us a vivid account of the scene at the Kimberley Big Hole.

As viewed from the edge of the surrounding clay walls, the appearance of one of the great diamond-fields is so peculiar as almost to defy any verbal description. It can only be compared to a huge crater, which, previously to the excavations, was filled to the very brink on which we stand with volcanic eruptions, composed of crumbling diamond-bearing earth, consisting mainly of decomposed tufa [porous rock]. That crater now stands full of the rectangular 'claims', dug out to every variety of depth. Before us are masses of earth, piled up like pillars, clustered like towers, or spread out in plateaus; sometimes

2. the different phases of the operation which took place from the establishment of a claim to the production of the diamonds;
3. how mining methods changed over time in order to deal with the new problems that arose;
4. what the effects of the above changes were on the pattern of ownership or economic control of the diamond industry.

e.g: — how did technology change?
— how did ownership change?
— how did labour change?
— why did monopolies come about?
— what were the political results of the changes referred to?

Life at the diamond-fields

We have selected one edited description of Kimberley to give a sense of the bustle and excitement. Rev. Tyamzashe was a Congregational clergyman who was sent to minister to a congregation at Kimberley in 1872. This account was written for the eastern Cape newspaper *Christian Express*, published at Lovedale College in Alice in 1874.

We have often heard of the industrious city — the Metropolis of Great Britain; the crowding of its streets, and the noise of the machinery and workmen. But I question if the noise there has ever been anything approaching what I have heard at the New Rush. The hurry and din of the wheels, pulleys, wires, and buckets, in conveying the diamondiferous ground out of the gigantic mine; the noise of waggons, carts, carriages, sieves, sorting tables, and all the like, combined with the ...yells of the ... labourers, and accompanied with a hurrah for every trifling thing that seems to be out of place, — these things are as familiar to us at Kimberley as the touch bells are to you at Lovedale.

On my first arrival at the New Rush [in 1871] I observed that nearly every evening was devoted to private and public amusements, insomuch that there seemed to be no room left for the great work for which we had come.[1] The evenings resounded with the noise of the concert, the circus, and all sorts of dances from one end of the camp to the other. The life then of both coloured and whites was so rough that I thought this place was only good for those who were resolved to sell their souls for silver, gold, and precious stones, or for those who were determined to barter their lives for the pleasures of a time. Diamond stealing was also regularly carried on a large scale by persons of colour as well as whites. Even in the present days of order, peace, and good government,[2] I fear that diamond stealing is still practised systematically and ingeniously[3] ...

During the short period of about two years there has been a wonderful change with regard to the moral condition of the Diamond Fields. The invincible power of the Gospel has made itself felt in the hearts of many, so that now there are two opposite forces acting against each other, whereas before only one — namely, the evil influence — seemed to be the one ruling power in this camp.

Instead of the bustle and confusion of 1872, we have now that quietude and security of life and property which is characteristic of proper legislation and good government. About two years ago human life was, so to speak, reckoned

1. i.e. preaching Christianity and tending his 'flock'.
2. Since the British Government annexed the area as the Crown Colony of Griqualand West in 1872.
3. For example, some people swallowed the diamonds in order to hide them.

241

as of less value than silver, gold, and precious stones. At that time you would hear nothing but cursing, swearing, screaming, and shouts of hurrah for new comers from the interior, for fighters, for a well dressed lady, for a diamond being found, and so forth. It is vain to expect order and smoothness here. The very purpose for which the people have rushed and crowded together in this camp, — to get rich rapidly, — speaks of itself that there can be neither order nor smoothness in such a rush as this. Add to this the severity of the climate and the unruly character of the diggers. All who have ever visited the fields will have complained of excessive heat, extreme cold, and choking dust occasioned by the every day storms of wind raising the gigantic heaps of sorted gravel, sometimes rendering the sun invisible, and breathing also difficult. You would be surprised to find at the Colesberg Kopje a person whom you knew to have been a respectable gentleman, dressed like a common labourer, with only a pair of trousers, a big flannel shirt purposely unbuttoned, and a big heavy belt round his waist. Every one who succeeds in making a fortune . . . will first have to be contented to live day after day like the Xhosa-Bakwetas or white boys¹. When they are all at work you can hardly distinguish the whites from the coloured, for they all resemble the diamondiferous soil they are working . . .

Day after day you hear shouts of hurrah for a diamond being found, for a rope or wire breaking, for a bucket falling and injuring some one, for a portion of a claim breaking down and burying some person or persons underneath it.

This is the reason why many persons wanting patience and perseverance have been thoroughly disappointed when they came here. To bear on for a year or so at this picnic life requires no ordinary degree of patience on the part of the digger. The summation of the above statements with regard to life at the Diamond Fields may be comprehended under the two English words, rough and hard . . .

In a mission point of view, it is not easy to deal with such a mixture of tribes as we have at the Diamond Fields. There are . . . [San], Koranas, . . . [Khoikhoi], Griquas, Bataping, Damaras, Barolong, Barutse, Bakhatla, Bakwena, Bamanguatu, [Pedi] . . . Magalaka, Batsuetla, Baganana, Basutu, Magwaba, Mazulu, Maswazi, Matswetswa, Matonga, Matebele, Mabaca, Mampondo, Mamfengu, Batembu, Maxosa, etc. Many of these can hardly understand each other, and in many cases they have to converse through the medium of either Dutch, Sisutu, or Xhosa. Those coming from far up in the interior, such as the Bakwena, Bamanguatu, [Pedi] . . . Matebele, etc., come with the sole purpose of securing guns. Some of them therefore resolve to stay no longer here than is necessary to get some six or seven pounds for the gun. Hence you will see hundreds of them leaving the Fields, and as many arriving from the north almost every day . . .

(Wilson and Perrot, pp. 19–21.)

Questions

1. In what ways does Rev. Tyamzashe compare 'the Metropolis of Great Britain' (i.e. London) to Kimberley?

2. Consider the account given here of mining operations and the illustrations in this chapter.
Write your own account of mining operations, taking care to demonstrate your understanding of the methods of mining and the work involved for mineowners and labourers in 1874.

3. Why was life so 'rough and hard' at Kimberley?

---

1. The young Xhosa men who go naked and paint themselves white to prepare for the initiation ceremony to manhood.

4. How, in Rev. Tyamzashe's opinion, had Kimberley changed between 1872 and 1874? What is the attitude expressed towards the 'moral condition of the diamond fields'? Do you think his attitude was justified? Give evidence to support your answer.
5. Can you explain the writer's attitude to the following groups on the diamond-fields?
   (a) The Xhosa;
   (b) the labourers from the 'tribes of the interior';
   (c) the whites.
6. Why, in Rev. Tyamzashe's opinion, did so many Africans come to work on the diamond mines? Do you agree with his explanation? Can you add to it?
7. What observations can you make about Rev. Tyamzashe on the basis of his writings above? What were his attitudes to the changing circumstances of life as he observed them in Kimberley?

The discovery and exploitation of the gold bearing reefs on the Witwatersrand from 1886 onwards intensified all the tendencies and pressures introduced into the South African economy and society by the exploitation of the Kimberley diamond mines.

(Nattrass, p. 136)

The development of gold mining on the Witwatersrand

Gold mining transformed the southern Transvaal into the economic heartland of Southern Africa in the last fifteen years of the Nineteenth Century. The development of the Witwatersrand mining camps into the largest urban area in sub-Saharan Africa represents a key aspect of our modern history. There are few issues so hotly debated by South African historians as the nature of the impact of the gold mining industry on South African society, politics and economics. The influence of the gold mining industry on the nature of work, employment, and labour relations* has been singled out for particular attention. Another important issue has been the influence of the gold mining industry on the relative living standards of whites and blacks during this century.

After a number of minor gold rushes in the Lowveld at Tati (on the border of present-day Zimbabwe and Botswana), Eersteling and Barberton (in the eastern Transvaal), payable gold was discovered on the farms Roodepoort, Landlaagte, Turffontein and Doornfontein along the Witwatersrand in 1886. A number of prospectors, including the Struben brothers, J. J. Bantjes, George Harrison, and George Walker are remembered for their role in the early discoveries.

At first the surface mining was relatively easy, but the complex nature of the underground mining operation on the Witwatersrand soon revealed that the process of creating the fabulous wealth of the gold mines was not to be at all simple. The gold was for the most part to be found deep under ground. In addition, there was only a small quantity of gold in the ore mined. The gold ore of the Witwatersrand was low grade ore*. This combination of circumstances, added to the fact that it was extremely difficult to extract the gold from the ore, meant that gold mining on the Witwatersrand was an extremely expensive business from the earliest days of the industry.

243

The mining of gold on the Witwatersrand

Read this description in conjunction with the illustration on the right.

1. Once gold is discovered, underground shafts are sunk. These shafts go hundreds of metres underground.
2. Then passages or stopes are dug out, leading off from the main shaft (A). These stopes cut into the line of the reef (or gold-bearing rock) that runs deep underground.
3. Miners drill holes into the gold-bearing rock before blasting it to create small tunnels.
4. The tunnels have to be cleared of the blasted rock. This process is called lashing (B).
5. The rock and ore is loaded onto small trucks or cocoa pans and transported to the main shaft. This job is called tramming (C).
6. The ore is lifted to the surface in a lift or cage, where it is loaded onto a train and transported to the crushing, processing and smelting plant. There the gold is separated from the crushed ore. Machines, chemicals and heat are used in this process (D).
7. The hot, liquid gold is poured into trays to produce gold ingots (E). The ingots are then transported (F) to Johannesburg and other major centres where they are sold.
8. Every ton of rock mined produces approximately one ounce of gold.

An underground stope in a gold mine.
(Photograph courtesy of the Johannesburg Africana Museum.)

The diagram below explains key aspects of the processes of surface and underground gold mining. Note that the gold reef always runs at the angle shown in this diagram.

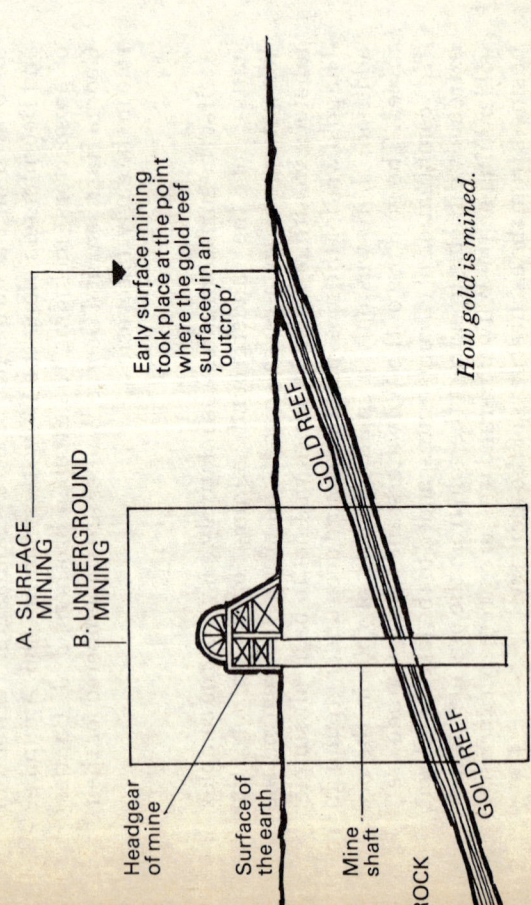

How gold is mined.

244

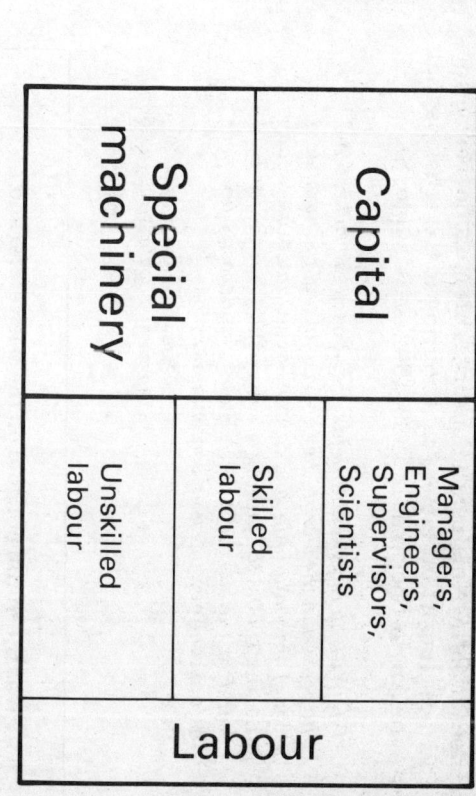

THE NEEDS OF THE GOLD MINES:

Capital		
Special machinery	Managers, Engineers, Supervisors, Scientists	
	Skilled labour	
	Unskilled labour	
	Labour	

The low-grade* gold ore was a key problem for the mineowners. On average one ounce of gold was recovered for every ton of ore mined. That meant that the mining operation was extremely expensive. Also, the gold-bearing reef slanted deep into the earth at an awkward angle, making the task of mining difficult. Mining could only be possible and profitable if heavy machinery and modern technology were used. As a result, the industry was dominated from an early date by the need to raise large amounts of capital, both internationally and from the mining magnates in Kimberley. Such funding could only be raised if the mines paid large profits to those who invested. The costs of mining gold were therefore high.

The mineowners were known as Randlords. They were supported by the British government in demanding conditions suitable for the growth of the gold mining industry. The informal alliance between the Randlords and the British administration in Southern Africa produced poor relations between Britain and the South African Republic (ZAR) in the last decade of the Nineteenth Century. This must be seen as one of the most important factors contributing to the tensions that led to the Anglo-Boer War in 1899–1902 (see Chapter 8).

> The Witwatersrand goldfields are at once the richest and the poorest in the world; they are rich in that the number of tons of ore containing gold cannot be calculated, and today [i.e. the 1950s] the mining areas extend from the far East Rand to the northern Free State; the deposits are poor because the average gold content is very low.
>
> (de Kiewiet, cited in A. N. Boyce, *Europe and South Africa*, p. 156.)

Why was the mining of gold on the Witwatersrand so costly?

1. Because costly machinery was needed:
   — to mine the ore;
   — to extract the gold from the ore.
2. Because labour costs were high:
   — skilled miners and engineers had to be imported and paid high salaries;
   — very large numbers of unskilled black labourers were needed for these mines.

of commodities for export to the world market, such as wool and sugar (see table on p. 235).

After 1870 there was undoubtedly expansion of agricultural production as a consequence of the development of a home market at the mining camps and ports. Yet it is equally clear that by 1899 South Africa was no longer self-sufficient in many basic food requirements. Wheat, maize, meat, eggs, milk and butter had to be imported in large quantities.

Why was this so?

1. There was a sharp rise in the urban population as a result of the mineral revolution. Immigrants from Europe and Africa swelled the population of the mining camps. Local agriculture was not geared to cope with the increased demand. The combination of skills and capital required for large-scale commercial farming was lacking amongst the rural population, both black and white.
2. The very *railways* that promoted the development of the mineral deposits had the effect of lowering the price of imported foodstuffs (see Basutoland case study on the right). It was as a consequence often unprofitable for farmers to produce some foods for the local market.
3. *Wages* on the mines and in the urban areas were often much higher than those in the rural areas. This tended to draw many people away from the rural areas and the farming sector.
4. *Drought and disease* plagued agricultural production and stock farming throughout this period.

1880s	— Drought
	— Horse sickness
1894–95	— Drought
1896–97	— Rinderpest
1900–01	— Drought
1910–11	— East coast fever

THE AGRICULTURAL REVOLUTION

Prior to 1870 there had been growth in commercial farming, especially in the Cape and Natal. The nature of that development was very largely in the direction of the production

All of these circumstances combined to hinder the growth of agriculture.

Basutoland (Lesotho) case study

Basutoland provides a useful case study of the complex nature of the relationship between agricultural growth and the mineral discoveries. In the 1870s Basutoland became the 'bread basket' of South Africa by producing large quantities of flour for the diamond-fields. The growing of wheat and the need for transport (transport-riding) led to a period of prosperity in the mountain kingdom. In 1875 the prosperity of Basutoland could be judged by the fact that there were approximately 2700 ploughs, 300 wagons and 35 000 horses in the territory.

Yet at the moment of crisis when the Southern Sotho (Basuto) were fighting for their political independence (1879–1880) they found their economic prosperity under threat as well. As the railways reached into the interior, the Americans replaced the Southern Sotho as the major suppliers of wheat to the diamond-fields, flooding the country with cheap flour from the prairies.

As Basutoland declined in importance as a major agricultural export area, there was an increase of poverty in the area. From being a major supplier of agricultural products, Basutoland became a major supplier of migrant labour for the mines.

Despite this lack of agricultural self sufficiency, in areas of communal ownership (the so-called 'tribal areas' or reserves) an important group of peasant* farmers emerged who were very successful in cultivating and marketing produce. The historian Colin Bundy has shown that this wealthy and successful peasantry was to be found in many parts of Southern Africa in the period up to 1910. (Also see below for more details: 'The creation of an industrial labour force', page 262, or Bundy's book, *The Rise and Fall of a South African Peasantry*.)

On freehold, or privately-owned land, which was largely owned by white farmers, there was a dramatic move towards production for the market. Much of the production here was in the hands of African peasant farmers who either rented the land or engaged in sharecropping*.

The economic potential of an expanding market meant that the value of land rose sharply, because land now became a valuable commodity. As a result many rural dwellers who either did not own land, or could not rent land, or did not have funds to farm profitably, were forced to leave their rural homes and move to town in search of work. The townward trek affected large numbers of people — poor whites, and poor blacks, who were unable to make a living in the rural areas.

The other side of the coin was that the expansion of commercial farming led to the emergence of a group of wealthy farmers. Large mining companies also bought up farm land and companies produced food for the mines as well as for the market.

In short, the character of farming changed in many areas during this period, from being largely for subsistence to being market-orientated. It was, however, not until well into the Twentieth Century that South Africa became largely self-sufficient in agricultural production.

247

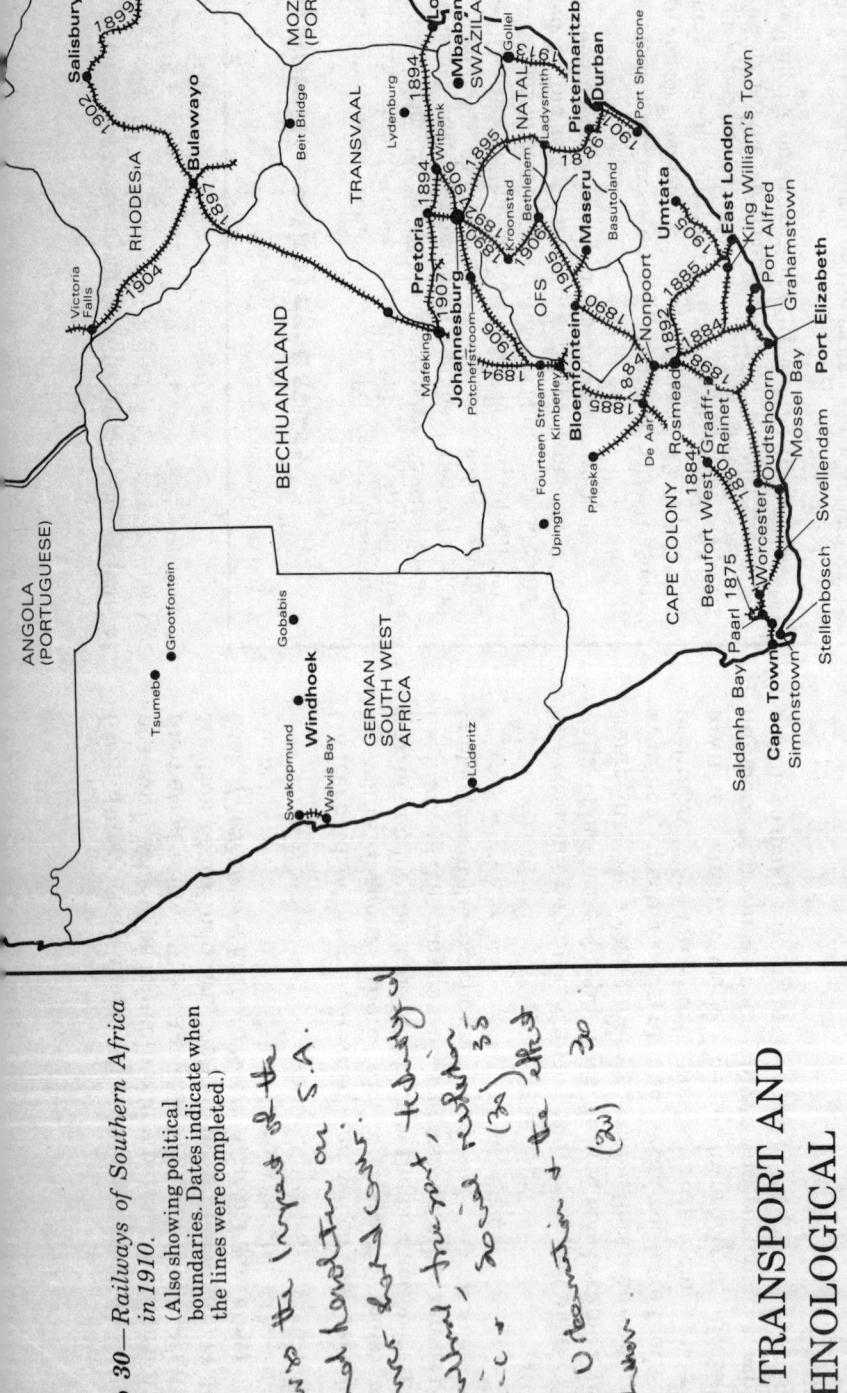

Map 30—*Railways of Southern Africa in 1910.*
(Also showing political boundaries. Dates indicate when the lines were completed.)

The rate of new railway construction in South Africa in decades

1860–1869 — 110 km
1870–1879 — 1 265 km
1880–1889 — 1 725 km
1890–1899 — 3 315 km
1900–1910 — 4 823 km

(Oxford History of South Africa, Vol. II, p. 20.)

(Compare these figures with those for the USA, p. 147.)

THE TRANSPORT AND TECHNOLOGICAL REVOLUTION

The opening up of the diamond-fields and the Witwatersrand gave rise to an urgent need for transport facilities from the distant coastal ports and areas of food supply to the mining areas. First white and black transport riders, who drove large ox-drawn wagons or mule coaches, supplied the mining camps with their needs. Later the technological and scientific revolution that was already far advanced in Europe and North America put the transport-riders out of business.

248

In the early 1890s railways were built from all the ports to the mining areas. By 1910 a network of railways covered most of Southern Africa (see Map 30), and motor cars were also becoming an important means of transport.

Ox wagons and horses were too slow for the modern mechanized age. Science came to the assistance of the mining industry in other ways. New machines were constantly being developed to improve the mining operation itself (for example the invention of 'horse whims', mechanical washing machines, and rock drills) and the extraction of the minerals (for example the introduction of the MacArthur-Forrest cyanide process of gold recovery).

These rapid advances in technology were also reflected in the military sphere. The importation of early repeater rifles and machine-guns had a decisive influence on the balance of power in Southern Africa. The white states, which were now wealthy, were able to buy the new weapons and so assert their power over the surrounding African states.

Questions

1. To what extent does the 'railway revolution' show the strengthening of an alliance between the state and capital (or big business)?
2. Could this alliance be shown to cut across political or 'national' boundaries?

THE SOCIAL REVOLUTION: URBANIZATION AND THE GROWTH OF TOWNS

In Britain, Europe and the USA the rise of industrialization and the growth of towns during the Nineteenth Century was accompanied by massive disruption of the rural population.

This change was also of great importance in South Africa. As a result of the rising value of land and the need for commercial farming, many large-scale landowners began to consolidate their agricultural lands, and in the process squeezed out both black and white small-scale peasant farmers. Those who lost their lands had to find work in the towns. There they sold their labour to factory owners and industrialists in return for wages.

From the 1870s, the rise of the mining industry in South Africa and the stimulus it gave to the development of other industrial and commercial enterprises, led to a transformation of social and economic life. These events provided the first major impetus towards the development of modern towns in South Africa. This gave rise to a process of urbanization which was caused, on the one hand, by the need for labour and the offer of employment in the mining camps and towns, and on the other hand, by the growing poverty in many rural areas.

Urban dwellers as percentages of the population (approximate)			
	1890-1	1904	1911
Whites	36%	53%	52% of the total white population
Africans		13%	13% of the total African population
'Coloureds'		46%	46% of the total 'Coloured' population
Indians		46%	46% of the total Indian population
Total		25%	25% of the total population

(Oxford History of South Africa, Vol. II, p. 173)

The table on the previous page shows that approximately a quarter of the population had become town dwellers by the time of Union. These figures do not show that, as a result of migrant labour, very large numbers of rural people came to work in the mining areas and towns on a temporary basis. The number of people resident in the towns at any one time was therefore much higher than these figures indicate.

The population of the towns, from the earliest times, was predominantly black, because of the large demand for labour. Considerable numbers of poor Afrikaners also drifted to the towns in search of employment. But the groups that dominated business and commercial life and placed their stamp on the cultural life of the towns, were drawn from the English-speaking community.

The towns often came to be associated in traditional Afrikaner folklore with the place of the oppressor and the gold mining industry was seen as an evil which had been a key element in the destruction of the traditional Boer way of life. The life of the towns was seen, wrongly or rightly, to have caused the moral decline of large sections of the Afrikaner *volk*.

For Africans, the life of the locations or townships, the urban slum-yard, and the compound, was also said to have destroyed the valuable fabric of traditional society and custom. Regardless of whether townlife was seen to be 'good' or 'bad', it became an important aspect of social life in South Africa during this era. The economic positions of the black and white groups were reflected in the environments in which they lived.

In this period Kimberley and Johannesburg were transformed from mining camps to cities. The photograph of a location in Kimberley around the turn of the century helps to remind us that, despite the absence of formal segregationist laws, most towns had locations by the turn of the century, which were occupied solely by blacks.

Kimberley location c. 1906.
(Photograph courtesy of the Kimberley Municipal Archives)

Du Toit's Pan, near Kimberley c. 1870.
(Illustration courtesy of the Cape Archives.)

This separation of the races was at first defended on the grounds of slum clearance, control of crime and control of disease, (in keeping with the models of town planning developed in Europe and the USA during the Nineteenth Century); but in fact it amounted to the social segregation of black and white people. Locations were really an extension of the compound system — where blacks were allowed to stay in an urban environment because they provided the labour essential to the functioning of industry. They were never provided with adequate social services and welfare considered essential to other groups.

Question

In what ways did the industrial revolution influence the process of urbanization in Southern Africa in the period 1870–1910?

Such an extraordinary city: Johannesburg, 1889

Never in the history of the universe was such an extraordinary city conceived or carried out as Johannesburg ... Day after day comes the news of fresh [gold] discoveries; week by week patience and the pick are teaching us what we may later expect. We are simply living in a sea of gold.

Johannesburg has now a population not far short of twenty-five thousand, to say nothing of countless [blacks], who ... [live] upon the surrounding ... [veld]. Poor fellows! their patience and hard work will never do more than they have done. They toil as slaves until ... [sufficient] capital accrues to their labours; when they quit for the distant Zulu or Suazi country, where, the proud possessors of four or five cows and a squaw [wife], they can dream of dynamite and the mad white man. Johannesburg would not be Johannesburg were the ... [African] unknown. He is the backbone of the country.

Johannesburg is barely two and a half years old; but as we drive across the tops of the hills, and gaze downwards, it seems impossible to believe it. Acre after acre, mile after mile, are covered with lordly buildings or the humble shanty. House-room is precious and costly, bricks are £4.10s.–£6 per thousand, and any place is expected to pay for itself in rent within three years. Builders are doing their utmost to cope with public wants, but the demand is infinitely greater than the supply. An ordinary eight-roomed house may total to £3,000 or £4,000, and a rental of £50 per month is by no means uncommon ... And remember every bit of machinery or furniture, or everything indeed that comes from the Cape, costs threepence per pound in freight alone. No wonder things are dear. Two hundred wagons a day come into the market-place, each one carrying a precious freight of 7,000 lb to 8,000 lb, and drawn by twenty patient oxen. A month they have been upon the road, and a month they will be in returning. But the back journey is an easy one, as the sole freight will be the drivers.

Men of every sort or kind can here find plenty of work if they wish it. It is no place for idling. Probably skilled artisans, carpenters, bricklayers, and suchlike, are wanted more than any other class. But farmers or market-gardeners ought to make a fortune. A teamster told us, on our way hither, that he netted £60 a trip. The book-keeper at an hotel we stayed at gets £600 a year, with all found. Waiters command £10 to £15 per month, an hotel cook £25 a month, all found, and lots of extras. A [black] cook expects £10 per month, a ... [black] servant £4 to £6, a groom £12 to £13. Money commands [can be invested] in certain circles [at] 5 per cent a month.

251

Meat is very good and cheap—about 6d. per lb. Eggs average about 5s. per dozen, butter 4s. per lb., and bread sixpence per lb. Cigars are 1s. to 2s. each, cartridges 30s. per 100, and forage bundles of between 4 lb and 5 lb [oat-straw, with the oats attached] 1s. Horses are cheap enough (small, but active and hardy), at about £10 to £20. Newspapers are 3d., and Stock Exchange offices anything between £20 and £100 per month. An office-boy is worth 30s. a week, and hard to get at that. Washing is 5s. per dozen 'all round'; and hotel keep is about £1 per day. Beer at 4s., champagne at £1, and whisky at 8s to 10s per bottle make many a man teetotal. Vin ordinaire claret 7s. 6d. a bottle. Vegetables are double or treble English quotations…

Everybody in South Africa speculates; the place is a living hell…It is simply ridiculous to doubt that ere long the city will be a wonder—that it will beat San Francisco, if not Oklahoma, into the shade. We say again the country is as yet barely scratched; it will be years before even a fraction of its vast wealth can be extracted. If the banket [gold-bearing ore] only holds good in depth, human foresight will be at fault as to the future of the Transvaal.

And this is the country Mr. Gladstone or his Government gave up!

(K. F. Bellairs, *The Witwatersrand Goldfields: A Trip to Johannesburg and Back*, London 1889, pp. 33–6, 334.)

Questions

1. In what ways was Johannesburg 'an extraordinary city' in the late 1880s?

2. What are Bellairs' views on the role of Africans in the making of Johannesburg?

3. Do his views agree with those expressed by Rev. Tyamzashe with regard to the same topic in the context of the diamond-fields in 1874? Back up your argument with evidence from the text.

4. What conclusions can you draw about the labour market in Johannesburg from the figures provided?

5. How was Johannesburg linked to the outside world at this time? What were the consequences?

6. What is Bellairs referring to in his final comment relating to Mr Gladstone, the British Prime Minister? Why is he disappointed with Mr Gladstone's actions?

The process of urbanization in South Africa

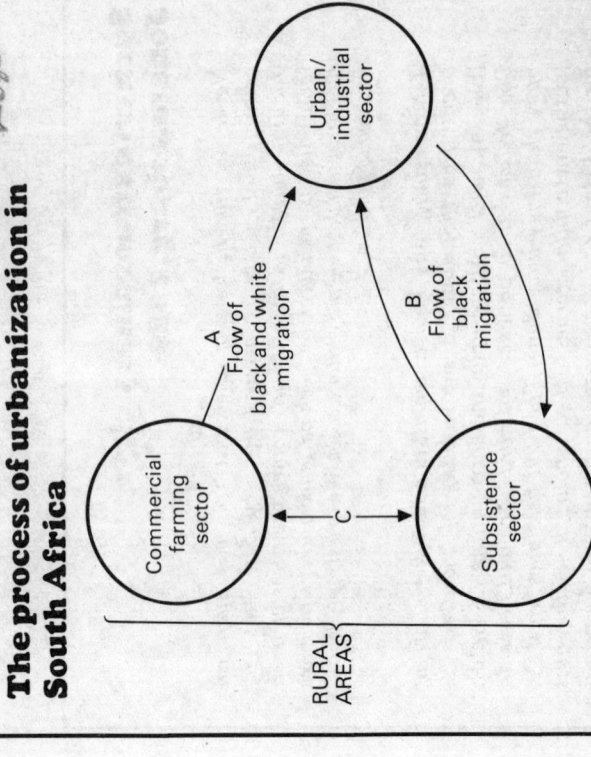

Questions

1. Explain the causes of the migration indicated by A.
2. Why is there a two-way flow of migration in B? Did all of those who went to town return to the rural areas?
3. Explain the two-way movement of people along C.

Why did people leave the countryside and move to the towns?

WHY DID BLACK SOUTH AFRICANS MOVE TO THE TOWNS?

At first Africans went to work on the mines out of choice, to obtain cash and purchase consumer goods. Historians have often argued that Africans were attracted to the diamond-fields because of the prospects of earning cash wages which enabled them to purchase guns with which to kill each other and/or the whites. Such arguments are, however, at bottom, simply descriptions of what happened at the time, and do not explain why those events occurred. Certainly Africans *were* buying increasing numbers of guns — which for the most part they obtained on the diamond-fields — but the expansion of the gun trade during the 1870s and 1880s itself needs to be understood within the context of the expansion of white rule and capitalist relations in Southern Africa (after D. Innes p. 25).

The threat posed to African societies by these developments meant that many men worked on the mines especially to obtain

Sketch of Commissioner Street, Johannesburg, in 1904.
(From the *Star* weekly edition, 23 April 1904.)

253

guns to defend their independent kingdoms. In some cases, such as that of the Pedi, whole regiments of warriors were sent to work on the mines for the specific purpose of equipping themselves with guns at a time when their society was under military pressure from the ZAR and the Swazi.

Once the African kingdoms had been conquered, many people had no choice but to go out to work. Societies had limited land and were impoverished, and the people now had to pay taxes to the colonial governments. Men (and later women) therefore had to go out to work in the mines or towns in order to ensure the survival of their families.

They went to work as migrant labourers or as permanent town dwellers because:

— the rural population was rapidly growing in size;
— the land of the African areas (eventually called the 'reserves') was insufficient to provide for the needs of its people;
— even where prosperous peasant farmers did exist, they soon became the victims of legislation which restricted their development (e.g. the Glen Grey Act of 1894; the Land Act of 1913);
— Africans in the reserve areas had to pay taxes in cash. Most therefore were obliged to go out to work to earn cash to avoid breaking the law;
— Africans, when given a choice, were in general unwilling to work on farms owned by whites. They associated them with poor employment conditions, low wages and long hours of work;
— the highest wages were obtainable in industry;
— people were acquiring new needs and wants. As they became acquainted with modern society, they wished to move to the towns in the hope of sharing the better opportunities provided by that new society, such as jobs and education.

254

WHY DID MANY AFRIKANERS MOVE FROM THE COUNTRYSIDE TO THE TOWNS?

The 'push-factors' that affected the movement of blacks to the towns also affected large numbers of whites, particularly the so-called poor white Afrikaners, in this period.

Many Afrikaner small farmers could no longer pursue the traditional Boer way of life and had to become *bywoners* or squatters on white farms, or move to live and work in the towns. Many had also been impoverished during the Anglo-Boer War (1899–1902) as a result of the devastation of the scorched-earth policy of the British army. A series of droughts and stock diseases also destroyed crops and herds. Changes in patterns of land ownership and in the practice of farming also had adverse affects on this group.

These people arrived in the towns without the language or the skills to cope with life in an urban society. Because of the specific circumstances in South Africa, whites and blacks found themselves in conflict over jobs, for although both were unskilled, poor whites had expectations of a privileged position in society. Much of the history of South Africa in the Twentieth Century revolves around this conflict.

THE LABOUR REVOLUTION: THE MAKING OF THE WORKING CLASS

The making of the Southern African working class — the group that provided the labour for the mines, factories and towns — is an aspect of our history that has often been overlooked. How was this working class created? This topic will not be dealt with in great depth here, but it is important to state that although foreign investment capital was a key factor in establishing the mining industry in South Africa from the 1880s, the mines depended for their operation and profitability on massive supplies of labour. The big companies that emerged to control the gold and diamond mines (Rand Mines, Consolidated Gold Fields and De Beers, to name a few) were extremely wealthy and powerful. They nevertheless faced great problems in making sufficiently high profits to keep their shareholders happy. Unlike other minerals, the price of gold was fixed by the large international banks. This meant that increases in the costs of gold mining could not be passed on to the buyer of the gold through higher prices. To keep their profits high these mining companies had to keep their costs low. The greatest of these costs was labour.

The labour force that emerged on the underground mines was divided into (a) a small group of skilled white workers, and (b) a very large, mainly unskilled, black labour force. In the 1890s half of the total production costs of many of the big companies were related to expenditure on labour. One of the main ways in which the gold mining companies tried to lower their costs was to reduce the costs of labour. They did this in two ways: they tried to reduce the numbers of expensive, skilled white miners from overseas; and they tried to reduce the level of wages paid to the majority of the unskilled black workers. There were also a variety of attempts to control the labour force more effectively, for example by enforcing the pass laws and by curbing the growth of trade unions. Three key aspects of the extension of control of black workers were: the evolution of the compound system; the development of a centralized recruiting system; and the expansion of the area from which labour was drawn to far beyond the borders of South Africa.

The situation of black mineworkers changed considerably during the early days of the diamond mining industry. At first, on the river diggings, there were numbers of black claim-

holders; this was not allowed on the dry diggings. In the early days black workers usually arrived on the fields and sold their labour to the highest bidder—given the acute shortage of labour, this meant that wages were relatively high. Also, if a worker did not like his employer he could simply 'desert' and move to another employer, or return home, at will. These conditions clearly favoured the workers and provided scope for considerable worker resistance to unacceptable conditions of work. (See below.) As mining became more organized into employer monopolies, these conditions did not please the mineowners, who demanded that the government (first the British government, and later the Cape government) exercise greater control over African labour. After 1874 that control was to become a reality. All blacks on the diamond-fields, barring citizens of the Cape Colony, were required to carry passes. This meant that their freedom of movement was restricted and they were obliged to honour labour contracts. These regulations were enforced by the newly formed Griqualand West police force.

The introduction of a policy of searching miners to prevent the theft of diamonds from the Kimberley mines in 1883–4 had important consequences for the history of labour relations. Both black and white miners joined to resist this move as they saw it to be an attack on their dignity. Led by the Working Men's Association of Griqualand West they went on strike—some 250 whites and over a thousand blacks were involved. Police fired on the workers and 6 whites were killed. The strike was broken. The mineowners learnt the lesson that they needed to prevent any future combinations of black and white workers.

This also led to the framing of new policies aimed at: (a) gaining greater control over black workers and preventing desertion, i.e. ensuring that workers stayed for the full period of their contract; (b) controlling drunkenness; and (c) preventing illicit diamond buying (I.D.B.).

255

Once workers entered the compound on legal contracts they were not allowed to leave for the six or eight months of their contracts. Though there was a strike to oppose the establishment of compounds, the white workers did not join the black workers because they were not affected. This marked an important beginning in the history of a racially divided industrial labour force, and set the pattern for labour relations which was to be followed on the goldfields of the Witwatersrand.

The mineowners developed a policy aimed at reducing the numbers of the more expensive skilled white miners, reducing the level of wages for the unskilled black workers, and obtaining a monopoly on labour recruiting. The consequence of various attempts to reduce wages in the 1890s was that the gold mines were always short of labour. South African blacks simply refused to do such heavy and dangerous work for such low pay.

The response of the Randlords was firstly to develop a centralized recruiting agency, the Rand Native Labour Association (later to be called the Witwatersrand Native Labour Association—W.N.L.A.) to avoid competition between the mines over the recruitment of labour and thus prevent the price of labour from rising. Secondly, they extended the area of recruitment far beyond South Africa's borders—to Mocambique, Nyasaland (now Malawi), Tanganyika (now Tanzania) and Bechuanaland (now Botswana). It was therefore possible to obtain more recruits who were prepared to work at the wages offered, since these countries offered fewer job opportunities.

After the Anglo-Boer War (1899–1902), during the period of Reconstruction (1902–1909), the labour situation remained critical for the mineowners. The British administration therefore agreed to the importation of over 60 000 Chinese

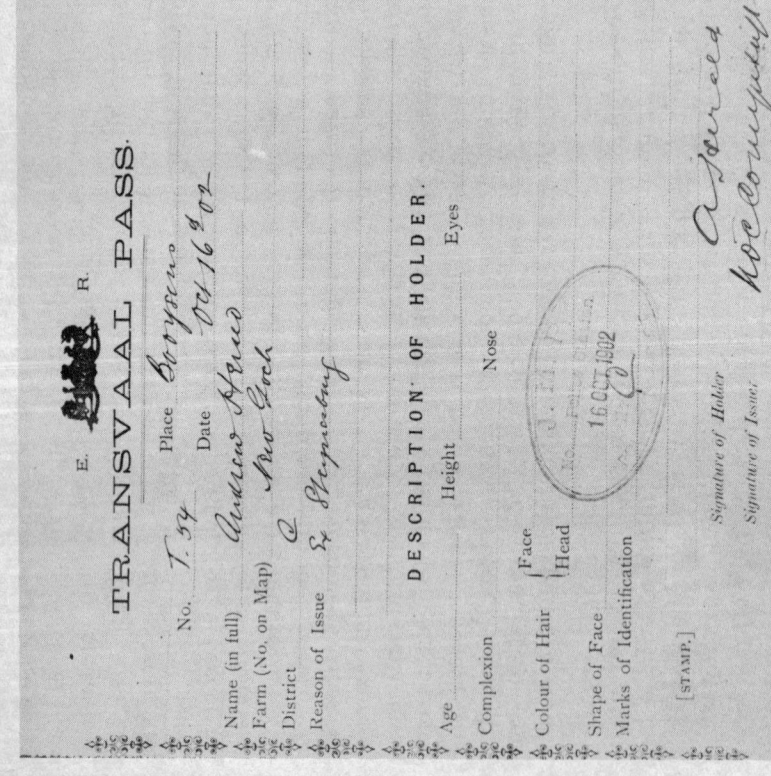

A pass issued in 1902.

(Photograph courtesy of the Johannesburg Africana Museum.)

In order to ensure that all these policies were carried out the government required all workers to carry passes and housed workers in 'closed compounds'. The lives of black workers could then be controlled both on and off duty. These compounds were modelled on prison compounds. They ensured tight control and supervision and secured a disciplined and regular labour force.

labourers to the Transvaal in an attempt to solve the problem. This was known as the Chinese labour experiment. (See Chapter 9.) Although the Chinese were returned to China by the end of the decade, due to pressure from the British government, they had assisted the Randlords to keep down the wages of unskilled workers on the mines. If you study the tables on pp. 259–260 you will see that the period 1904–1909 was indeed very important in expanding the number of blacks who presented themselves for work on the gold mines for very low pay. The Chinese labour experiment, the introduction of poll tax for adult Africans, the general decline in the agricultural condition of the Reserves, stock disease and drought, and rising population in the rural areas, all help to explain this trend.

A group of Chinese miners.
(Photograph courtesy of the Johannesburg Africana Museum.)

Labour in the early days of the diamond diggings (1872)

The immense demand for labour, created by the rapid growth of the Diamond Diggings, and the splendid wages given, have attracted to our camps thousands of ... [men] belonging to all the tribes around and a long way north of the Vaal River ... [Africans], Koranas, ... [Khoikhoi], of every colour ... swarm at the Fields. Formerly ... [blacks from the interior] used to contract with the Boers and other farmers for a year's services, at the end of which time they considered themselves well rewarded with a cow, value £3 or £4; now good ... [labourers] are freely paid on the diggings 30s. per month, and well fed into the bargain. They are all indiscriminately spoken of as 'nigger', and addressed as 'boy', quite irrespective of age. [Among the Africans] ... the Zulus have the ... reputation [as the best and most trustworthy labourers] and perhaps the Basutos next ...

Large parties of ... [Africans] are constantly coming up 'on their own hook', and ... [arrive at] the camp in search of a ... 'master', which they are not long in finding, the demand for ... labour being continually on the increase. Old colonists and traders frequently make money by going into the interior, bringing down lots of ... [Africans], and introducing them to masters with whom they contract for three months' services, the trader charging per head for the ... [service][1]; but anyone who has been long on the diggings will not have much difficulty in obtaining ... [labourers]. If he is a 'good ... [master]', his own 'boys' will frequently bring to him relatives or friends who will offer their services ...

---

[1] This was called 'touting'.

Questions

1. Read the extract carefully. Then make notes under the following headings to assist you in discussing the extract:
   (a) Recruitment
   (b) Housing
   (c) Food
   (d) Leisure
   (e) Work
   (f) Names or descriptions for labourers and employers

2. While describing and discussing each of the above, attempt an assessment of the attitudes of the author (and other white miners) to their employees. Give evidence to back up your arguments.

Compounds and migrant labour*

Early Johannesburg compound.
(Photograph courtesy of the Johannesburg Africana Museum.)

With regard to sleeping accommodation for the ... [labourers], some generous diggers provide them with a rough tent; but if the 'boys' are smart and active they will soon make a comfortable little hut for themselves with branches, bushes &c., which they can go into the country to fetch on Saturday afternoons and Sundays. In any case one or two cotton blankets should be given them, for the nights are often very chilly, and they suffer much from cold. With regard to food, the digger must buy for them mealies (Indian corn or Maize), crushed mealies, or mealie meal ... About 100 lb ... or half a muid, is a fair monthly allowance for each ... [labourer]. Mealie meal fluctuates on the Fields from 25s. to 35s. per muid; crushed mealies and whole mealies are a good deal cheaper. A large iron cooking-pot should also be bought ... It is as well to give them a little coarse meat ... once or twice a week, and a glass of brandy (Cape Smoke) on Saturdays or Sundays. If the tent is anywhere near a slaughtering place, they will frequently provide themselves with an extra in the shape of offal, ... Good 'boys' should be encouraged with a small present, say a shilling every time a diamond is found. The work that ... [an African labourer] is expected to perform at the claim is — picking, shovelling, hauling, and sifting. It is not desirable to let them sort, both because it is throwing too much temptation in their way, and because they are very slow sorters; ...

Two ... [African labourers], if they understand their work, ought to be able to keep two white men constantly employed in sorting, and this is a very good division of labour for the hot weather, while in the winter the ... [master] will often find it pleasant and warming to take a hand at the pick, shovel, or sieve himself.

(Charles A. Payton, *The Diamond Diggings of South Africa*, pp. 137–9.)

Questions

1. Look carefully at the photographs of compounds on the left and right and then attempt to answer the following:

    (a) Describe the environment of the compound.

    (b) What does the architecture of the compound tell you about its function?

    (c) What impression do you have of the social life of the inhabitants of the compounds?

    (d) How had the conditions for black labourers changed between the 1870s (see the extract from the writings of Rev Tyamzashe pages 241–42 and the description by Payton page 257) and the 1890s?

2. Do you think the drawing below conveys an accurate or inaccurate impression?

An artist's drawing of the meeting of Basuto going to and from the diamond-fields.

Interior of compound.
(Photograph courtesy of the Johannesburg Africana Museum.)

Percentages of miners by racial group: 1904–1909

Year	Whites	Blacks	Chinese
1904	13,6	76.8	9.6
1905	10,9	63,7	25,4
1906	10,3	74,3	15,4
1907	9,6	63,3	27,1
1908	9,7	79,2	11,1
1909	10.8	86,0	3,2

From the above table offer suggestions regarding the consequences of the Chinese labour experiment.

Conclusion

The characteristics of the first phase of modernization or the first industrial revolution

THE CONTEXT OF MODERNIZATION

It is important to see the changes outlined above in the context of two dominant features of world history in the late Nineteenth Century:

(a) The industrial revolution in South Africa was part of a much larger set of changes that were a feature of this period. When South Africa entered the first stages of an industrial revolution, countries of the 'north', like Britain, France, Germany and the USA, were already far advanced along that road. South Africa's entry into the international industrial revolution was, therefore, very much as a junior partner. Developments in South Africa were in many ways dependent on developments in the advanced industrial countries, and South Africa's major products (gold and diamonds) were only important because they were given a somewhat artificially high value in the world economy.

(b) The industrial revolution in Europe was accompanied by a period of intense rivalry amongst the major industrial countries which took the form of nationalism. That rivalry in Europe became a world-wide rivalry as the European nations fought each other for a share of the wealth generated by colonies and international trade. This rivalry between the major capitalist states was called imperialism*, and the 'Scramble for Africa' in the 1870s and

---

Composition of the black labour force on South African gold mines: 1896–1912

Year	from South Africa	Foreign black Mozambique	Labour from other countries	Total
1896	18 000	32 000	4 000	54 000
1904	18 000	52 000	8 000	78 000
1905	12 000	59 000	10 000	81 000
1906	18 000	53 000	9 000	80 000
1908	58 000	82 000	9 000	149 000
1909	61 000	85 000	10 000	156 000
1912	65 000	92 000	18 000	175 000

Foreign workers (i.e. black workers who came from beyond South Africa's borders) as a percentage of the total

1896	67 %
1904	76 %
1905	85 %
1906	77 %
1908	61 %
1909	61 %
1912	57 %

1880s was an aspect of imperialism. Both types of change — the development of industrialization and the emergence of nationalistic imperialism — had important effects on the development of political, social and economic forces in South Africa.

THE PRICE OF MODERNIZATION

The first phase of modernization, or the extractive phase of industrialization, took place between 1870 and the 1920s. (See table on p. 231.)

The early phase of Southern Africa's first industrial revolution had characteristics in common with similar developments in other industrialized nations.

The first industrial revolution is defined by the nature of the economic activity and social change during this period. Namely the extraction of raw materials, a mining revolution, the growth of towns, the construction of a modern transport system, and changing forms of work and labour relations. The raw materials or primary industrial products, whether obtained from agriculture or mining, were exported to the new industrial nations of Europe and North America, where they were processed and made into manufactured goods.

The sale of the raw materials, increased employment opportunities, the expansion of the market and the need for increased food and services, linked to the growth of the towns, all led to the creation of wealth on a scale that had never before been possible. All this was part of the positive effect of the process of modernization.

Yet the transformation of the economy and society during the period 1870–1910 had its price in four major areas.

1 The decline of the African economy:

The loss of political autonomy by the independent states of Southern Africa and the forcible transformation of African and Boer society.

While a modern capitalist society and economy were being rapidly created in line with developments in northern industrial nations, African and Boer societies put up large-scale resistance to their incorporation into the new economic and political structures on the terms imposed upon them by the imperial power — Britain. The independent African states of the region fought the white Boer states or the British in an attempt to defend their way of life and their political independence, but they were defeated and incorporated into the new pattern of political domination and economic 'modernization'. It was, indeed, only the wealth created by the mineral discoveries that tipped the balance of power in favour of the white states. Prior to 1870 that balance had been very even or had, in some areas, been weighted in favour of the black states.

The independent Boer republics, in their turn, came under the rule of the Union Jack after 1902. The major consequence of the mineral discoveries was therefore that by 1906 all the black people of the region had, directly or indirectly, come under white rule, and the Boer states of the interior had been conquered by Britain.

In the process a significant proportion of the rural population was transformed into an industrial working class in a single generation — either as migrant labourers or as permanent urban dwellers. Their incorporation into the modern economy was an important feature of the whole process of transformation, as they supplied a vital and necessary component of the new industrial society — namely, cheap unskilled labour.

through education and increased agricultural guidance, and through assistance with scientific farming methods. The implication was that this state of poverty and poor agriculture was largely a legacy of the pre-colonial past. This was in line with the general European belief that African culture was inherently inferior.

More recently the backwardness explanation has been challenged, and increasingly evidence has been put forward to show that precisely the opposite explanation seems to be more valid. The rural areas like the Transkei and the Ciskei were not poor prior to the last quarter of the Nineteenth Century. They included tracts of highly productive agricultural land and extensive herds of cattle that were quite capable of sustaining the population.

Indeed, as has been shown, areas of Lesotho and the Transkei (see Box p. 247) were so productive that their surpluses of foodstuffs contributed substantially towards supplying the markets of Kimberley and the Witwatersrand in the period after 1870. The historian Colin Bundy has shown how:

> ... the early 1870s saw a virtual explosion of peasant economic activity ... Five hundred wagons of corn were sold by Fingoland peasants in 1873, as well as a crop worth £60 000; and in 1875 the trade of Fingoland at lowest estimate was adjudged to be worth £150 000. From Gaikaland, Gcalekaland, Tembuland and East Griqualand came similar reports; peasants were selling cattle in order to invest in sheep (to produce wool); the number of traders across the Kei River trebled; African produce in 1875 was estimated to be worth £750 000. A single firm bought £58 000 worth of African produce while a merchant's house in Port Elizabeth boasted an annual turnover of goods for the African trade of £200 000. New methods and resources rippled from tribe to tribe, and even amongst the most 'backward' tribes crop diversification and wider cultivation were common by the 1880s.

(Bundy, pp. 376-7.)

2 The creation of an industrial labour force

From 1870, and even more dramatically, from 1886, the economy of Southern Africa developed along the lines of a modern industrial state. The evidence outlined above shows an impressive record of achievement in the areas of commercial farming, mining and industry. Great wealth was created. Yet it is also true to say that by 1910 there were areas of the country, in particular the so-called reserves, where poverty was just as sharply on the increase. More and more families were being forced to leave their homes in the country districts permanently and go to live in the town where they could find work. Alternatively the young men and women had to become migrant labourers in order to earn sufficient to keep the rural family alive. In short, the rural areas could no longer support the people who lived there. How is the production of wealth in the cities and in the mining towns, side by side with impoverishment in the countryside, to be explained?

In the past one of the key explanations for this state of affairs was that Southern Africa was a *dual economy* — in other words, within one region (and even in one country) there were two economies, side by side. The one was the modern, industrial, capitalist economy; the other, to be found in the reserves, was the 'primitive' economic system that was derived from the pre-conquest era. The reserve economy was marked, it was said, by a primitive system of agriculture and animal husbandry, and primitive forms of communal land ownership. In short, the poverty of these areas was said to be due to the backwardness of the people, their lack of modern education and absence of technology. Such arguments were applied to poor whites and blacks alike.

The remedy for the situation was simply to 'bring the rural areas into the Twentieth Century'. This was to be achieved

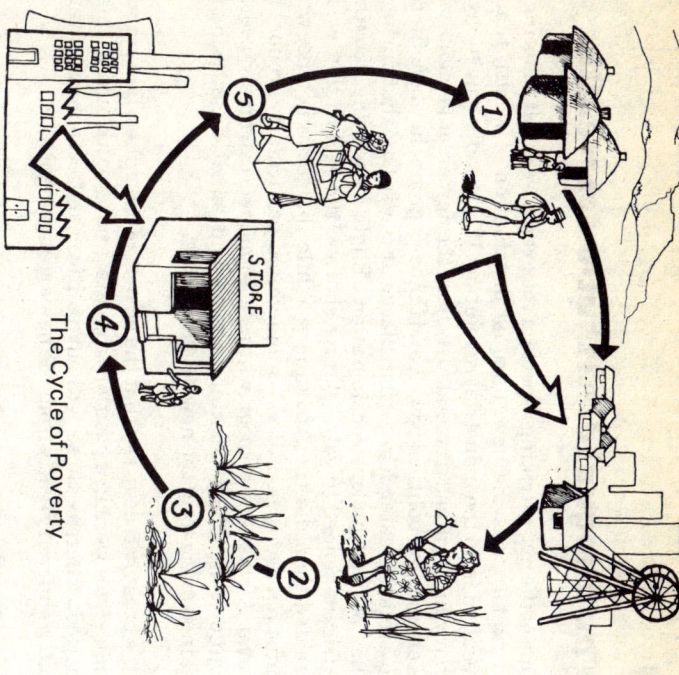

The Cycle of Poverty

1. Labourers migrate to towns and mines to earn wages.
2. Women and old people work insufficient land.
3. The land gets poorer.
4. People have to buy commodities from stores which are supplied by factories in towns.
5. Money becomes necessary for daily needs.

The process of industrialization and urbanization initially had the effect of creating marketing opportunities for a small class of African peasants who were able to take advantage of the opportunities offered. Black peasants were so successful, in fact, that white farmers used their political power as voters to prevent the expansion of African farming. In particular, they succeeded in preventing African peasants from purchasing or hiring land in areas outside of the reserves (the Glen Grey Act 1894; the Land Act 1913), and limiting marketing facilities and credit available to African farmers.

The more the Transkei was incorporated into the modern economy in the period after 1870, the more it began to show signs of growing poverty. The restricted area of land available, the growing population, the devastating effects of the severe droughts and stock disease, all meant that agriculture declined. In addition much of the wealth created went into the hands of a relatively small and privileged elite, while the rest of the population became increasingly poor.

Much of the economic wealth created was also removed from the area in the form of profits by white-owned trading companies and middlemen, or in the form of government taxes. This all helps to explain the general decline.

In short, by the early years of the Twentieth Century, the Transkei was in sharp economic decline, and apart from a small group of wealthy peasants, the population of this area was unable to support itself. The majority were therefore forced to move to town to become industrial workers (the pass laws prevented too many from following this option), or to become migrant labourers on mines or in factories. This picture of the Transkei is more or less true for the other reserve areas of South Africa as well, and applies to other areas beyond the boundaries of South Africa.

In terms of these arguments, the poverty of the reserve areas is therefore not a consequence of their isolation from the modern economy or the backwardness of these areas and peoples. The reserves are poor precisely because they have been so deeply involved in the modern economy, firstly as producers of foodstuffs for the market and then as suppliers of labour for the industrial economy. This is the explanation for their state of decline by 1910. This process of underdevelopment* has been accelerated dramatically in the Twentieth Century.

Question

Why was there such a brief period of prosperity for an African peasantry in Southern Africa?

3
Dependency: The limits to industrial development

Despite massive increases in the production of wealth, the third major drawback to modernization in South Africa was that it remained strongly *dependent* on imported capital in the early years of industrialization. Very large amounts of overseas (mainly British) capital were attracted to South Africa for the purpose of the development and exploitation of mineral resources. But profits were usually tied to the repayment of foreign investors and not to the promotion of local economic development. As in other colonies in an era of imperialism the economy stopped short of the full industrialization typical of the advanced industrial nations. South Africa was primarily an exporter of raw materials. Little heavy industry was developed during this period, and even by the late 1920s the economy was still based on mining, export agriculture and light industry.

Only after Union in 1910, and more particularly after the defeat of the South African Party in 1924, was there any real attempt to reverse the above trend. General Hertzog's Pact government set out specifically to encourage local manufacturing industry. In the long run these policies had the positive affect of reducing South Africa's dependency on mineral exports. This policy was so successful that minerals accounted for only 10 per cent of the gross national product (GNP) in 1970.

4
The unequal distribution of wealth

One of the most striking aspects of the events we are attempting to explain was the new, unequal distribution of wealth that resulted from the industrial revolution. It is broadly true to say that whites gained tremendously from the new arrangements of economic and political power, and that as a group they benefited to a much greater degree than blacks. It is also true that during the period under consideration English-speaking South Africans tended to gain a larger share of the wealth that was created than did the Afrikaners. While the above is true, we must not over-generalize — some whites, particularly groups of rural Afrikaners or poor whites — remained extremely poor, while some black peasant farmers and small businessmen gained much from the new developments.

It is broadly true to say that the owners of the mines, farms and industries were in a position to create great wealth during this period, whereas those without political and economic power often suffered greatly from the new arrangements.

SUMMARY

The development of the modern Southern African economy

1. Southern Africa's economic growth and development during the key period of its industrial revolution from 1870 to 1910 was closely linked to a major period of economic transformation in the world economy. Southern Africa's economic growth was in many ways dependent on the growth of the world economy.

264

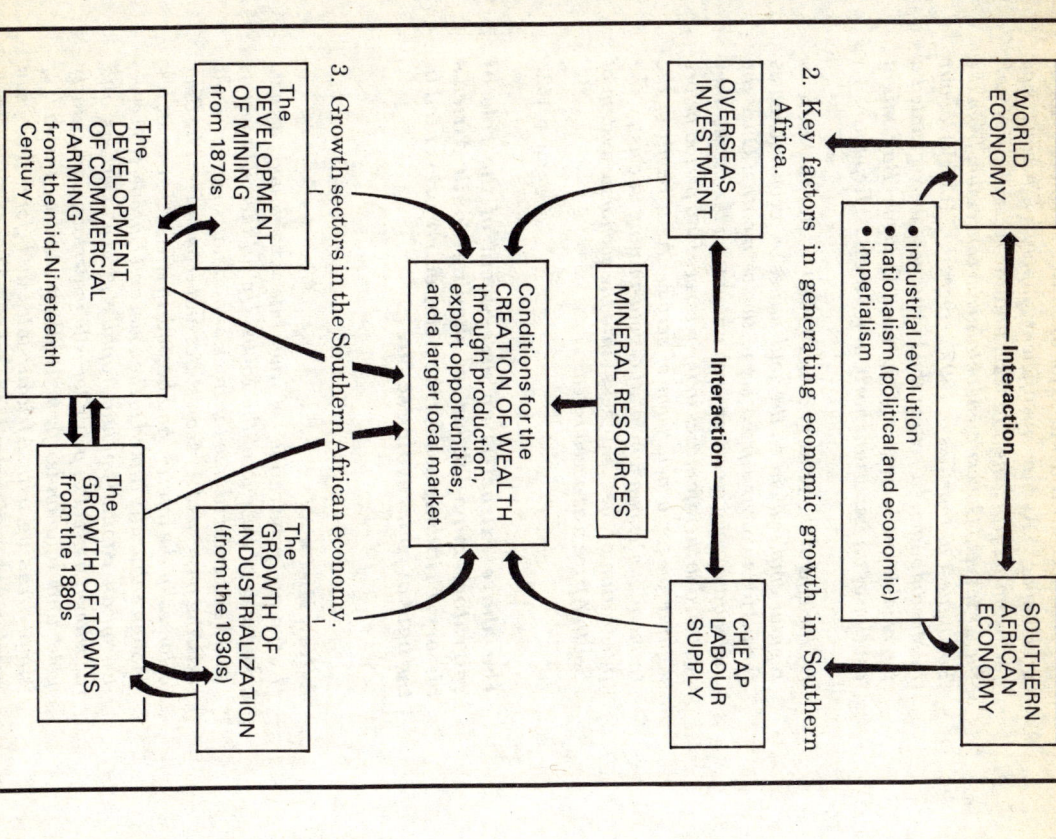

Revision Questions

1. Some social results of diamond mining in Griqualand West, as described in a school textbook.

The development of mining resulted in a great redistribution of the white population in South Africa. Large numbers of men were drawn to the new mining areas which developed into towns within a short space of time. On the bare veld Kimberley came into being with, by the end of 1871, a population of some 50 000. This trek from the rural areas became a feature of the new Mining Era. Urbanization of the white population proceeded at a greater pace with the development of the gold industry on the Rand. The same phenomenon was evident in the growing seaport towns. By the end of the 19th century the urbanization of the Afrikaner population was well underway, largely as a result of the emergence of the Mining Era.

Although many of these people were from the coastal colonies and the republics, large numbers also came in an increasing stream as immigrants from Britain, her colonies and the countries of Western Europe.

Many hoped to win a fortune as diggers, but many also came to fill positions as shopkeepers, merchants, tradesmen or to take up professional posts as the economy developed. These people from overseas came with new ideas, customs and traditions. The isolation which South Africa had experienced for more than two centuries was drawing to a close by 1870. In the new towns lawlessness, organized crime and the like became new features of urban life, which up to this point had been peaceful and orderly. Many enterprising immigrants began successful careers and became wealthy men. Cecil Rhodes, Alfred Beit and Barney Barnato are examples of successful men in commerce and industry. There were many others, however, who were not able to adapt themselves to the new and strange urban conditions. They became mere wage earners, struggling to make a living, as the factory hands in Britain had done in the earlier part of that century.

Large numbers of ... [blacks] were also attracted to the towns. Many did not return to the reserves, but settled on the outskirts of the new towns in slum townships. Their mode of life changed and this led to the disruption of their tribal organisation and customs. They developed into a detribalized ... class which had accepted some forms of Western customs and dress. A new social and economic problem therefore emerged. Mention has already been made of the illicit trade in firearms. Unrest was created in various parts of South Africa, far removed from Griqualand West, when these people returned to their kraals [homesteads].

The Mining Era therefore had far-reaching results on the political, economic and social structure of South Africa. All ... were affected by this new industrial revolution that had emerged in our country.

(Smit)

The above extract is a summary of the social results of the mining revolution on the diamond-fields.
(a) How does this account differ from that given above (pp. 249–253).
(b) Explain the different emphases on evidence in each account.

2. **Migrant labour***

The ... [black] population was restricted chiefly to migratory labourers who worked in the mines for a period and then returned to their homes in the reserves. Few ... [black] families at that stage left the reserves to find permanent work in the new towns. With the development of the gold-mines the demand for unskilled ... [black] labour grew apace. As an insufficient supply of labour was forthcoming from the Transkei and the reserves in Natal, the Transvaal Government obtained a concession from the Portuguese authorities in 1897 to recruit ... [black] labour in Mozambique. In return the Portuguese were granted a favourable railway tariff. so that Delagoa Bay might develop as an important harbour for the S.A. Republic.

By the end of the century over 100 000 ... [blacks] were in regular employment on the gold-mines on a contract basis for periods varying from six to twelve months. Once the men had earned a certain cash amount on the mines, they returned to their families in the reserves for a period before signing on for a new term of service. As a result of the tremendous expansion of the gold-mining industry the integration of the ... [blacks] into the economic system of South Africa was accelerated.

(Smit p. 152.)

The above extract is an assessment of the role of 'migratory mine labour' in shaping South Africa's history. Critically assess the perspective presented in the light of your reading so far.

3. **A 'New History'?**

European penetration of the interior gained a new character at the end of the 1860s. Up till then Europeans who had ventured into the interior had had to adapt to the existing pattern of African states and economies. The Boer colonies in the interior had become in effect African states, though culturally linked to the coast and Europe. However, European capitalism had rapidly grown overseas and developed a great appetite for raw materials, particularly gold and diamonds, from southern Africa. Instead of simply trading with African states as before, European capitalists began to move in to take over land and minerals for production using advanced technology and local unskilled labour. The African states that already owned the resources and controlled the labour were reluctant to lose control of land and labour. The European imperialists on the other hand became more and more involved in African politics to secure or extend their investments. The clash of African and European interests eventually led to wars of conquest, or treaties of 'protection', which robbed African states of their sovereignty.

(N. Parsons, p. 141.)

(a) *In what ways does Parsons' interpretation of Southern African history differ from a more conventional account?*

(b) *Do you agree or disagree with Parsons' interpretation of history? Give evidence to back up your answer.*

Glossary

Capitalism — an economic system based on private ownership of the wealth and the system of production, distribution and exchange; the individual owners of wealth (the capitalists) operate and manage their property for profit in competitive conditions.

Extractive phase of modernization/primary industry — the early phase of industrialization when there is an emphasis on the extraction of raw materials from the earth — either in the form of mining or agriculture.

Homestead production — communal production based on pre-colonial forms of social and economic organization.

Imperialism — the extension of power by one nation over another nation.

Industrialization — the process of the development of industry on an extensive scale.

Industrial revolution — the transformation, first of Britain (in the Eighteenth and Nineteenth Centuries) and later of Europe, the USA and other countries, including South Africa, from a feudal to an industrial or 'modern' system of economic production, along with changes in culture, social life and politics.

Job reservation — the reservation, by law, of specific jobs for whites only.

Labour relations — relations between employers and employees in an industrial enterprise.

Manufacturing phase of modernization — the later stage of industrialization, when there is an emphasis on manufacturing industry.

Migrant labour — a system of labour which depends on the recruitment of rural workers for industrial work; and ensures that the rural workers do not settle permanently in urban areas.

Peasant — small-scale agriculturalist who produces partly for sale in the market and partly for subsistence.

Low grade ore/low grade gold mines — ore or mines where the rock mined contains only a very small proportion of gold.

Randlords — the name given to the wealthy owners of the Witwatersrand gold mines.

Reserves — areas reserved by law for African occupation, for example, the Transkei.

267

Sharecropper — an agricultural producer who lives on the landowners' farms and cultivates crops in an independent manner, but has to pay a portion of his crops to the landowner. (Also known as 'farming-on-the-halves'.)

State — the organized political power that rules a specific geographical area.

Underdevelopment — 'The process by which any given region of today's Third World was progressively incorporated into a permanent relationship of exploitation with the expanding capitalist world economy' (after C. Leys, *Underdevelopment in Kenya*, p. 8).

Bibliography

Bundy, C. *The Rise and Fall of the South African Peasantry* (Heinemann, London, 1979)

Callinicos, L. *Gold and Workers, 1886–1924*, Vol. I (Ravan Press, Johannesburg, 1980)

Davenport, R. *South Africa: A Modern History* (Macmillan, Johannesburg, 1977)

de Kiewiet, C. W. *A History of South Africa* (Oxford University Press, London, 1957)

Denoon, D. *Southern Africa since 1800* (Longman, London, 1972)

Doxey, G.V. *The Industrial Colour Bar in South Africa* (Oxford University Press, Cape Town, 1961)

Guy, J. *The Destruction of the Zulu Kingdom* (Ravan Press, Johannesburg, 1983)

Houghton, D. H. *The South African Economy* (Oxford University Press, Cape Town, 1976)

Houghton, D. H. & Dagut, J. (eds), *Source Material on the South African Economy*, Vol. I, (Oxford University Press, Cape Town, 1972)

Innes, D. *Anglo* (Ravan Press, Johannesburg, 1984)

Kallaway P. and Pearson, P. *Witwatersrand Germinal: A social History of Johannesburg through Photographs* (Ravan, 1986)

Lanning, G. and Mueller, M. *Africa Undermined* (Penguin, Harmondsworth, 1979)

Nattrass, J. *The South African Economy* (Oxford University Press, Cape Town, 1981)

Palmer, R. & Parsons, N. (eds) *The Roots of Rural Poverty*, (Heinemann, London, 1977)

Parsons, N. *A New History of Southern Africa* (Macmillan, London, 1982)

Roberts, B. *Kimberley: Turbulent City* (David Philip, Cape Town, 1976)

Smit, G. J. J. *History for Standard 9* (Maskew Miller, Cape Town, 1975)

Southall, R. *South Africa's Transkei* (Heinemann, London, 1982)

Trapido, S. "South Africa in a comparative study of industrialization", in *Journal of Development Studies*, III, April 1971

van der Horst, S. T. *Native Labour in South Africa* (Oxford University Press, London, 1942)

Wilson, F. & Perrot, D. (eds) *Outlook on a Century* (Lovedale Press, 1973)

Wilson, F. *Labour in the South African Gold Mines 1911–1969* (Oxford University Press, London, 1972)

Wilson, M. & Thompson, L. (eds) *The Oxford History of South Africa*, II (Oxford University Press, London, 1971)

8 IMPERIALISM, REPUBLICANISM AND THE INCORPORATION OF THE AFRICAN KINGDOMS

Introduction 270
   South Africa 1880–1900

Imperialism and the incorporation of independent African kingdoms 272
   The Anglo-Zulu War and the imperial factor
   Rhodes and the Road to the North
   Rhodesia
   The Matabeleland Native Police

Republicanism and conflict with independent African kingdoms 282
   Goshen and Stellaland
   The Ndzunda Ndebele
   Zululand
   Swaziland
   North of the Limpopo
   The subjection of the last African kingdoms
   Conclusion

Africans within white-ruled Southern Africa 294
   Migrant labour
   Peasant farming
   The Glen Grey Act of 1884
   Reactions:
   Defiance in Pondoland
   Resistance in the Langeberg
   Africans and the franchise
   Conclusion

Britain, the Boer republics and the making of a war 299
   Governing the gold-fields: clashing opinions
   The Railway War
   The question of customs duties
   The Jameson Raid
   The Uitlanders
   Prelude to war
   The end of an era
   The Anglo-Boer War and the Peace of Vereeniging
   The Anglo-Boer War

Chronology of wars fought by Africans against colonial forces
Glossary
Bibliography

Introduction

SOUTH AFRICA 1880–1900

The political map of Southern Africa changed radically in the last twenty years of the Nineteenth Century. The remaining independent African kingdoms were crushed and incorporated into white-ruled Southern Africa. Political and economic power shifted steadily into the hands of the wealthy South African capitalists, although Britain, the major colonizing nation, also played an important role in shaping the course of events. Relations between the Afrikaner republics and the British colonies, which had never been friendly, now grew very tense. The pace of South African economic life quickened. Mines extracting rich gold ore were established on the reef and agriculture was expanded. An explanation of these changes must be seen against the background of international and local developments.

The major international forces of change at this time derived from the economic transformation of Europe. First Britain and then the whole of Europe experienced an industrial revolution. The effects of European industrialization rippled outward and countries as different as Russia and Japan were slowly encouraged to leave the feudal age and enter the new era of capitalism. In Africa the spillover of Europe's industrial revolution took the form of intensified colonial activity which became known as the 'Scramble for Africa'.

To understand why the 'Scramble' took place we need to investigate the nature of economic and political changes taking place in Europe at the time. Industrialization and mechanization had occurred on an unprecedented scale. The mass production of goods and the intensification of economic competition caused increasing degrees of political friction between the new nation states.

By 1880 the local markets of Europe and the USA were nearly saturated* by all the goods produced and industrialists began to look around for markets further afield. They singled out the continent of Africa for special attention.

The increase of European interest in Africa changed that continent's relationship with the outside world. For the fifty years prior to 1880 a policy of free trade* had operated. Britain had been the leader in international trade, but in the 1870s rival capitalist states (France, and to a lesser extent, Germany, Italy, Belgium and Spain) emerged to challenge British trading superiority. The new competitors cut Britain's trading profits by taxing British imports, muscling in on foreign trade and seizing overseas possessions. Britain was no longer able to trade freely and so responded aggressively by annexing colonies wherever it could. Other states followed this example.

Conditions in Southern Africa differed from those elsewhere in Africa. From the mid-Seventeenth Century there had been a European presence in the Cape. European rule had gradually spread northward and in the process a powerful white settler community had established itself. This distinguished South Africa from most of the rest of Africa, which lacked large settler populations. By the late Nineteenth Century the resident colonial power in South Africa, namely Britain, was no longer able to dictate policy to the white settlers. The white inhabitants of the Cape and Natal had close ties with the mother country, but they also had their own goals which often clashed with those of Britain. In 1853 the Cape gained partial political independence when it was granted representative government. Thereafter it was increasingly able to control its own affairs and resist British interference.

The settlers in the Orange Free State (OFS) and the *Zuid-Afrikaansche Republiek* (the ZAR, also known as the South African Republic, and as the Transvaal) were politically independent of Britain. They had removed themselves from British rule in the 1830s and jealously guarded their status. Although the ZAR, OFS, Natal and the Cape had differing degrees of political independence, we should not forget that they all felt Britain's economic power and were therefore never completely free from British influence.

As long as the Boer republics remained beyond its control, Britain was dissatisfied. It feared that the independent republics would ally with foreign rivals to challenge Britain's position in South Africa. Britain also feared that Boer expansion would increase the chances of expensive wars. At the same time there was increasing pressure on Britain from English-speaking settlers, especially in the Cape, for further say in local government. Britain hoped to solve all its problems with one simple policy: federation*. Federation would enable Britain to:

(a) unite the sub-continent under its control; and
(b) give some political power to the colonists.

The first federation attempt by Sir George Grey ended in dismal failure in the 1850s. In the 1870s Lord Carnarvon, Britain's Secretary of State for Colonies, revived plans for federation. Carnarvon's immediate concern was to shift the burden of administration and finance on to the South African colonists. This had already been done in Australia and Canada, and the discovery of diamonds in the Cape made the same thing possible in South Africa. (See Chapter 7.)

In Carnarvon's opinion, for federation to work, the whole of South Africa would have to be brought under British rule. Colonists could then be admitted as junior partners in the project of empire building, and prevent any foreign power from gaining a foothold in South Africa. (There were rumours at that time of possible German intervention.) A federation constructed by Britain but ruled by loyal colonists could also be relied upon to safeguard Britain's strategic interests centred on the Cape sea-route. In 1877 the first step towards bringing the whole of Southern Africa under British rule was taken when the Transvaal was annexed. Carnarvon's ambitious scheme did not ultimately succeed. It was wrecked in 1879 by the defeat of British forces at Isandlwana in Zululand.

Britain ultimately won the war against the Zulu, but these events caused the failure of the federation scheme. Britain's embarrassment did not end there. Shortly after federation was abandoned, Transvalers took up arms and regained their independence by inflicting a humiliating defeat on the British army at Majuba in northern Natal in 1881. British fortunes were at a low ebb. Widespread African opposition to white rule compounded Britain's problems.

Many clashes resulted elsewhere in Africa when Europeans attempted to impose their rule over African kingdoms which had hitherto been independent. In South Africa, conflict between Africans and incoming settlers had been common for two centuries. Some of the African peoples, like the Cape Khoikhoi, had been defeated, but there were still many groups that remained independent.

Although independence was fiercely defended, the development of the South African economy led to an intensification of the challenge to African kingdoms. Modern military technology was used against Africans and their independence was cut short.

The study of history is always changing, never static. It responds continuously to new discoveries and insights. The way

271

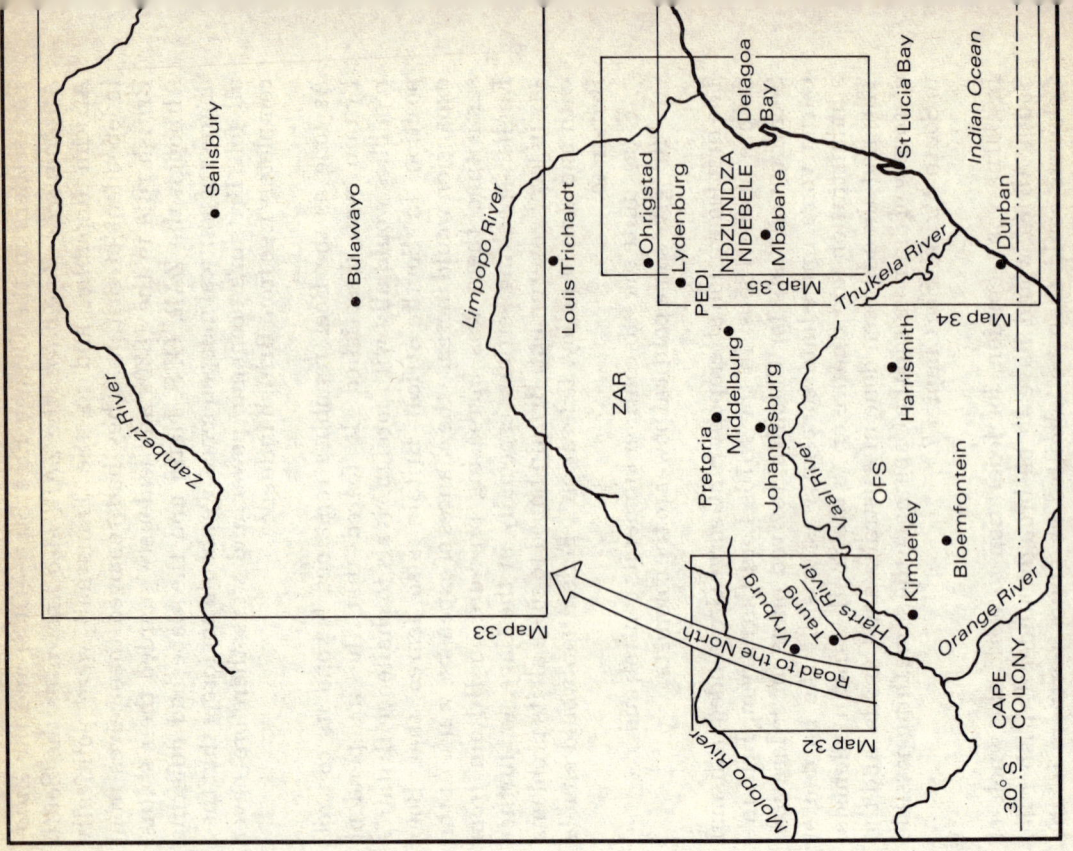

Map 31 — South-eastern Africa in the 1880s.

in which standard South African textbooks explain the South African past has for a long time focused on the activities and achievements of white colonists and frontiersmen. As a result of recent research, however, new perspectives have been developed which offer new interpretations. Certain economic and local factors are now given greater explanatory emphasis. This chapter attempts to shed new light on this period of Southern African history by reflecting the findings of the latest research.

This chapter is divided into sections. The first looks at the impact of British and colonial forces on African kingdoms. The second examines relations between African kingdoms and the ZAR. The third deals with the activities of Africans who already found themselves within the boundaries of white-ruled South Africa. The fourth section investigates the relationship between the Boers, on one side, and the Cape, Natal and Britain, on the other, leading to war.

Imperialism and the incorporation of independent African kingdoms

The years 1877–1880 were busy years for the British forces in Southern Africa. In these years they fought the Zulu, Pedi, Tswana, Kora, Griqua, Southern Sotho, Xhosa and the

272

Transvaal Boers. Each campaign was accompanied by eventual British victory, except in the case of the ZAR. This was significant because some of these African powers (for example the Zulu and the Pedi) had histories of successful resistance. They were defeated only because of the entry into South African politics of the 'imperial factor'* in the form of the British army.

The spate of wars in the late 1870s reflected increasing pressures on African kingdoms and their resistance to this pressure (see the chronology at the end of this chapter). The wars had two basic causes. One was Carnarvon's attempt to bring about a federation, which has already been referred to. The other was the influence of the mining industry and the demand for black labour.

Up until 1880, however, the demands of the Randlords were overshadowed by Britain and its imperial representatives. The most important of these was Lord Carnarvon, who was still attempting to bring the whole of South Africa under British rule.

THE ANGLO-ZULU WAR AND THE IMPERIAL FACTOR

The War of 1879 was a direct result of Carnarvon's federation plan. Britain believed that its rule in South Africa could be threatened by independent African kingdoms. It was therefore prepared to take steps against potential opponents.

Cetshwayo's Zulu kingdom was the most powerful in Southern Africa and consequently excited the most concern. The white settlers of neighbouring Natal were directly in the line of any possible Zulu advance. They therefore had an interest in the breaking of Zulu power. This would also help them to obtain some of the fertile lands north of the Thukela (Tugela) River. They urged the headstrong and aggressive High Commissioner, Sir Bartle Frere, to assert colonial authority over Zululand and to end the reign of the Zulu king.

Frere, along with Lord Chelmsford, the commander of British troops in Natal, accordingly made it clear to the Zulu that they

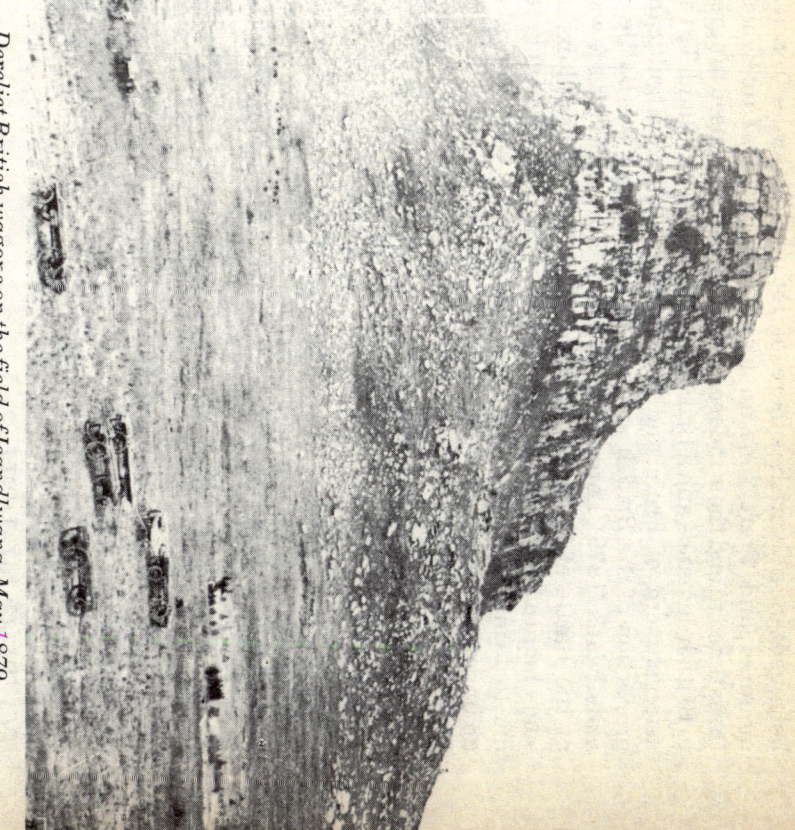

Derelict British wagons on the field of Isandlwana, May 1879.

273

belonged in a British sphere of influence. Border tension mounted and Frere sent an ultimatum to the Zulu which threatened to end their independence. The Zulu refused to agree to British demands and a British army invaded Zululand. To the astonishment of Frere and the British public, a significant proportion of the British army was wiped out at the Battle of Isandlwana (1879). Later in the year, Britain concluded the war at the Battle of Ulundi. Cetshwayo was captured and exiled some months later. The British success was, to a large degree, due to its military superiority, but Zulu food shortages were also an important factor in explaining why they did not fight on. The Isandlwana defeat had demonstrated to the British the dangers and expense of enforced federation. The wars with the Xhosa, Basuto, Kora and Pedi had also been expensive and the prospect of further cost restrained the Colonial Office in London from pursuing federation further. This did not mean the end of unifying strategies or a halt to assaults on African kingdoms, but it did signal the rise of local personalities who now took the initiative.

RHODES AND THE ROAD TO THE NORTH

In the previous chapter we saw how the development of diamond mining at Kimberley revolutionized the economy of South Africa. Not only did diamonds rapidly become the most valuable South African export, but wealth was created which came to be under the control of a small group of mineowners.

Cecil Rhodes was the most prominent and influential member of this group. The son of an English parson, he came out to South Africa for health reasons and then made his fortune on the diamond mines. By 1882 he headed De Beers Company, which soon secured a monopoly over the diamond industry. In 1887 he became leading director of the Consolidated Gold Fields Company in Johannesburg.

Rhodes had the reputation of being the greatest imperialist Southern Africa had seen. It was his proud boast that he would 'paint Africa red, from Cape to Cairo', meaning that he would bring it under British rule. Recent assessments of Rhodes have modified this picture and presented him rather as an ambitious capitalist who used British imperialism for the benefit of his private fortune. He undoubtedly advanced the British imperial cause, but only when his own interests were not harmed. His success as a British imperialist was in no small measure due to the attitude of the British government which allowed him to be 'its man in South Africa'.

While some historians have suggested that Rhodes was working as an agent of the British Empire, others have shown how his actions served his economic interests. For example, his attempts to regulate labour supplies in Bechuanaland, his quest for gold in Rhodesia, and his bid to install a sympathetic government over the richest gold-fields in the world in the ZAR, all testified to his consuming drive for profit. This is not to say that profit was the only consideration at work; Rhodes's friendship with British colonial officials and members of the Cape government influenced his actions as well. In addition, opponents often forced Rhodes to reconsider his decisions. The argument here is simply that Rhodes cannot be understood without first taking into account his economic interests and ambitions.

The first area to attract Rhodes's attention was the Kimberley hinterland. In the 1870s diamond mineowners were often short of labour. One of the reasons for the shortage was that labourers migrating to and from Kimberley were often robbed or taxed en route to the mines and this discouraged them from continuing to work on the mines. Labourers on their way to the diamond-fields were often waylaid in the Transvaal along the Road to the North (see Map 31).

In the 1870s the area that is today the northern Cape, western Transvaal, Bophuthatswana and Botswana, was the site of a number of independent states such as those of the Kgatla, Kwena and Ngwato. These Africans had been pushed into confined areas and as a result, frequent disputes arose over land. This troubled region was a focus of Cape politics at this time. The area provided labour but it was also a problem to its neighbours. For example, upheavals there might spread southward and disrupt diamond mining or influence labour suppliers in the Transvaal. The Boers, who had recently won the first Anglo-Boer War, appeared intent on expanding westward and this complicated matters further.

In 1881 Rhodes became a member of the Cape Parliament. Both Rhodes and the High Commissioner, Frere, believed that annexation was the best way of producing stability. By bringing the lands north of Kimberley under colonial control, labour supplies would be guaranteed, peace ensured and Boer expansion halted. The influential missionary, John Mackenzie, supported the idea. For a while Cape border police patrolled the area but when they were withdrawn in 1881, fighting flared up.

The origins of the violence that erupted in 1881 are complicated, but they can basically be summarized in this way. Boers began moving into the area and, in the process, aggravated a local land feud. A civil war broke out. Some British advisers helped the Tlhaping of Mankurware and Montshiwa, but the Kora of David Massouw and the Rolong of Moswete received Boer aid, which won them victory in 1882.

The Boer allies of Massouw and Moswete received land as a reward. The Boers established two small republics—Goshen and Stellaland—on this land in 1882/3 (see Map 32 on the next page). But the conflict did not end.

Mankurwane and Montshiwa gathered forces to try and wrest back the land they had lost. It was at this point that Britain intervened by appointing John Mackenzie as resident agent for the area in April 1884.

Meanwhile, on the west coast of Southern Africa, a German presence had been established. Lüderitz, a German explorer, had occupied the natural harbour of Angra Pequena (later called Lüderitz) in 1883, and shortly afterwards Germany stepped in to annex the whole of southern Namibia. The possibility of a German-Boer link-up, together with the continuing turmoil along the Road to the North, prompted Britain to dispatch 4 000 troops under General Warren to

275

the High Commissioner in South Africa. It became part of the Cape Colony in 1895. The *Bechuanaland Protectorate* was the area to the north of the Molopo which was bounded in the west and north by German South West Africa and in the east by the ZAR. It eventually became the Republic of Botswana in 1966.

Once the protectorates had been set up, a Land Commission was appointed by Sir Sidney Shippard, the Administrator of British Bechuanaland. The Commissioners had to decide on the distribution of land and heard evidence from many claimants. No representative of the local African population was appointed to serve as a member of the Land Commission. This was a serious omission because they were the region's original inhabitants. Some extracts from the Land Commission's report are given on pp. 277–8.

As a result of the Land Commission's judgement (1886) white settlers received a large portion of the best lands. The local Africans lost a lot of land, especially those areas served by springs. These springs supplied the water necessary for dry land agriculture. In the 1870s large amounts of grain had been exported, but now the loss of agricultural land to Africans ended this profitable occupation. Opportunities for hunting were also greatly reduced and access to firewood lost. Both these activities had been a source of income and an integral part of the subsistence economy. In addition, Mankurwane alone lost between 30 000 and 60 000 cattle. A committee under the chairmanship of the missionary, John Mackenzie, investigated the situation and concluded:

> ...*the present condition of Mankoroane's* [Mankurwane's] *tribe is one of extreme and increasing poverty ... The greater part of the tribe is now crowded in the immediate neighbourhood of Taungs living from hand to mouth, and deprived of any regular means of subsistence or of purchasing food. Some of the men of the tribe have entered*

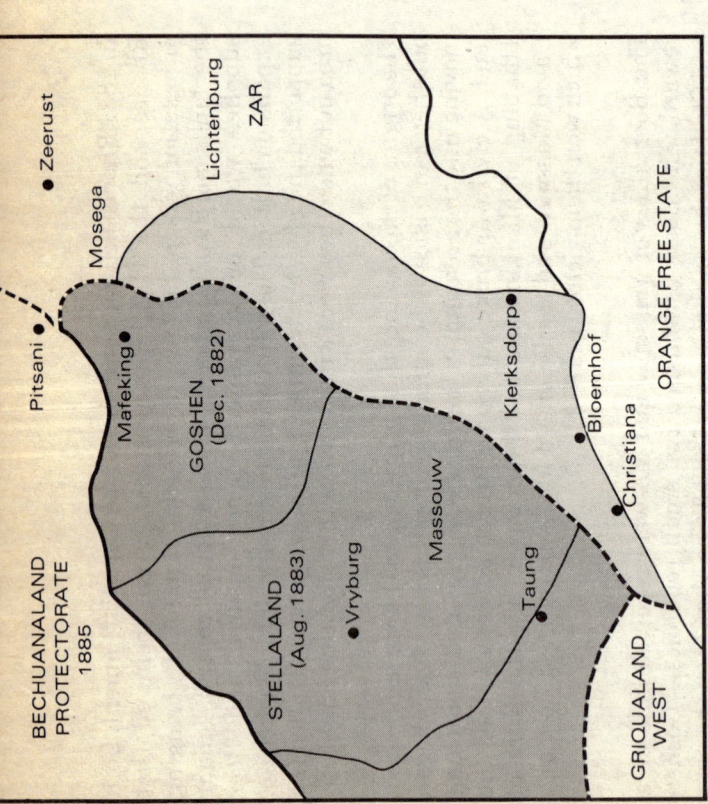

Map 32 — Stellaland and Goshen.

(The dates on which the various protectorates and republics were created are indicated in brackets.)

Vryburg in 1885. Rhodes became the commissioner of the area for a while, but after quarrelling with Warren, he resigned. In the mean time the Cape refused to take over the costly administration of the desert-like area, so in 1885 Britain formally proclaimed two protectorates*. *British Bechuanaland*, stretching from the Molopo River southward to the Cape and including Goshen and Stellaland, came under the jurisdiction of

276

the service of the British army, others have gone in various directions to find work, and have left their families behind....

(Quoted in Davenport and Hunt.)

General Warren enters Vryburg in 1885.
(Illustration courtesy of the Killie Campbell Africana Library.)

Questions

1. What impression is given by the artist regarding the attitude of the townspeople to the annexation?
2. Do you think this impression is accurate? Give reasons to back up your answer.

King Mankuruane rides down with his escort to view the British army camp at Taung, Bechuanaland.
(A contemporary impression, c. 1885; courtesy of the Killie Campbell Africana Library.)

Land Commissions

Land Commissions played an important part in the history of Southern Africa. Later on in this chapter we refer to two other Land Commissions — those that deliberated in Zimbabwe and in Swaziland. A Land Commission was also established in Zululand in 1905. (See Chapter 9.) In virtually every case, Land Commissions gave judgements that favoured the interests of white settlers over those of the African inhabitants. In other words, Land Commissions were a significant part of the process by which land was occupied by whites. Here are some extracts from the evidence heard by the Bechuanaland Land Commission in 1886.

A very large number of witnesses have told deliberate falsehoods while under examination. Claimants who had filed written statements in support of their claims have confessed under cross-examination that the facts therein stated were untrue, documents purporting to bear the marks of native chiefs have been produced which had never been placed before those chiefs for signature....

277

...It must be obvious that Mankurwane had not the slightest idea that he was giving away so much land...

... Chiefs who actually signed the documents had no knowledge of what they were doing and they frequently were persuaded to sign documents which had not been read over to them, and that even when documents were read over to them their full importance and meaning were rarely explained.

(Extracts from Agar-Hamilton, pp. 432–4.)

Questions

1. What was the aim or purpose of a Land Commission in the context referred to?
2. Was it possible for a Land Commission to arrive at a just allocation of land? Give evidence to support your answer.
3. Was reliable evidence presented to the Land Commissions? Explain your answer.
4. What was the outcome of the presentation of Land Commission reports?

of gold at Tati in 1867 and Lydenburg in 1872 had led to rumours of fabulous wealth in central Africa.

In 1886 gold was again found, this time on the Witwatersrand in the ZAR. Rhodes and other investors soon realised that the discovery was a rich one and began to buy up mining land and invest vast sums in mining operations. Mining on the Witwatersrand was risky because there were still many new technical problems to overcome. (See Chapter 7.) Aware of this, Rhodes wanted to protect himself from possible losses by finding a 'Second Rand'* in the Ndebele and Shona occupied territory of present-day Zimbabwe*.

Many people believed that gold was abundant north of the Limpopo River because objects made of gold had been discovered in the ruins of Great Zimbabwe. The problem was that prospectors were prevented from searching freely for gold by Lobengula, king of the Ndebele (Matabele). Lobengula feared the penetration of whites into his lands because he had heard of the downfall of many African powers as a result of conflict with white settlers. He could not exclude whites altogether but was very careful to limit their entry as much as possible. He did this by giving permission (granting concessions) to only a few carefully selected people. Yet, as interest in the area grew, Lobengula was approached by many concession seekers and found it increasingly difficult to maintain control over them.

Amongst those who pestered Lobengula for concessions was Charles Rudd, Rhodes's representative. Lobengula was cautious especially as he had just signed a treaty of friendship with the ZAR's representative, Piet Grobler (1887). In October 1888, King Lobengula eventually signed a concession which gave permission to Rhodes to prospect in those parts of his domain which he specifically pointed out. The concession was known as the Rudd Concession. It was obtained with the help of

RHODESIA

The extension of British influence into the Kalahari and up to the Limpopo opened the way for prospectors and fortune-seekers to penetrate the area to the north. Many were lured by the hope of finding diamonds or gold, especially as the discovery

John Moffat, Assistant Commissioner of the Bechuanaland Protectorate. John was the son of Robert Moffat, the missionary at Kuruman who had at one time been the adviser of Lobengula's father, Mzilikazi. Rhodes exploited his links with British colonial representatives to obtain an agreement that was to be the basis for the foundation of the British South Africa Company (BSAC). This company, based on the model of West African chartered trading companies*, was created by royal charter and had the power to 'make treaties, promulgate laws, preserve the peace, maintain a police force and acquire new concessions'. It owed its existence not only to Rhodes's agents, but also to the willingness of the British government to give local agents like Rhodes a great deal of responsibility.

Recently the historian Cobbing has called into question the validity of the Rudd concession. He shows that a crucial part of the deal was the consignment of 1 000 rifles promised to Lobengula by Rhodes. Although the rifles were delivered, Lobengula refused to accept them. The reason was that Lobengula found out that the agreement he had made verbally with Rudd had been distorted in the written version of the concession. Rhodes had been given much more power than had been agreed upon. He realized that accepting the rifles would have signified consent to the concession and this he refused to give. Notwithstanding the doubtful validity of the concession, the BSAC came into being late in 1889.

As soon as Rhodes had gained the concession and had been granted a trading charter* by the British government he began to plan the occupation of Mashonaland. Lobengula had not given permission for prospecting in Mashonaland or for the occupation of Mashonaland, but Rhodes calculated that such a move would not be opposed because Mashonaland was some distance from the Ndebele heartland in western Zimbabwe (see Map 33).

A proposal for the colonization of Rhodesia

F. C. Selous, an explorer who entered Rhodes' service, gives reasons for choosing to settle in Mashonaland. The following is an extract from a letter he wrote to prospective settlers in October 1889.

It is folly to plan wild schemes for the colonization of Central Africa, and to leave a country with the glorious climate and great natural resources of Mashunaland [sic] out in the cold. In Mashunaland Europeans can live and thrive and rear strong healthy children ... Once get a footing in Eastern Mashunaland, and the country will be quickly settled westwards, and before very long the Matabili [sic] Question will settle itself. Now or never is the time to act. Make a southern road to eastern Mashunaland. Have the country thoroughly prospected and reported upon this coming year; and if the reports are favourable pour in men and machinery, and at the same time establish cattle and agricultural farms. In a word, work the gold, and open up and occupy the country. If Mashunaland is not worth this experiment, then there is no country in the interior of Africa that it will pay any company to spend money upon.

(Selous, p. 311.)

Questions

1. From the above passage, list the advantages that Selous thought would promote white settlement in Mashonaland.

2. What do you think Selous meant by the 'Matabili Question'? In what way do you think it would quickly 'settle itself'?

279

3. What were the major economic attractions offered by Mashonaland to white settlers?

4. By referring to pp. 278–282 of this chapter, indicate what the dangers of occupying Mashonaland were.

5. Perhaps the most interesting aspect of this letter is its failure to mention important factors such as:
   (a) the Rudd Concession;
   (b) Lobengula;
   (c) the Shona inhabitants of Mashonaland.
   Explain the importance of these omissions.

6. To what extent was the advice of Selous followed when Rhodesia was occupied in 1890?

When Lobengula heard about Rhodes' plan to occupy Mashonaland, he was furious.

> *How is it that the Doctor [Jameson] agreed at Bulawayo [the place where the concession discussions took place] to dig only in a place pointed out by the king? And now he wants to dig in Mashonaland where the king objects — and will not allow ... [the] king asks whether the Doctor understands the King's language.*
>
> (Cobbing, p. 45.)

When Rhodes eventually took possession of Mashonaland in 1890 he used a heavily armed group of men called the Pioneer Column. Cobbing explains:

> *... the heavy arming of the Pioneer Column was ... a result of the knowledge that Lobengula had not given any prospecting rights in Mashonaland to the Company.*
>
> (Cobbing, p. 42.)

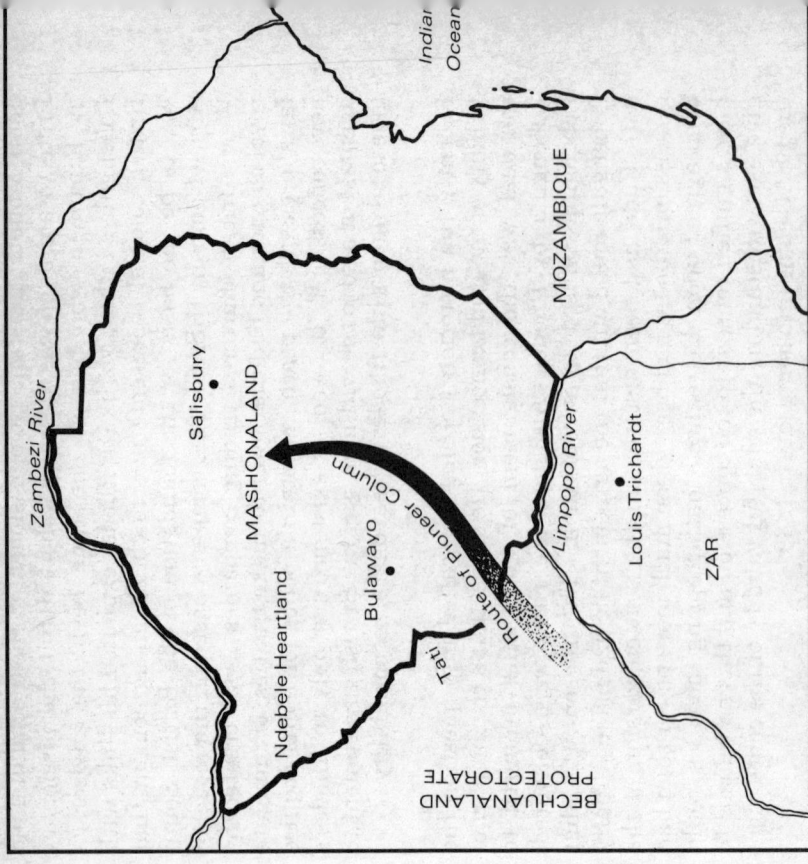

Map 33 — Rhodesia (Zimbabwe).

The Pioneer Column set up the Headquarters of the BSAC at Salisbury [present-day Harare] in 1890 and began to consolidate white rule in the area. Land was occupied and prospecting extended. The Ndebele were still perceived as the major threat to settlement. After a number of clashes between Ndebele warriors and white settlers, a war broke out in 1893. Rhodes tried to justify the war as an attempt to secure a peaceful settlement with the Ndebele. Recent historical research has revealed, however, that Rhodes sought the downfall of the Ndebele and that the 650 men who volunteered to fight in the war, did so in the hope of making a fortune in loot, cattle, gold claims and land.

(Stigger, pp. 22–3.)

The Pioneer Column in laager at Tuli River, before commencing the trip to Mashonaland.

The war was won by the BSAC 'police'. Lobengula fled, and died soon afterwards in 1894. Matabeleland was added to Mashonaland and the entire area was named Rhodesia in honour of Rhodes.

As in the case of the Tlhaping on the fringes of the Kalahari, the Ndebele were now also subjected to a Land Commission. The Commission's task was to decide on areas for white settlement and set out reserves for Ndebele occupation. The Commission was not impartial. For example, it was chaired by Joseph Vintcent, a judge of the High Court of Rhodesia, who believed that the British government obtained:

... *no revenue from the natives in return for the protection it affords to them, and further, Europeans though anxious to occupy vacant land are unable to do so.*

(Stigger, pp. 103–4.)

To remedy this situation, Vintcent believed that Africans should be forced off the agricultural land and that this should be handed over to white farmers. On the basis of the Commission's recommendations, the best arable land was given to white settlers, while the Ndebele lands were for the most part sandy, infertile and malaria infested. This was hardly a good way of ensuring peace as it made the Ndebele extremely bitter.

A factor that further angered the Ndebele was the conduct of the newly created Native Affairs Department (NAD). Although the NAD claimed that it was there to help the Ndebele, some of its officers (the 'native commissioners') and those who enforced the new laws — the Matabeleland Native Police — often abused their positions.

In addition, their official task of providing labour for the local gold mines brought them into conflict with a defiant local population which did not wish to enter wage labour.

The Matabeleland Native Police

In 1896 the deadly rinderpest epidemic swept down from north Africa killing nearly all the cattle in its path. This was a catastrophe for the Ndebele. They had already suffered severe land losses under white settler domination, and the loss of their cattle now made the situation intolerable. In 1896 the Ndebele rose and attacked white settlers, members of the NAD and the Matabeleland Native Police. The Chimurenga War had begun.

281

Republicanism and conflict with independent African kingdoms

In the previous section we saw that to understand Rhodes' motives for the political domination of the Road to the North and Rhodesia it was necessary to take into account broader economic factors. Economic factors are also of importance in a study of the ZAR.

The ZAR was founded by *Voortrekkers*. The main wealth of the state that they built lay in the land. It is not surprising therefore that the pursuit of land and conflict over land with neighbouring African kingdoms was a major and ongoing theme in the ZAR's history. The gradual rise to power of a class of Boer 'notables' or landed gentry was important because they acquired large tracts of land which in the end led to a shortage of land among the poorer white settlers. They also used their political power to pursue policies aimed at securing more land and ensuring a supply of labour for agriculture from neighbouring African chiefdoms. Such policies caused conflict between groups of Boers, and between the ZAR and its neighbours. A combination of these factors resulted in a policy of expansionism by the ZAR government.

Another important consideration for the ZAR was the establishment of independent links with the outside world. The fierce republicanism of the Boers meant that they wished to avoid being economically dependent on the British colonies of

The Ndebele were soon afterwards joined by the Shona. BSAC forces were unable to defeat this alliance. Eventually imperial troops were brought in and after a long struggle they forced first the Ndebele and then the Shona to surrender (1897). Once again Rhodes had relied on his imperial connections to achieve his ends.

The subjugation of the two powerful Zimbabwe kingdoms took only seven years. What had been the cause of the sudden white interest and involvement in this area? The evidence we have looked at seems to point to a number of factors, the most significant of which was the mining revolution.

Mining created a new, ambitious and exceedingly wealthy class of capitalists, in search of further investments and profits in Southern Africa. It also attracted imperial interest. This complex mix of forces was responsible for the creation of Rhodesia.

Rhodesia was not the only region affected by these changes. The ZAR, the home of gold mining, was transformed during this period from a pastoral nation into the most prosperous power in Southern Africa. This had serious consequences for the African kingdoms within the Transvaal. We now turn to this area.

South Africa. To achieve this they tried to gain a port outside British-controlled areas.

President Burgers of the ZAR (1872–77) tried to expand his country's territory. He succeeded in one area by securing the annexation of some Tlhaping land along the Harts river in 1875. He failed elsewhere when, he temporarily lost control of the early gold diggings in the northern Transvaal. White miners paid tribute to the local chief and thereby gained control of the area for a while.

An inability to control territory worried the ZAR government. It was still too weak at this point to challenge the adjacent independent African kingdoms. Ironically, it was the ZAR's enemy, Britain, that eventually subdued the African kingdoms.

In 1877 Sir Theophilus Shepstone and 25 mounted policemen peacefully annexed the ZAR and made it a British colony, in keeping with British plans for a federation, and in an attempt to bring political stability to the area. Two years later, British forces attacked one of the most powerful African kingdoms in the Transvaal area — Sekhukhune's Pedi. In 1876 the ZAR had been unable to defeat Sekhukhune, but now the British forces achieved a victory that was to rid the Boers of one of their most formidable opponents. The defeat of the Zulu in the Anglo-Zulu War of 1879 also helped the Transvaal (ZAR) government. Boers on the south-east borders of the Republic had lived a tense existence alongside the Zulu. The weakening of Zulu power gave them a chance to strengthen their position and even to expand their territories into Zululand itself.

The British occupation of the Transvaal did not last long. Growing Boer resentment of British rule came to a head in 1880. Boer commandos were called up and the British expelled. The war was called the *Eerste Vryheidsoorlog* (First Freedom War)

by the Boers, though it is more generally known as the First Anglo-Boer War (1880–1). The Pretoria Convention concluded the war in 1881. Partial independence was restored to the ZAR but Britain insisted on retaining a degree of informal control — sometimes called suzerainty — over the affairs of the ZAR. In particular, Britain wanted to manage the ZAR's foreign policy; to place some of the costs of war on the ZAR; to ensure the flow of labour to the diamond-fields; and to cut off ZAR support for the new mini-republics of Goshen and Stellaland in the western Transvaal.

In 1884 the Pretoria Convention was the subject of discussion in London. The ZAR wished certain aspects of the 1881 Convention to be revised. Britain conceded a number of points. It allowed its claim of suzerainty to lapse although it retained some say in foreign policy. Restrictions on the ZAR's policy towards Africans were dropped and the ZAR's war debt was reduced.

The exit of Britain from the Transvaal was a cause of much rejoicing in the ZAR. Nevertheless, British occupation had been of great value to the Boer republic. Britain had conquered two of the ZAR's major antagonists — the Pedi and the Zulu. Government and administration had been improved. Stability had been restored to the republic's finances. All in all, the ZAR was given a firm footing to embark on a vigorous policy of strengthening its internal and external position under its new President, Paul Kruger.

The history of the period between the London Convention of 1884 and the outbreak of the Anglo-Boer War (*Tweede Vryheidsoorlog*) in 1899 has often been summed up in terms of the conflict between British attempts to maintain supremacy in South Africa and the ZAR's expansionist policy. On the one hand Britain has often been accused of following a policy of

283

Paul Kruger came from a trekboer family that had originally lived in the Transgariep (northern Cape) area. His family had joined in the Great Trek in the 1830s and had eventually settled in the Rustenburg area, where they became prosperous notables. Kruger was a hunter and a farmer and became an assistant field-cornet at the age of seventeen. He was closely involved in the politics of the ZAR from that date. In the 1860s he became the Commandant-General. He was a leading figure in the First Anglo-Boer War (1880–81). At the conclusion of the war he was chosen as one of the three members of the Triumvirate who took charge of affairs after the Pretoria Convention. In 1883 he was elected State President.

The following two extracts represent a widely accepted interpretation of Kruger's career from this juncture.

The encirclement of the South African Republic

Kruger's political objectives

It was the aim of Kruger to preserve the independence of the S.A. Republic at all costs. Thus he desired to maintain friendly relations with Britain and also to make the Republic economically independent of British influence. Like Burgers, his predecessor, he wanted the Republic to be freed of the necessity of making use of the ports of the two British colonies in the south. To this end the Republic should gain access to a neutral port of a friendly Power, such as Delegoa Bay, or secure a port within republican territory by expansion eastwards to the coast of Zululand. Kruger also wished to make the ZAR the dominant political influence north of the Orange River. For this reason various attempts were made to extend the boundaries of the Republic westwards into Bechuanaland and northwards across the Limpopo into Matabeleland-Mashonaland.

(C. de Fowler and G. J. J. Smit, *Senior History*, p. 330.)

'encirclement' of the ZAR to prevent it from gaining control of neighbouring African kingdoms, or gaining access to the sea and the outside world. On the other hand the ZAR is seen by many to have been following expansionist policies, in keeping with the interests of the notables, in their quest for land and wealth. The so-called 'encirclement of the Transvaal' has often been described as the consequence of this clash between:

... South African imperialism and South African nationalism as exemplified in the policies of Rhodes and Kruger respectively.

(Boyce p. 149.)

The accuracy of this interpretation needs to be examined closely. The political and economic strategy of the British and Cape governments—often strongly influenced by Rhodes—has been discussed above. The role of Kruger and the policies of the ZAR government now need to be explored.

The policy of encirclement

With the re-establishment of independence in the Transvaal in 1881 and the London Convention in 1884 it appeared that Britain, as in 1854, was about to withdraw from the interior of South Africa. This, however, was not so; Britain could not allow the two Boer Republics to develop into powerful states and threaten British supremacy in South Africa. Britain now adopted a new approach and attempted to surround the republics with British territory to prevent any chance of their gaining independent access to the sea and the outside world. The republics had to be so restricted economically and otherwise, that they would be compelled to seek closer union with the British colonies. The imperial factor as well as the Cape Colony and Natal were to play a part in this encirclement.

The policy of encirclement should not, however, be viewed merely as a narrow British South Africa policy. It should also be viewed against the background of the rising new imperialism and the consequent partition of Africa ... Rhodes's capitalist-imperialist ideal was opposed by the nationalist ideal of President Kruger. Kruger united all Afrikaner nationalist forces ... Kruger was to run into much opposition. His desire to expand the Transvaal and find a way to the sea was to alert Rhodes and the other imperialists and hasten their attempts to encircle the Transvaal.

(M. C. van Zyl, "States and Colonies in South Africa, 1854–1902" in C. F. J. Muller *500 Years: A History of South Africa* pp. 273–276.)

Questions

1. In the opinion of the above writers, what are the key aspects of ZAR policy in the 1880s?
2. Is it accurate to suggest that Kruger himself was largely responsible for the policies followed by the ZAR government, or were other influences important in shaping the course of events? Explain.
3. In terms of your reading so far, and in the light of what follows below, would you agree that the 'policy of encirclement' is the key factor in understanding Southern African politics during the period 1880–1960?

GOSHEN AND STELLALAND

In 1881–2 some ZAR burgers moved westward into Tlhaping country. As we have already seen, violence erupted between Massouw and Moswete on the one hand and Mankurwane and Montshiwa on the other (see p. 275). Two small trekker republics of Goshen and Stellaland were created out of this turmoil (see Map 32). The newly elected ZAR President, Paul Kruger, tried to turn the situation to his country's advantage.

A group of Stellalanders, with Vryburg in the distance.
(Illustration courtesy of the Killie Campbell Africana Library.)

285

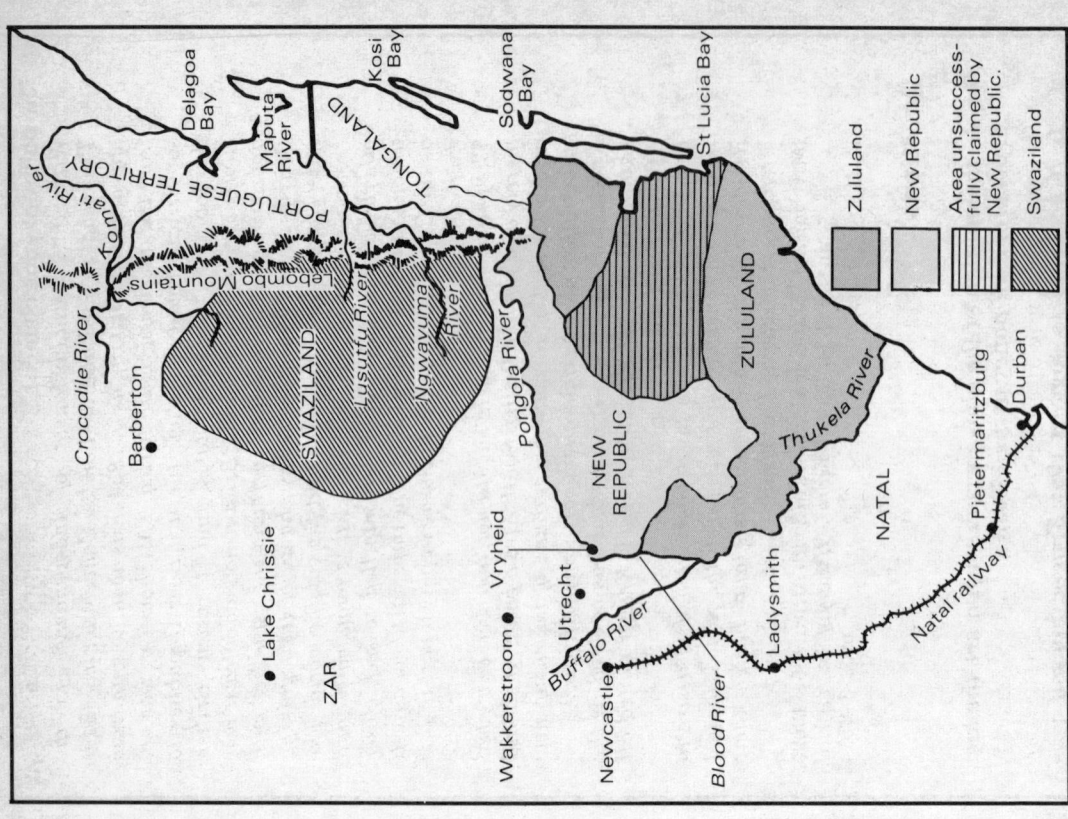

Map 34 — Zululand and the New Republic, 1887.

The Pretoria Convention of 1881 had already extended the ZAR's territories in the west, and Kruger now sought to acquire more land by annexing the two republics. These plans were halted by the arrival of the British army in 1885, under the command of General Warren. Goshen and Stellaland were annexed and became part of British Bechuanaland. The former allies of the Boers, Massouw and Moswete, drifted into obscurity, much the worse off after white involvement in their affairs.

THE NDZUNDZA NDEBELE*

Within the ZAR itself there were many African groups which were to all intents and purposes independent. Most of these were situated in isolated areas of the Transvaal where they did not really disturb the slow-moving life of the Boer Republic. In the eastern Transvaal, however, the Ndzundza Ndebele were close to areas of white settlement (see Map 31). The major power in the area — the Pedi — had been defeated in 1879, and only the Ndebele stood in the way of Boer attempts to ensure their authority over the area. There was the attraction of land and labour, but mainly the eastern Transvaal gold mines needed to be protected from possible disruption. In 1883 General Piet Joubert assembled a large force. Up until this time Mabhogo, King of the Ndebele, had led a successful defence against the Boers, but now the Boers were stronger and Mabhogo had been succeeded by his son Njabele. After an eight-month siege and extensive use of dynamite, the Ndebele were forced from their mountain hide-out and surrendered. They were left with no land and the entire population was pressed into forced labour on Boer farms on the highveld.

ZULULAND

As was the case in the western Transvaal, Boer pastoralists on the south-east borders of Transvaal were also on the move in

286

search of grazing land. Their expansion into north-western Zululand along the upper Pongola valley was aided by the absence of organized Zulu resistance. This was a consequence of the British defeat of the Zulu in 1879. Not only had Britain inflicted a military defeat on the Zulu, but it had also disrupted their political system. Britain had dethroned Cetshwayo. This meant that there was no longer one undisputed King in Zululand.

Two major factions rivalled one another for power in Zululand. One was led by Cetshwayo, whom the British had allowed to return from exile in 1883; the other by Zibhebhu. In 1884 a civil war broke out between the two and Zibhebhu emerged victorious. Although Cetshwayo died soon after being defeated, his son Dinizulu continued the struggle. Dinizulu was too weak to overcome Zibhebhu by himself, and so he asked for help from Lucas Meyer and the white settlers in the Wakkerstroom/Utrecht areas. With their aid, Dinizulu was able to defeat Zibhebhu in August 1884. Meyer's Boers were paid for their assistance with large tracts of land. This land became the New Republic.

In 1884 German businessmen began showing an interest in Zululand. Britain became suspicious. It realised that it would lose the natural harbour of St Lucia should Germany annex the area. In addition the Boer republics would be provided with alternative access to the sea. This would break Britain's monopoly over South African shipping and trade.

The Boer presence in Zululand annoyed Natal's settlers. As in the case of Goshen and Stellaland, English settlers feared that the New Republic would interfere with their claims to Zulu labour and land which they believed to be their rightful heritage. They also felt that the New Republic barred the way to the eastern Transvaal goldfields and the central African interior. They therefore agitated for Britain to clamp down and restrict the Boer presence in Zululand. Before acting, Britain had to consider the position of the Zulu.

The 'native question' in Zululand

Sir Henry Bulwer, Governor of Natal, realized the importance of the 'native question'. Here is an extract taken from one of his memoranda, written in 1886.

The solution of the native question of Natal lies in Zululand; and I will go further and say that a solution for every native question in South East Africa lies through Zululand because of this area's links with the vast African continent beyond the region of European occupation.

Zululand is like a golden bridge that leads to a solution of the native questions of the future. But let this golden bridge be closed or destroyed, and there will remain pent up within our borders, unable to escape, the elements of burning questions which, for want of their natural outlet, must some day be kindled into flames in our very midst.

(Quoted in Guy, p. 234.)

The 'native question' was a term used to refer to African affairs, and particularly to the relationship between Africans and whites. When Bulwer talked of 'elements of burning questions' he was referring chiefly to Zulu independence, Zulu landholdings, and the need to prevent a recurrence of conflict in Zululand with the New Republic and the history of Zululand. Neither is there much evidence of a systematic British attempt to encircle the ZAR as such. The ultimate result of the episode was that the Zulu lost a huge amount of land to the burgers of the New Republic.

SWAZILAND

Transvaal Boers had been involved with the Kingdom of Swaziland for a long time. Since the 1840s, when they had tried to establish settlements at Ohrigstad and Lydenburg, they had negotiated with the Swazi, who were a force to be reckoned with in this area. The Boers and the Swazi frequently fought side by side against the Pedi, the other major power in the area. The decline of Pedi power coincided with the rise of the ZAR, so that by the 1880s the Boers were beginning to dictate to the Swazi. King Mbandzeni (1874–89) tried to avert conflict with the ZAR. His solution was to grant concessions which would bring him revenue, while pleasing the Boers at the same time.

In 1880 Mbandzeni began to grant concessions on a large scale to speculators, Boer and Briton alike, and by the time of his death had virtually signed away the entire wealth of his country. Mbandzeni's actions proved to be disastrous. He lost control of his country and failed to receive the anticipated financial benefits from the sale of concessions. Swaziland was invaded by prospectors and, though gold was discovered at Piggs Peak and Forbes Reef in 1884, the deposits were poor and the Swazi kingdom derived little benefit from them. To control the concessionaires, Mbandzeni employed Offy Shepstone. Offy was the son of Theophilus Shepstone who had long been in charge of 'native affairs' in Natal. The Swazi King's trust in Offy Shepstone was misplaced and the fortunes of the Swazi did not improve. Swaziland became an 'economic satellite and unofficial Protectorate of the ZAR', especially after the London

Questions

1. Why did Bulwer think that Zululand was the key to the solution of the 'native question' in the whole of Southern Africa?

2. Bulwer described Zululand as a 'golden bridge'. Why did he use this metaphor? Why did he use the colour 'gold'?

3. If the 'native question' in Zululand was not solved, what did Bulwer think would happen? What did he mean by a 'solution to the native question'?

Though defeated in the 1879 war, Zulu military power was still a force to be reckoned with.

The demands for land made by the New Republic on the Zulu were extremely harsh, and very likely to provoke a further period of hostilities in Zululand if they were not toned down by British intervention. (See Map 34.)

As a result of all these factors, Britain negotiated with the New Republic Boers in 1886. It succeeded in restricting their land claims to north-western Zululand. They were forced to drop their demands for land right up to the coast. In 1888 Britain allowed the ZAR to incorporate the New Republic.

Zulu interests were less well served. In 1887 the colony of British Zululand was created. The Zulu lost the last remnants of their political independence and came under the direct authority of the Governor of Natal. New laws were passed to control their activities and new taxes were levied. In 1897 Zululand became part of Natal.

The episode of the New Republic is sometimes interpreted as a defeat for Kruger as he attempted to break out of the British encircling manoeuvre. In fact Kruger himself had little to do

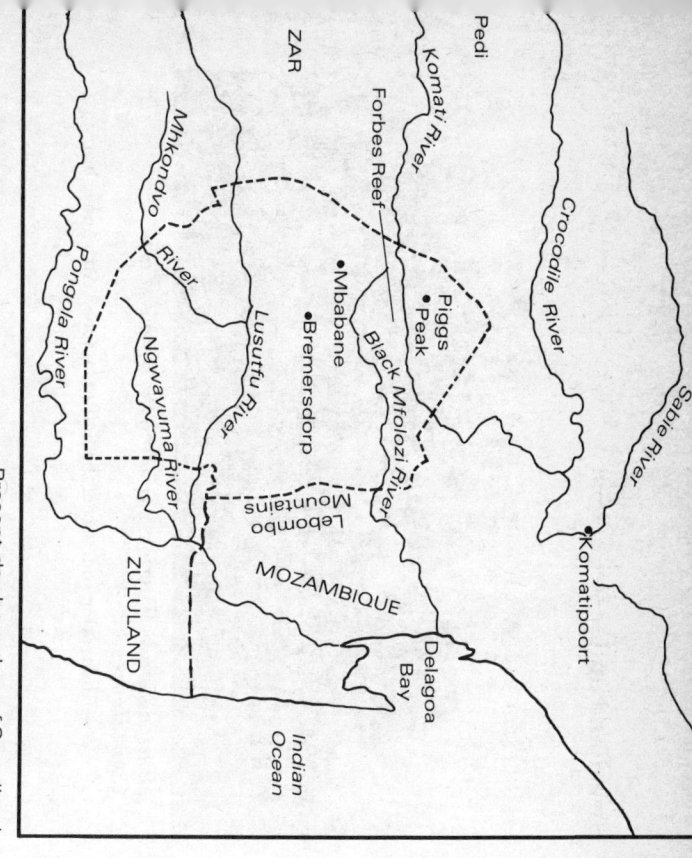

Map 35 — *Swaziland.*

---- Present-day boundary of Swaziland

Convention of 1881 which gave the ZAR 'a more or less free hand' in Swaziland.

The wealth of Swaziland itself was enough to keep Boer interest in the kingdom alive, but there was the added attraction of a possible route to the sea via the natural harbour of Sodwana Bay on the Tongaland coast. In 1887 Tongaland was annexed by Britain, thus ending Boer dreams of a port of their own. There was an alternative harbour on the east coast, namely Lourenço Marques in Delagoa Bay. In 1875 the French President, Macmahon, had settled a dispute between Britain and Portugal over the ownership of the port. Portugal had been declared the rightful owner.

The ZAR was keen to use the Lourenço Marques harbour in order to escape the British monopoly of sea trade. The ZAR and Mozambique shared a common border, and Delagoa Bay was not far from the border town of Komatipoort. The construction of a railway line to the coast could finally link the ZAR with the sea.

One of the most direct routes to Lourenço Marques was through Swaziland. In 1887 the ZAR negotiated a railway concession through Swaziland (p. 291). In 1894 the ZAR finally completed a railway to Delagoa Bay; but for a variety of reaons it went through Komatipoort, just to the north of the Swaziland border.

After the Anglo-Boer war the British occupied Swaziland. It was treated as an African reserve within the Transvaal. Lord Milner, Governor of the Transvaal, encouraged the settlement of English farmers in Swaziland. In 1906 Swaziland finally became a separate British colony ruled, like Basutoland and Bechuanaland, as a protectorate.

Swaziland concessions syndicate in Bremersdorp in 1891. This was the first business office in Swaziland.

(Illustration courtesy of the Killie Campbell Africana Library.)

Swaziland under siege, 1898

Swazi defiance. Warriors surround the Bremersdorp Court House.
(Illustration courtesy of the Killie Campbell Africana Library.)

White defences. Government offices in Bremersdorp sandbagged.
(Illustration courtesy of the Killie Campbell Africana Library.)

The decline of Swazi power

By 1888 Boers occupied and controlled land throughout Swaziland. In fact, they had virtual control over the economic life of Swaziland.

Mbandzeni seemed powerless to prevent the ZAR takeover. As a recent historian put it:

> Feeling his own life ebbing away from him, and his country slipping out of control, Mbandzeni seems quite simply to have given up.
>
> (Bonner, p. 189.)

In 1889 Mbandzeni died. A succession crisis developed and Britain, the ZAR and Offy Shepstone stepped in to prevent political disorder and violence.

In 1890, 1893 and 1894 a series of three Swaziland conventions decided the fate of Swaziland. Although Britain also cherished ambitions in Swaziland, it agreed to recognize the ZAR protectorate over the Swazi. Swazi objections lodged by the Queen Regent, Labotsibeni Mdluli, were ignored.

The ZAR's control of Swaziland gave it independent access to the sea. As we shall see later this was crucial in its campaign to sidestep the attempts of the Cape and Natal to monopolize sub-continental rail traffic. The ZAR's success was achieved at the expense of Swazi independence. In 1898 the added hardships imposed by the rinderpest epidemic brought Swaziland to the brink of rebellion. The arrival of a force under General Joubert silenced Swazi opposition and further reduced royal authority. Swazi rulers were as a result obliged to govern with the consent of the ZAR commissioner.

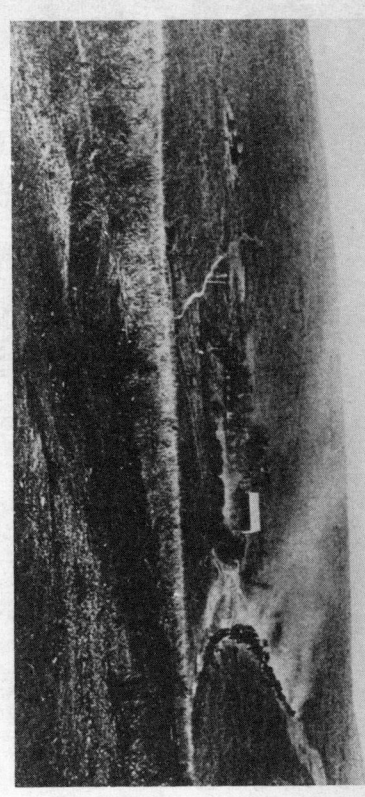

White reinforcements. General Joubert's column arrives (right-hand side of picture).
(Illustration courtesy of the Killie Campbell Africana Library.)

The Swazi railway concession

Although Offy Shepstone was employed by Mbandzeni to look after Swazi interests there were suspicions that he was involved in double-dealing.

The first hint of anything improper came to light in July 1887, when Offy secured a Swaziland railway concession for agents acting on behalf of the ZAR. Once this became public knowledge it gave rise to widespread speculation that Offy was acting in collusion with the ZAR, and this was further fuelled by a visit Shepstone made to Pretoria in November 1887. There was some truth behind these allegations. Shepstone had helped the ZAR to obtain an important concession, but he realised that this concession was largely worthless until the ZAR was able to exercise direct physical control over that part of Swaziland through which the railway was to pass. Offy therefore avoided becoming a tool of the ZAR. Although the ZAR made overtures for his services, he was careful not to sell himself completely. Instead, he kept a foot in both camps. On the one hand he pleased the ZAR by helping it get a railway concession. On the other, he retained Mbandzeni's trust by refusing to assist the ZAR in taking control of Swaziland and thereby converting the railway concession into a railway. In other words the concession remained a dead letter and Mbandzeni kept control of his kingdom.

Offy could not go on indefinitely in this manner. In 1888 Swaziland lost a border dispute to the Portuguese who claimed lands in the Lebombo mountains in eastern Swaziland. This proved fatal to Shepstone's political credibility. Not only had he failed to keep control of Swaziland's turbulent white population, and pocketed most of the king's revenues, but now he and his family had proved incapable of combating the feeblest imperialism of them all.

(Bonner, pp. 187–8.)

Questions

1. What was the first piece of evidence which suggested that Shepstone was double-dealing?
2. What was the second piece of evidence which suggested that Shepstone was double-dealing?
3. To what extent had Shepstone actually helped the ZAR?
4. To what extent had Shepstone protected the interests of Mbandzeni?
5. Explain the importance of the railway concession (a) for Shepstone, (b) for Mbandzeni, (c) for the ZAR.
6. What finally convinced Mbandzeni that Shepstone was not a very useful agent?

Boers found land difficult to acquire because of the activities of land companies. These companies bought large amounts of land in the hope of finding minerals, and for speculation purposes as well. They hoped to sell the land at a profit when prices rose. The factor that finally prompted Boer moves into Zimbabwe was the report of gold discoveries and the possibility of gaining permission from Lobengula to prospect and mine.

In 1887 Piet Grobler, an agent of the ZAR, succeeded in getting a treaty of friendship from Lobengula, but ZAR hopes of exploiting the mineral wealth of Zimbabwe came to nought. Grobler was killed while returning to the Transvaal and Rhodes succeeded in extracting the Rudd concession from Lobengula in 1889. This double blow prevented the ZAR from tapping Zimbabwe's mineral wealth.

In 1890 some Boers received a land concession from a Nyai chief. They saw this concession as giving them the right to establish a 'Republic of the North' beyond the Limpopo River, without fear of Ndebele aggression. Led by Bowler, they therefore planned to migrate into Zimbabwe. Their major aim was to secure grazing lands. Kruger restrained them in the hope of gaining British goodwill and thus consolidating his advantage in Swaziland.

THE SUBJUGATION OF THE LAST AFRICAN KINGDOMS

The discovery of gold on the Witwatersrand in 1886 not only swelled Republican coffers but also stimulated agriculture in the Transvaal. The growing Johannesburg population provided a large market for agricultural goods. Many Boers began to cultivate crops in order to meet the new demands. Agricultural success hinged on a sufficient supply of labour and internal political stability. Commercial farmers could not afford to be

---

7. What was the 'feeblest imperialism of them all'?

8. What reasons might Mbandzeni have had for employing Shepstone?

9. Do you think that Offy Shepstone helped the Swazi cause? Use evidence to back up your answer.

10. Refer back to the section on Swaziland. Explain how and why the ZAR became involved in the affairs of Swaziland.

11. Are there any similarities between the Rudd concession (1889) and the Swaziland railway concession (1887)?

NORTH OF THE LIMPOPO

We have already seen how Boers moved beyond the borders of the ZAR into the fringes of the Kalahari, into Zululand and Swaziland. In the case of the Tswana and the Zulu they had exploited divisions between African groups, and the Swazi, trying to avoid conflict, had given concessions.

In the north, however, the Ndebele were neither divided nor intimidated by the prospect of white expansion. Ndebele power was therefore a major deterrent to Boer expansion.

In the 1880s circumstances changed in such a way as to encourage Boer settlement north of the Limpopo. Within the ZAR itself, there was an increasingly urgent problem of land shortage for the growing white population. Much land in the northern Transvaal was occupied by the Lobedu and Venda who prevented Boers from taking farms there. In addition, many

constantly called out on commando, nor would they cultivate in areas that were still beyond the effective control of the ZAR. Thus it was that a number of campaigns were waged against chiefdoms in the northern Transvaal. Without exception these chiefdoms were defeated by General Joubert. Forced to pay taxes, many were then obliged to become labourers in order to earn sufficient to meet their tax commitments. In 1898 Mphephu, the Venda leader, became the last African King within the Transvaal area to lose his independence. He had refused to pay taxes to the Transvaal government. As a consequence he was attacked and fled across the Limpopo.

Armed peace in the Zoutpansberg

A state of armed peace and vigilance in the northern Transvaal around 1890. The original caption reads 'Iron fort and fortified residence of the Native Commissioner, Zoutpansberg District'.

(Illustration courtesy of the Killie Campbell Africana Library.)

CONCLUSION

The history of the ZAR has frequently been explained in terms of British encirclement. A recent South African schools' textbook, for example, claims that 'the [Boer] republics were encircled and their existence as independent states threatened'. This explanation suggests that (a) there was a systematic British policy to isolate the Transvaal, and further (b) that Rhodes and Kruger were the people who, alone, decided the destiny of the ZAR. In other words, it is suggested that some grand design* or master-plan was at work. Although few would deny that Kruger and Rhodes were important figures in their times, we should be careful not to attribute them with super-human ability and extraordinary powers of perception.

ZAR politics should not be seen as the design of one man — Kruger; nor should the history of the period be reduced to the British encirclement of the Transvaal. As we have seen, these themes only tell part of the story.

This section has shown that relationships with neighbouring African kingdoms were crucial in shaping the history of the ZAR. It has also attempted to demonstrate that ZAR Boers were not simply the unthinking puppets or representatives of Kruger. These Boers were burgers of the ZAR, but they were also self-interested farmers trying to make a living. Only when we appreciate this economic factor and place proper emphasis on local circumstances can we fully understand the history of this period.

Africans within white-ruled Southern Africa

So far we have looked at the way in which independent African kingdoms were affected by Britain, the British colonies of Southern Africa and the ZAR. We have not yet examined the economic and political changes that took place in African societies that had been defeated and incorporated earlier on and were situated within white-ruled Southern Africa. These changes were profound and were accelerated by the mineral revolution. Africans responded to the change in economic climate in two major ways. Increasing numbers became migrant workers. Many others supplied the growing markets with vegetables and cereals, especially maize. Others remained subsistence farmers, though taxes and declining agricultural productivity in the areas of land that remained for African occupation in time forced most of them into the labour market as well.

MIGRANT LABOUR

Migrant labour is today a well-established and important aspect of the South African economy. It had its origins in the early 1800s when both Xhosa and Pedi men sought agricultural labour on white-owned farms. (See also Chapter 7.) Initially this form of labour was a voluntary act on the part of the migrant. He hoped to earn enough to either buy consumer goods, pay *lobola* (bride price paid by husband to wife's family) or obtain guns which were otherwise very difficult to get. In time many others were forced to become migrant labourers by the levying of taxes by the Trekker republics and the colonies, and by the loss of land and devastation wrought by war and stock diseases. This process was speeded up by the discovery of minerals because mining required much cheap labour. The mineowners searched far and wide for labour. They established recruiting agencies in the rural areas which forwarded labourers to the mines.

PEASANT FARMING

Subsistence agriculture. Here women and children hoe a field. The work is done by large groups rather than individuals. This is called communal agriculture.

(Illustration courtesy of the Killie Campbell Africana Library.)

While the number of migrant labourers rose steadily, there were still many who earned a good living by peasant farming (see Chapter 7 for further information). African cultivators had long conducted a flourishing trade amongst their own communities and were therefore quick to respond to the opening-up of the colonial market. Among the first to do so were the Mfengu in the eastern Cape and Transkei in the 1830s and 1840s. As the local market in South Africa grew, more and more subsistence farmers began to aim their agricultural production towards the urban markets. After the discovery of diamonds and gold, this process accelerated. White farmers were also

A sharecropper speaks

Until recently it has been difficult to reconstruct the lives of peasant farmers in South Africa. They left little in the way of written records. The collection of oral history has made possible the reconstruction of this history. By interviewing old people it is possible to get a good idea of how peasant farmers lived.

The extract below comes from Nkgono (grandmother) Mma-Pooe, who was interviewed in 1979 when she was 99 years old. As a child in the late Nineteenth Century she lived with her parents on a white farm in the OFS.

Pooe. *I know about the disease* [rinderpest]. *I remember precisely that many cattle died.*

Interviewer: *Did you eat the meat of these dead cattle?*
P. No.
I. *Did you have cattle in your household at that point in time?*
P. Yes! *My father had cattle. He and many others did keep cattle. I still remember the period when the disease was rampaging through the area. We would wake up in the morning to find some of our oxen had fallen headlong and stone dead in the kraal manure ... My father started sharecropping. His eldest brother, Rankwe, continued to farm on a small piece of the farm Rietfontein which he rented from the white owner. Rankwe argued that he wouldn't go to settle on a farm where he would work so hard to cultivate the lands to produce a lot of crops that he would have to share with the white man, 'a Boer!' He disagreed completely with my father.*

My father, on the other hand, felt very strongly about leaving Rietfontein. He said that like many others he was going to take a chance at sharecropping. 'Even though there are not enough oxen to pull the plough, I am going to.' It was a bad time. The rains had failed and many people at Rietfontein had not even ploughed.

It was a lot of work to cultivate the soil and handle the harvest and that was not to be taken lightly—'to share your full harvest with a Boer!' That Rankwe wouldn't do. He advised my father to look for another farm to rent if he could no longer stay at Rietfontein and grow his own crops.

(Matsetela pp. 2–5–8.)

Questions

1. Make a list of the difficulties that African farmers encountered.

2. Describe the impact of rinderpest on the African economy. Check on p. 281 for further information.

3. What were the two brothers arguing about?

4. Outline the argument for and against becoming a sharecropper.

5. Do you think oral testimony is a good source of historical information? What advantages and disadvantages does it have?

295

producing for this market and they resented African competition. In addition white farmers required farm labour but African families who were self-sufficient could afford not to enter wage employment. A labour shortage developed.

All the white governments in Southern Africa reacted to the shortage of labour by passing anti-squatting legislation. A squatter was an African peasant farmer who lived on a white farm. Squatters would either pay rent to the landowner or would be required to provide labour for the landowner at certain times of the year. Alternatively he might be a sharecropper* who would farm the land and give the owner a percentage (a share) of the crop. These new laws were designed to force African families into purely wage employment on white farms. The laws also limited the number of Africans allowed to reside on any one farm. Those who lacked permission to remain on a farm were forced to seek work elsewhere. This legislation was the predecessor to the 1913 Natives Land Act and later segregationist apartheid laws.

THE GLEN GREY ACT: 1894

One of the best known of the Acts which attempted to change the lives of African peasants was the Glen Grey Act of 1894. This was an Act passed in the Cape Parliament by Rhodes' government. It proposed to introduce individual land tenure for Africans to replace their communal or tribal tenure system in certain areas. The traditional African system had ensured that all would be provided with land and a means of subsistence. Individual tenure — where small plots of land would belong to individuals — involved the danger that many might be unable to afford land. Alternatively since there was a restricted amount of land, children of succeeding generations might find themselves without plots. For these people there would be little option other than to become migrant workers, and indeed this is what Rhodes had in mind when he proposed the bill. He said:

> *Every black man cannot have three acres and a cow ... it must be brought home to them that in future nine-tenths will have to spend their lives in daily labour.*
>
> (Quoted in Parsons p. 184.)

A further aspect of the individual land tenure provided for by the Act, was that it prevented Africans from owning more than one plot. This was intended to prevent progressive peasants from expanding their operations.

In addition to the land reforms, there was a labour tax which also aimed at 'forcing out' labour. Such was the resistance to these measures that the labour tax was dropped and only in the Glen Grey (now the Cala district of Transkei) district itself was the new individual form of land tenure applied.

REACTIONS

Defiance in Pondoland

Africans opposed the measures taken against them on a wide scale. There was some peaceful resistance. Some Africans hid from tax collectors, ignored instructions or simply moved away from areas where laws were being enforced against them. In many cases, however, there was open confrontation.

The Mpondo were the last chiefdom on the east coast to remain independent. Cape rule had steadily been extended from the south for nearly two centuries. Nine wars had been fought between the Xhosa and the British government on the eastern

296

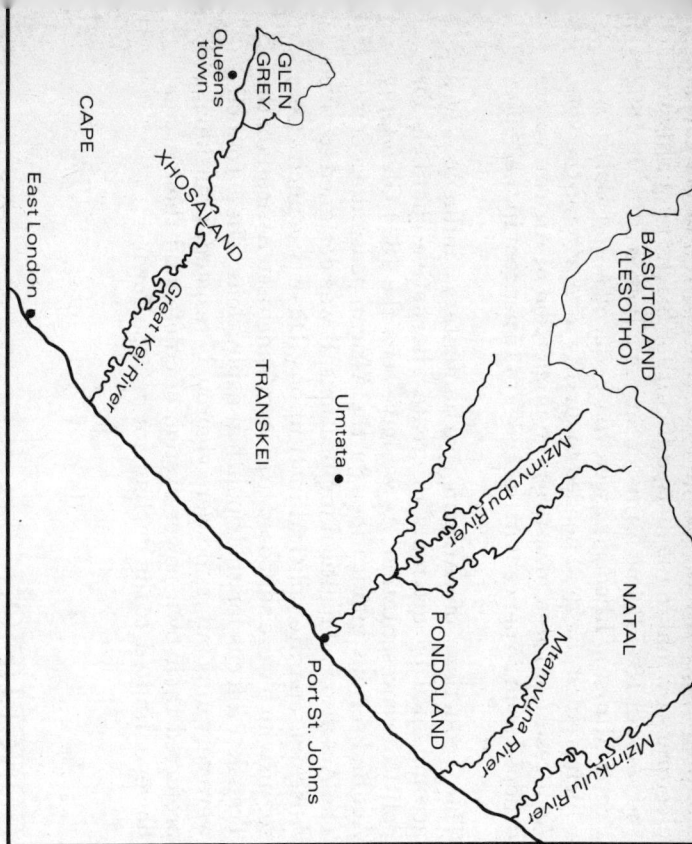

Map 36 — *Pondoland and Transkei.*

frontier. The most recent war had ended in 1878. As a result of these wars, Xhosaland was conquered and annexed to the Cape. Cape rule was not popular in the Transkei and a rebellion broke out against colonial rule in 1880. The rising did not spread to neighbouring Pondoland where a British agent had been stationed in 1878. Nevertheless the Mpondo were also unhappy about the prospect of falling under British or Cape rule. They were resentful of Cape customs duties which restricted their trade. They responded to this by levying duties on the passing wagons and by seeking the support of local white traders who feared that Cape rule might jeopardize their positions. When these tactics failed, the Mpondo chief, Mhlangaso, approached German agents for aid in 1885. The British were nervous about German involvement, especially after their recent annexation of Namibia and their involvement in Zululand. They therefore proclaimed an imperial protectorate over the Pondoland coastline. This served two functions: it warned off the Germans; and it prepared the way for stepped-up colonial involvement in the area. The Mpondo decided to resist these British moves and in 1886 mobilized an army of 15 000. Faced with superior military power, the Mpondo eventually backed down. Both the extension of informal colonial control into Pondoland and the activities of the Cape traders served to undermine the power of the chief and to limit the ability of the Mpondo to control their economy and remain independent.

Pondoland remained tense and in 1891 a civil war broke out between rival chiefs, Sigcau and Mhlangaso. Sigcau wanted a conciliatory policy with the Cape whereas Mhlangaso did not. Fearing that its power would be challenged, the Cape intervened and annexed Pondoland in 1894. The Mpondo were henceforth subject to the policies of the Cape Colony.

Resistance in the Langeberg

The western Tswana, including the Tlhaping, had been subjected to colonial rule in the 1880s (see p. 275). This experience had not been a happy one as they had lost much land and many cattle in the process. In 1896 rinderpest, a devastating cattle disease, began to afflict their area. Cape officials shot large numbers of Tlhaping cattle, arguing that this was necessary in order to prevent the spread of the disease to the herds of the white farmers.

297

This infuriated the chiefs Phetlu and Galishiwe, who led their people in rebellion. They were joined by other groups in the area.

They took up positions in the Langeberg mountain range, the site of earlier battles in the war of 1878–9. They were besieged and defeated by a force of settlers and Cape soldiers. Phetlu was executed and Galishiwe imprisoned on Robben Island. The rebels who were captured were distributed as forced labour amongst local white farmers.

AFRICANS AND THE FRANCHISE

Many African kingdoms when they lost their autonomy, looked for ways of replacing their political structures which had been destroyed. They wanted some form of political representation. Most white settlers were strongly opposed to sharing power with blacks. Blacks, they believed, should be held in positions of subservience so that they could serve the needs of South Africa's white population.

The Boer republics had no black voters at all. Natal had virtually none, but in the Cape, where the structures of political representation had had time to develop and mature, some blacks were allowed to vote. Blacks in the Cape had been under white rule for over two hundred years and they had, during that time, successfully appealed for some political rights. A system of qualified franchise was in operation which allowed all men who earned a particular amount or who owned a certain extent of land to vote. As Cape Africans began to enter commercial farming on a large scale, many qualified for the vote. This alarmed Cape parliamentarians who feared the influence of black voters. In 1886, Prime Minister Upington's administration attempted to slow the growth of the black electorate by making it more difficult for blacks to qualify for the vote. In 1887 Prime Minister Sprigg followed suite. In 1892 Prime Minister Rhodes passed his Franchise and Ballot Act which trebled the land needed to qualify a person for the vote. As a result of these measures the proportion of African voters dropped from 25 per cent in the 1880s to 15 per cent in the 1890s.

The reduction of African parliamentary influence was accompanied by attempts to create alternative channels for political representation. As we have seen the 1894 Glen Grey Act had serious implications for the African peasant economy. The Act also had political implications. It was designed to give Africans separate political institutions. District councils were set up which were supposed to give enfranchised Africans of the Transkei a focus for their political aspirations. These councils were very unpopular and were vigorously resisted. Transkeians preferred their own power system of chiefs, and their access, however limited, to the Parliament in Cape Town.

CONCLUSION

In the late Nineteenth Century there were still signs of African prosperity and progress in Southern Africa. Peasants continued to supply a large proportion of South Africa's agricultural needs, and the numbers of educated and professional Africans began to swell. There were also, on the other hand, disturbing developments that threatened African advancement.

Reserves were created in the rural areas. These were zoned for tribal inhabitation. They were far from markets, cities and major transport routes. Some were already becoming overcrowded by the end of the Nineteenth Century and signs were present that, far from being able to support the African population, the reserves would soon become poverty-stricken.

Many Africans were already feeling the strains of being tied to the land and some of them headed for the cities. Here they tried to find permanent jobs and homes. Some were unsuccessful and after living in the cities for a short time were forced back into the rural areas. Some Africans had no intention of settling in the cities — these were the migrant labourers who returned to their homes in the countryside when they had completed their contracts on the mines. City life was not easy for either permanent urban dwellers or migrants. Laws were passed to restrict them and most were prevented from settling down permanently to an urban life.

Africans who had chosen to fight the intrusion of white power soon discovered the uselessness of armed resistance. The settlers' technological military superiority condemned uprisings to failure. Other ways of resolving the problems which plagued their lives were explored. The vote became a source of hope for many blacks. Although only a few Cape blacks enjoyed the vote, blacks elsewhere in South Africa strived optimistically for the extension of the franchise. A later section will take up the story of African hopes, and disappointments.

Britain, the Boer republics and the making of a war

The relations between Britain and the Cape, on the one hand, and the ZAR on the other, had not been very cordial since the First Anglo-Boer War (1881–2). There had been disagreements over Goshen and Stellaland (1884–5), the New Republic (1884), Rhodesia (1887–90) and Swaziland. In the 1890s, the gold mines were the source of tension. Although the mines were inside the ZAR, they were owned mainly by British capitalists. A dispute therefore developed over the distribution of mine profits.

Gold had been discovered in 1886. The socio-economic results of this have been explored in Chapter 7. It remains for us to investigate how the discovery affected relations between the British colonies and the ZAR.

GOVERNING THE GOLD-FIELDS: CLASHING OPINIONS

Gold mining required vast capital resources. The business men who had the resources and invested in the Transvaal included Lionel Phillips, Alfred Beit and Cecil John Rhodes. Known as 'Randlords', these men expected government support for their undertakings. President Kruger's government was not always able to please the Randlords. It must be remembered that the ZAR was still essentially a poorly developed state, capable of handling a pastoral economy and little else. The ZAR

299

nevertheless passed labour legislation to help the mines control their labourers. The provision of certain services, on which the mines relied, often proved to be impossible for the ZAR government. Such services were made the responsibility of private contractors who were granted concessions*. In this way, for example, railway transport and the supply of dynamite came to be monopolized by Boer businessmen. This system tended to benefit the contractors more than it did the mines. Indeed, the dynamite concession, held by Lippert, was estimated to cost the mines £600 000 a year.

As far as the majority of Randlords was concerned, the government of the ZAR was in many ways unsatisfactory. Government policy inflated mining costs. The ZAR administration, they said, was inefficient and corrupt, and this meant the support they required to make mining profitable was not always present. In addition they begrudged the ZAR the taxes levied to finance agriculture and government. Finally they felt threatened by the existence of a hostile press in the ZAR. The newspaper, *Standard and Diggers News*, for example, stirred up the passions of white miners against the Randlords. The Randlords therefore wanted a sympathetic government installed which would respond to their requests.

Kruger was in two minds about the mines. On the one hand they provided badly needed income, but on the other, the influx of foreigners (uitlanders) and the activities of powerful capitalists threatened the existence of an Afrikaner republic.

For a long time Britain had been trying to form a federation in South Africa. These plans necessarily hinged on the inclusion of the Transvaal. When gold was discovered, Britain was tempted to renew its plans for unity because the precious metal could be used to finance federation. Britain also feared that Transvaal gold might fund an anti-British federation. This possibility made Britain's task all the more urgent.

THE 'RAILWAY WAR'

The job of integrating the Transvaal into a British-dominated, capitalist economy system was initially undertaken by the Randlords. Their attempts to mould the Transvaal into a mineowners' paradise were, however, resisted by the ZAR government. Disagreements between the Randlords and the ZAR government came to a head over railway policy. The ZAR was anxious to make profits from the transport business that grew out of the mining industry. In addition it was still committed to finding an independent route to the coast. It fused

The first railway under construction in the Transvaal, 1888.
(Illustration courtesy of the Killie Campbell Africana Library.)

these goals with its plan to construct a railway line to Lourenço Marques.

The ZAR was short of capital for the venture so it gave a monopoly on railways in the ZAR to German and Dutch contractors who in 1887 founded the Netherlands South African Railway Company (N.Z.A.S.M.). (The company was later to be known disparagingly as 'No Zeal and Slow Motion'.) At the same time, however, railway lines to Johannesburg were being built from the British colonial ports of Cape Town, Port Elizabeth and Durban.

Kruger prevented the Cape railways from reaching the Rand by refusing to allow them to cross the Vaal River. In 1892 mounting Randlord pressure prevailed on Kruger to consent to the Cape line being extended to Johannesburg.

In 1894 the Lourenço Marques line was finally completed. The line had been very expensive to build and the N.Z.A.S.M. sought to make good its losses by charging high rates. Since the N.Z.A.S.M. had a monopoly of the railways in the ZAR it was able to charge very high prices for the 64km section of line linking the Cape route to the Rand. The point of this was to force rail traffic to use the N.Z.A.S.M.'s own line through Lourenço Marques rather than the Cape routes.

The Randlords reacted angrily to the new policy by transporting goods from the Vaal River to the Rand by wagon to avoid the inflated rail charges. Indignant at this defiance, Kruger 'closed the drifts'. In other words, he tried to force all traffic to use expensive railway transport within the ZAR by preventing wagon traffic across the Vaal River. This action was condemned by the Cape, Britain and even the OFS, and the ZAR was forced to back down.

Tension: Randlords versus Republicans

The 'drifts crisis' was just one of the clashes between Kruger and the Randlords in a series of developments that increased tension on the Rand.

In 1892 the Transvaal National Union (T.N.U.) was formed. It represented many of the Randlords and the wealthy Uitlanders, rather than the ordinary white miners who made up the bulk of the Uitlander population. The T.N.U. set itself the task of improving conditions for Uitlanders. Its members, who would ordinarily have exercised influence in government, felt their exclusion from administrative and policy matters in the ZAR was unjust. They agitated by constitutional means, petitions and gatherings, to remove President Kruger from office as they saw him as their major opponent.

By 1895 the T.N.U had attracted the active support of Britain. Lord Loch, British High Commissioner, visited Pretoria in June of that year to investigate T.N.U. grievances. Kruger interpreted Loch's trip as active British support for the T.N.U. In December 1895, Charles Leonard, a Johannesburg advocate and the chairman of the T.N.U., distributed a document called the 'Uitlander Manifesto' which set out their grievances. Within a month the Jameson Raid was launched to overthrow the ZAR government.

THE QUESTION OF CUSTOMS DUTIES

The question of customs duties had been an issue in South African politics since 1885 when Kruger had approached the Cape to form a customs union. Customs duties are an important source of revenue. Countries with ports generally levy charges

301

THE JAMESON RAID

The Raid was launched from the Bechuanaland village of Pitsani by a force led by Dr Leander Jameson, the administrator of the British South African Company. The force was made up of B.S.A.C. police and began its raid on 29 December 1895. The raid was supposed to coincide with an Uitlander rising in Johannesburg. This never materialized. When news of the invading force was received, the ZAR government reacted swiftly, and it was defeated on 2 January 1896 at Doornkop near present-day Roodepoort. The Johannesburg conspirators were arrested and four, including Sir Lionel Phillips of the Corner House mining group, received the death sentence. Kruger wanted to avoid British hostility and so wisely commuted these sentences to fines of £25 000, which were paid by Rhodes. In addition, Kruger elected to hand over most of the rebels to the Cape for trial, where they received light sentences.

Dr Leander Jameson
(Illustration courtesy of the Killie Campbell Africana Library.)

(customs duties) on foreign cargoes to raise funds. They also impose these duties in order to control imports so that new or struggling industries can be protected from foreign competition. The inland states of the ZAR and OFS wanted a share of the customs duties but these were initially denied to them. From 1886 onward gold provided the ZAR with a reliable source of money and so it held aloof from the customs debate from this point on.

The Cape, Natal and the OFS continued to disagree and so in 1888 a customs conference was held in Cape Town. This resulted in a customs union being formed between the OFS and the Cape in 1889. The OFS would now get some of the duty charged on goods imported through Cape ports. The OFS had close economic ties with the Cape, especially since the opening of the Kimberley diamond mines, and this led to the joint action with the Cape.

When Rhodes became Prime Minister of the Cape in 1890, he believed that a customs union was a good way of bringing about a Cape or British-dominated federation. We have already seen (in Chapter 1) how the German Zollverein helped German unification in the 1860s, and Rhodes might have thought that something similar was possible in South Africa. His major target was the ZAR, but the now wealthy republic rejected all suggestions of a national customs union.

In 1892 the ZAR began taxing British imports heavily in order to protect its own industries. This step made Cape agricultural goods more expensive on the Rand markets and this angered Cape farmers, including members of the Afrikaner Bond which had previously been sympathetic to the ZAR.

Jameson Raid prisoners waiting at Volksrust for rail transport to take them to the Cape.

(Illustration courtesy of the Killie Campbell Africana Library.)

There has been much debate surrounding the Raid. Two major questions that have concerned historians have been:

1. Did the British government know about and support the Raid?
2. Why were the Randlords divided on this issue? Some supported the Raid but others believed it to be misguided and unjustified.

Research has shown conclusively that Joseph Chamberlain, Britain's Secretary for Colonies, knew about and secretly gave permission for the Raid. (See box.) At the time, however, loyal British commentators were outraged at suggestions that Britain helped engineer the raid. One commentator wrote:

Mr. Chamberlain has pledged his word of honour and has sworn upon oath that he knew nothing of the Raid ... but even so members of the public have with evil spirit attributed the most selfish and the most sordid* motives to Mr. Chamberlain's actions.

(Iwan-Muller, pp. 373–4.)

Joseph Chamberlain and the Jameson Raid

In 1961, J. S. Marais' book *The Fall of Kruger's Republic* appeared. The book was significant because it proved beyond doubt that Chamberlain had played a part in the Jameson Raid.

There are three counts in the indictment against Chamberlain. The first charge is that although aware that Rhodes, Prime Minister of the Cape Colony and managing director of the B.S.A. company, was playing a principal part in the Johannesburg insurrectionary* movement against the government of the ZAR and that such action on Rhodes's part constituted a breach of international good conduct, Chamberlain not only did nothing to stop him (as was his duty as British representative in South Africa) but actually collaborated with him to the extent of giving him advice as to the date of the rising. The second charge is that he intervened before the rising took place, in order to ensure that the British flag would be hoisted in the Transvaal. He also envisaged dictating a settlement which involved the immediate termination of Boer control of the ZAR. This would probably have provoked war. The third and final charge is that Chamberlain was aware that Rhodes wanted to secure an immediate transfer of the borderlands of the Bechuanaland Protectorate to the B.S.A. company to allow Jameson to launch the raid from Pitsani. Chamberlain went so far as to facilitate the transfer of the territory in question, as well as a portion of the territory's police. He then deliberately left Rhodes a free hand to use his troops as he thought fit in support of the Johannesburg rising. Chamberlain denied these charges on oath before the committee of the House of Commons. I have shown that Chamberlain's word was worthless.

(Marais, p. 94.)

303

owners mined at great depths. They required expensive machinery to mine successfully. Other mineowners worked at the surface. They mined the outcrops and this was a much cheaper way of extracting gold. The Australian historian, Blainey, found that the Randlords like Phillips and Rhodes who owned deep-level mines were the main conspirators. The Randlords with outcrop interests like Joseph Robinson remained aloof from the Raid.

Deep-level mineowners had reason to otherthrow the ZAR government. Inefficient government on the part of the ZAR threatened their finely balanced profits more than it did the outcrop mineowners whose operations were much cheaper to run.

The deep-level mines were expected to yield gold over a long period. This expectation alone justified the heavy expense of deep-level mining. The deep-level Randlords were uncertain about the future of their mines as long as the ZAR remained independent. They were therefore tempted to safeguard their long-term prospects by overthrowing the ZAR and helping to install a sympathetic (British) government. The outcrop mines on the other hand had limited lifespans and their owners were consequently less inclined to act against the ZAR.

The second school of historians places less emphasis on economic factors. They prefer to stress political factors (for example, political party allegiance), in explaining the divisions within the mining industry. They have shown that divisions amongst the Randlords were not as simple or as clear-cut as the historians of the opposing camp made them out to be.

The importance of the Raid is that it showed how willing at least some of the Randlords were to resort to a violent overthrow of the Republic. The Raid also showed how closely the British government was prepared to work with them. This working relationship continued even after Rhodes's resignation as Prime Minister of the Cape in 1896. The failure of the Raid signalled the return of Britain to the political arena in Southern

Questions

1. *What part did Rhodes play in the Raid?*
2. *How did the village of Pitsani feature in the history of the Raid?*
3. *What was the role of the B.S.A.C. in the Raid?*
4. *What was the 'Johannesburg rising' to which Marais refers?*
5. *Compare the view of Iwan-Muller (p. 303) with the findings of Marais on Chamberlain's part in the Raid. Comment on the viewpoint of each.*
6. *What advantage did Chamberlain hope Britain would gain from the Raid?*
7. *Why do you think Chamberlain tried to hide British involvement in the Raid?*
8. *Could the Jameson Raid have been launched without the help of Chamberlain? (Your answer should include details of Chamberlain's involvement in setting up the Raid.)*

Why were the Randlords divided?

Historians still disagree about reasons for the division of Randlords. These historians can be roughly divided into two camps.

The first camp holds that different economic interests separated the Randlords. Their argument goes as follows: Some mine-

Africa. After the failure of Carnarvon's federation plans, Britain had retreated into the background, but the defeat of Jameson once again brought the imperial factor to the forefront of politics in Southern Africa.

THE UITLANDERS

Despite the failure of the Jameson Raid, and the removal of many of the chief enemies of the Kruger regime from the ZAR, agitation did not come to an end. Now, instead of the Randlords leading the condemnation of the ZAR, Britain took over. One of the causes which Britain championed was that of the Uitlanders (literally, those from outside the land).

Uitlanders, as we have mentioned before, were foreigners living in the Transvaal. They have often been cited as a major cause of the Anglo-Boer War which broke out in 1899. Recently, however, this view has been questioned. Uitlanders in Johannesburg were not without complaint but on the whole many were satisfied with conditions. One contemporary observer wrote:

As for general liberty and even licence of conduct, it existed nowhere if not in Johannesburg. Every luxury of life, every extravagance of behaviour, every form of private vice flourished unchecked; every man and woman ... said and did what seemed good in his or her own eyes ... The entire wealth of the country, drawn from the bowels of the earth by ... [black] labour, passed easily into his hands, with the exception of a toll taken by the Government, which he resented as if it were the fruits of the toil of his own hands; in a land of simple mannered, plain-living farmers he alone had material luxury and the leisure to enjoy it.

(T.C. Caldwell quoted in Robinson, p. 39).

It is frequently suggested that the Uitlander demand for political representation was a major grievance and source of irritation. To qualify for the vote in the ZAR, Uitlanders had to be over 40 years old and have resided fourteen years in the Transvaal. It was thus extremely difficult to become a voter. Although much has been made of this burden, it needs to be seen in perspective. Sir Lionel Phillips for example, said: 'As for the franchise, few of us care a fig for it.'

The strict franchise regulations were formulated by the ZAR to ward off the possibility of the burgers being swamped by Uitlanders. In effect, however, Kruger was not antagonistic to the Uitlanders and many Uitlanders believed they had more in common with the Boers than the Randlords.

PRELUDE TO WAR

Between 1896 and 1899 war fever was drummed up in the Cape. Lord Alfred Milner, who became Governor of the Cape and High Commissioner of South Africa in 1897, was partially responsible for this. Milner was an imperialist who believed that it was necessary for the ZAR to become a British colony if the interests of Britain were to be secured. The difficulty facing Milner was to manufacture convincing reasons for war.

The most popular tool used by Milner to create a climate of war was the Uitlander question. He frequently criticized the terrible conditions of the Uitlanders, even though these were not nearly as bad as he made them out to be. In his famous 'Helot* telegram' of May 1899, Milner set out his views on the inevitability of war.

305

'Squealing and Squeezing'

A. Colonial Secretary   B. High Commissioner 1897

Mr Chamberlain and Sir Alfred Milner: *Why do you keep on squealing 'Suzerainty'?*
Kruger (Brer Rabbit): *I can't help squealing, you squeeze me so hard!*

(*Westminster Gazette,* 9 September 1899.)

Questions

1. Why are Chamberlain and Milner 'squeezing' Kruger?
2. How in practice did Chamberlain and Milner 'squeeze' Kruger?
3. Why is Kruger depicted as squealing 'suzerainty'?

The spectacle of thousands of British subjects kept permanently in the position of helots, constantly chafing under undoubted grievances, and calling vainly to Her Majesty's Government for redress, does steadily undermine the influence and reputation of Great Britain and the respect for the British Government within its own dominions.

(Milner, quoted in Robinson, p. 37.)

Suzerainty was another of the issues exploited by Milner to engineer a war. Suzerainty is a vague term implying that one power has influence over another which is recognized by the latter. Milner's argument rested on the interpretation of the Pretoria and London Conventions of 1881 and 1884. In the 1884 Convention Britain had not renewed her suzerainty claim over the ZAR, although Milner claimed that Britain still in effect had the right to dictate to the ZAR in certain matters.

Milner also criticized the ZAR government and suggested that its inefficiency severely jeopardized the profitability of the gold mines. He alleged that the ZAR was aggressive and a threat to peace. Indeed the ZAR had begun to arm on a massive scale. By 1896 it was spending £500 000 a year on French and German arms. Milner also played on fears of German involvement. The Kaizer had congratulated Kruger on defeating the Jameson Raiders and this irked Britain. In addition German capital and the presence of 15 000 German nationals in the ZAR gave some credibility to these claims. In 1898, however, Britain and Germany came to an agreement over British paramountcy in south-east Africa. From then on the chance of active German involvement seems to have been remote. (See p. 307.)

As the prospects of war grew, Kruger attempted to defuse the situation. He met Milner in Bloemfontein and offered to make it much easier for Uitlanders to get the vote. Milner stood firm and

'My friend the Kaizer'

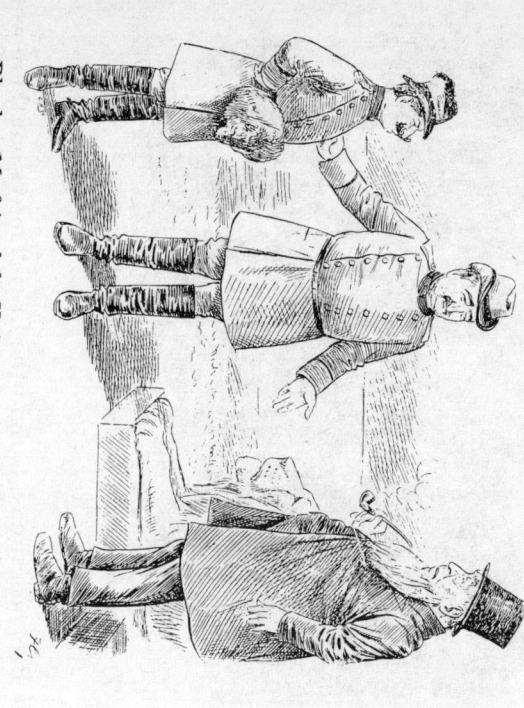

Rhodes: *My friend the Kaizer.*
Kruger: *'Your friend! I thought he was mine.'*

(*Westminster Gazette*, 16 March 1899.)

In March 1899 Rhodes visited Kaizer Wilhelm II of Germany in Berlin. This was the first sign that the Kaizer was changing heart. The Kaizer subsequently met with his great-aunt, Queen Victoria, and Chamberlain, and agreed not to actively support the ZAR in the event of a war. This cartoon shows Kruger's disappointment at being deprived of a potential ally.

refused to accept these offers. Kruger complained of the aggressiveness of Britain.

> Imagine that a man has given his blood and his substance for a farm, and says to someone else — you can come and live on my farm as a squatter and make a profit from it. But if this bijwoner now starts to declare that he has the same rights to the farm as the owner; then, if this matter were brought before a court, the verdict could never be given in favour of the bijwoner....Now this farm is all that we have left of what our forefathers inherited.
> The stranger comes here to make his profit, and would it be right to hand over to him the voortrekker's rights of ownership?

(Kruger, quoted in Robinson, p. 46.)

Negotiations finally broke down, and war broke out on 11 October 1899.

THE END OF AN ERA

The period 1880–1900 was crucial in South African history. The most obvious changes in this period were wrought by the mining revolution. Industrialization began and wealthy capitalists and penniless miners alike flocked to the mine city of Johannesburg.

The effects of mining also spread beyond Johannesburg. African kingdoms that had maintained a tenuous independence were enveloped by the new developments. Before, members of those kingdoms had been economically self-sufficient and had entered wage labour voluntarily. Now the massive demands for mine labour placed new stresses on them. The colonial quest for land and minerals added further to the pressures on these kingdoms. Finally, Britain attempted to bring the whole of the sub-

307

Three generations in the Boer army, 1900.

continent directly under its control, while white settlers supported moves to complete the subjugation of Africans.

The downfall of the African kingdoms coincided with the rise of a powerful capitalist class. The Randlords became not only wealthy but extremely influential. For much of this period they took over from Britain in promoting the colonial cause. It was only their failure in the Jameson Raid that ushered in the imperial factor once again and created the conditions for a South African war.

The richest gold mines in the world were situated in the ZAR and it was this Boer Republic that appeared most likely to be the major benefactor of the discovery. Virtually penniless in 1877 when it was annexed by Britain, the ZAR twenty years later was the most powerful state in southern Africa. It had stabilized its internal position and expanded its territory at the expense of independent African kingdoms. It then faced an even greater challenge as the Randlords attempted to disrupt its new-found political stability. Britain openly supported the mining interest because it feared the emergence of a powerful Republican bloc in South Africa. The polarization of forces led to war in 1899. (See pp. 310–11.)

THE ANGLO-BOER WAR AND THE PEACE OF VEREENIGING

By the beginning of 1902 it was becoming clear that the prospects of an ultimate Boer victory were slight and receding with every passing day. Thousands of British soldiers were engaged in destroying Boer farm houses, rounding up cattle and imprisoning women and children in concentration camps. There they would no longer be able to help the Boer war effort.

The Boers continued to fight the British forces but there were some who felt there was more to be gained by siding with the British. They joined units like the National Scouts* and fought against their former comrades. They became known as *hensoppers* (hands-uppers). They were generally quite poor and switched sides in the hope of some reward in the event of a British victory. On the other hand, many Boers who owned farms thought they would lose them if they were defeated. Those who believed defeat would be disastrous were called *Bittereinders**, because they were prepared to fight until the end. President Steyn of the OFS, who favoured continued resistance, led the Bittereinders. In April 1902 the Boers met in Klerksdorp to discuss surrendering. Many still wanted to fight, but Generals Jan Smuts and Louis Botha argued that nothing would be gained from this. They won over Generals J. B. M.

Hertzog and C. de Wet to their way of thinking and this paved the way for the Peace of Vereeniging on 31 May 1902.

At Vereeniging the Boers surrendered. They lost their independence and had to acknowledge the authority of the new British monarch, King Edward VII. The former republics came under the rule of British governors. The OFS was renamed the Orange River Colony (O.R.C.). In addition, the Transvaal lost Vryheid which was incorporated into Natal. The Cape rebels, who had supported the long-distance commando raids of men like Smuts, temporarily lost the right to vote. Apart from these measures, the Boers received relatively generous treatment. They were given £3 million to repair the war damage. Burgers were allowed to keep their farms. Interest-free loans for two years were provided to help Boer farmers. The defeated republics were excused from having to pay reparations (war debts). The Boers feared that Africans would be given the vote. This did not happen and the question of the African franchise was left unresolved. Finally, both the Transvaal and the O.R.C. were promised self-government in the not too distant future.

Two months before the conclusion of the war, Rhodes died at his home in Cape Town. And in July 1904 Kruger died in self-imposed exile in Switzerland. South Africa thus lost two of its most prominent figures. The roles of Kruger and Rhodes in South African history have sometimes been exaggerated when historians have explained an entire period of South African history (1880–1900) in terms of their personal rivalry. This 'great man' approach to understanding history can sometimes hide the complexity of a situation. Nevertheless these two personalities had a big impact on South African history, and for this reason their deaths can be viewed as ending a particular epoch. A new age of South African history unfolded between 1902 and 1910.

The foundations of modern South Africa were successfully laid. In 1910 the Union came into being, and Britain's attempt to create a stable and modernized state compatible with the needs of mining capital finally [met with success] . . .

(Adapted from Warwick, p. 5.)

British troops at the Orange River Station, 1902.

The Anglo-Boer War

The first phase 1899–1900

1. The Boer army was made up of part-time soldiers formed into commandos. The ZAR imported arms from Europe before the war and its forces were therefore well armed. The commandos' greatest asset was mobility. They were mounted and astonished the slow-moving British army with their speed.

2. After the start of the war, Boer armies advanced to besiege Kimberley, Ladysmith and Mafeking.

3. British armies attempted to relieve these sieges and in one week (called 'Black Week') in December 1899, suffered three defeats at Colenso, Stormberg and Magersfontein.

4. The Boers were unable to break down the defences of the besieged garrisons and got bogged down. By forfeiting their advantage of mobility, many commentators believe the Boers lost their only chance of victory.

5. Determined attempts were made by Sir Redvers Buller in Natal to relieve Ladysmith. These ended in bloody defeat at Spion Kop (January 1900).

6. In February 1900 the siege of Kimberley was raised and Gen. Cronje was defeated at Paardeberg. Boer forces were also defeated at Ladysmith and Mafeking and the Boers were forced to abandon their sieges.

7. Massive British reinforcements meant that the war eventually tilted in Britain's favour. On 5 June 1900 the new commander, Lord Roberts, entered Pretoria without encountering resistance.

Boer soldiers in trench.

Boers firing lyddite guns at the enemy's trenches at the Battle of Colenso. (© J.E.M.)

British soldiers at Modder River. (Courtesy of the Killie Campbell Africana Library.)

British Cape garrison artillery at Modder River. (Courtesy of the Killie Campbell Africana Library.)

Contemporary British Cartoon.

The second phase 1900-1902

8. In August 1900 Kruger felt that defeat was inevitable and fled to Delagoa Bay, and from there into exile in Switzerland.
9. A new phase of the war began after August 1900 — the guerrilla phase. No pitched battles were fought and Boer forces limited themselves to hit-and-run attacks and sabotage. Britain responded by destroying Boer farmhouses to prevent Boer soldiers from receiving aid.
10. In the mid-winter of 1901 Boer civilians were herded into concentration camps. They were thus prevented from taking part in the war. Conditions were terrible and 26000 died, most of whom were children.
11. In mid-1901 Smuts led a Boer invasion of the Cape in the hope that Boers there would rise up in sympathy. Some did, but most remained passive.
12. By 1902 there were 10000 blockhouses in South Africa. These were designed to limit Boer mobility and cut up the veld into manageable portions. These portions were then swept by British troops and any Boer soldiers within them would be captured or killed, being unable to flee because of the blockhouses.
13. The war cost Britain much more than originally anticipated. Nearly half a million soldiers were eventually deployed in South Africa. Even so, predictions of victory were often premature, and frequently followed by small defeats inflicted on imperial troops by Boer commandos.
14. On 31 May 1902 the war ended. Much of South Africa was in ruins, and the task that lay ahead was to repair the damage and unite the country.

A British blockhouse.

Boer soldiers at Modder River, waiting to be assigned to tents in the prison camp. (Courtesy of the Killie Campbell Africana Library.)

Contemporary British cartoon, showing the bewilderment of the average British citizen after British losses at Nooitgedacht, especially in view of the fact that Lord Roberts had recently sent a cable promising that the war was nearly over.

Boer children in a concentration camp.

Contemporary British cartoon reflecting British view of the Boer surrender.

311

Chronology of wars fought by Africans against colonial forces

1879: Anglo-Zulu War, Anglo-Pedi War, Kora resistance on the Orange River crushed, Moorosi rebellion (Lesotho)
1880: Transkei rebellion, Basotho Gun War, East Griqualand rebellion
1882: Montshiwa and Mankurwane defeated by Massouw and Moswete with Boer assistance
1883: Ndzundza Ndebele defeated
1893: Anglo-Ndebele War
1894: Mudjaji's Lobedu revolt in the northern Transvaal put down, Malaboch revolt put down, Germans attack Witbooi's Nama in Namibia
1895: Makgoba's Tlou crushed in the northern Transvaal
1896: Chimurenga War, Langeberg rebellion
1897: Venda defeated, Andries le Fleur's revolt in East Griqualand nipped in the bud, Portuguese defeat the Gaza in Mozambique
1898: Swazi threaten to rebel
1900: Kgatla attack the Boers in western Transvaal, Pedi attack the Boers
1902: Zulu attack Boers in Vryheid district
1904: Germans embark on war of extermination against Herero in Namibia (1904—7)
1905: Germans attack Nama (1905—7)
1906: Bambata's rebellion

Glossary

Bittereinders — those who continued to fight the British to the 'bitter end' during the Anglo-Boer War.

Charter — a trading charter from the British government which gave the holder exclusive rights to trade in a specific area.

Concession — a contract which gave the recipient (concessionaire) certain privileges. These privileges covered many aspects of economic life, from prospecting rights to grazing lands, and were generally purchased from the ruler of an area.

Federation — a loose grouping of states, as opposed to a union.

Free trade — a situation in which there are no restrictions on trade.

Grand design theory — a tendency to explain history in terms of great men and their all-encompassing plans for the destiny of a country.

Helot — a member of a slavish class.

Imperial factor — refers to the influence of British imperialism.

Insurrection — a rising against established authority.

National Scouts — the military unit created for Afrikaners who abandoned the Boer cause and joined the British.

Ndzundza Ndebele — not to be confused with the Ndebele of Zimbabwe, with whom they have no direct links.

Protectorate/colony — a protectorate implies colonial protection for the local people but does not involve the colonial power in administration costs. In a colony, colonial control is direct and therefore more expensive.

Saturated — filled to overflowing.

'Second Rand' — a second rich goldfield somewhere else in Southern Africa.

Sharecropper or 'squatter' — an agricultural producer who lives on the landowner's farm and cultivates crops in an independent manner, and either pays rent or a portion of his crops to the landowner.

Sordid — meanly selfish.

Suzerainty — informal political control of one state over another.

Trading companies — companies based in the British colonies or in Europe, which traded with the interior.

Zimbabwe — area between Limpopo and Zambezi Rivers, divided geographically into Matabeleland and Mashonaland. After it was subjugated by the B.S.A.C. it was named Rhodesia.

Bibliography

Agar-Hamilton, J.A.I. *The Road to the North* (Longman)

Beinart, W. *The Political Economy of Pondoland 1860 to 1930* (Ravan, 1982)

Blainey, G. "The lost causes of the Jameson Raid" in *Economic History Review No. 2* (1965)

Bonner, P. L. *Kings, Commoners and Concessionaires* (Ravan, 1983)

Boyce, A. N. *Europe and South Africa Part 1* (Juta, 1974)

Bransky, D. "The Causes of the Boer War: Towards a Synthesis" (unpublished)

Cobbing, J. R. D. "Lobengula, Jameson and the Occupation of Mashonaland 1890" in *Rhodesian History No. 4* (1973)

Davenport, T. R. H. *South Africa: A Modern History* (Macmillan, 1977)

Davenport, T. R. H. and Hunt, K. S. *The Right to the Land* (David Philip, 1974)

Delius, P. *The Land Belongs to Us* (Ravan, 1983)

Gale, W. D. *One Man's Vision, The Story of Rhodesia*

Guy, J. *The Destruction of the Zulu Kingdom* (Ravan, 1982)

Iwan-Muller, E. B. *Lord Milner and South Africa*

Jeeves, A. "The control of migratory labour on the South African Gold Mines in the era of Kruger and Milner" in *Journal of Southern Africa Studies No. 1* (1975)

Kubicek, R. "Finance Capital and South African Gold Mining, 1886–1914" in *Journal of Imperial and Commonwealth History No. 3* (1975)

Marais, J. S. *The Fall of Kruger's Republic* (Oxford University Press, 1961)

Matsetela, T. in Marks S. and Rathbone R. *Industrialisation and Social Change in South Africa* (Longman, 1982)

Mendelsohn, R. "Blainey and the Jameson Raid: The Debate Renewed" in *University of London Institute of Commonwealth Studies Collected Seminar Papers: The Societies of Southern Africa in the Nineteenth and Twentieth Centuries* (1976)

Parsons, N. *A New History of Southern Africa* (Macmillan, 1982)

Phimister, I. R. "Rhodes, Rhodesia and the Rand" in *Journal of Southern African Studies No. 1* (1974)

Ranger, T. O. *Revolt in Southern Rhodesia 1896–7* (Heinemann, 1967)

Robinson, D. *The Causes of the Anglo-Boer War*

Selous, F. C. *Travel and Adventure in South East Africa* (Rhodesiana Reprint, Books of Zimbabwe Publishing Co.)

Smit, G. J. J. *History for Standard 9* (Maskew Miller, 1975)

Stigger, P. "Volunteers and the Profit Motive in the Anglo Ndebele War, 1893" in *Rhodesian History No. 2* (1971)

Stigger, P. "The Land Commission of 1894 and its membership" in *Rhodesian History No. 8* (1977)

Wilson, M. and Thompson, L. *Oxford History of South Africa Vol. 2* (Oxford University Press, 1971)

Van Jaarsveld, F. A. and van Wijk, T. *New Illustrated History Std. 9* (Perskor, 1974)

9 RECONSTRUCTION TO UNION: SOUTH AFRICA 1902–1910

Introduction 315
Economic and political reconstruction 315
  Economic recovery under Milner: 'Picking up the pieces'
  Further political and social changes
  The growth of political parties in the Transvaal and the Orange River Colony
  Self-government for the former Boer republics
  Poor whites and the white working class
  Political parties in the Cape
  Natal
'A melancholy situation': The position of blacks after the war 325
  Africans and the Anglo-Boer War
  Africans on the land
  Africans in the town: Urbanization
  The birth of African nationalism
  Bambata's rebellion: Armed resistance
  Indian discontent and opposition
South Africa 1908–1910: The achievement of unification 332
  The groundwork for unification
  The obstacles to unification
  The National Convention and its work
Conclusion 337
  Glossary
  Bibliography

Introduction

The independent Boer republics were finally crushed in the Anglo-Boer War. The war left thousands dead and huge areas devastated. Unlike the Franco-Prussian War (1871) which was the final act in the unification of Germany, the Second Anglo-Boer War merely set the stage for a drama that unfolded over the next eight years and eventually came to a climax in the unification of South Africa. The war brought all of South Africa under British rule, but there were still many problems to be ironed out before further unification could be considered.

The destiny of Africans was one of the rare areas of broad agreement between the colonies. They all believed that African labour would contribute to the economic fortunes of the new South Africa. There was however disagreement over the political rule of Africans, and this was to be vigorously debated in the years preceding union.

There was also debate over the way in which South Africa was to be economically developed. Massive amounts of aid were made available for the restoration of the war-damaged economies. The way in which the aid was to be used had yet to be decided. In addition there were many people who hoped to receive assistance and the distribution of aid therefore became a hotly debated subject.

The form that the unification of South Africa was to take was disputed by the different colonies. Each colony had its own traditions, history and economic interests and wanted to preserve these as far as possible. Unification demanded that some of these customs and powers be surrendered to a central government. There were therefore those who proposed federation, a loose form of union which would allow members to retain much of their independent character. Others, however, opted for union, which would bind members tightly together in unity. This would iron out the earlier differences between the white states of South Africa.

This chapter is divided into sections. The first deals with economic recovery, in which the damage of the war was repaired and the foundations for economic growth were laid. It also looks at the growth of political parties. The second section focuses on the position of blacks. During and after the war, Africans tried to improve their position in society, but these efforts largely ended in failure. This failure was the starting point for new forms of opposition to white rule. Although new urban-based organizations emerged to lead opposition, resistance in the rural areas could still utilize traditional organizations like the chiefdom. This section therefore investigates the Bambata rebellion of 1906, perhaps the last instance of armed tribal resistance in Southern Africa. The final section examines unification and the debates that were aired at the National Convention in 1908-9.

Economic and political reconstruction

ECONOMIC RECOVERY UNDER MILNER: 'PICKING UP THE PIECES'

The centre of the South African economy was the Witwatersrand and the most important industry was gold

315

mining. It was thus to the Transvaal that the most attention was paid in the years following the Second Anglo-Boer War. Gold mining and agriculture had both come to a virtual standstill. Lord Alfred Milner, the new Governor of Transvaal, set himself the task of getting economic life in motion once again. His project, which lasted until 1907, was called 'reconstruction'.

Milner first addressed the problems of getting gold mining onto a secure and profitable footing again. In doing so, he confirmed the Randlords' hopes that the overthrow of the Boer government in the Transvaal would be beneficial to the gold mining industry. Milner's first job was to obtain labour. In December 1901 he came to an agreement, known as the *modus vivendi**, with the Governor of Mozambique. This secured large amounts of 'Shangaan' labour from this Portuguese colony and helped to solve the labour crisis.

For the rest of the decade the mines continued to enjoy privileged status. In 1904 black labour was still in short supply and this led the British government to agree to the importation of Chinese labour. Workers were indentured* for short periods of time and returned to China on completion of their service. There was much opposition to this step because of fears that it would complicate South Africa's race problems. Liberal party politicians in Britain labelled the exercise 'Chinese slavery'. Local Transvaal Labour party members condemned the importation of labour because they argued that it would reduce the number of jobs available to white workers. Nevertheless, over 60 000 Chinese workers arrived. With their help, gold production was raised from its 1901 level of £1 million to £32 million in 1910. Ceaseless political campaigning by opponents of 'Chinese slavery' eventually led to a complete withdrawal of the Chinese workforce by 1910.

Farming in the Transvaal had also been severely disrupted by the Second Anglo-Boer War. The Milner administration — aided by a group of young Oxford graduates known as 'The Kindergarten' — set about restoring agricultural production. As we shall see in the following section, African occupation of white farmlands initially prevented the reconstruction of agriculture. The British administration of the Transvaal helped farmers to forcibly eject Africans. After the land had once again been placed firmly under white control, efforts were made to reform farming techniques and practices.

Departments of Agriculture and Lands were formed. These distributed aid and advised farmers on a wide range of matters varying from veterinary care, to land use, to the clearing of weeds. In addition a Land Bank and a Land Settlement Board were established in 1907. The Land Bank provided credit on easy terms for farmers. The Land Settlement Board helped to establish white farmers on the land. Farming was not easy and

Chinese labourers in a mine compound.
(Illustration courtesy of the Killie Campbell Africana Library.)

laws were passed to reduce the chance of failure amongst white farmers.

Agricultural yields amongst white farmers were low — lower in fact than comparable African yields. A government campaign was therefore launched to increase the quantity as well as the quality of white farmers' crops.

Up until this time farmers had for the most part sold their crops locally. They were satisfied to sell to the local storekeeper and showed little interest in increasing their market involvement. They were ignorant about marketing practices and showed little inclination to expand production. In the decade that ended in 1910, farmers began to take an interest in selling not only to the big cities of South Africa, but to international markets as well.

Absentee landowners or those who used their land neglectfully were pressured through taxation to begin cultivation or to sell to people who would farm. To further encourage the swing to commercial agriculture, £8 million was spent on public works. Most of this was spent on the building of 2 000 km of railway branch lines. The extension of the rail network made it easier for farmers to sell their goods on the urban markets.

African cultivators were not given similar assistance and struggled to improve their agricultural productivity. They often lost their land and therefore had to work for white farmers.

FURTHER POLITICAL AND SOCIAL CHANGES

Milner's Transvaal administration wanted a significant proportion of the rural white population to be British. Imperial plans for the unification of South Africa demanded that significant numbers of British families be settled on the land. The intention of this was to undermine potential Afrikaner nationalist opposition to British rule by implanting British communities in the heart of the Boer population. Two measures were initiated to achieve this.

Wealthy people from Britain were encouraged to immigrate. Officers and soldiers who were no longer needed by the British army were urged to settle on small plots as yeomen. (Yeomen are farmers who cultivate on small plots and provide nearby towns with their fresh fruit and vegetable requirements.)

Neither plan succeeded to any significant extent, but Milner had a further strategy to ensure English dominance — the control of the schools. He used this to promote the English language and encourage imperial values, while at the same time he hindered the teaching of Dutch. This policy was known as Anglicization. It was supported by the writings of novelists like John Buchan and Rider Haggard, who wrote books that glorified certain aspects of British life and attempted to unite Afrikaners and Englishmen in common South African nationalism. Perhaps the most important book in this style was John Buchan's *Prester John* which appeared in 1910.

THE GROWTH OF POLITICAL PARTIES IN THE TRANSVAAL AND THE ORANGE RIVER COLONY

Economic changes were accompanied by political developments. The Second Anglo-Boer War added to a legacy of bitterness that went back to the Great Trek (mid-1830s) and the First Anglo-Boer War (1880–1).

317

Late in 1900 Milner was already planning the future of the Transvaal.

> Next to the composition of the population, *the thing which matters most is its education*...Dutch should only be used to teach English, and English to teach everything else. Language is important, but the tone and spirit of the teaching conveyed in it is even more important. Not half enough attention has been paid to school reading books. To get these right would be the greatest political achievement conceivable. I attach especial importance to school history books. A good world-history would be worth anything. At present children are only taught the history of South Africa, with at most a little English history, of the narrowest purely English type, thrown in. Everything that makes South African children look outside South Africa and realize the world makes for peace. Everything that cramps and confines their views to South Africa only (limits their historical reading, for instance, to Slagter's Nek and Dingaan's Day, and Boomplaats and Majuba) makes for Afrikanderdom and further discord.
>
> (Thompson, p.7.)

Questions

1. Why was the 'composition of the population' so important to Milner?
2. What was the role of education in Milner's Anglicization policy?
3. Was Milner's Anglicization policy successful? Give evidence to support your answer.

Many Afrikaners felt extremely bitter about the British treatment of Boer civilians and this laid the foundation for the later emergence of Afrikaner nationalism. (Although there were many Afrikaners who despised their *hensopper* compatriots and these sentiments delayed the emergence of a unified Afrikaner nationalism.) The stirrings of nationalist feeling found expression in the revival of Christian National Education, which attempted to combat Milner's Anglicization programme. Language was the major issue used to mobilize support. Afrikaans, as opposed to Dutch, was promoted as the language of the people (the *Volk*). Afrikaans poets who glorified the virtues of Boer life, such as Eugene Marais and Jan Celliers, became popular. In 1909 the Afrikaans Academy for Language, Literature and Art (*Akademie vir Taal, Letterkunde en Kuns*) was formed. Although it focused on cultural matters, it also contributed to the upsurge in political feeling amongst Afrikaners. This was to pave the way for the emergence of powerful political forces in the years to come.

Here is a report of a speech which demonstrates the growth of Afrikaner nationalism. It was given in 1904 by the Moderator of the Dutch Reformed Church, Dominee H. S. Bosman. The occasion was the burial of Paul Kruger, ex-President of the ZAR.

> The speaker likened the people of this country to those men of God and urged them to obey the Bible...He urged them, by the God of Paul Kruger, not to let that national feeling die out...
> Paul Kruger was dead, but his people were not dead. Neither was his spirit dead and they could go along the lines that he had laid down under the flag that now waved over them, and still be true to it, but they would always remain Afrikanders, God helping them.
>
> (Thompson, pp. 18–19.)

318

Amongst South Africa's English-speakers there were serious divisions. Some were 'jingoes'*—pro-British people who wished to convert the victory on the battlefield into political supremacy. There were others, however, who believed that conciliation* with their former enemies was the only way to assure a lasting and stable peace in Southern Africa.

The first political party to appear was the *Transvaal Political Association* (T.P.A.) in 1902. Headed by diamond magnate Dale Lace, it called for Uitlander support over the issue of the capital of the Transvaal. Pretoria, the old ZAR capital, not Johannesburg, had been made capital and this irritated the *Uitlander* population which was concentrated in Johannesburg. In 1904 the T.P.A. split because some members wanted representative government while others wanted responsible government. Representative government entailed giving the inhabitants of a colony some political influence. Their views would be represented to the colonial administration and they would sometimes be consulted in the framing of legislation. Administration would remain in the hands of the colonial power (in the case of the Transvaal, a British governor was in authority). Responsible government entailed giving colonists more power to control their own affairs. Not only would they be able to make laws, but they would also be able to execute them. The granting of responsible government was seen as marking the gradual withdrawal of the colonial power from a colony's affairs. Colonists would then be expected to shoulder more of the financial and administrative responsibilities.

The T.P.A. members who favoured representative government wanted continued British supervision of Transvaal affairs. Those who preferred responsible government wanted the rapid transfer of political power to representatives of the Transvaal population and the steady withdrawal of Britain from active administration.

Two organizations emerged to cater for the different points of view. The *Transvaal Progressive Association*, headed by Randlord Sir Percy Fitzpatrick, wanted to delay self-government until English dominance in the colony was assured. The *Transvaal Responsible Government Association*, headed by E. P. Solomon, a Transvaal lawyer, preferred the rapid transfer of rule to the colony's own legislators. In this they agreed with the *Het Volk* party, founded in January 1905.

Het Volk was an Afrikaner party led by Louis Botha and Jan Smuts. The party condemned restrictions on the use of Dutch in schools. It also agitated for the distribution of relief to Afrikaner poor whites. Since many of Het Volk's supporters were farmers, the party devoted a lot of attention to agricultural matters. It sought to provide white farmers with adequate supplies of labour and to ensure that they received sufficient credit from government funds. Het Volk realized the importance of white conciliation and therefore encouraged Boer and Uitlander to resolve their differences.

Het Volk also enjoyed some support from the mining industry, notably that of Randlord Joseph Robinson. Mining interests clashed with those of the poor whites on the issue of Chinese labour. In order not to offend either group of supporters, Het Volk adopted a vague and undecided stance with respect to the use of Chinese labour on the mines.

In the Orange River Colony, the *Oranje Unie* party was founded in 1906 as a preliminary to responsible government in the following year. J. B. M. Hertzog, who soon became leader of the party, was initially opposed to conciliation. He yearned for the old Republican days and set his mind on protecting Dutch-Afrikaans traditions and preserving the identity of the volk.

Louis Botha, leader of Het Volk, is the central character of the cartoon which appeared in *The Star* in February 1907 prior to the first Transvaal general election after the achievement of self-government.

'A dual attitude.'

The attitude of Het Volk towards the Chinese question is still a dual one — Pro-Chinese in the mining constituencies and anti-Chinese elsewhere.

On the Rand —

And off.

(*The Star*, 2 February 1907.)

(Illustration courtesy of the Killie Campbell Africana Library.)

Questions

1. What do the towers and smoke in the distance represent?
2. The Chinese labourers are holding 'contracts'. What do these represent?
3. From the cartoon, what were the main characteristics of Het Volk's policy towards the Chinese?
4. Why did Het Volk have this policy?
5. What is the attitude of the cartoonist towards Botha and Het Volk?

Self-government for the former Boer republics

The struggle for responsible government leading to self-government was resolved in 1906 by the victory of Campbell-Bannerman's Liberal party in a British general election. The Liberals wanted Britain to retire from South Africa and supported plans for self-government in the colonies. The West Ridgeway Commission was appointed to make recommendations on a new constitution for the Transvaal. By then Lord Selborne had succeeded Milner as governor. Like Milner, Selborne opposed the rapid transfer of power to the colony's white population, but was unable to prevent it once the Liberals came to power.

After the granting of self-government an election was held in 1907. The Het Volk party triumphed, winning 37 of the 69 seats in the new Parliament, and Louis Botha became Prime Minister. Het Volk's allies, E. P. Solomon's National party, which had previously been known as the Transvaal Responsible Government Association, won six seats. The major opposition came from the Progressive party which won 21 seats.

The elections were a disappointment to British imperialists who had hoped for an Uitlander victory. The Het Volk government, however, did not take revenge on the English-speaking inhabitants, as many expected them to do. The mining companies which had backed the Progressives out of fear of Afrikaner political domination, found on the contrary that they were well served by Louis Botha's government.

In the Orange River Colony responsible government was granted in June 1907. Elections were held early in 1908 and the Oranje Unie party easily won the election. Abraham Fischer became Prime Minister and Hertzog became Minister of Education.

> *It is quite clear that Het Volk was presenting itself as something wider and larger than an exclusive Boer nationalist party. Many of the Het Volk's English-speaking supporters were dissident* capitalists (like Joseph Robinson).*
>
> (Denoon, pp. 326–7.)
>
> (The dissident capitalists were a minority of mineowners who had opposed Rhodes and the Jameson Raid of 1896. They were well-disposed towards those Afrikaans leaders, like Botha, who desired conciliation.)

Poor whites and the white working class

Not all whites supported the growth of these political parties. Indeed there were many whites who were unenthusiastic and in some cases even hostile to those parties which did not seem to consider their interests. These people were known as the poor whites. Many had been poor before the war and the war ensured that they stayed poor. In most cases, poor whites were illiterate and lacked the skills necessary for employment in industry, especially mining. They blamed government for their misfortune and bore a grudge against the rich, especially the Randlords.

Many poor whites still lived on the land as *bywoners* (sharecroppers). They lived and worked on farms belonging to white farmers and paid for the privilege with their labour, rent or part of their crop.

The white poor enjoyed some sympathy in government circles. This was because the Milner administration wanted to keep white farmers on the land to raise the colony's agricultural production. Another consideration was the possibility of poor white unrest in the towns. Officials believed that the best way of preventing this was by keeping people on the land. Poor whites therefore received incentives* to keep them farming. Credit, assisted land purchase and cattle loans were all extended to them. The aid was not really adequate and few were able to become productive and independent farmers.

There were still other avenues of help for those wanting to remain in the countryside. The establishment of labour colonies marked one important experiment in this direction. In 1897 the first labour colony had been established at Kakamas in the northern Cape. It was a home for failed farmers and evicted bywoners. In 1907 another labour colony was founded at Dejagersdrif in the eastern Transvaal.

321

Labour colonies were often sponsored by the Dutch Reformed Church. The state gave assistance but even so labour colonies could only provide employment and a home for a small number of people. They were not a long-term solution to the poor white problem. A last option in the countryside was relief work: poorly paid manual labour. From 1907 onwards the South African Railways gave preferential employment to whites, and there were also other jobs on public works such as road and dam construction.

Despite the aid granted to keep poor whites on the land, the urban poor white population continued to grow. Johannesburg was particularly attractive to poor white job-seekers and its population expanded rapidly. The Transvaal administration was concerned and appointed an Indigency* Commission (1906-8) to investigate the worsening situation. It recommended the creation of more jobs for whites in the cities. A lack of funds prevented these recommendations from being implemented. A major reason for the shortage of funding was that substantial amounts of money were spent on helping the gold mines. Many poor whites were aware of this and condemned the mineowners and their allies in the government.

Unemployment and desperation were highest amongst Johannesburg's poor whites. Conditions were hard and many blamed the government for their plight. In the poor suburb of Vrededorp, for example, poor whites called upon the Prime Minister, Louis Botha:

> ... to meet the masses in order to show cause why land was not opened up for the purposes of agriculture, and why work should not be immediately supplied to starving white workers.

(van Onselen, p. 154.)

The government and the mining industry provided charity and relief work but not on a large enough scale to prevent the spread of poor white frustration. This was often expressed in a rejection of existing political parties. A contemporary observer commented:

> ... There was growing up a population poverty stricken, ignorant and a danger to the community. This population was the bane of all political effort. Every political party pandered* to this mass of voters and endeavoured to find employment for them. The mass had overturned every political party, and would overturn any political party which might be in power unless a remedy was provided to remove their appalling poverty and degradation.

(van Onselen, p. 158.)

At this time one party alone had significant white working class support and this was the Labour party. It was founded in 1904 and led by mine manager, F. H. P. Creswell. Like the Labour parties in Britain and Australia, the Labour party in the Transvaal was the political arm of the working class, in this case the white working class exclusively. The party's goal was political power for white workers. Political power was in the hands of wealthy mine and landowners, which the Labour party viewed as the ruling class. The ruling class, and the political parties which represented it (for example, Het Volk and the T.P.A.), were therefore, according to Labour party policy, the enemies of the workers. The bulk of the party's membership was made up of skilled foreign white miners. They were experienced in the ways of trade unions and political organization, and so joined together to protect their well-paid positions in the mining industry.

Two groups threatened the monopoly over skilled mine jobs which the foreign miners sought to preserve; poor whites and Africans. In 1907 a strike was called by white miners on the Rand after a dispute with management. About 3 000 unemployed poor whites accepted scab labour* offers on the mines and the strike disintegrated. The introduction of poor white Afrikaners into the mining industry infuriated white mine labour which was largely British in origin. In the longer term, however, the result of the influx of poor whites into industry led to broader support for the Labour party.

The cartoon on the right appeared in *The Star* in response to the strike. *The Star's* cartoonist was however wrong about the long-term consequences of the strike. Poor whites and foreign mine workers sank their differences and joined together to oppose African mine labourers. Poor whites absorbed by industry felt themselves best represented by the Labour party. In this way divisions between the urban poor whites and white miners were lessened to some extent.

The threat that African labourers posed to the privileged position of white labour within the mining industry was that they could be used to replace both skilled and unskilled white workers. Randlords found this option attractive because they could pay Africans lower wages.

When Afrikaners joined the mining industry they added their voice to those of the other white miners in protesting against the increasing use of black labour in jobs that had previously been done by whites. The respective places of white and black miners in the labour process on the mines remained a sensitive issue which was not finally settled until the 1922 Rand Revolt.

A SWIVEL ARRANGEMENT.

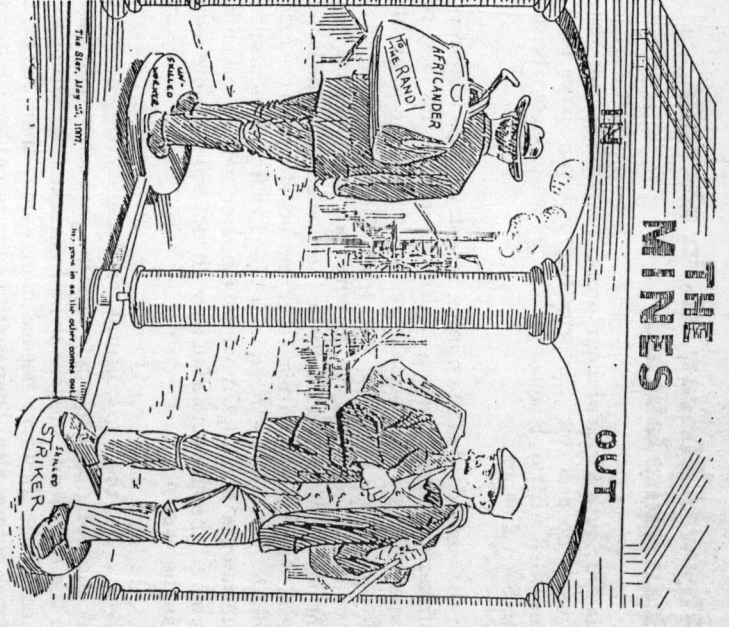

One goes in as the other comes out.
(*The Star,* 25 May 1907.)

(Illustration courtesy of the Killie Campbell Africana Library.)

One of the most serious effects of the strike, so far as the strikers themselves are concerned, is that by their action in leaving the mines they are ushering into their places the Afrikander miner, who will henceforth become a keen competitor in this field of employment, of which hitherto the workers from oversea have held a virtual monopoly.

323

POLITICAL PARTIES IN THE CAPE

The Cape had a long tradition of elections and self-government. It had gained representative government in 1853 and responsible government in 1872. During these years, no clear-cut political party system had emerged, although the *Afrikaner Bond* had grown to be the most influential political grouping. Although the Afrikaner Bond stood for the promotion of Afrikaans culture and the realization of Afrikaner political goals, the leaders of the Bond never expressed disloyalty to Britain, and they never formed a government because they believed that this might scare away the support of English-speakers.

The Jameson Raid profoundly altered the political situation at the Cape. The Bond, led by J. H. Hofmeyr, condemned the attempted raid and its architect, Rhodes, who had long been a friend of the Bond. At the same time, some of the Cape's English-speaking population formed the Progressive party and went into open opposition to the Bond. The Progressive party drew support from the South African League which had succeeded the jingoistic Empire League.

The Progressives lost the 1898 election, but after the Second Anglo-Boer War their fortunes rose because the 'Cape rebels'* who generally supported the Bond, were deprived of the vote. In 1904 the Progressive party won its first election and gained power. L. S. Jameson, leader of the Raid, became the Prime Minister.

The Progressives' period in office was short-lived. By the time of the next election in 1908, the Cape rebels had had the vote restored to them. They supported the South African party (S.A.P.), the name taken by the Afrikaner Bond and its English-speaking allies. The S.A.P. led by John X. Merriman won the

---

Why was African labour cheaper than white labour?

Most of South Africa's labour force today is made up of Africans. This is no accident. Historically, employers have preferred unskilled African labour to unskilled white labour because it has been cheaper.

In the early days of the mining industry, white labourers and African migrants competed with one another for jobs. In the majority of cases, especially on the mines, the migrant was chosen. The argument was that migrant labourers were prepared to work for less than white labourers because they did not have to support a family on their wage. Migrant labourers resided alone in the cities. Their families stayed in the reserves where they were assumed to be able to support themselves by subsistence farming. A white labourer, on the other hand, generally had his whole family with him and therefore required a higher wage.

Over time the agricultural productivity of the reserves declined. Migrants began to send money back to their families in the reserves to prevent them from starving. Although this meant that they now needed more money than before, their wages did not rise. They continued to be paid much less than white labourers. This phenomenon can be explained by the laws which prevented them from organizing to demand wage increases. (White labourers were allowed to form trade unions and were able to negotiate for pay increases.) In addition the families of migrants were prohibited by the pass laws from coming to live in the towns. In this way they were forced to remain in the reserves. Since the migrants' wages continued to be seen as supporting one individual rather than an entire family, levels of poverty rose in the reserves. (For further information, refer to Chapter 7.)

1908 election. Its goals were the creation of a united South African nationalism for English and Afrikaans-speaking whites, and the preservation of a self-respecting Afrikaner identity. In addition it was committed to unifying South Africa.

NATAL

In 1893 Natal gained responsible government. The first Prime Minister was John Robinson. This meant that policy would henceforth largely be determined by locally elected members of parliament. The power of rural voters soon became apparent as government aid was channelled into white agriculture. After 1902, agricultural development was stepped up. The Transvaal's reconstruction programme was faithfully applied in Natal. In 1904 the Agricultural Development Act was passed and it was followed in 1907 by the Land and Agricultural Development Act. These acts helped white farmers to establish farms and improve their operations.

Prospective African farmers were meanwhile prevented from buying land and in 1905 had the further burden of a new £1 poll tax added to their tax load. In the same year, a Delimitation Commission decided to cut two-and-a-half million acres out of Zululand and make it available for white purchase. This was a terrible blow to Zulu cultivators and was a major contributing factor to the rebellion that followed.

'A melancholy situation': The position of blacks after the war

In 1916 Sol Plaatje, an African journalist from Kimberley, wrote a book called *Native Life in South Africa*. In it he looked at South Africa through the eyes of a black man and described what he saw as 'a melancholy situation'. He was writing at a time when the Natives Land Act had just come into effect. But even before this Act, the 'black man's burden' as Plaatje described it, was heavy.

AFRICANS AND THE ANGLO-BOER WAR

When the war began, many Boer and African cultivators were in a similar position. They were on the brink of poverty and had to go to the cities to seek work. During the course of the war many lost their land and cattle. To avoid becoming even poorer, some of the poor Boers joined the National Scouts, a Boer unit which helped the British. They were regarded as traitors by their former comrades, but their actions can be explained in terms of their economic positions. They simply joined the side which they believed was most likely to restore their fortunes. Africans were possibly in a worse position than these whites. Like the poor whites, they regarded the war as a chance to improve their position, and acted accordingly.

325

The Anglo-Boer War has commonly been presented as a war exclusively between Boer and Briton. In fact, there was also significant African participation. All over South Africa, Africans responded to war-time conditions in a manner calculated to improve their own circumstances. This meant that some supported the Boers and some the English. It would, however, be true to say that the power of British arms and the reputation of British liberalism drew most of the African participants onto the side of Britain.

African spies who worked for the Boers taken prisoner by British troops.

(Illustration courtesy of the Don Africana Library.)

Many groups which had only recently lost their independence, mobilized regiments in order to take back land which they had formerly occupied and to which they still laid claim. By 1900, Chief Lentshwe's Kgatla regiments controlled the Rustenburg area. The Pedi and Sekhukhune dominated the Steelpoort River area in the eastern Transvaal. In 1902 Dinizulu's Zulu attacked a Boer commando at Holkrantz in northern Natal. Fifty-six Boers were killed when the Zulu attempted to reclaim the Piet Retief area — which they had lost to the Boers of the New Republic in the 1880s.

Africans elsewhere also supported Britain. In Transkei over 4 000 jobless tribesmen joined the British forces. Many had been impoverished when they lost their cattle in the rinderpest epidemic (1896–7). Many others had lost their jobs on the gold mines when these closed down at the onset of war. Others, like transport riders, were unemployed as a result of the spread of

An African messenger has a message attached to his coat by British troops.

(Illustration courtesy of the Don Africana Library.)

railways. There was therefore good reason for signing up at 2 shillings a day. (This was a very high wage and should be contrasted with the 10s to £1 per month paid to agricultural labourers.) Many who joined were motivated by political considerations. The Mfengu and Thembu who made up the bulk of the force had traditionally supported the Cape Colony in return for political and economic privileges.

In the Transvaal and Orange Free State, African cultivators used the cover of the British army to take cattle from unoccupied or abandoned Boer farms. In addition they frequently spied for the British and provided them with provisions (though not always willingly). Those that gave support expected some form of payment. They also hoped that the British would help them reclaim their lands after the war.

African participants in the war were mainly non-combatant* but on some important occasions such as at Holkrantz in 1902, they took up arms. By 1902 the African war effort posed such a threat to the Boers that it was one of the reasons they gave for agreeing to peace terms. Yet when the peace had been signed, the British failed to reward Africans for the assistance they had given. The British even agreed to withhold the vote from Africans in the former Boer republics. They prevented Africans from regaining their lands and compensated them very poorly for the losses sustained in support of the British war effort.

AFRICANS ON THE LAND

Immediately after the war there were isolated African attempts to take land by force. Boer farms were occupied and large areas became unsafe for the returning Boers. Britain's response to this situation was to allow the Boer commandos to keep their weapons and to support their efforts to quell the attempted risings. When stable conditions returned to the region, Africans were left with very little land. The general assumption of whites was that Africans should not own land outside white-designated reserves.

In 1905 an important Transvaal Supreme Court judgement in the case of *Tsewu vs. Registrar of Deeds*, ruled that Africans could own land in 'white' areas.

Some wealthy Africans took advantage of the decision to buy land individually or in syndicates. They intended to continue with their profitable farming operations. Much land in the Transvaal was owned by land companies like the Transvaal Consolidated Land and Exploration Company. These companies allowed Africans to rent the land, but rarely to buy it. Opposition by white farmers to African competition and complaints about labour shortages eventually led to the passing of the Natives Land Act in 1913. This took away African rights to buy or rent land in 'white' areas.

AFRICANS IN THE TOWNS: URBANIZATION

In the aftermath of the war, many Africans migrated to the towns. Many had been evicted from their lands, others had been swept up in the general turmoil that follows war. They all had a common goal as they flocked to the cities: work. Great sprawling suburbs grew up around the cities. Urban authorities were opposed to Africans living amongst whites and so Africans were forced into adjacent areas which became known as 'townships' or 'locations'.

327

THE BIRTH OF AFRICAN NATIONALISM

By the beginning of the Twentieth Century, it became quite clear that there was strong white objection to the growth of a racially integrated society. African opposition began to emerge in the first decade of the Twentieth Century. It was normally passive, not well organized and geographically isolated. Nevertheless a force that was to unite opposition and give direction to African resistance did appear. This was African nationalism, with a growing feeling of African solidarity or Pan Africanism*. This early form was encouraged by contact with black Americans, and was known as 'Ethiopianism', Ethiopia being an African Empire which had withstood the onslaught of colonialism.

The church was one of the centres of protest. African clerics became dissatisfied with the mission churches, finding white churchmen to be patronizing* and accepting of racial discrimination of one sort or another. As early as 1884 Rev. Nehemiah Tile broke away from the Wesleyan Church to found the Thembu National Church. His initiative sparked off similar breakaways which culminated in the Ethiopian Church (The Order of Ethiopia) of the early 1890s. Between 1904 and 1907 the national unity of the African ecclesiastical movement crumbled because regional churches broke away from the mother body. The growth of independent African churches however helped to foster the development of African national awareness.

In the Transkei and the Orange River Colony, Vigilance Associations were formed. They were civic organizations which united Africans in defence of their rights. They held mass meetings and wrote letters to newspapers complaining of their plight. This form of protest made little impact. White politicians

---

The Cape Prime Minister, W. P. Schreiner, explained the official Cape government viewpoint on African urbanization in Cape Town at a public meeting in 1899.
(Refer back to Chapter 7, pp. 253–254 for further information.)

We have in the neighbourhood of Cape Town, some 10 000 ...[black people]. (Hear, Hear.)

They lived all over the place ... And they were learning all sorts of bad habits through living in touch with European or Coloured surroundings. We could not get rid of them: They were necessary for work. What we wanted was to get them practically in the position of being compounded [placed in compounds]. (Hear, Hear.) Keep ... [them] out of harm's way; let them do their work, receive their wage; and at the end of their term of service let them go back to the place whence they came — to the ... territories, where they should really make their home. (Hear, Hear.)

The present Bill would at least make provision in this direction. The great difficulty was the enforcement of compounding which was really the solution of the whole question.

(Quoted in Swanson, p. 395.)

Questions

1. Why do you think there were 10 000 Africans in the neighbourhood of Cape Town in 1899?

2. What, in Schreiner's opinion, were the important results of African urbanization?

3. What arrangement did Schreiner favour with regard to the future of the African population in the Cape?

were already in the process of deciding that African political activity should be separate from white political activity. They believed that the African population could best be controlled through the use of compliant African officials. This philosophy had indeed already been incorporated in the Natal Native Code of 1891 and in Rhodes's Glen Grey Act of 1894 (see Chapter 8).

Here is one of the early letters of protest written in 1892 by an OFS correspondent W. N. Somngesi. It appeared in the Bloemfontein newspaper, *De Express*.

His Honor the President [of the Orange Free State] says: ... 'The days of slavery are gone, and let us be thankful that it is so'. I may ask first what is a slave. A slave is any one in bondage. Are the ... [Africans] free in the Free State? Are the ... [African] ministers and other respectable people not bound to carry passes which they are bound to pay for? Are the ... [Africans] free to go and see their friends who are living on farms close by? I say no. It does not matter whether your friend was dying on a farm, you dare not pass the boundaries of the town commonage without a sixpenny pass. ... [African] preachers dare not forget their passes on Saturdays, if they have to go out preaching on Sundays, pass op, for a fine of £3 or one month's imprisonment with hard labour. Do they not pay a poll tax, and [get] nothing in return done for them; whilst the white man is free from the tax, and his children's schooling supported by Government?

Secondly, a slave means one wholly under the will of another. Now, Mr. Editor, an ... [African] has no voice in politics here not even in things concerning themselves. They have to do the will of a white man, and the will they must do, and what return do they get for their servitude? Nil.

Thirdly and lastly, a slave means one who has lost all power of resistance. What I have said on the first and second points will explain the third, and I will, therefore, dwell no longer on this painful subject of "The Native Question", with the prayers and hopes that the Lord will hasten the time when all nations will be entirely freed from bondage.

(Quoted in Odendaal, p. 22.)

Questions

1. How does Somngesi define slavery?
2. Why does Somngesi regard Africans in the O.F.S. as slaves?
3. Why do you think Somngesi wrote to the newspaper?
4. How accurate is Somngesi's observation that Africans had lost all power of resistance?

In all the colonies there were Native Congresses. The first was formed in the Cape in 1902. These bodies were the predecessors of the South African National Native Congress, later called the African National Congress (ANC). Initially the Congresses had little support and their influence was slight. Their chief function was to represent African opinion to local government and to government commissions.

The most well-organized movement was the Cape-based African Peoples' Organization (A.P.O.), founded as a Coloured political organization in 1902. In 1904 Dr. Abdurahman became leader of the A.P.O. He vigorously opposed discriminatory legislation but his organization's effectiveness was retarded by

One notable instance of armed African resistance was the Bambata rebellion which occurred in Natal in 1906. This was the last major revolt by rural people against white rule, and it was in some respects reminiscent of the Nineteenth Century tradition of Zulu resistance. The Zulu tribesmen who rebelled had endured years of hardship. A combination of colonial laws, cattle diseases and drought had whittled away their wealth. The last straw for them was the new poll tax in 1905. There was widespread defiance of the tax. Eventually Chief Bambata of the Zondi in the Greytown area went into open rebellion. He was joined by a large number of rebels including the aged Chief Sigananda. The rebels were attacked and defeated at Mome Gorge, suffering heavy losses. Sporadic outbreaks of resistance followed, but the rebellion petered out. Three thousand Zulu and 30 whites were killed. The Zulu defeat paved the way for the enforcement of the policies of the Natal government.

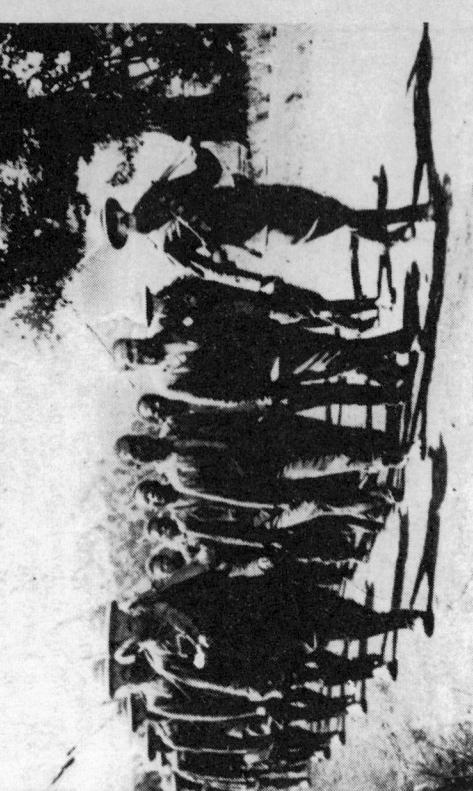

Some participants in the Bambata rebellion marching to their execution.

(Illustration courtesy of the Killie Campbell Africana Library.)

its inability to decide which white political party to support. The hallmark of all these movements was a belief in negotiation and a determination to avoid violence. There was no thought of armed resistance — this lay in the future.

BAMBATA'S REBELLION: ARMED RESISTANCE

The 1906 rebellion caused many white Natalians to panic. They feared a Zulu attack at any time and prepared themselves accordingly. In these two pictures, sandbags and barbed wire have been used to fortify residences.

(Illustration courtesy of the Killie Campbell Africana Library.)

What were the causes of the Bambata rebellion? (Also refer back to Chapter 8.) The Bambata rebels differed from the members of the Congress and Vigilance Association movements. They were fighting to protect their hold on the land that made it possible for them to survive as cultivators or farmers. They were defending a rural way of life. The Congresses and Vigilance Associations on the other hand were largely urban-based organizations. Their members had already left the land and were living in the cities. Their aspirations, grievances and ways of operating were different. They wanted to exercise political influence; to have the vote. They demanded the right to work. They resented laws like the pass law which interfered with their attempts to get jobs and made their lives difficult. Their mode of expression was through petitions and meetings, not through the spear or the gun.

INDIAN DISCONTENT AND OPPOSITION

Amongst the most impressive steps taken against white domination in the decade after the Anglo-Boer War were those taken by the Indians. The Indians, like other blacks in South Africa, suffered economic exploitation and political oppression which gave them reason to oppose the government. In Mohandas Gandhi, the Indians found an outstanding leader who was able to attract a large following and who used peaceful means to pressurize the government on issues of concern to Indians.

Since the early days of Indian settlement in Natal, efforts had been made to prevent them from having a say in politics. A qualified franchise system existed which recognized Indians as British subjects but nevertheless prevented the majority from voting. Towards the end of the century wealthier Indians began qualifying for the vote in increasing numbers. The majority of Natal's whites feared the growing influence of Indians. Indians had already made a big impact on trading. The possible spread of their economic competition to other spheres of business made whites feel threatened. In order to contain the political and economic challenge of Indians, most whites in Natal wanted to restrict them from voting.

In 1893, the year in which Natal was granted responsible government, Mohandas Gandhi, a lawyer from India, arrived in Durban. Gandhi dedicated himself to resisting the attempted disenfranchisement of Indians. In 1894 he formed the Natal Indian Congress to bring educated and wealthy Indians together to fight for Indian rights. He edited the newspaper, *Indian Opinion*, to publicize the Indian cause.

Mohandas Gandhi

331

South Africa 1908–10: The achievement of unification

THE GROUNDWORK FOR UNIFICATION

In 1907 all the South African colonies were self-governing and a movement rapidly grew amongst them for unification. Members of Milner's Kindergarten, Patrick Duncan and Lionel Curtis, gave the movement some momentum by forming Closer Union Societies all over the country. In 1907 F. S. Malan, the new leader of the Afrikaner Bond in the Cape, suggested that the question of union be considered by all the South African colonies. Shortly afterwards, the Selborne Memorandum appeared. The memorandum, which was supported by Leander Jameson, Prime Minister of the Cape, sounded a note of warning against continued disunity. It urged South African politicians to get together and sort out their problems.

THE OBSTACLES TO UNIFICATION

Problems that had dogged South Africa for over two decades still barred the way to co-operation and union. Railway and customs policies and the political rights of blacks were the main sources of dispute.

The Anglo-Boer War did not end railway rivalry. After the war the railway from the Rand to Lourenço Marques became the

Gandhi was unable to prevent the passing of the 1896 Franchise Act which deprived Indians of the vote. Natal legislators claimed that the Act was 'colour-blind'. By this they meant that the Act did not discriminate on the grounds of race. In fact the Franchise Act affected Indians alone by disqualifying everybody whose country of origin did not have parliamentary institutions. (White settlers from Britain therefore had the vote, whereas settlers from India, a country without a parliament, were deprived of the vote.)

Many Indians were traders. They were industrious and often sold goods more cheaply than their white counterparts. In 1897 the Natal parliament favoured white traders by allowing for Indian trading licences to be cancelled without recourse to a court of law. After the Anglo-Boer War, Indian merchants suffered further setbacks which culminated in the prohibition of Indian immigration into the Transvaal and the registration of Indians by their fingerprints.

These measures were humiliating. Gandhi led opposition to them in a series of passive resistance* (more correctly called *Satyagraha*, which means 'the force of truth') campaigns from 1907. Passes were burnt and mass meetings and political marches were held. Yet political rights were not granted.

most popular route in South Africa, carrying 67 per cent of the Rand's traffic in 1905. This was a profitable business and one which the rival colonies of the Cape and Natal eyed enviously. Each tried to win more traffic for their own railways, but to no avail, and the only result was a growth of tension between the colonies concerned.

While the colonies argued about railway policy, they were also engaged in a vigorous debate over customs duties. The problems associated with customs duties also stemmed from the pre-war period. The Transvaal had tried (but failed) to gain a greater share of the income from the customs levied by the ports of Natal and the Cape. After the war, the Transvaal was still dissatisfied with the situation. A Customs Union joining all four colonies was formed in 1903. The Transvaal was not satisfied with the new arrangements.

Customs duties were levied at colonial ports on goods destined for the interior. This raised the Transvaal cost of living and mining costs. The Transvaal therefore wanted the duties reduced. The Cape and Natal were not really in a position to agree to this demand because they were short of money, and income from customs duties was of major importance to them both. In 1907 the Transvaal threatened to withdraw from the Customs Union. The threat was eventually withdrawn but it became clear that a national policy on customs was the only chance of ending the dispute.

The other important obstacle to unification was the question of political rights for blacks. The place of the black voter in a united South Africa was a perplexing problem. Franchise regulations differed markedly from one colony to the next. Africans and Coloureds in the Cape had a qualified franchise. In Natal, it was technically possible for blacks to have the vote, but in practice very few ever qualified. In the Transvaal and the O.R.C., no African was allowed to vote.

The British set up a commission of enquiry to investigate the whole question. In 1905 the South African Native Affairs Commission, appointed by Milner and headed by Sir Godfrey Lagden, issued its report. The report recommended geographical and political segregation; i.e., African political aspirations should be met using 'traditional' institutions rather than the white parliament. If this was to be the blueprint for the future development of African political institutions, it still required the consent of all four colonies. Their differing traditions in black politics suggested that an easy solution was unlikely. One of the best ways of thrashing out the problems would be at the conference table.

THE NATIONAL CONVENTION AND ITS WORK

In mid-1908 an inter-colonial customs conference was held in Pretoria and Cape Town. Although agreement over the customs question was not achieved, the conference was successful in setting up a National Convention to which each colony sent representatives to discuss unification.

The Convention first met in Durban in October 1908. It later sat in Cape Town and Bloemfontein. By this time, J. X. Merriman and the S.A.P. had come to power in the Cape. All the colonies were self-governing and so were able to put their cases with equal force. There were several problems to be overcome. The first was the form that a united South Africa was to take.

There was a choice between union—a powerful centralized government—or federation—a looser form of government which allowed for greater regional autonomy*. Natal was the only colony which wanted a federal or a decentralized form of

333

government. It cherished its English character and feared Afrikaner domination. Its preference was supported by Lionel Curtis, W. P. Schreiner, his novelist sister, Olive Schreiner and J. H. Hofmeyr, all of whom wanted to protect the Cape African franchise. They felt that a union dominated by the former Boer republics would jeopardize this.

The second problem was the creation of constituencies* and the distribution of parliamentary seats. There are two basic ways of deciding the size of constituencies for which Members of Parliament will be elected. The key question is what criteria to use in deciding the area of constituencies. One can divide up the voting *population* into equal constituencies, or one can split up the *land area* into equal constituencies.

Afrikaner voters who lived mostly in the countryside wanted the latter method to be applied. This would create enough rural seats to balance the English voting power based in the cities. English-speaking voters on the other hand felt that the former method would give them the best representation and restrict Afrikaner political domination.

The Transvaal delegation was the best organized and the most influential at the Convention. They insisted on a system in which political superiority would be determined by the rural vote. As a result it was decided that the number of voters in country constituencies could be as much as 30 per cent less than the number in urban constituencies. This meant that the number of rural seats far exceeded the number based in the cities.

The third problem was the African vote. Africans were the big losers in the process of unification. Instead of the Cape franchise being extended to the whole of South Africa, as Schreiner, F. S. Malan and others had passionately argued for, the franchise provisions which existed before Union were retained.

Here are some extracts from the convention diary of F. S. Malan, the Cape parliamentarian:

Tues. 20 Oct. 1908

Mr. Merriman (Cape Prime Minister) spoke against the drawing of a colour bar with regard to the franchise. He proposed that the franchise be left as it was in each Province, not to be changed except by a three-fourths majority of the Union Parliament.

Col. Stanford (Transkei) wished to have the colour bar abolished throughout the Union.

Mr. Moor (Natal Prime Minister) wished to abolish the Native franchise in the Cape Colony.

Sir Percy Fitzpatrick (Transvaal Randlord) wanted the introduction of a high qualification—open also for Natives provided that the Natives first acquire a certificate-of-civilization—issued by a special Commissioner.

Mr. Smuts indicated the objections of a practical kind—to all these suggestions. In his opinion Mr. Stanford's was unacceptable to the three Colonies other than the Cape. That of Mr. Moor would be rejected by the Imperial Government and Parliament. That of Sir Percy would meet with opposition both in the Cape Colony and the other Colonies and would therefore seriously imperil the unification of South Africa. He suggested that the franchise be left as it stood in the various Colonies, but that it be left to the Union Parliament to amend it by a simple majority.

The debate was adjourned until tomorrow.

Wed. 21 Oct., p. 49

The debate on the franchise was continued, Mr. Greene (Natal) made a strong speech against the granting of any political rights to Natives and Asiatics. He proposed that only the descendants of Europeans be eligible as members of the Union Parliament. Mr. Fischer (OFS Prime Minister) was in favour of keeping the Natives and the Europeans — in different kraals. He was not, however, in favour of altering the franchise in the Cape Colony. Mr. Sauer (Cape) delivered an eloquent plea for granting the franchise to the Natives. He defended the policy of the Cape Colony.

Messrs. Walton (Editor, E. P. Herald) and Jagger (Cape Liberal) defended the policy of the Cape Colony; while General Hertzog thought that the Cape Colony did not realize the danger of the Native franchise, just as somebody playing near a river sometimes did not see the danger of the flood which would sweep him away.

Thurs. 22 Oct., p. 55

The debate on the Native franchise was continued. As a result of the discussion as a whole it was clear that all the ideas that were expressed were grouped round three main thoughts:

Firstly: To maintain the paramountcy of the European in South Africa.

Secondly: To see to it that a uniform system was obtained for the whole of South Africa; and

Thirdly: To leave the franchise as it was in each Colony.

white races first and then to tackle the Native franchise question but a union of this kind would not be a genuine union. The germs of discord would continue to exist. General Botha (Transvaal, Prime Minister) then spoke and said that Mr Malan's speech had made him fear for the Union because he saw in it a desire to force the rest of South Africa to accept the principle of the Native franchise of the Cape Colony. If this were done he might just as well go home. He could not go further than the recognition of the rights of the Natives in the Cape Colony.

Mr. F. S. Malan then said that he regarded it as his duty to make a last earnest appeal to the Conference to try and arrive at a uniform system. This was a crisis in the history of the people of S.A. It had taken a hundred years of strife and tears to bring the Europeans to unification. By not facing squarely the disagreement over the Natives they were once again heading for a struggle and tears and suffering. People spoke about the necessity to unite the

Questions

1. Make a list of those who favoured the African franchise and those who did not.

2. How did Fitzpatrick propose to limit the numbers of African voters?

3. What was the main difference between the recommendations of Smuts and Merriman?

4. In what way was Greene's view of the black vote affected by the 1896 Natal Franchise Act? (See p. 332.)

5. In what light did Hertzog view the African franchise?

6. To what extent was Merriman's suggestion accepted by the National Convention? (See below in this chapter to help you answer this question.)

7. To what extent did the question of the African franchise threaten unification?

335

The constitutional structure of the Union of South Africa

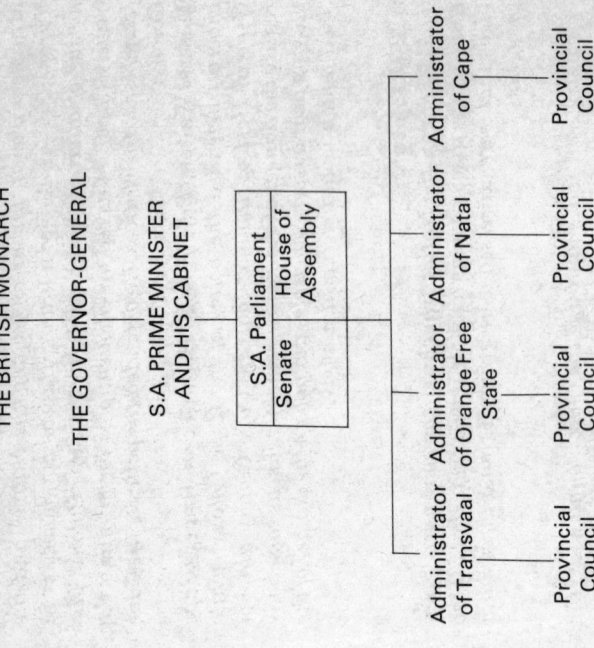

The franchise provisions of the Convention meant that the only Africans who were eligible for the vote were those who lived in the Cape. This privilege was protected by an entrenched clause* similar to the one governing the official languages (see below). The Cape did not win the battle to protect the status of its African voters altogether. It agreed that Africans could not become members of Parliament. This set the country on the road that was eventually to deprive all Africans of representation in the white parliament. Although delegations including black leaders like Jabavu, Rubusana, Abdurahman and Gandhi visited London to protest, they had no success in changing the conditions of union. African hopes for a better political deal under British rule were shattered.

The fourth problem in the attainment of unity was that of the official language. There was much debate on this issue and in the end, to avoid offending either group, both English and Dutch became official languages. They were protected by an entrenched clause* in the constitution which meant that they could only be changed by a two-thirds majority in a joint sitting of both houses. Afrikaans became an official language instead of Dutch in 1925.

The final problem was that of the capital of the country. All the provinces wanted to host the capital so a compromise solution was reached. Pretoria was to be the executive capital (symbolized in Sir Herbert Baker's Union Buildings), Cape Town, the legislative capital (and seat of Parliament), while Bloemfontein became the judicial capital (and seat of the Appeal Court). Pietermaritzburg was given monetary compensation for being neglected.

While the National Convention did succeed in bringing South Africa together in a political union, it did not succeed in solving all the problems which beset the country.

336

Conclusion

The first decade after the South African War saw remarkable advances in the political unification of South Africa and set the scene for much further development. There was also an acceleration of economic life. Despite a depression lasting from 1906 to 1908, the gold mines were working well. Industry was developing and thousands of people were finding homes in the cities.

Johannesburg, the hub of the South African economy, was expanding in all directions. The wealth of Parktown and Houghton, the two prestige suburbs of Johannesburg, only told half the story of South Africa's economic growth. The other half was to be found in the squalor of suburbs like Vrededorp where the workers and the unemployed lived cheek by jowl.

The wealth seen in the streets of Johannesburg was also to be seen in the countryside. There white farms showed off their rippling wheat fields and waving maize lands. But in the rural backwaters where the railways did not reach, Africans and poor whites battled on small plots to grow an acre of maize and raise a beast or two.

Given these sharp contrasts between rich and poor, it is not surprising that the political victory of unification concealed much disappointment. Many groups found little to applaud. Africans, Indians and Coloureds came off worst. Many had little to look forward to but a grim struggle against impoverishment and political subordination. In 1912 the South African Native National Congress was founded to fight for land and political rights.

The poor whites in the countryside became increasingly disenchanted. In 1914 many turned to Hertzog's breakaway National party while others took up arms in the Afrikaner rebellion (1914). White miners on the Reef had nothing to be thankful for either. They continued to clash with the Randlords and began developing worker organizations wh.ch were eventually strong enough to paralyse the mining industry and challenge the government in the rebellion of 1922.

Glossary

Cape rebels — people who lived in the Cape and sided with the Boer republics by taking up arms against the British during the Anglo-Boer War.
Conciliation — dedication to a policy of goodwill and peaceful reconciliation between the Boers and the British.
Constituency — a designated area which a member of parliament represents.
Dissident — a person who disagrees with the established government.
Entrenched clause — a part of a constitution which is difficult to change. Normally such clauses protect the rights of certain groups.
Incentive — a benefit granted to promote a particular course of action.
Indenture — an agreement which binds a person to an employer by contract.
Indigency — poverty.
Jingoes — people who take extreme pride in their nation or group, often espousing an aggressive foreign policy.
Modus vivendi — a temporary working arrangement, usually between people who differ on some issue.
Non-combatant — someone who, during time of war, does not fight, but serves the army indirectly by providing food, transport and services.
Pan-Africanism — a movement for the unity of *all* Africans.
Pander — act in a subservient manner, seek the approval of.
Passive resistance — to oppose something peacefully.
Patronize — to treat someone one is helping as an inferior.
Regional autonomy — self-government within a region.
Scab labour — workers who defy a strike and replace those out on strike.

Bibliography

Brookes, E. H. and Webb, C de B. *History of Natal* (Natal University Press, 1965)
Denoon, D. *A Grand Illusion* (Longman, 1973)
Denoon, D. "Capitalist Influence and the Transvaal Government during the Crown Colony Period, 1900–06" in *The Historical Journal* (1968)
Marks, S. *Reluctant Rebellion* (Oxford University Press, 1960)
Marks, S. and Trapido, S. "Lord Milner and the South African State" in *History Workshop Journal No. 8* (1979)
Nassou, B. *Isau's War: The making of a Cape People's war 1899–1902* (Not yet published)
Odendaal, A. *Vukani Bantu. The Beginnings of Black Protest Politics in South Africa* (David Philip, 1984)
Pakenham, T. *The Boer War* (Weidenfeld and Nicolson, 1979)
Phimister, I. *Capital and class in Zimbabwe 1890–1948* (To be published by Longman)
Plaatje, S. *Native Life in South Africa* (Ravan, 1916)
Spies, S. B. *Methods of Barbarism* (Human and Rousseau, 1977)
Swan, M. *Gandhi: The South African Experience* (Ravan, 1985)
Swanson, M. "The Sanitation Syndrome: Bubonic Plague and Urban Native Policy in the Cape Colony" in *Journal of African History No. 3* (1977)
Thompson, L. M. *The Unification of South Africa* (Oxford University Press, 1960)
Van Onselen, C. *Studies in the Social and Economic History of the Witwatersrand 1886–1914 Vol. 1 New Babylon* (Ravan)
Van Onselen, C. *Vol. 2 New Nineveh* (Ravan, 1982)
Warwick, P. *Black People and the South African War* (Ravan, 1983)
Willan, B. *Sol T. Plaatje: A Biography* (Ravan, 1984)

Chronology of Southern African history: 1870–1910

ECONOMIC AND SOCIAL	POLITICAL	MILITARY
1867–70 Discovery of diamonds and opening up of diamond-fields	1868 Death of Mzilikatzi; Lobengula King of Ndebele; Basutoland becomes a British Crown colony	
	1870 Diggers Republic at Barkly West; Death of Mosheshwe	
	1871 Keate Award	
	1872 Responsible government for the Cape; Griqualand West becomes a British Crown colony; Burgers President of ZAR; Cetshwayo becomes Chief of Zulu	
1873 Gold discovered on the Lowveld		
	1876 OFS paid compensation for loss of diamond-fields	
	1877 Britain annexes ZAR; Carnarvon's federation scheme	
		1878–80 British/Pedi War; 9th Frontier War (Xhosa); Griqualand West rebellion; Griqaland East rebellion; Orange River rebellion
	1879 Afrikaner Bond established	1879 Anglo-Zulu War; Basuto Gun War
	1880 Griqualand West annexed to the Cape Colony	1880 Trenskei rebellion
	1881 Pretoria Convention	1881 First Anglo-Boer war; Death of Majuba
		1882 Montshiwa + Mankurwane vs Massouw + Moswete (S. Bechuanaland)
	1883 Kruger becomes President of ZAR	1883 Nazundza Ndebele defeated
	1884 London Convention	1884 Zulu civil war; Germany annexes SWA
	1884–5 Stellaland/Goshen dispute; Britain annexes Bechuanaland; Shippard's Land Commission in Bechuanaland; Law to restrict African vote in the Cape (Upington)	
1885 Depression and collapse of the diamond market		
1886 Rhodes gains control of De Beers Mining Company; Discovery of gold on the Witwatersrand; Johannesburg founded	1887 Grobler treaty with Ndebele; Tongaland annexed by Britain; Law to restrict African vote (Sprigg)	
1887 Swazi railway concession to ZAR	1888 Rudd Concession	
	1890 Pioneer Column to Mashonaland	
		1891 Pondo civil war
	1892 Law to restrict African voters in the Cape (Rhodes)	
	1893 Second Swaziland Convention	1893 Anglo-Ndebele War

Chronology of Southern African history: 1870—1910

ECONOMIC AND SOCIAL	POLITICAL	MILITARY
1894 Glen Grey Act	1894 Rhodesian Land Commission; Third Swaziland Convention 1895 Rhodes resigns as Cape Prime Minister	1894 Lebedu revolt in N. Tvl; Malaboch revolt in N. Tvl; Nama revolt in SWA 1895 Jameson Raid 1896 Langeberg rebellion
1896–7 Rinderpest	1897 Zululand annexed by Natal	1896–7 First Chimurenga War 1897 Venda defeated/Gaza defeated by Portuguese 1898 Swazi threaten to rebel 1898–1902 Herero rebellion in SWA 1899 Second Anglo-Boer War 1899–1902 Kgatla attack Boers in western Transvaal; Pedi attack Boers
	1902 Treaty of Vereeniging; Britain annexes Swaziland	1902 Zulu attack Boers at Vryheid 1904 Germans embark on a war of extermination against the Herero in SWA (1904–7)
1904–7 Chinese labour experiment		
1905 East Coast Fever		1905 Germans attack Nama 1905–6 Bambata's rebellion
1906 Customs Union 1907 Gold miner's strike	1906 Customs Union 1907 Self-government for Transvaal and Orange River Colony 1908–9 National Convention 1910 Union	